P9-DGS-629

mobituaries

GREAT LIVES WORTH RELIVING

Mo Rocca
and Jonathan Greenberg

Illustrations by Mitch Butler

SIMON & SCHUSTER

NEW YORK   LONDON   TORONTO   SYDNEY   NEW DELHI

Simon & Schuster
1230 Avenue of the Americas
New York, NY 10020

Copyright © 2019 by Maurice Rocca
Illustrations by Mitch Butler

First Simon & Schuster hardcover edition November 2019

SIMON & SCHUSTER and colophon are registered trademarks of Simon & Schuster, Inc.

For information about special discounts for bulk purchases, please contact Simon & Schuster Special Sales at 1-866-506-1949 or business@simonandschuster.com.

The Simon & Schuster Speakers Bureau can bring authors to your live event. For more information or to book an event, contact the Simon & Schuster Speakers Bureau at 1-866-248-3049 or visit our website at www.simonspeakers.com.

Interior design by Timothy Shaner, NightandDayDesign.biz

Manufactured in the United States of America

1   3   5   7   9   10   8   6   4   2

Library of Congress Cataloging-in-Publication Data has been applied for.

ISBN 978-1-5011-9762-8

ISBN 978-1-5011-9764-2 (ebook)

CONTENTS

CONTENTS

As a lover of obituaries, these are the kinds of questions that weigh on my mind:

How did Founding Father Thomas Paine, the man who inspired the American Revolution with his pamphlet *Common Sense*, end up with just six people at his funeral and an obit summed up in the line "He had lived long, did some good and much harm"?

Did Sammy Davis Jr. and Jim Henson really have to die on the *same day*? Didn't each of these brilliant talents deserve a news cycle all to himself?

Is it even possible to diagram a sentence as long as what will likely be the first line of Bill Cosby's obit? Seriously, that's going to be one heck of a dependent-clause-heavy sentence:

Bill Cosby, the Philadelphia-born stand-up comedian who broke barriers when he became the first black actor to star in an American television drama before going on to star in his own blockbuster eponymous sitcom, but whose legacy was eclipsed by a torrent of accusations of drug-facilitated sex crimes and whose 2018 conviction on aggravated indecent assault sent him to prison where he lived out his days in disgrace, died today.

My father loved the obits, too. It was his favorite section of the newspaper. I think he liked the sweeping drama of a life packed into a few inches of print. Indeed a great one can feel like a movie trailer for an Oscar-winning biopic, leaving the reader breathless.

Consider the story of Madame Chiang Kai-shek, who died in 2003. At 105(!), the widow of Chinese Nationalist leader Chiang Kai-shek had long outlived general interest in her. Even the people still around who knew her name had forgotten she was alive.

But Madame Chiang's life was consequential, hence the gripping 2,600-word saga penned by the *New York Times*'s Seth Faison. Beautiful, brainy, and driven, she was one of three sisters from the Soong family, which "dominated Chinese politics and finance in the first half of the 20th century." Quoted in the obit is a famous Chinese ditty about the sisters: "One loved money, one loved power, one loved China." (Madame Chiang was the "power" one.) The Gabor sisters were slouches next to these three.

Madame Chiang barnstormed the United States during World War II, electrifying Congress, winning Americans to the side of the Nationalists over the Communists, charming the masses with her southern-accented English, which she learned growing up for a time in Georgia.

Underneath the charm was a ruthlessness, though, which Faison captures. This is my favorite paragraph:

> *Although Madame Chiang developed a stellar image with the American public, President Franklin D. Roosevelt and other leaders became disillusioned with her and her husband's despotic and corrupt practices. Eleanor Roosevelt was shocked at Madame Chiang's answer when asked at a dinner at the White House how the Chinese government would handle a strike by coal miners. Madame Chiang silently drew a sharp fingernail across her neck.*

Can't you just hear Eleanor Roosevelt gasping as Madame Chiang pantomimes a beheading? Reading that paragraph I am there at that table!

She eventually fled to the posh Upper East Side of New York. At ninety she plotted a comeback but it failed and she lived out her days being waited on by guards in the Nationalist uniforms of old. (I knew one of her neighbors, and he was convinced she and those guards were running an off-the-books takeout service out of her apartment.)

Her obit is a twofer: an engrossing personal story and a riveting history lesson about China during World War II. And a fitting send-off for someone who was, like it or not, once a pivotal figure. But not everyone has gotten the send-off they were due—which is where this book comes in.

A Mobituary is an appreciation for someone who didn't get the love she or he deserved the first time around. This person could be a well-known name. Audrey Hepburn had the misfortune of dying not only way too young but also on the day Bill Clinton was inaugurated. Her own wartime experience—and how it shaped the woman we all fell in love with—is unknown to many. (You may have heard Audrey Hepburn's story on the first season of the *Mobituaries* podcast. But there's way more to discover in this book that wasn't covered in the podcast.)

There are Mobituaries for people who were once very famous but whose names are barely remembered today. Nineteenth-century composer Giacomo Meyerbeer practically invented grand opera. But he never recovered from an anonymous and virulently anti-Semitic hit piece written by his once-friend Richard Wagner.

And throughout the book there's a series of "Forgotten Forerunners." These are Mobits for people whose great achievements have never been truly recognized—people like Ada Lovelace, the woman who wrote the world's first computer program, way back in 1843.

There are also Mobits for people who aren't people at all. Dragons were for a long time thought to be real. (*Game of Thrones* fans may want to skip that chapter.) Ditto the behemoth known as the station wagon, which didn't get any kind of obituary when it passed on in 2011. It gets a Mobit.

Distinctions between who is famous now, who used to be famous, and who was never famous are ultimately moot. Back in 2002, my friend and colleague Rita Braver interviewed the late, great writer-director-wit Nora Ephron (*Sleepless in*

Seattle, When Harry Met Sally) for *CBS Sunday Morning*. (I would later on become friends with Nora.) The segment was tied to the Broadway premiere of Nora's musical *Imaginary Friends*, about the titanic feud between the larger-than-life writers Lillian Hellman and Mary McCarthy. The interview included this sobering exchange:

> RITA: What would you like people to say about Nora Ephron's work in years to come?
>
> NORA: Oh, well, I think one of the things you realize when you write a play about Lillian Hellman and Mary McCarthy, who were in their time way more famous than I am—and who almost no one knows who they are and they've only been dead what, ten or twelve years?—is that there's no point in thinking about what people are gonna say about you . . . because they probably aren't gonna say anything!

Nora was right. None of the people under thirty who helped put the *Mobituaries* podcast on the air (and these people are whip smart) knew who Nora Ephron was—and she's only been dead for seven years.

So I'm pretty sure that all the people in these pages are new to someone—and one day sooner than we realize they'll be new to everyone. They'll all be Forgotten Forerunners. All except Audrey Hepburn. I mean, c'mon, Ariana Grande tweets about her.

So please enjoy this book. But first, here is a sentence diagram of the first line of Bill Cosby's obit:

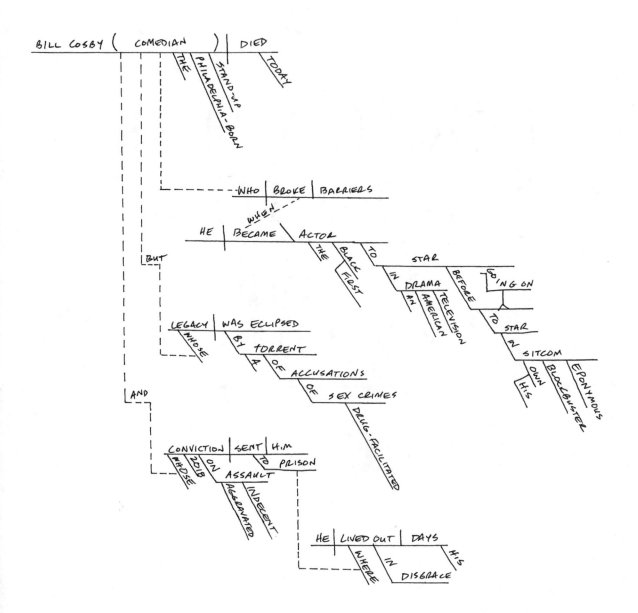

DEATH OF THE FANTASTIC

DRAGONS
{3000 BC–1735}

I know what you're thinking: Mo, you can't write an obit for dragons because dragons never existed. I mean, what's next? Obits for those silly cartoon animal appliances on *The Flintstones*? To which I have a three-part response:

1. I, for one, loved the animal appliances on *The Flintstones*. My favorites were the woodpecker camera and the pelican dishwasher.
2. This isn't an obit; it's a Mobit.
3. Dragons may be imaginary but here's the thing: people used to believe they were real.

For most of Western history, in fact, dragons were considered part of zoology or "natural history," no more mythical than horses or chickens. Ancient writers describing dragons never questioned whether they were real. In the year 77, Pliny the Elder, in his *Natural History*, a model for the encyclopedia, described epic battles in India between dragons and giant elephants with the professorial tone of a biology teacher detailing how a cheetah runs down an antelope. For the Greeks, in fact, the word *drakon* simply meant "snake." Over time, bits of folklore and religious symbolism got mixed in with the natural history of the ancients. Writers started to describe dragons of exotic colors that could breathe fire and fly and that Peter, Paul, and Mary would one day sing about. (St. Augustine seems to be the main authority for claiming that dragons can fly. By the eighth century it was normal to see dragons represented with wings.) But no matter how magical these beasts seemed to get, historians still struck the tone of the worldly zoologist whom no marvel could faze. In the early third century, for example, Philostratus, a Greek teacher and orator, sounds as if he sees these flame-belching terrors every day while he's out walking the dog:

> *The dragons of the mountains have scales of a golden color, and in length excel those of the plain, and they have bushy beards, which also are of a golden hue; and their eye is sunk deep under the eyebrow, and emits a terrible and ruthless glance.*

In 1025, the Persian philosopher Abu Ali Ibn Sina (aka "Avicenna") added marine species of the dragon to his *Canon of Medicine.* He was probably referring to moray eels and stingrays. Fifteenth-century maps warned explorers, "Here be dragons," and featured drawings of both land and sea dragons. And again, in Conrad Gessner's *Schlangenbuch,* a Renaissance treatise on snakes, a dragon was just another reptile. As late as the early eighteenth century, it was not strange for university-educated men to believe in dragons.

Enter the great Swedish botanist-slash-dragon-slayer Carl Linnaeus (1707–1778). Perhaps you didn't know there were any great botanists, let alone great Swedish botanists. But back then the Swedes were powerhouses in the world of science and Linnaeus was tops. I recognized his name because AP Bio was my favorite course in high school and Linnaeus was the father of modern taxonomy, the scientific system for classifying plants and animals that I was required to learn. (I was ridiculously proud of how well I memorized my levels of classification and still look for any excuse to show off. That's not a sponge in my kitchen sink. It's *Phylum Porifera*!)

Linnaeus showed an interest in the natural world from early childhood. At age five his father gave him his own little plot of land to tend. As a teenager he was well-versed in the existing literature on botany. At Uppsala University he began to stand out for his work in classifying plants. His reputation continued to grow as he continued to study and to observe the natural world.

Then in 1735, while still a young man, Linnaeus and a friend traveled to the Dutch Republic to pursue degrees in medicine. En route they stopped for a stay in Hamburg (today a city in Germany, then a prosperous independent city-state). The mayor at the time, Johann Andersson, was eager to show the young scientists a prized possession—a taxidermied hydra. Both weird and terrifying looking, it was said to be a small version of the species, with seven symmetrical long necks capped off by heads that contemporary Swedish scholar Professor Gunnar Broberg thinks look like ET. (Actually in the drawing I've seen each head looks like the chest-busting monster in the movie *Alien*.)

The creature had first been displayed in Prague on a church altar, but when the city was sacked by the Swedes in 1648, its treasures were seized. It eventually made its way via a Swedish count to Mayor Andersson's collection in Hamburg. But it truly became famous when Albertus Seba, the great Dutch naturalist, included a drawing of the creature in his *Cabinet of Natural Curiosities,* a lavish four-volume compendium of plant and animal illustrations that sold throughout Europe.

When young Linnaeus saw this "dragon," he immediately discerned that it was a fraud. As author Marc Cramer has detailed, Linnaeus's knowledge of zoology was such that he could see clearly that the creature's skin was that of several snakes, sewn together and stretched over various mammal parts, including the jaw and feet of a weasel. He reasoned that this patchwork animal had been assembled by Catholic monks some centuries back in order to represent the Beast of Revelation described in the New Testament—an object manufactured with the deceitful aim of inspiring fear in gullible congregants. "God never put more than one brain in one of [His] created bodies," remarked the young scientist, demonstrating his knowledge of both zoology and theology at once. He quickly published his findings in a Hamburg magazine. Mayor Andersson was not too thrilled with this verdict, since he was trying to sell the thing, hoping that its inclusion in Seba's popular book would juice the price. At one point, the king of Denmark was said to have offered ten thousand thalers. (A thaler was a silver coin currency. If it sounds familiar, that's because its name lives on in the "dollar.") Linnaeus's article exposed the inauthenticity of the hydra and ended the mayor's hopes for a windfall. As he related years later in his autobiography, Linnaeus and his friend had to flee Hamburg under Andersson's threats.

Of course Linnaeus may have been exaggerating the danger he was under, since he was painting himself as a hero. And, as Professor Broberg argues, he wasn't just any hero. He was a dragon-slayer. In Linnaeus's Europe, the dragon-slayer was just as iconic a figure as the dragon itself. The city of Stockholm still possesses a prominent wooden statue of St. Goran (George) slaying a dragon that dates to the fifteenth century. Linnaeus surely knew the statue, which had been commissioned to commemorate a defeat of the Danes. He also would have understood the allegorical meaning of slaying the dragon. In Christian tradition the dragon had become a symbol of Satan, in the form of both the serpent of Eden and the beast of the Apocalypse, and the dragon-slayer was Christ, or a servant of Christ. Moreover, for Protestants like Linnaeus (whose father was a Lutheran minister), the dragon had come to symbolize the Antichrist, or what they saw as the false religion of the pope. Thus Linnaeus stressed that the hydra was a papal fraud—a symbol of Catholicism's deception. In slaying the dragon, Linnaeus was striking a blow for the Protestant Reformation.

But with the rise of modern science, Linnaeus, maybe unconsciously, was investing "slaying the dragon" with yet another meaning: science triumphing over superstition. In his autobiography Linnaeus described himself as the first person to recognize that the hydra was a creation of art, not of nature. For him, science was not about freaks or marvels, but about the everyday wonder of creation. According to the new school of thought called "natural theology," it was the order and regularity of nature that revealed God's plan, not onetime miracles and certainly not frauds. The way to understand nature was through careful, empirical observation of details.

Linnaeus soon published his own masterwork, the *Systema Naturae*, where he established that taxonomical system that I loved so much in high school. (Quickly:

if you're looking for a good mnemonic to remember the rankings of Kingdom, Phylum, Class, Order, Family, Genus, Species: King Philip Came Over For Good Spaghetti!) Among many other accomplishments, the book was the first taxonomy to place humans in a group with other primates. The book, which he would expand and revise in many editions over the course of his life, included a section called "Animalia Paradoxa" (animal absurdities), devoted to frauds and impossibilities. Chief among these is the Hamburg hydra. Additional entries of imaginary animals include the dragon, the unicorn, the phoenix, the satyr, and, um, the pelican. (Clearly Linneaus never watched *The Flintstones*.) Referencing his moment of triumph in Hamburg, Linnaeus wrote: "Nature is always true to itself and never naturally produces several heads on one body. When seen for ourselves, the fraud and artifice were most easily detected, since the teeth of a wild weasel differ from the teeth of an amphibian." The dragon had become the symbol of medieval, unscientific thinking, and the zoologist a knight, pledged to the service of reason and enlightenment, the quest for which would reveal the presence of God on earth.

Mermaids People had been believing in the existence of mermaids for thousands of years when in the 1840s the great showman P. T. Barnum exhibited his "Fiji Mermaid," an artifact constructed from the upper body of a monkey and the tail of a shark. Barnum was more like an *anti*-Linnaeus, seeking to convince people that this fake was real. Although his specimen looked nothing like Daryl Hannah in *Splash*— it was shriveled and grotesque—Barnum sold a lot of tickets, even supporting his exhibition with lectures given by a scientist named Dr. J. Griffin. (Griffin was actually a lawyer and Barnum associate named Levi Lyman.) It wasn't until the 1880s, when the English naturalist Henry Lee published *Sea Fables Explained* and *Sea Monsters Unmasked*, that science was untangled from myth: Lee suggested that most mermaid sightings were probably manatees, seals, or other marine mammals.

Kishi One of these days the Kishi of Angolan folklore is going to make a great movie, or at least a cool comic book. The Kishi is two-faced. Really. On one side of its head is the face of a very handsome man and on the other, the face of a very unhandsome hyena. The Kishi is also one smooth operator: it saunters out of the hills into an unsuspecting village, all the while presenting its young man's face. It then charms the most beautiful young woman it can find, takes her off into the hills . . . then eats her savagely with its hyena face. So remember, insist on seeing *both* his faces before you swipe right.

The Roc Originating in Persian and Arabic mythology, this giant bird with a wingspan that blocked the sun shows up in *One Thousand and One Nights*, where Sinbad the Sailor describes its egg as fifty paces around. To escape a deserted island, Sinbad ties the cloth from his turban to the bird's leg. Marco Polo claimed to observe one during his thirteenth-century travels through Asia. "It was for all the world like an eagle, but one indeed of enormous size . . . so strong that it will seize an elephant in its talons and carry him high into the air and drop him so that he is smashed to pieces; having so killed him, the bird swoops down on him and eats him at leisure." It's unclear what exactly Marco Polo saw, but a real-life inspiration might be the enormous Haast's eagle, native to New Zealand, which died out around 1400. Either way, it's indisputable: the Roc is dead.

Unicorns Unicorns did exist: The Siberian unicorn is an extinct species of mammal that resembled a furry brown rhinoceros. It died out about 39,000 years ago. But the unicorn you're thinking about never existed, though it was for many years thought to be real. The ancient Greeks described a swift, white-coated animal with a single spiraling horn and which supposedly lived in India. Pliny the Elder (yes, him again) somehow concluded that the unicorn possesses "the body of a horse, the head of a stag, the feet of an elephant, the tail of a boar, and a single black horn three feet long in the middle of its forehead." The creature gradually acquired associations with purity and became a fixture in religious art alongside a virginal maiden. But belief in unicorns was largely dispelled by the Scientific Revolution.

Frankenberry We may never know what Mary Shelley's monster ate for breakfast. We do know that Frankenberry didn't come into existence until 1971, when General Mills launched its line of monster-themed cereals, which over time included Count Chocula, Booberry, Fruit Brute, and Fruity Yummy Mummy. The strawberry-flavored Frankenberry was soon discovered to contain a dye that turned children's feces pink. According to medical researcher John V. Payne, "The stool had no abnormal odor but looked like strawberry ice cream." This horrifying (to parents), hilarious (to children), and harmless (to doctors) condition was named "Frankenberry Stool." While Frankenberry still lives, Frankenberry Stool seems to have, as it were, passed out of existence when General Mills tried a new dye in its recipe.

DEATH OF A FOUNDING FATHER

THOMAS PAINE
{1737–1809}

One of the perks of working at CBS News is I can submit questions to our polling unit to ask a random sampling of a thousand people over the phone. (That's *ten times* the number of people surveyed by *Family Feud*. Take that, Steve Harvey.) "What issue matters most to you?" "Are you happy with the direction of this country?" "Would you like to see me in more earth tones?" (Once you've been with the network for ten years, you're allowed to use the polling unit to float wardrobe ideas.)

Not long ago I wanted to know how many Americans could identify Thomas Paine as a Founding Father. And so I put our polling unit on it. The results were sobering: From a lineup of eight (seven of whom were most assuredly not Founding Fathers) only 32 percent of respondents selected Paine. Forty-three percent chose Abraham Lincoln. On the bright side, only 2 percent chose James Tiberius Kirk.

Tom Paine doesn't get nearly as much love as bona fide Founding Fathers George Washington, Thomas Jefferson, John Adams, Benjamin Franklin, or the post-musical Alexander Hamilton. I call these men FTFFs: First-Tier Founding Fathers. But make no mistake, Paine wasn't just a Founding Father; he was the intellectual engine that powered the American Revolution. His incendiary pamphlet *Common Sense*, calling for independence from Britain, sold half a million copies in 1776. (In proportion to the population back then, it remains the best-selling American title of all time.) A moral and political call to action, written in clear, simple prose to be read aloud, it spread revolutionary fervor throughout the continent, convincing ordinary farmers and merchants and tradesmen that small-time tax reductions weren't enough: what the colonies needed was a complete and total break from England and its monarchy. In the words of FTFF John Adams, "Without the pen of the author of *Common Sense*, the sword of Washington would have been raised in vain." Or as I like to say—and I hope you'll help make this catch on—"No Paine, No Gain . . . of Independence!"

That same year, at Christmastime, when Washington was camped with his ragtag, dispirited troops on the banks of the icy Delaware River, he roused their patriotism by reading them passages from a pamphlet called *The American Crisis*:

> *These are the times that try men's souls. The summer soldier and the sunshine patriot will, in this crisis, shrink from the service of their country; but he that stands by it now, deserves the love and thanks of man and woman.*

Yup, Paine wrote that, too. Some historians even give Paine credit for naming the country the "United States of America," a phrase he was the first to use publicly when writing under the pen name "Republicus" in a Philadelphia newspaper.

But look for Paine's place in the American pantheon and you'll find him buried in the second tier of founders, maybe even the third, vying for attention with such forgettables as the over-voweled Gouverneur Morris (who was never actually governor of anything), Roger Sherman (author of the calamitous three-fifths compromise), and John Paul Jones (father of the American Navy and later bassist for Led Zeppelin). Many Americans aren't even sure whether Paine counts as a Founding Father at all, since he didn't sign either the Declaration of Independence or the Constitution. To make things worse, Paine died impoverished and reviled—likened by the press to Benedict Arnold, scorned by the very American nation he had helped birth. Thousands thronged the funeral of Paine's mentor, FTFF Benjamin Franklin, but the writer who had marched down Broadway in triumph in 1783 with General Washington drew only six mourners at his death—three of whom were his housekeeper and her two sons.

How did such a world-changing writer end up on the back of a *Trivial Pursuit* card instead of the front of a quarter? Clearly Paine needed a better PR person—someone who could have told him the "Rules for Becoming an FTFF."

Rules For Becoming a First-Tier Founding Father

RULE 1. One Revolution Is Enough for One Lifetime

When the War of Independence was won, and the bad old British chased from the land, the FTFFs turned their attention to building the new republic, fashioning the Constitution, and getting the government off the ground. But not Paine. He saw the cause of freedom as not merely an American affair, but a revolution in the history of humankind. American independence was just the beginning. The whole world would eventually follow the colonies' example, throwing off tyranny and allowing ordinary men and women to rule themselves. "Where liberty is, there is my country," Franklin reputedly said; Paine answered, "Where liberty is not, there is my country." And so Paine sailed to England to stir up trouble.

When the French Revolution broke out across the Channel in 1789, Paine published *The Rights of Man*, a manifesto for universal human rights. The new book laid out radical ideas, including universal suffrage, free public education, progressive taxation, guaranteed basic income, limits on property, and South American independence from Spain. This was seen as hooliganism pure and simple to the conservative regime of Prime Minister William Pitt the Younger, who was already worried that the revolution might spread to England and that King George III might suffer the fate of the recently deposed Louis XVI. Pitt commissioned a slanderous, rumor-filled biography of Paine, whipped up mobs to burn him in effigy, and indicted him for seditious libel. Tipped off by the poet William Blake of his impending arrest, Paine fled to France.

Paine was at first quite popular in France thanks to his defense of the revolution. In fact, he had already been named to the National Assembly, despite the fact that he spoke almost no French. But even in revolution-crazy France, Paine's radical

17

ideas got him into trouble. Paine was a steadfast opponent of capital punishment, and argued that King Louis should be exiled to the United States instead of being executed. The French revolutionaries, however, were enthralled with their new invention, the guillotine, which sliced off aristocratic heads with a crisp, satisfying efficiency. The nonviolent Paine found himself denounced as a counterrevolutionary and thrown in prison. The new American government did little to help him; in fact, the American ambassador, that same over-voweled Gouverneur Morris, probably conspired to have his old political enemy arrested in the first place.

Meanwhile, back in the United States, the other founders were making the transition from activists to statesmen—landing jobs as cabinet secretaries in Washington's administration, laying down roots in the swamp, enjoying the nascent Georgetown Cocktail Party Circuit. That's how you stake a claim as an FTFF.

RULE 2. Maybe Don't Trash George Washington

Paine was no dope. As he was rotting in a French prison, he figured out what was going on: FTFF Washington, now President Washington, didn't want to spend a lot of political capital helping the radical firebrand. You know how it's sometimes just easier to pretend you've never met that drunken loudmouth at the end of the bar, even though he's your best friend—and you yourself bought him the last round of Bushmills that pushed him over the edge? That's how Washington felt about Paine. Washington's government was trying to patch things up with Britain and negotiate its place in a new political order. Helping Paine light the fuse of a global revolution was very low on the to-do list.

Paine had served Washington in the Revolutionary army and supported him even when the Continental Congress wanted to take away his military command. He even dedicated *The Rights of Man* to Washington. So he was steamed when the biggest of the FTFFs let him languish in prison under threat of execution. Paine eventually got out of prison in 1794, when, in one of history's ironies, Robespierre—the architect of the French Revolution's Reign of Terror—was himself guillotined. Then FTFF James Monroe succeeded STFF Gouverneur Morris as ambassador to France and secured Paine's release. But Paine never forgave Washington. "He thinks the president winked at his imprisonment and even wished he might die in gaol," Monroe later wrote to FTFF James Madison, unaware that the spelling of "jail" would soon be Americanized. To make things worse, Washington had sided with Hamilton, Adams, and the Federalists in adopting a pro-British, anti-French stance, which Paine saw as backsliding on the egalitarianism that had animated his belief in American independence. To Paine, the conservative retrenchment of FTFFs Hamilton and Adams was little different from monarchy.

Writing from Monroe's Paris residence, Paine authored an open letter to Washington that accused the father of his country of losing touch with the ideals that sparked the revolution. Monroe warned him not to publish it, but Paine would not be counseled, and in 1795 sent it to Franklin's grandson, Benjamin Franklin Bache, who shared Paine's view.

In the letter, Paine laid into George Washington with the same relish with which he had savaged George III two decades earlier in *Common Sense*. "You commenced your Presidential career by encouraging and swallowing the grossest adulation, and you traveled America from one end to the other to put yourself in the way of receiving it." He called Washington a man too cold-hearted to form friendships, an unprincipled chameleon in politics, an indifferent military commander who sucked up glory that should have gone to others, concluding with these choice words:

> *And as to you, Sir, treacherous in private friendship (for so you have been to me, and that in the day of danger) and a hypocrite in public life, the world will be puzzled to decide whether you are an apostate or an impostor; whether you have abandoned good principles, or whether you ever had any.*

It was a bad move. Paine's letter became a political hot potato in the very ugly 1796 presidential election, the first contested election in American history. Adams's Federalist Party painted Jefferson's Democratic-Republicans as sympathetic to the out-of-control violence in France, and linked them to Paine's intemperate letter. It became another way for the Federalists to tarnish Jefferson with associations of wild-eyed radicalism. Jefferson lost the election, and Paine's chances at the first tier took a serious hit.

RULE 3. Whatever You Do, Don't Trash Jesus

For anyone seeking a legacy as an FTFF, calling George Washington an apoſtate and an impoſtor (see Mobit for Long ſ) is an incredibly stupid move. But it wasn't even the stupidest thing that Paine did. There's one person in American life more untouchable than the Father of his Country. That person, of course, is the Son of God. Paine went after Jesus with his new book, *The Age of Reason*, which he had begun to write in his French prison cell. In the book—which Paine biographer Craig Nelson calls a "terrible terrible sort of nutty book" for its political ineptitude—Paine rejected the divinity of Christ and argued for the authority of reason over revelation. And he decried "the adulterous connection of church and state." Of course, belief in the separation of church and state was mainstream enough in early America, but Paine's fervent rejection of Christianity pushed things too far for many. To be fair, Paine was an equal opportunity offender, rejecting the authority of all "churches," Christian, Jewish, and Muslim:

> *I do not believe in the creed professed by the Jewish church, by the Roman church, by the Greek church, by the Turkish church, by the Protestant church, nor by any church that I know of. My own mind is my own church. All national institutions of churches, whether Jewish, Christian or Turkish, appear to me no other than human inventions, set up to terrify and enslave mankind, and monopolize power and profit.*

The Long s (1500–1803)

If you come across an early edition of Common Sense, *you'll notice a funny-looking letter that keeps popping up. It's not a typo. It's a long-dead letter of the alphabet, and here is its Mobit:*

I firſt came acroſs the long *s* while peruſing a facſimile of the Declaration of Independence. "When in the Courſe of human Events" it ſtarts. As ſomeone with a liſp I was pſyched to ſee an *f* where I expected an *s*. Could it be, I wondered, that the ſuperſmart Thomas Jefferſon alſo had a liſp? Alas, it turns out the long *s* is a ſtrange ſymbol that merely reſembles the letter *f*.

The long *s* came into ſtyle during the ſixteenth century when printers got fed up with 𝕭lackletter 𝕿ype—you know, the font you ſtill ſee today in newspaper nameplates that makes you feel as though ſomeone ᴀ repeatedly clanging a ſledgehammer on a giant anvil. This ſtupid typeface was inſufferably oſtentatious, ſo they ſtarted to ſwitch to roman fonts to ſimplify things. If you look on the firſt page of the famous Firſt Folio of Shakeſpeare's works, you'll ſee the long *s* all over, in words like *ſeeſt*, *ſurpaſſe*, and, of courſe, *Shakeſpeare*.

Moſt letters didn't poſſeſs different forms, juſt lowercaſe and uppercaſe. (Neſ-café came along much later.) But for ſome ſilly reaſon, *S* got two verſions. The short *s* was uſed at the end of a word, but the long *ſ* was uſed at the ſtart or in the middle. If the word had a double *s*, people ſometimes uſed a long *s* followed by a short *s*, like this: ſs. If you can ſurmiſe how they ſpelled "Miſſiſſippi," all I can ſay is "Godſpeed."

We don't fully underſtand why people finally got fruſtrated with this ſtupid f---ing letter, but it's not ſurpriſing. The *Times* of London ſtopped uſing it on September 10, 1803.

That's the long and the ſhort of it!

Even worse, he laid the blame for social injustice on the Holy Book itself: "It is from the Bible that man has learned cruelty, rapine, and murder; for the belief of a cruel God makes a cruel man." Paine's old mentor Ben Franklin urged him to set fire to the manuscript, even though he probably sympathized with much of what it said. This kind of rhetoric was simply too dangerous. "I would advise you," Franklin wrote, "not to attempt unchaining the tiger, but to burn this piece before it is seen by any other person; whereby you will save yourself a great deal of mortification by the enemies it may raise against you, and perhaps a good deal of regret and repentance." But once again, Paine would not be muzzled.

Publishing *The Age of Reason* earned Paine a reputation as an infidel, an atheist, and even an Antichrist (though it most certainly would've got him booked on Bill Maher). In truth, Paine considered himself a deist. Much like Jefferson, Franklin, Washington, and many other educated men of the time, he believed in a Divine Creator but not in supernaturalism or the authority of priests. Paine actually asserted his belief in a single God several times in the book. Yet FTFFs John Adams and Samuel Adams saw the book as impious, and many other lower-tiered FFs, including Paine's old friend Benjamin Rush, condemned it. But Paine was unrepentant in rejecting the authority of revelation, the possibility of miracles like the Virgin Birth, and the tenets of specific religions, including the divinity of Christ. In a letter to FTFF Jefferson, he even impishly referred to Christmas as "the Birthday of the New Sun."

All of this came home to roost in Paine's dying days. In 1809, knowing his end was near, Paine requested a burial in a Quaker cemetery. His father had been a Quaker and Quaker teachings had been a source of his egalitarian politics and his fervent abolitionism. But, as the *New York Evening Post* wrote, Paine "declined a renunciation of his deistical opinions," and so "his anxious wishes were not complied with." Paine had the bad luck, too, of dying during the Second Great Awakening, when the rationalism and secularism of a generation earlier were in retreat and modern American evangelicalism was emerging. In his last days he was repeatedly

that feature his gaunt, creepy face and hunched shoulders. Paine, needless to say, is not pictured on any currency.

When the United States started issuing "greenbacks" to help fund the Union cause during the Civil War, the rehabilitation of Paine's reputation still had a ways to go. In the years after the war, as banking and the printing of currency were nationalized, FFs of various rankings made appearances on paper bills—Madison, Henry Clay, Robert Morris, even John Quincy Adams, who was more of a Founding Son than a Founding Father. Most of our present-day lineup reflects choices made following the establishment of the Federal Reserve in 1913, but even then Paine's reputation was nowhere near currency-worthy. Face it, he lost out to Jackson, the guy behind the Trail of Tears.

But even if you can't manage to get your face on a coin or a bill, then at least get your name on something that will sell. Samuel Adams did pretty well by getting his name and face on a craft beer in 1984. Hamilton shot up the power rankings thanks to eleven Tony Awards and a triple-platinum album. John Hancock snagged himself an insurance company, which is now owned by a Canadian company. And, really, would anyone have any clue who Ethan Allen is if not for the furniture store? (FYI, he helped capture Fort Ticonderoga.)

RULE 6. Get a Real Monument

The single best way to get yourself a place in the public memory is to make sure that you have a prominent monument commemorating your life and achievements. Most experts recommend building a 555-foot-tall granite obelisk* that towers above surrounding structures, centrally situated in the nation's capital (which should also be named after you, if at all possible), at the end of a grassy lawn designed to attract tourists by the thousands. If you can't do that, go for the neoclassical domed marble

---

* If you want to needle your second-tier presidential history buff friends, point out that the Washington Monument is technically not an obelisk, since it's composed of many stones, rather than one.

structure with lots of pillars, surrounded by cherry blossoms and a tidal basin. But no matter what the shape, there's no surer sign of an FTFF than a great monument with a line of sweaty tourists snaking its way to the entrance, selfie sticks at the ready. The Benjamin Franklin National Memorial features a 20-foot-tall, 30-ton marble statue of the man, set in the center of an 82-foot-long hall in Philadelphia's Franklin Institute that is capped with a 1,600-ton domed ceiling.

Paine's got nothing comparable. Partly that's because his reputation was at a low when he died, so there was little public ceremony surrounding his death, which took place in a small wooden house on 59 Grove Street in Greenwich Village. Because the Quakers wouldn't admit him to their cemetery, he was interred under a tree on his New Rochelle, New York, farm. Ten years later, his bones were dug up by the British radical William Cobbett, who brought them back to England with plans for a proper monument. But Cobbett somehow never got around to it. He dumped Paine's bones in a large trunk that sat in his attic for the next twenty years gathering dust. On Cobbett's death, his son and heir actually inscribed his own name on some of the larger bones, but when he ran into debt, the remains were confiscated by the court. They eventually passed to a day laborer, then a furniture dealer, and from there they seem to have been dispersed. Some bones may have been made into buttons. In the 1930s, a woman in Brighton, England, said she owned the jaw, while about twenty years ago an Australian claimed to be in possession of the skull. But most of the bones are lost. Some say they're buried somewhere in Manchester, England. A "Citizen Paine Restoration Initiative" was launched in 2001 with the aim of reconstituting the skeleton, but little progress has been reported. While there is a certain poetic justice to the scattering of Paine's bones, like his words, all across the globe, this is a terrible plan if your goal is to attract families on summer vacation to your memorial.

Instead of a grand dome or 500-foot-tall phallic symbol in the middle of the nation's capital, Paine received an assortment of sorry remembrances. An early biographer, Gilbert Vale, put up a pedestal in New Rochelle in 1839, which over the next fifty years was "often mutilated by fanatics" (*New York Times*, 1910) who still regarded Paine as an infidel. Efforts at commemoration picked up a bit as Paine's reputation began to rebound through the nineteenth century. Abraham Lincoln and Mark Twain were both admirers, and his unorthodox religious views became less radical as various Protestant denominations began to accept many of his beliefs. In 1899, the monument in New Rochelle was restored and a bronze bust of Paine added. Somewhere around 1900, Moncure D. Conway, an abolitionist, freethinker, and friend of Lincoln's, acquired Paine's brain stem in England, and brought it, along with a lock of Paine's hair, back to America. The brain stem was interred underneath the restored monument and the hair eventually placed on display in the charming Thomas Paine Cottage Museum, which bills itself as "the last existing building in North America that was owned by Thomas Paine." There's also a seven-foot-long obelisk dedicated to Paine that a construction worker discovered in 1976 while installing a drainage ditch for a septic tank in Tivoli, New York. It broke when it was being removed from the ground and few people visit it today. (Oh well, at least it's a true obelisk.)

For better or worse, New Rochelle is far better known as the fictional home of Rob and Laura Petrie in *The Dick Van Dyke Show*. Or if you're a musical theater junkie like me, you may know "New Rochelle" as one of the better songs in the very fine Frank Loesser score for *How to Succeed in Business Without Really Trying*. Which brings us back to the location of the Greenwich Village house where Paine actually died. It's now the site of a beloved piano bar called Marie's Crisis, named in homage to his patriotic pamphlet *The American Crisis*, the work from which Washington read to his troops in December 1776. A nice honor, but Paine's ghost doesn't get much rest these days: while the place may be named for him, it's the score of *Hamilton* that the kids from NYU are caterwauling into the wee hours of the morning.

And now for a side-by-side comparison of Founding Father Thomas Paine and rapper, producer, and Auto-Tune pioneer T-Pain. Because why not?

A TALE OF

THOMAS PAINE		T-PAIN
Thomas Pain	BIRTH NAME	Faheem Rasheed Najm
Thetford, East Anglia	HOMETOWN	Tallahassee, Florida
Quaker	FAMILY RELIGION	Muslim
Deism	ASSUMED RELIGION	Everything
Benjamin Franklin	DISCOVERED BY	Akon
Common Sense	NUMBER ONE HITS	*Epiphany*
The American Crisis *Rights of Man* *The Age of Reason*	IMPORTANT WORKS	"I'm Sprung" "I'm N Luv (Wit a Stripper)" "Buy U a Drank"
Jefferson elected President, welcomes Paine back to USA	COMEBACK	Wins *The Masked Singer*, welcomed back to R&B elite
Almost executed by Robespierre	NEAR-DEATH EXPERIENCE	Lost four teeth in a golf cart crash
Plain, simple style	INNOVATIONS	Use of Auto-Tune
Godless Infidel	ONCE CRITICIZED AS	Novelty Act

2 PAIN(E)S

Which T. Pain(e) Said It? *You decide!*

❝I don't think I like religion. I think it's another form of separation. You know what I'm saying? You can have your beliefs and do your thing but I don't think anybody should be separated. You know what I'm saying? So I try not to put a label on my beliefs, you know what I mean? I believe in God, I believe in Jesus, I was raised Muslim, you know what I'm saying? I believe, I believe in everything. I believe in Buddha, you know what I'm saying? I believe in whatever it is. You know I think it's all about what you want to believe.❞

❏ **T. Paine** or ❏ **T-Pain**

❏ **T. Paine** or ❏ **T-Pain**

❝I shall, in the progress of this work, declare the things I do not believe, and my reasons for not believing them. I do not believe in the creed professed by the Jewish church, by the Roman church, by the Greek church, by the Turkish church, by the Protestant church, nor by any church that I know of. My own mind is my own church. All national institutions of churches, whether Jewish, Christian or Turkish, appear to me no other than human inventions, set up to terrify and enslave mankind, and monopolize power and profit.❞

... and Other Famously Disembodied Body Parts

Einstein's Brain When Albert Einstein died in 1955, scientists wondered, "If we remove and examine his brain, will we discover any clues as to his unique genius?" The meticulous photographing and dissection was conducted by Dr. Thomas Harvey, after which the brain . . . disappeared! Yes, really. Had Einstein's brain escaped, perhaps in search of a new host body? No. It was found twenty-three years later, preserved in two mason jars, stored inside an old cider crate . . . at the home of Dr. Thomas Harvey. The mystery was solved, which was terrific for fans of science and really disappointing for fans of science fiction. To this day scientists are still studying the brain, which turns out to have an unusually thick corpus callosum. Also, it's missing part of its Sylvian fissure, a condition that turns out to have been congenital and can't be blamed on Dr. Harvey.

That painting has heart!

Relative to what? — EINSTEIN

Grover Cleveland's Jaw In 1893, shortly after beginning his second term, President Grover Cleveland discovered a tumor in his mouth that was growing much faster than America's struggling economy. Not wanting to add to the Wall Street "Panic of 1893," Cleveland hatched a plan to keep his illness secret: his surgery would take place aboard a yacht out on Long Island Sound. The tumor, along with a large section of his upper palate and five teeth, would be removed through his open mouth. (Any external cuts would be confined to his upper lip and concealed by his copious mustache.) Then the gap inside would be filled with a custom-built rubber prosthesis so that no one would ever be the wiser. The plan was incredibly ridiculous, of course. And even more incredibly, it worked perfectly. Cleveland's jaw tumor is on display at Philadelphia's Mutter Museum, within spitting distance of "Siamese Twins" Chang and Eng Bunker's conjoined livers.

Galileo Galilei's Middle Finger Arrested, tried, condemned, forced to recant his ideas about the revolutions of the planets, and finally dying under house arrest, Galileo Galilei had reason to be a little grouchy. Which may or may not explain how he contrived, ultimately, to give the world his middle finger. Literally. As it happened, ninety-five years after his death in 1642, his body was moved from a small room in the Basilica di Santa Croce in Florence to a larger room with a proper monument. However, the middle finger of his right hand fell off during the move, and it ended up touring Europe for a few hundred years. It eventually came to rest in its current home, Florence's History of Science Museum, where I like to think it continues to send the message, "Hey, Pope Urban VIII, revolve around *this*!"

Louis XIV's Heart It wasn't remarkable that the Sun King's heart was removed and preserved (after his death, of course). The French started doing that with the hearts of their dead monarchs in the thirteenth century. What was remarkable was that seventy-seven years after Louis's death, when the French Revolution came, the victorious rebels took the time to track down and destroy all those old hearts. But what truly takes *la gateau* is the fate of Louis's heart. It was taken from its resting place at l'Église Saint Paul–Saint Louis, where it had been enshrined next to the heart of his dad, Louis XIII. Both hearts were then sold to a painter named Alexandre Pau, who ground up the Sun King's heart to make a popular shade of paint called Mummy Brown—a shade ordinarily made from, you know, ground-up Egyptian mummies.

The Rosa Parks of New York

ELIZABETH JENNINGS
{1827–1901}

Most of us know the story of civil rights pioneer Rosa Parks, whose refusal to give up her bus seat in Montgomery, Alabama, in 1955 helped to end Jim Crow laws in the American South. But a century before Rosa Parks stood her ground by sitting, another African American woman struck her own blow for justice. Her name was Elizabeth Jennings. Most Americans have never heard of her.

On the sweltering day of July 16, 1854, Elizabeth headed to church to practice the organ with the choir. She was walking through the Lower Manhattan neighborhood known as Five Points. You may remember it from the Martin Scorsese film *Gangs of New York*. The area was called "the Gates of Hell," and for good reason: the streets were covered in horse manure with hogs running rampant alongside open sewers. Jennings must have been particularly uncomfortable; she was wearing a long-sleeved jacket over an ankle-length dress with layers of petticoats and corsets. After all, despite the heat, this was the 1800s and Jennings was an upstanding, churchgoing young woman—a schoolteacher, no less.

Running late, Jennings was looking to board a horse-drawn streetcar—the public transportation of the day—with her friend Sarah Adams. At that time, certain streetcars in New York were designated as "colored" cars, for African American passengers. Although a black person could ask to board the cars ridden by white passengers, any white person could object to the presence of a black person and have them ejected. The first car to arrive was for white passengers. There were empty seats, so Elizabeth climbed aboard. But the conductor told her she had to wait for the colored car trailing one block behind. But that car, it soon became clear, was full.

Elizabeth wasn't budging from the white car. In her own words, "I answered again and told him I was a respectable person, born and raised in New York." (The conductor was an Irish immigrant.) Things turned physical. The conductor tried to pull her off; she grabbed the window sash and held on, but the man was too strong. Jennings says she "screamed murder with all [her] voice" but was pushed down off the streetcar. Undeterred, she climbed back on. The driver then headed full speed to the nearest police officer. Before she could plead her case, the officer pushed Elizabeth to the ground for a second time. This time she didn't get back on. She was bruised, dirtied, and humiliated. She later referred to the men who assaulted her as "monsters in human form."

The men had messed with the wrong person. As University of Oregon historian Leslie Alexander told me, Elizabeth Jennings came from a family of activists. Her parents were vocal abolitionists, and she grew up amid discussion of politics. Her father, Thomas Jennings, was also a wealthy businessman, believed to be the first African American to hold a patent, for an early version of dry cleaning. And with her father's support, Elizabeth decided to sue the Third Avenue Railroad, the private company that ran the streetcar. She raised funds from her church community and set out to find a lawyer. And this is how *I* found out about the Elizabeth Jennings story.

You see, I have a thing for obscure nineteenth-century presidents, the guys between Lincoln and Teddy Roosevelt. Lots of facial hair, usually from Ohio, one of them was knocked off by an anarchist, another by an aggrieved office-seeker. If you've watched *CBS Sunday Morning*, you've probably seen me do reports on a few of them. Anyway, one day I was riffling through one of my presidential trivia books because that's what I do on the weekends to unwind, and I read about this Mobit's heroine and her representation by a future very obscure nineteenth-century president, Chester Alan Arthur. Arthur was only twenty-four years old and he had been practicing law for about six weeks. But he was an abolitionist and believed in Jennings's cause.

Instead of pursuing a criminal case, Jennings and Arthur brought the suit to a civil court. This meant that a victory wouldn't merely punish the men who assaulted Elizabeth; it could change the whole system of segregation.

The case was argued before a jury of white men, naturally. Jennings's case was bolstered by eyewitnesses and her own first-person account. Moreover, the judge pointed out to the jury that rail companies were required to carry all "respectable passengers" so long as they "were sober, well-behaved and free from disease." In the end, the jury sided with Jennings, awarding her $250. The Third Avenue Railroad Company was found liable and moved to integrate their cars. Meanwhile, the city's other rail companies were put on notice that they could be sued as well. The *New York Daily Tribune* ran the headline: "A Wholesome Verdict." And while desegregation in New York City public transportation wouldn't become official until after the Civil War, Jennings's lawsuit had prepared the ground.

The victory that Jennings won was a victory for the people of New York. But the battle was one that would have to be fought over and over again in other cities and states. In Philadelphia, Robert Smalls—you'll read about him as one of the first black congressmen in the nation—helped lead the fight for integrated public streetcars. He was on leave from the US Navy in 1864 when, on a rainy December day, he was told by a streetcar conductor that he had to ride on the outside platform rather than sit inside the car. Smalls chose to walk to his destination, but he organized a boycott that led to legal integration of public transportation in the City of Brotherly Love in 1867.

For a while, Elizabeth Jennings was celebrated. As Professor Alexander notes, for women of any race to have been involved in political activism at this time was rare. But after the court case, Jennings's life returned to normal. She continued teaching and even opened the city's first black kindergarten. She married a man named Charles Graham; they had a son, but he died as a young child. Over the years her name faded from history.

It seems that Elizabeth was not a person who promoted herself. Yet the deeper reason why so few of us know her story today may lie in the way we still think about slavery. As Alexander said, "Elizabeth Jennings' story doesn't fit with the narrative that we like to tell about the North." Her life, rather, reminds us that "slavery existed in the North for almost as long as it did in the South." (Slavery existed in New York State all the way up until 1827.) Jennings's courage may be inspiring, but it upsets our belief that the North was mainly innocent—rather than acknowledging that the North also participated in slavery, segregation, and other forms of oppression.

Jennings died on June 5, 1901. I didn't expect to find much mention of it in the papers of the time, but there were a few short obituaries. Here's the *New York Times* headline: "Aged Colored Teacher Dead: Mrs. E. J. Graham Was Prominent in Antebellum Race Troubles Here." The item takes note that "her whole life was devoted to the improvement of her race."

DEATH OF AN INFLUENCER

BEAU BRUMMELL

{1778–1840}

I loved the costumes in *Dangerous Liaisons*, the 1988 movie about lust, seduction, and revenge among nobles in eighteenth-century Paris. I'm also eternally grateful that each morning, before I head to work, I *don't* have to put on knee breeches, stockings, colorful silks with flounces and ruffles, a waistcoat, and a long powdered wig. For that, I have George Bryan Brummell to thank.

Brummell went by the nickname "Beau," and today the name "Beau Brummell" is a somewhat outdated synonym for a fashion plate or clotheshorse. You'll hear his name in the lyrics of the musicals *Annie* and *Gypsy*—and in the old Billy Joel song "It's Still Rock 'n' Roll to Me." (If anyone can tell me where to find pink sidewinders to go with my bright orange pair of pants, I'd be mighty appreciative.) You might not have even realized he was a real person.

But Brummell's legacy is very much with us. Variations of the adage "Clothes make the man" (or as Shakespeare put it, "The apparel oft proclaims the man") predated Brummell, but no one more famously used fashion to rise to the top of society. And once there he helped rewrite the rules on how men dress. Rules that are still with us nearly two hundred years later.

Brummell was born in 1778 in England into a world in which capitalism was creating new opportunities for social mobility. His grandfather was a servant who became a shopkeeper. His father, William, climbed still further in society, becoming private secretary to an aristocrat named Lord North, who served as prime minister for twelve years. Aspiring to have his own sons continue the family's ascent, William sent his boys to Eton, one of the most prestigious of British private schools (which are actually called "public schools" in England in order to confuse Americans). At school, the young George Brummell distinguished himself for his wit and style, and earned the nickname "Buck." ("Beau" came later, when he moved to London.) He went on to Oxford, where, despite being recognized for his skill in Latin, he was a largely indifferent student, and left at age sixteen after a single term.

At this point Brummell's ascent through the tiers of British society really began. He decided to join the army. But the position he secured was not just any ordinary post. He managed to have himself named as a low-level officer in a cavalry regiment called the 10th Royal Hussars, a unit assigned personally to George, Prince of Wales, the heir to the British throne. ("Hussar" was originally a Hungarian term for a cavalryman, but it sounded so bad-ass that it spread throughout Europe.) Officers in the 10th Regiment generally came from the upper crust of society, and were expected to pay lavishly for their own horses and ornate uniforms. Beau was able to afford these expenses due to an inheritance left to him upon his father's death in 1795. And while the inheritance was modest in comparison to those of most other officers, the position was worth the expense, since service in the regiment allowed access to Prince George himself. (Pro tip: dress for the job you want . . . and keep dressing up to keep it.)

Brummell, with his tendency to arrive late and his reputation for laziness, was not a natural fit for the military, but he cultivated the prince's favor and charmed his way up through the ranks, soon gaining the rank of captain. The prince was a hard-partying bad boy whose louche enjoyment of women, drinking, gambling, and food (his weight reached 280 pounds) irritated his father, King George III, and left a trail of scandals. In 1795, as a condition of paying off the prince's debts, the king forced his son to marry his cousin, Caroline of Brunswick, whom the prince detested. Beau attended the wedding and later, at least according to the disgruntled Caroline, helped to ruin the honeymoon with unspecified drunken antics.

Soon the Hussars were assigned to put down a strike by impoverished mill workers in the northern industrial city of Manchester, and Beau resigned his commission, claiming that Manchester was too much of a backwater for a man of his taste and style to abide. (It has been speculated that he actually wanted no part of the violence that the troops would have to inflict on the striking workers.) In 1799, he moved to a relatively small house in the expensive and fashionable London neighborhood of Mayfair, where, in the words of an article written shortly after his death, he "established himself as a refined voluptuary." Drawing on his friendship with the Prince of Wales, Brummell became a central figure in the highest echelons of London social life.

It helped that Brummell had developed a reputation as a bold wit. At one fashionable dinner he was seated immediately to the right of the prince. When he annoyed the prince with a snarky remark, the future King George IV threw his wine in Brummell's face. Thinking fast, Brummell immediately tossed his wine into the face of the person on his right, exclaiming, "The Prince's toast! Pass it round!" The table broke out in laughter. Brummell had turned a potential humiliation into a triumph. Some years later, after George's father had been incapacitated with mental illness, George, who was now quite heavy, was named prince regent. By this point he and Brummell had completely fallen out. When Beau encountered his former friend and sponsor at Watier's, the fashionable men's club to which they both belonged, Prince George greeted Brummell's companion Lord Alvanley but snubbed Beau completely. Never at a loss, Brummell turned to his companion and asked, "Alvanley, who's your fat friend?" (Why do I only think of the perfect thing to say the next morning when I'm in the shower?)

Along with his sharp tongue was a look to match. England was in the middle of a great change in style that was later called "the Great Male Renunciation," with men abandoning their formerly ornate forms of dress. While this great shift is not solely attributable to Brummell, he became its most visible figure.

To appreciate this change in style, you need to picture what male fashion looked like before it took place. In the late 1700s, male dress was still heavily influenced by the French royal court of Louis XIV, the Sun King—long powdered wigs, white makeup with spots of rouge, lots of lace and silks, oversized and frilly cuffs on sleeves, high-heeled shoes . . . you get the idea. Men, in other words, dressed as lavishly as women. In eighteenth-century England and France, the leaders in taste were rival squads of aristocratic young men who gave themselves names such as the Incredibles (no, not the superhero family) and the Muscadins.

One of the trendiest groups was the Macaronis. True, that name sounds pretty ridiculous today, but think what they'll say in 250 years about terms like "Mac Daddy" or "Glamma." The Macaronis earned their name from their grand tours of Italy, where they acquired a taste for Italian pasta, and also for the fashions there. These young men wore towering, ornate wigs. Sometimes they would even balance on top of these wigs a little three-cornered hat, called a chapeau bras, placed so high that it could only be reached with the point of a sword. These outlandish updos were literally the height of fashion. Macaronis naturally received their share of mockery in the London press. The word *macaroni* even became a synonym for "fashionable," as in, "Those peacock green breeches are very macaroni, Sir Fopling." If you've ever wondered about the seemingly nonsensical lyrics to the song "Yankee Doodle" ("Stuck a feather in his cap and called it macaroni"), they refer to this kind of macaroni, not the Kraft kind. A Yankee doodle dandy is a badly dressed American fool, who is being mocked for being so clueless and provincial that he puts a feather in his cap for decoration and thinks he has achieved the high style of the chapeau-wearing Macaronis. (Basically those lyrics are throwing some pretty serious nineteenth-century shade.)

This was, more or less, the reigning taste when Brummell entered London society. Now it's true that in some circles fashions were already beginning to change, becoming simpler, less ostentatious. The spirit of the American Revolution may even have been a partial cause of the change—bringing about an anti-elitist, more democratic attitude. (Benjamin Franklin had stopped wearing a powdered wig during the war.) But the takeaway here is that even though Beau Brummell is remembered today as a fashionista, his innovation was actually to implement a new code of *restraint*, rejecting the rococo excesses of style derived from the French royal court. Beau was decidedly not a Macaroni.

Brummell's style was all about elegance achieved through simplicity. Instead of satins, silks, and velvets, embroidered with expensive gold and silver threads, he favored simple fabrics like wool and buckskin that suggested a rustic naturalness. He dispensed with the garish rainbow palette of the Macaronis and other fops, favoring just two colors, blue and buff—the first for his jacket, the second for his vest. Full-length trousers, a clean white linen shirt, and spotless black Hessian boots (polished to a shine with champagne) completed the outfit. And no wig.

As Isaac Mizrahi told me, "Beau Brummell helped the world find its way clear of dusty, fancy frock coats and breeches and heavily ornamented clothes into plainer coats and stock-tie shirts and long pants. Also, he put an emphasis on cleanliness and even hygiene. His toilette introduced the idea of bathing daily, which wasn't a common thing. Clean shirts. Clean teeth. Coiffed hair instead of dirty old wigs. For that I'm forever grateful."

That's right, Beau scorned the heavy perfumes that men wore to mask their body odor. Instead he insisted on the most radical innovation of all—a daily bath.

Brummell's friend and fellow dandy the poet Lord Byron said that there was nothing exceptional in Brummell's attire, only "a certain exquisite propriety." In other words, his style was not really about the clothes themselves, but about the grace, even the perfection, with which he wore them. The cut of the cloth, the elegance of the tailoring, mattered far more than the expense of the fabric. (Brummell insisted on different tailors—specialists, in effect—for each item in his outfit.) Rather than burying the male figure under layers of fabric, his well-tailored clothes would follow the human form, emphasizing the body's natural elegance.

While Brummell's look was far simpler than the rococo fashions that preceded it, it was achieved only through notoriously painstaking labor. He used tweezers rather than a crude razor to meticulously remove his facial hair from the roots. He was similarly fastidious about the cleaning of his teeth. In what may seem awfully intimate for two friends who aren't having sex with each other, the Prince of Wales himself would sit and watch his friend's morning-long rituals of hygiene and preparation. Most meticulous of all was the attention devoted to the tying of his cravat; he spent hours on the knot until he got it just right. He expended all this effort, in short, to achieve the effect of effortlessness. And even though he dispensed with silks threaded with gold, he still spent enormous sums of money—estimated to be as much as £100,000 per year, or about £1,893,000 in today's money.

Eventually Brummell's lifestyle caught up with him and his reign atop London society came to an end. In 1816 he fled to France in order to escape his creditors. After a number of years he managed to patch things up with his old fat friend George (King George IV beginning in 1820), who helped him out with a do-nothing diplomatic post, but he could never regain his former glory. When the diplomatic position was abolished, his creditors resumed their pursuit, and he was sent to debtors' prison. The next stop was a French sanitarium, where he was placed for dementia that was probably caused by untreated syphilis. The story goes that Brummell spent his waning years acting out parties for the London luminaries of his earlier life whom he imagined were present with him in his room. When he died in 1840 his glittering career in society had faded to a dim memory.

But his legacy was substantial. Said Lord Byron, in an epic humblebrag: "There are three great men of our age: myself, Napoleon and Brummell. But of we three, the greatest of all is Brummell." The change in men's dress that he helped bring about eventually evolved into the coat and tie; the necktie, like Brummell's cravat, is still the focal point of men's fashion. (As Beau's ghost is my witness, before my time on earth has ended, I *will* achieve the perfect dimple.) More than this, however, he reinvented the very idea of the man of fashion. The first true "dandy" in the modern sense, he created an elite of taste, not of wealth. As the French poet Baudelaire put it, a little grandly, "Contrary to what a lot of thoughtless people believe, dandyism is not an excessive delight in clothes and material elegance. For the Perfect Dandy, these things are no more than a symbol of the aristocratic superiority of his mind." Put another way, clothes don't make the man, so much as they reveal him.

Confession: In the summer, I wear Tevas to work. That's my decision and mine alone. Don't blame Brummell for that.

Fur Coats Once a statement of luxury and a staple of high fashion, by the late twentieth century fur coats had become a target of the burgeoning animal rights movement—literally. Stars found themselves barraged by eggs, dye-bombs, dead animals, and withering insults. Soon, celebrities like Mariah Carey, Mary Tyler Moore, Anjelica Huston, and Sharon Osbourne were donating unwanted fur coats to PETA. The lone holdout was Aretha Franklin, who maintained fur coats as a signature accessory until her death in 2018, even performing in one before President Obama at the Kennedy Center Honors in 2015. And nobody seemed to mind. Why? Because she was Aretha Franklin, that's why. PETA did address an angry open letter to her in 2008, writing that her Grammy outfit made her look "like a walrus in a cat costume." But this was not well received, as most fans thought P-E-T-A needed to show a little R-E-S-P-E-C-T.

Corsets For centuries, fashion dictated that European and American women wear corsets. The corset, an incredibly binding garment, created a waspish waist and amplified a bulging bosom by forcing the wearer's internal organs upward. (It's probably not coincidental that corsets passed from the world at the same time as "fainting couches.") But it wasn't health concerns that killed the corset; it was World War I. The need for metal for ammunition led the US War Industries Board in 1917 to urge women to stop buying corsets. Serendipitously, the very first modern bra had been patented only three years earlier, by debutante Caresse Crosby. She wore it to a ball, and all the other women noticed that she could actually breathe and were like, "Yeah, *that*!"

Hobble Skirts Around the time corsets were poised to disappear, a toxic fashion took America by storm: the hobble skirt. Tightened or cinched near the knee or calf, this hot item was named for the crippling effect it had on its wearer. Because what's the point of strangling a woman's torso with a corset if you're just going to let her legs go free? Some women even tied their legs together at the knee to avoid ripping their skirts while attempting to walk. Because hobbled women could no longer step onto public transportation, special "no step" hobble-skirt-friendly streetcars began running in New York and Los Angeles. The hobble skirt had tottered off into the sunset when America needed women with functional bodies to help with the war effort. Which is why, for American women, "the Great War" really *was* kinda great.

The Codpiece Like a lot of men's fashions, the codpiece was born out of practicality. And like anything men do, it was soon carried way too far. It emerged in the sixteenth century to literally fill a sartorial gap. To wit, once you've pulled your hose onto each leg, and secured them to the doublet or tunic that covers your torso, how the devil do you cover your most favorite anatomical region? *Voila—le codpiece!* Soon, however, this fashion accessory tumesced to enormous sizes, lest someone think the wearer wasn't well-endowed. They became stiff and up-pointing, lest someone think the wearer wasn't virile. And they became embroidered and bejeweled, because why the hell not at this point!? Just as quickly, court fashion became fixated on more feminized, "elegant" looks like balloony breeches, and the codpiece was gone by 1600, giving men smarter fashion choices and depriving women of a good laugh.

DEATH OF AN AMERICAN STORY

CHANG AND ENG BUNKER
{1811–1874}

Nestled in the foothills of the beautiful Blue Ridge Mountains sits Mt. Airy, North Carolina, population 10,347. It's the birthplace of beloved American actor Andy Griffith and the model for Mayberry, the setting for his classic sitcom *The Andy Griffith Show*. Griffith played Sheriff Andy Taylor, dispensing homespun wisdom to his son, Opie, played by young "Ronnie Howard," and keeping watch over his sleepy town. Growing up my family watched the show in reruns, 6:30 p.m. weeknights on channel 5.

If you're a visitor to Mt. Airy, you can get treated to the whole Mayberry experience: a pork chop sandwich at Snappy Lunch, a ride around town in a replica Mayberry police car, and an afternoon at the Andy Griffith Museum itself. It's filled with costumes (like Sheriff Andy's uniform) and props (the courtroom doors from the set) from the show. The museum, just like the series itself, conjures a fantasy of a bygone America—made up from a little bit of history, a good portion of nostalgia, and some very high-quality 1960s Hollywood television writing.

But just downstairs from the Andy Griffith Museum, in the basement, there's another exhibit that tells a very different story. Conjoined twins Chang and Eng Bunker, the original "Siamese Twins," were born in Thailand (then called Siam) and settled in this quiet hamlet more than a century before Sheriff Andy's deputy, Barney Fife, ever locked himself in his own jail cell. Theirs is a complicated—and not always happy—story. But this story is real. And it tells us a lot about nineteenth-century America, the nature of a sibling bond, and what it means to be human.

In the summer of 2018 I traveled to Mt. Airy for the annual Bunker family reunion, where hundreds of Chang and Eng's descendants gathered at the town's

First Baptist Church for a delicious southern meal of, what else—pad thai, shumai, and chicken penang. (Bunker is the name the brothers adopted when they settled in North Carolina.) The Thai food is an homage to their ancestors; even though the Bunker family's North Carolina roots stretch back nearly two centuries, its Thai roots stretch back even further. The Bunkers who converge on Mt. Airy for this reunion are proud of where they came from. Some even sport T-shirts that read "Our Family Sticks Together," with a picture of Eng and Chang on the back. But their unique ancestry wasn't always something the family celebrated, and for many generations what is now a source of pride was considered something closer to a shameful family secret.

The twins' story began on the other side of the planet, in a fishing village in Siam. The boys were born on a houseboat in 1811—I know what you're thinking, what kind of ob-gyn recommends a houseboat birth?—to ethnically Chinese parents, perfectly healthy . . . except for a four-inch-long band of flesh and cartilage joining them at the midsection. If you trace your finger down the lower part of your chest and find the spot where the bone stops, you're right at the place where Chang and Eng were conjoined. They shared one belly button, right in the center of that band.

Surprising as it might sound, the two boys had relatively normal childhoods. They learned to walk, then to swim—together, of course. And to help the family make ends meet they raised ducks and sold the eggs at market. As biographer Joe Orser told me, "they weren't raised as curiosities." In fact, "they were given a great amount of freedom to run around and play."

Then one day, when the boys were just twelve years old, a British merchant named Robert Hunter came sailing down the river as the sun was setting. That's when he spotted something mysterious swimming in the distance—two-headed and four-armed, it appeared to be, as he put it, "a monstrosity." Hunter soon realized that he was looking at two boys joined together. And immediately he realized that he could make a lot of money exhibiting these boys in the West. But to take the twins from their homeland, he needed the permission of the king of Siam. (And if you're picturing Yul Brynner in the musical *The King and I* right now, sorry. The king that character was based on didn't come on the scene for a few more decades.) Finally, in 1829, after five years of lobbying, and after Hunter had teamed up with Boston ship captain Abel Coffin, the king gave his consent. The brothers, now eighteen, signed a contract with the men and set sail for America. They had little idea where they were going. They would never again see their family or their homeland.

For four and a half months on Abel Coffin's ship, Eng and Chang learned to climb the mast, to play chess, to speak English, and to do a backflip (presumably during calm seas). When they arrived in America, the young nation was in the middle of a transformation. Andrew Jackson had just been elected president, the country was industrializing, and . . . it was a super-boring place. There were basically three options for entertainment: card games, hard cider drinking, and cockfights. That was pretty much it.

It's no surprise, then, that Chang and Eng became instant stars, two of the first big-time entertainers in the country's short history. No one had ever seen anything like them. Within months they were household names. The term "Siamese twins" entered the vernacular to describe the rare condition of conjoined siblings. (About one in 200,000 births produce conjoined twins, with about 50 percent stillborn and 33 percent of live births dying within twenty-four hours. And that's today. All of this is to say, in the nineteenth century Chang and Eng were extreme rarities.)

By now that four-inch band that connected the brothers had stretched to five and a half inches—no small difference—and so they were able to stand side by side. If you've ever seen pictures of them, they're dressed nicely, and each has one arm over the other's shoulder. That was the most comfortable position for them. To me they look kind of like two best friends coming home from a late night out.

Under Hunter and Coffin's management, they toured the country, putting on a show. In New York City they were exhibited at the grand saloon of the Masonic hall. In small towns and villages, they performed in living rooms or tents, as people came from all over in wagons to see them. Although people turned out simply to gawk at them, they would give the audience their money's worth by performing acrobatic acts—turning somersaults or playing badminton against each other. According to Orser, "Some of the commenters said that they had a great sense of humor, that they were very quick-witted, so you could ask a question and they would be quick with a response." During one show, they noticed a one-eyed man in the audience. They told him they would refund half his admission fee because, after all, he was only seeing half the show.

As a society today, we like to think that we've grown more sensitive to people's differences and disabilities, but we're still fascinated with rare conditions like conjoined twins. In many ways, these siblings appear ordinary, just like the rest of us. But of course, in a fundamental way, they're not typical. They share a body, creating a level of intimacy and connection between them that is utterly foreign to the rest of us. Everywhere they went, Eng and Chang encountered this fascination, making their tour of the United States into what Orser calls "an early version of what ultimately will become known as a freak show." During the next century, in fact, freak shows would grow enormously popular in the United States, famously under the management of P. T. Barnum.

Philosophers opined about the brothers' souls; doctors prodded them with needles. There was a romantic comedy written about them. Herman Melville even alluded to them in *Moby-Dick*. The narrator, Ishmael, is at one point literally tied together with a harpooner from the Pacific Islands named Queequeg. Ishmael realizes that as their bodies are tied together, so are their fates at sea. He and Queequeg are connected, he says, by "an elongated Siamese ligature," a bond that is not just physical but metaphysical:

> *For better or for worse, we two, for the time, were wedded; and should poor Queequeg sink to rise no more, then both usage and honor demanded, that instead of cutting the cord, it should drag me down in his wake. So, then,*

an elongated Siamese ligature united us. Queequeg was my own inseparable twin brother; nor could I any way get rid of the dangerous liabilities which the hempen bond entailed.

This Siamese connection, in fact, is a "mortal wound" to his "free will." Mark Twain, who was always a little more plainspoken than Melville, speculated on them, too: "When one is sick, the other is sick; when one feels pain, the other feels it; when one is angered, the other's temper takes fire."

Although the twins never wrote their own story down—a loss for those of us who want to know how *they* experienced life, *their* thoughts and feelings—it's said that the two had opposite personalities: Eng was supposedly more gentle and well-mannered; Chang was cranky and loved a fight. Sometimes they fought with each other . . . and sometimes that temper was directed at those who got in their faces. Increasingly their ire was aimed at Abel Coffin, who had bought out Robert Hunter for full ownership of the twins' contract. As the boys matured into manhood, they came to realize they were, in Orser's phrase, "bonded labor," working to earn money for Coffin. They were, in effect, his property. When the brothers traveled to England, Coffin and his wife luxuriated in first class while Chang and Eng stayed in steerage with the servants. Before long, they'd had enough. (Can we just take a moment to acknowledge the eerie allegorical nature of some of these names: Robert *Hunter* finds the boys and takes them to the West. Abel *Coffin* essentially strips them of most of their rights.)

At the age of only twenty-one, they fired Coffin and decided to manage their own affairs. If they were going to suffer the indignity of being exhibited and stared at, at the very least they should be the ones to reap the material rewards. After several years of exhibiting themselves (and stashing away their earnings), the brothers traveled through rural North Carolina. When they saw the Blue Ridge Mountains in the distance, they were reminded of Siam. It was a sign. They were now twenty-eight and ready to settle down and make new connections. And this is where the story gets really interesting.

After a decade on the road Chang and Eng retired to North Carolina, where they could start building a life, undisturbed by curiosity seekers. They became American citizens, and as they established themselves in town they started looking around for potential wives. The story goes that at a friend's wedding, Chang fell hard for a woman named Adelaide Yates. It was mutual. But as one half of a conjoined pair, Chang realized the relationship was going to be extremely awkward unless Eng also found a spouse. The good news was that Addie Yates had a sister, Sarah. The bad news was that Sarah didn't particularly like Eng.

So the twins hatched a plan: have all the women from neighboring towns over for a quilting party. Remember, they couldn't watch Netflix back then but they could chill. During the festivities, Eng doted on Sarah, regaling her with tales of life on the road. It worked. The twins had found their other halves.

It didn't hurt that the twins were funny, and, well, rich. It also didn't hurt that Addie and Sarah were used to not caring what other people thought about them or their family. They had grown up with a mother who was obese, so large that she constantly attracted attention. It's said that she was the biggest person in their community, weighing over five hundred pounds. I'm just speculating here, but it seems very possible that the sisters, having lived their lives in the presence of someone who was regarded as different, were less judgmental than others might have been—and more able to shrug off the stares or whispers of the community.

It was around this time that the twins considered being separated. They figured if they were going to have normal lives, this was the moment. Adelaide and Sarah were against it. Having fallen in love with these men, they didn't want to run the risk of losing them during the surgery. As doctors discovered after the twins' deaths, it turns out that they shared a liver, and the operation would have failed. Today, that same surgery would almost certainly be successful.

Both couples were ready to tie their respective knots, but this was uncharted legal territory—and not because the brothers were conjoined. Eng and Chang were among the very first Asians in America—this was decades before Chinese immigrants came to work on the railroads—and marriage between whites and nonwhites was illegal. The situation was unprecedented: the twins were not white but they also weren't black. So in this case, hoping to avoid any problems, each brother posted a bond of one thousand dollars. And in April 1843, in a small double wedding—and can I just say, I love double weddings—Chang and Eng Bunker married Adelaide and Sarah Yates and commenced building their families.

The story of Chang and Eng taking the country by storm, gaining their freedom, then marrying and settling down is so triumphant that it's a little surprising that some of the family members at the reunion I attended grew up not even knowing about their famous ancestors. Alex Sink, a descendant on Chang's side, told me her grandmother wouldn't even permit their names to be mentioned. I asked her why the subject was so taboo. "Nobody wanted to talk about how they created twenty-one children," said Alex.

Yes, between them, Chang and Addie and Eng and Sarah had twenty-one children. But exactly how *did* they do that?

I asked Yunte Huang, a professor at the University of California, Santa Barbara, and author of a biography about the twins called *Inseparable*, for the skinny. According to him, the two couples eventually set up two separate households, and moved between them on a set schedule. For three days and nights, they stayed at one brother's house . . . and then they moved to the other brother's. When they were at Chang's house, Chang would be in charge. If he wanted intimate time with Addie, then, when husband and wife got busy, Eng would go into a passive, meditative state. Imagine a computer in sleep mode—not shutting down, but inactive. Huang describes the arrangement as one of "alternate mastery." It's what allowed each brother to enjoy relations with his spouse while the other brother was right there.

If you're giggling at the description of this unorthodox arrangement, I get it. It must be hard to get comfortable with your brother right there . . . let alone your brother-in-law. But it's also kind of beautiful . . . the very definition of selflessness, to surrender free will, to sacrifice like that to give your brother some meaningful time with his wife. The marriages were fruitful: Chang and Adelaide had ten kids. Eng and Sarah edged them out with eleven. According to Alex Sink, they were very loving parents. And indeed, the body language that you can see in the old family photographs shows real affection between the fathers and their many children. For Chang and Eng—brought to this country for exhibition—even to have children and raise families strikes me as nothing short of radical.

But being landed gentlemen in the antebellum South also meant something else. While Chang and Eng had objected to being seen as slaves, it turns out they had no problem *owning* slaves. As Yunte Huang points out, slavery was "a fact in the Antebellum South," and for the brothers, owning a plantation run on slave labor became "their ticket . . . into the Southern white world." If you're like me, up until this part of the story, you've probably been rooting for them. But once they become slave owners, it gets much more complicated. To make matters worse, the brothers were slave traders of a sort—they would buy young slaves, raise them, and sell them at a profit. The slaves were essentially investment properties for them. They ended up owning thirty-two slaves, including children. Yunte Huang told me that becoming wealthy slave owners allowed Chang and Eng—who as Chinese did not fit into America's racial binary—to position themselves as "honorary whites."

After Abraham Lincoln was elected president in 1860, the nation was thrown into crisis as seven Southern states seceded. The twins once again became a kind of public symbol, a convenient literary device for journalists, a metaphor for a nation with two separate wills that could not be divided. As the *Baltimore American* wrote, "If one of the Siamese brothers, disgusted with his lifelong contact with the other, rudely tears himself away, snapping asunder a bond that God and nature intended to be perpetual, he inflicts upon himself the same precise injury that he inflicts upon his fellow . . . He commits fratricide and suicide at once."

But make no mistake, the twins were united in their allegiance to the South. They sent two of their sons off to war and converted their fortune into Confederate currency. This, unfortunately, proved a disastrous decision that wiped them out

Tiny Lavinia Warren (1842–1919) Lavinia Warren was one of America's most famous entertainers in the nineteenth century. As an adult she stood thirty-two inches tall due to a pituitary disorder that probably resulted from intermarriage. Inspired by the huge success of Charles Stratton, aka "General Tom Thumb," Lavinia worked as a singer and performer, eventually for P. T. Barnum. Both Stratton and another little person, "Commodore" George Nutt, pursued her. The general won her heart, and, with Barnum playing wedding planner, the two were married in 1863, with a lavish reception at New York's Metropolitan Hotel attended by ten thousand people. In what may be the greatest Vows column in history, the *New York Times* devoted 5,200 words to the "Loving Lilliputians." (". . . no one need be surprised that two little matters should create such a tremendous hullabaloo, such a furore of excitement, such an intensity of interest in the feminine world of New-York and its neighborhood, as have the loves of our Lilliputians.") During their honeymoon, Lincoln received them at the White House. Lavinia amassed great wealth and generally accepted the costs of living life in the public eye, but still insisted on her dignity, always chafing at being petted like a child.

Captain Martin Van Buren Bates (1837–1919) While many public performers who made a living displaying their unusual physical attributes gave themselves phony titles, the 7'7½", Kentucky-born Bates actually earned the title of captain fighting for the Confederacy during the Civil War. After the war, he joined a circus. As he wrote, "I decided, for want of something better to do, to exhibit myself as a curiosity." Bates was the rare giant who married a woman taller than himself—the 7'11" Anna Swan, an accomplished pianist whom he met while the circus was touring Halifax, Nova Scotia. The 1871 wedding, while not as grand as that of General Tom Thumb and Lavinia Warren, still made headlines. It was held in London, and the happy couple was given a pair of enormous gold wristwatches by Queen Victoria. They bought a farm in Ohio, and had a house and all its furniture built to proportions that would comfortably accommodate them; Bates himself compared the house to something out of Brobdingnag, the Land of Giants in *Gulliver's Travels*.

3-EYED
IVAN

MIMI the
MUSTACHIOED

NORMA with
a NAIL in
her HEAD!

Normal
Ned

Victor, the Wild Boy of Aveyron (1788–1828) In 1799, hunters discovered a feral child living in the woods of southern France. Approximately twelve years old, he ran naked and lacked speech. He was put into the care of a widow, but escaped and returned to the woods. Recaptured, he was taken to Paris for study. Some doctors believed that he was mentally impaired from birth and had been abandoned only recently, but Jean-Marc Gaspard Itard, the chief physician at the National Institute for Deaf-Mutes, believed he had lived a long time in the wild, and perhaps had been abandoned by alcoholic parents when he was very young. He also believed that in the proper environment "Victor," as he named him (he had heretofore been known as the "wolf child"), could acquire speech and social skills. Itard made little progress in developing Victor's language but made more in helping him to forge bonds. Itard's methods became pioneering techniques in what would become the field of special education.

Sara Baartman, the Hottentot Venus (1770s–1815) Sara Baartman, a Khoikhoi woman born in what is now South Africa, was displayed in England and France as "the Hottentot Venus"; her large buttocks and genitals were the objects of prurient fascination. (*Hottentot* is the derogatory Dutch term once used to describe the Khoikhoi.) The degrading treatment of Baartman epitomized colonial exploitation based on sexual and racial stereotypes. That's not just hindsight; even in 1810 her exhibitions drew protests from British abolitionists who decried her treatment and sued unsuccessfully for her freedom. Baartman defended her "employers," either because she was coerced or because a return to South Africa meant a return to servitude. (She was earning a small wage being exhibited.) Even after death, her exploitation continued: her brain, skeleton, and genitals were displayed in a Paris museum in 1974. It was only in 2002, at the request of Nelson Mandela, that her body was returned to South Africa for burial.

DEATH OF REPRESENTATION

THE BLACK CONGRESSMEN OF RECONSTRUCTION

{1870–1901}

Quick, when was the first African American elected to Congress? The 1950s? The '60s? Nope. The answer is the '70s. The *1870s*. During that decade sixteen African Americans, more than half of them enslaved only a few years before, strode the halls of power in the US House and Senate. And many more took the reins in state and local offices across the country. It was a time of sky-high hope for four million newly freed black Americans and for American democracy itself—a period that ended and faded from memory almost as quickly as it sprang to life.

If it sounds like I'm describing some mythical time and place—less Washington and more Wakanda—I assure you it's real. These men were very much heroes. They deserve to be in textbooks *and* comic books. They are the Black Congressmen of Reconstruction.

Many of these guys would be worth celebrating simply for their very cool nineteenth-century names—Hiram Rhodes Revels, Robert C. De Large, Richard "Daddy" Cain, Louisiana governor P. B. S. Pinchback—and for their absolutely fierce facial hair. But their story is much bigger than that. Reconstruction is one of the most significant and misunderstood chapters in American history.

Here's how it went. After the Civil War, the formerly rebel states were reabsorbed into the United States. And with the passage of the Thirteenth, Fourteenth, and Fifteenth Amendments to the Constitution (aka "the Reconstruction Amendments") between 1865 and 1870, former slaves became citizens, with African American men gaining the right to vote—and exercising it. (Women of all races had to fight for another half century before the Nineteenth Amendment guaranteed their right to vote.) Eric Foner, Columbia University historian and author of the landmark *Reconstruction: America's Unfinished Revolution, 1863–1877*, estimates that a remarkable 90 percent of eligible black voters in the South cast ballots during Reconstruction. "Today we're very lucky if we get fifty percent turnout in any election. But black people were tremendously enthused about voting and having some say in the government that was going to rule over them." Conventions—really, boisterous mass meetings—attended by black men and women throughout the South voted on resolutions and issued demands. "We tend to think of slaves as ignorant or unsophisticated," Foner told me. "But you know, they had been living in American society for their whole lives, and their parents had too." The slave trade from Africa had ended in 1808. "These people were Americans. They knew what democracy was, they observed the larger society. They knew what it was to be a free person in America, and they wanted the same rights, the same opportunities as free white people had."

During Reconstruction as many as two thousand black men attained positions ranging from sheriffs and school superintendents to a justice on the South Carolina Supreme Court. Fourteen were elected to the US House of Representatives and two to the US Senate. "I think of it as a pivotal moment in the history of American democracy," Foner said. "It's the first time in this country, or really anywhere, that an interracial democracy was created."

And then it was over. A dispute over who won the presidential election of 1876 (think *Bush v. Gore* but without the hanging chads) led to a deal: Republicans could have the White House as long as they agreed to the demands of the Southern Democrats (aka the former Confederates) to withdraw federal troops from the South. Those federal troops were essential to protecting the rights of the newly emancipated black population. Rights that included voting. This so-called Compromise of 1877 brought Reconstruction to a swift conclusion as insidious voting restrictions—many of which lasted until 1965—were instituted across the South.

Black representation in Congress (all of it Republican) quickly dried up. Between the retirement of Senator Blanche K. Bruce of Mississippi in 1880 and the election of

Edward Brooke of Massachusetts in 1966, not a single African American served in the US Senate. A few African Americans managed to be elected to the US House during the 1880s and 1890s. But there, too, representation disappeared for decades afterward.

Worse still, the *memory* of this moment faded. The North won the war, but the South won the textbooks (blink and you might have missed Reconstruction in high school history class) and the movie house: in one scene in D. W. Griffith's 1915 landmark and deeply racist film *The Birth of a Nation*, black legislators are depicted drinking, eating chicken, and putting their bare feet up on desks in the South Carolina statehouse. The movie's message was clear: black people were inherently corrupt and unequipped to lead.

But the message of the biographies of the *actual* men who served is of possibility. Being a "first" matters. It signals to people who are historically shut out that they belong. It inspires them to unlock their own potential. It's hard to think of a more dramatic example than this one. What had been unthinkable just a few years before— black men, some of them former slaves, serving in elective office—was suddenly real with the Black Congressmen of Reconstruction. Here are some of their stories:

Robert Smalls (1839–1915)

Perhaps the most famous of the Black Congressmen of Reconstruction was Robert Smalls. Smalls was a war hero before he was a congressman. He was born to a slave named Lydia Polite in South Carolina; his father was probably the son of her owner, which may explain why his servitude was relatively lenient.

As Robert got older, his master began to hire him out for various jobs, allowing him to keep a fraction of his pay. He learned sail-making and seamanship and eventually became the pilot of a steamer called the *Planter*. After marrying a woman named Hannah Jones, he began saving his pennies to purchase freedom for themselves and their young daughter. Then the Civil War broke out, and Robert was pressed into service by the new Confederate navy, using the *Planter* to mine Charleston harbor.

Smalls's crew members used to joke about his physical resemblance to the ship's captain, a white man named C. J. Relyea, and the jokes inspired a daring plan. In the early-morning hours of May 13, 1862, while the white officers of the ship slept on shore, Smalls dressed himself in a straw hat and long overcoat resembling Captain Relyea's. He and his black crew quietly took the *Planter* out into the harbor, stopped to pick up their families, and made their way out to sea. The stakes couldn't have been higher. Had he been found out, Smalls would have been made a particularly cruel example of by Confederates, before surely being put to death.

The seventeen black passengers, including five women and three children be-lowdecks, made their way through the harbor, Smalls signaling confidently past several checkpoints. The final barrier to freedom: the formidable Fort Sumter, where the Civil War had begun. "When we drew near the fort every man but Robert Smalls felt his knees giving way and the women began crying and praying again," one passenger later said.

Smalls was prepared: he knew the whistle signal ("two long blows and a short one") that would grant him the right of way. Once past the defenses, the crew fired up the boiler and headed for open waters. Knowing he was in the clear, Smalls cried out in jubilation. He took down the Confederate flag, ran up a white bedsheet, and surrendered to the perfectly-named-for-the-occasion USS *Onward*. The Union forces had suddenly gained a heavily armed ship ideal for navigating Charleston's harbor. Even more valuable than the ship and its military supplies, though, was the pilot's expert knowledge of the harbor's shallows and shoals—including the loca-tion of those mines he had planted.

The escape plan hatched by Smalls caused a sensation in newspapers throughout the fractured nation. "It really blew people's minds," Smalls's great-great-grandson Michael Boulware Moore told me. "It was just beyond what people thought an enslaved person could do." Smalls's brave and ingenious plan constituted a living, breathing argument for the intellect and ability of black Americans.

At this point, early in the war, President Lincoln did not want to employ runaway slaves in the Union military. He worried that doing so would cast the war incontrovertibly as a struggle for emancipation and hurt his support among slaveholders in the border states. But Lincoln's generals had been witnessing firsthand the passion that African Americans brought to the cause of freedom, and pushed Honest Abe to change his policy. On August 16, 1862, General David Hunter sent the new war hero Smalls to meet with Secretary of War Edwin Stanton and the Great Bearded One himself. Smalls helped make the case for recruiting blacks to serve in the Union ranks. Eventually 200,000 African American soldiers served the cause. (Music up: Theme from *Glory*.) Smalls himself went on to fight for the Union in seventeen naval battles, rising to the rank of captain.

After the war, Smalls could have moved to the North, but he returned to his native South Carolina. In fact, he purchased the Beaufort home of his former master and in 1868 helped to ratify a new state constitution that banned discrimination "on account of race or color, in any case whatever." He won a seat in the state legislature and fought for compulsory public schooling—for all children, white and black. And in 1874, he ran for Congress to represent the Sea Islands district, known informally as "the Negro Paradise."

But for many whites in states like South Carolina and Mississippi, the prevailing mood was indignation and outrage. Men they had been trained to regard as subhuman were now their representatives in Washington, not to mention their governors, judges, sheriffs, and schoolmasters. In reaction, the region saw the flourishing of domestic terrorist groups like the Red Shirts in South Carolina, the White League in Louisiana, and the White Liners in Mississippi. Violence became part of everyday politics. Black politicians and the whites who supported them were threatened, kidnapped, even assassinated. In Yazoo City, Mississippi, the election of a Republican postmaster led to a riot that left several men dead. Black political assemblies and gatherings were attacked by white mobs, who often outnumbered and outgunned the state militias.

Smalls himself became a target of Democrats seeking to roll back Reconstruction. After the Compromise of 1877 had emboldened the former Confederates, he had to fight off a trumped-up bribery charge and repeated efforts to force him out of power by redrawing his district. By 1886 the power in the state had shifted definitively, and Smalls lost his last election for federal office. In all he had served five terms in the US Congress.

By 1895, without the supervision of the federal government, political control of South Carolina had completely reverted to the Democrats. Red Shirt governor "Pitchfork Ben" Tillman held a new constitutional convention with the intent to secure "the blessings of Anglo-Saxon civilization." He denounced the "Reconstruction deviltry" of black Republicans and northern abolitionists. Since black voters still outnumbered whites, he pushed through an "understanding clause" that allowed registrars to prevent citizens from voting on the basis of a constitutional quiz. Smalls attended this convention, and I can only imagine what he must have felt to see history reversing itself before his eyes, as hard-earned rights and liberties vanished in a matter of days. He and the few other black delegates put up a noble protest, but lost the vote on the new constitution by 116 to 7. Smalls refused to sign the final document. The US Supreme Court upheld the "understanding clause," and similar ones soon spread across the South as Jim Crow segregation laws took root.

Blanche K. Bruce (1841–1898)

Blanche Kelso Bruce was born in 1841 in Virginia to Polly Bruce, an African American slave, and her white owner. As a boy, he was assigned to be a personal servant to his white half-brother. He sat at the table during his brother's lessons, and, as one report has it, "held every scrap of knowledge that came his way," while his brother turned out to be an indifferent student. By the time the Civil War broke out, the family had relocated to Missouri, and when his master enlisted in the Confederate army in 1861, Blanche, now twenty years old, fled to the free state of Kansas, where he got a job teaching school in Lawrence.

But being on free soil didn't ensure safety. Ever since the Supreme Court's infamous *Dred Scott* decision in 1857, escaped slaves could legally be forcibly returned to their owners. Bruce was nearly captured by William Clarke Quantrill, a "bush-whacker"—essentially a vigilante—who led an armed gang seeking to reenslave runaways. Bruce, dressed only in his underwear, escaped by hiding in the vegetation of the bank of the Kaw River.

After the war, Bruce briefly attended Oberlin College in Ohio, but when he read about Oscar Dunn and P. B. S. Pinchback, two black men rising to prominence in Louisiana politics, he headed south with thoughts of a career in public service. He settled in a majority-black district in Mississippi and was elected to a series of posts—tax collector, sheriff, superintendent of schools; at the same time he grew wealthy from a plantation he'd purchased. Like many of the African American politicians of his era, Bruce toed a more moderate line. He argued that educating blacks would be good for race relations, but didn't push to integrate schools, which might erode white support. Bruce's ascent in the state Republican Party led, in 1874, to his being elected by the state legislature as the second African American US senator, and the first to serve a complete term. (Until 1913, US senators were chosen by state legislatures, rather than by general elections.) And how's this for a sign? He occupied the very seat once held by Jefferson Davis, who had left the Senate to become the president of the Confederacy. (After the war Davis had been apprehended attempting to flee to Cuba, disguised in his wife's clothing.)

The other senator from Mississippi was James Alcorn, a white man who had been something of a mentor to Bruce earlier. But the two men had since fallen out. Now, in 1875, when the time came for Bruce's swearing-in at the Capitol building, Alcorn refused to escort his junior colleague to the podium, as was customary. Bruce later recalled: "When the names of the new Senators were called out for them to go up and take the oath, all the others except myself were escorted by their colleagues. Mr. Alcorn made no motion to escort me, but was buried behind a newspaper, and I concluded I would go it alone. I had got about half way up the aisle when a tall gentleman stepped up to me and said: 'Excuse me, Mr. Bruce, I did not until this moment see that you were without an escort. Permit me. My name is Conkling,' and he linked his arm in mine and we marched up to the desk together." It was Roscoe Conkling, Republican of New York. In gratitude, Bruce later named his son Roscoe Conkling Bruce.

As a senator, Bruce advocated not only for the rights of blacks, but also for Native Americans and for Chinese immigrant laborers. Living in Washington, DC, Bruce married Josephine Wilson, a beautiful wealthy black woman from Cleveland's social elite. Wilson had been raised with private tutors and her marriage to Bruce was covered by both black and white newspapers. Their DC town house became a fashionable hub for the growing black upper class. Bruce, with his genteel manners and wealth, embodied the heights to which a former slave could aspire. But violence back home in Mississippi was reaching a crisis point, with armed battles breaking out between Republicans and Democrats and the state militia outgunned by vigilante groups. It must have seemed to some that the Civil War had erupted all over again. Bruce urged President Grant to send federal troops, but the request was ultimately denied; the northerners' taste for fighting the battles of Reconstruction was waning.

It's not clear whether Bruce was defeated in 1880 or simply chose not to run for reelection, but literacy tests and other voter suppression efforts altered the Mississippi electorate so dramatically that black people no longer enjoyed significant representation. His seat went to a former Confederate colonel.

Bruce, born a slave, had been the first African American to serve a full term in the Senate, the first to preside over the Senate, and the first to chair the Republican National Convention. Once out of office, he and Josephine remained for much of their lives in Washington, where she founded the Colored Women's League, a civil rights organization, and he was named by President Garfield as Register of the Treasury. In that role he became the first African American to have his signature printed on US currency.

Hiram Rhodes Revels (1827–1901)

Hiram Rhodes Revels was senator for only a year, from 1870 to 1871, but he was *the* first African American to serve in the US Congress. He was born free in North Carolina to parents of mixed racial background, with African, Scottish, and Native American bloodlines. His father was a preacher. As a young man Revels moved north to Indiana and then Ohio to attend seminary, and was ordained in the African Methodist Episcopal (AME) Church. In Ohio he married a free black woman, with whom he had six daughters.

Having always been free, Revels asserted his rights boldly even before the war, breaking the law in Missouri by openly preaching to blacks, and refusing to give up his seat in a first-class railway car. His career as a pastor and schoolmaster had fostered an interest in politics, and after the war he settled in Natchez, Mississippi, where he was elected to the state legislature. At the encouragement of John Roy Lynch—another future black congressman—he ran for the US Senate. According to Lynch, it was when Revels was called upon to lead the state legislature in a prayer that he impressed them with his eloquence and secured his future as a US senator. The legislature elected him by a vote of 85–15 and he headed to Washington.

Revels's time in the Senate was brief. He was pragmatic and moderate when he needed to be. He supported amnesty for the former Confederates, and even protested to President Grant about the influx of northern whites into the South. When he completed his term, he returned to a career in education, serving as the inaugural president of Alcorn University (now Alcorn State), a newly established black-serving land-grant institution named for the man who would succeed Revels in the Senate.

The power of the symbolism of his being first is impossible to overstate. In 1870 the great abolitionist Frederick Douglass was sent a portrait of the dignified Hiram Revels—a chromolithograph (a kind of colored print) of a painting of the first black man to serve in Congress. In a letter, Douglass responded approvingly:

> *Whatever may be the prejudices of those who may look upon it, they will be compelled to admit that the Mississippi Senator is a man, and one who will easily pass for a man among men. We colored men so often see ourselves described and painted as monkeys, that we think it a great piece of good fortune to find an exception to this general rule.*

Robert Brown Elliott (1842–1884)

Elliott, a congressman from South Carolina, was most famous for his sterling oratory on the floor of Congress. His effortless display of classical learning and his eloquence in debate made him an object of fascination. His background was something of a mystery: he was said at different times to have been born in Boston, in Liverpool, and in the West Indies. He claimed to have graduated from Eton College, but probably didn't. He might have served in the Royal Navy. His parents were possibly Jamaican or South Carolinian. Both, however, were of apparently unmixed African descent, and Elliott stood out among his mixed-race colleagues for his dark skin.

In any case, by the end of the Civil War, Elliott was working as a typesetter in Boston and by 1867 he was an editor at South Carolina's first black newspaper, the *Leader*, which was owned by another future black congressman, Richard "Daddy" Cain. Like Robert Smalls, Elliott attended the state constitutional convention and made universal public education a top priority. He became a successful lawyer and served two terms in Congress, from 1871 to 1874.

Elliott was less conciliatory than some of his black colleagues, more reluctant to offer amnesty for the former Confederates. His greatest moment on the floor of Congress came in support of Charles Sumner's Civil Rights Act of 1875—the capstone legislation of Reconstruction, sponsored by probably the Senate's greatest champion of equal rights. The bill outlawed discrimination based on race in public places such as hotels, theaters, and railway cars—eighty-nine years before the Civil Rights Act of 1964. As the bill was debated, Sumner himself was dying, and Elliott took the lead in pressing his cause. (Fittingly Elliott held the congressional seat that before the war had been held by the champion of slavery Preston Brooks, now remembered for viciously caning Sumner during a debate over the Kansas-Nebraska Act.)

Adding to the drama: the Democrats' case was being argued by none other than Alexander Stephens, the former vice president of the Confederacy, now an aged congressman from Georgia.

But in what historian Philip Dray called "arguably one of the most daring addresses ever proclaimed in Congress," Elliott faced down the cretinous Stephens and his colleagues, calling them out for their Confederate pasts, insisting on the inalienable rights of his own race, and citing biblical precedent. The speech, wrote the *New York Times*, "electrified the nation," and the press hailed him as "the Genius of Freedom," on a par with Sumner and Lincoln himself. That night a celebratory crowd assembled outside Elliott's residence, cheering, playing music, and giving tributes to the silver-tongued champion of civil rights. President Grant signed the bill into law the next year.

But if the passage of the bill was the final triumph of Reconstruction, it was also the last gasp. Sumner died in March 1874. Elliott returned to local politics when his term was up. Grant signed the bill but did almost nothing to enforce it, and the Supreme Court invalidated it in 1883.

By the turn of the century Jim Crow laws were firmly in place and there was just one African American in Congress—North Carolina's George White. He was defeated in 1900. In his farewell address of January 29, 1901, White, a vocal advocate for civil rights and education, addressed the US House in words that managed to capture both the deep disappointment of Reconstruction and the fierce determination for a better future it had inspired.

This, Mr. Chairman, is perhaps the Negroes' temporary farewell to the American Congress; but let me say, Phoenix-like he will rise up some day and come again. These parting words are in behalf of an outraged, heartbroken, bruised, and bleeding, but God-fearing people, faithful, industrious, loyal people—rising people, full of potential force . . . The only apology that I have to make for the earnestness with which I have spoken is that I am pleading for the life, the liberty, the future happiness and manhood suffrage for one-eighth of the entire population of the United States.

Susanna Madora Salter (1860–1961)

First Woman Mayor in the United States

Salter was elected as the nation's first female mayor on April 4, 1887, by the town of Argonia, Kansas, population 500. The local Women's Christian Temperance Union favored enforcement of new state prohibition laws, and a group of anti-prohibition men, seeking to embarrass and discredit the temperance women, put Salter on the ballot as a prank. But the joke was on them. She won, making international news. (Women in Kansas had only weeks before been given the franchise in local elections, a development the pranksters may have overlooked. Maybe they were drinking?) A reporter for the *New York Sun* observed her during a city council meeting and praised her for several times checking irrelevant discussion. After one year in office, she chose not to seek reelection.

Ebenezer Don Carlos Bassett (1833–1908)

First Black American Diplomat

Bassett was born in Connecticut to a mixed-race father and a Pequot Indian mother. His father's father had been a slave who won his freedom by fighting in the American Revolution. While a young man, the college-educated Bassett struck up a friendship with Frederick Douglass. Following the Battle of Gettysburg, he joined with Douglass in enlisting African Americans in the US Army. After the war, President Grant wanted to recognize black leaders who had been essential partners in the struggle for the Union. At Douglass's suggestion, he appointed Bassett as minister to Haiti and the Dominican Republic—the equivalent of an ambassador.

Charles Curtis (1860–1936)

First Native American Vice President

Even more forgotten than hapless Herbert Hoover is his veep. Although Curtis joked that he was "one-eighth Kaw Indian and 100% Republican" it turned out that he was closer to half American Indian. Descended from the Kansa-Kaw chief White Plume, who had offered assistance to Lewis and Clark during their 1804 expedition, Curtis spent a portion of his childhood on a reservation with his maternal grandparents. (His mother had died when he was three.) He trained in the law, and at age thirty-two won a seat in Congress. He served seven terms in the House, followed by four in the Senate. While in Congress he sponsored the first version of the Equal Rights Amendment. As vice president, he was quoted as saying that "good times are just around the corner." The line was attributed to Hoover and became a liability in their historic 1932 defeat.

Harvey Milk (1930–1978)
First Openly Gay Elected Official in California

Born to a middle-class Jewish family in the suburbs of New York, Milk worked as a navy lieutenant, an actuary, a securities analyst, and a volunteer on the Goldwater campaign before finding his calling as an activist and politician in San Francisco. Milk showed a knack for bringing together the city's diverse constituencies in pursuit of common goals. After running unsuccessfully for office several times, he won a seat on the San Francisco Board of Supervisors in November 1977. Among his achievements was sponsorship of a local law that protected gays and lesbians from discrimination in hiring, housing, and public accommodations. But Milk worked on a range of issues, saying, "I'm showing people here that the gays are involved with taxes, and dog shit, and Muni [public transit], and everything else." Less than a year after his swearing-in, Milk, along with his ally Mayor George Moscone, was assassinated by a disgruntled former supervisor named Dan White.

Romualdo Pacheco (1831–1899)
First Hispanic Member of the House of Representatives

Born in the California territory when it was still a part of Mexico, Pacheco was a *Californio*, a word that I love and which means a descendant of the original Spanish-speaking colonists. A member of the wealthy landowning class, Pacheco "was indisputably the most illustrious Californio of his time," noted a contemporary, "a magnificent physical specimen whose brain matched his brawn." He became an American citizen in 1848, at the conclusion of the Mexican-American War. His views were mainly supportive of big landowners, but he was also an outspoken opponent of slavery. His political ascent was rapid: he became lieutenant governor in 1871 and in 1875 he became California's first native-born and first Mexican American governor. After completing the term, he turned his sights on the House of Representatives, and won his majority-Hispanic district by a single vote. After some tussles in the courts, Pacheco became the first Hispanic member of the House of Representatives from a US state.

Shirley Chisholm (1924–2005)
First African American Woman Elected to Congress

The daughter of immigrants from the Caribbean, Chisholm was a prize-winning debater at Brooklyn College. As a young woman she ran a day care center, an experience that significantly influenced her: early education and child welfare became key issues for her after she won a seat in Congress in 1968. Assigned to the House Agriculture Committee—not exactly a plum assignment for someone representing New York City—Chisholm made the most of it, using her power to help expand the Food Stamp Program. In 1972 she made history again when she became the first woman of any race to seek the Democratic nomination for president. "I ran," she later wrote, "because somebody had to do it first. In this country, everybody is supposed to be able to run for President, but that has never really been true." Discounted by the media, she had to file a complaint with the Federal Communications Commission to be included in a debate with McGovern and Humphrey. She made further news when she visited segregationist candidate George Wallace in the hospital after he'd been shot. Chisholm told Wallace that even though she knew she was taking a political risk, "I wouldn't want what happened to you to happen to anyone." Wallace broke out in tears.

forgotten forerunner

When a Woman Ruled Hollywood

LOIS WEBER
{1879–1939}

I t's projected that for 2019, a mere 18 percent of Hollywood studio films will be directed by women. And consider that that paltry number is a dramatic *improvement* over 2018. Only one woman has won the Academy Award for Best Director. Pay inequity is a stubborn problem. But in the Hollywood of a hundred years ago, one of the most respected and highest-paid directors was named Lois Weber. Not *Louis* Weber. *Lois*. She was the first American woman to direct a feature film, a 1914 adaptation of *The Merchant of Venice*. She directed more than one hundred short films and, in one year alone, she wrote and directed ten feature-length productions. If it sounds as though the Hollywood I'm describing is some mythical place like Camelot, it's not.

To understand Weber's career, you have to understand the beginnings of the movie industry. It was sort of like a land rush. Anyone with the resources, the will, and the talent could get in the game. And because demand was rising so rapidly, the business couldn't afford to discriminate. So, as the film historian Shelley Stamp told me, the industry became a magnet for women seeking careers both creative and lucrative. These women would help shape this new form of storytelling.

Lois Weber was one of those women. She was born in Allegheny City, Pennsylvania, in 1879 to a religious middle-class family. She started off as an accomplished pianist, then moved on to the theater, where she met her husband, Phillips Smalley. He started working in the movies, and they soon teamed up—as writers, actors, and directors. And it became clear that in this duo, Lois was playing the lead.

Weber succeeded because she grasped the potential of film as a visual medium. One of her most popular early shorts is *Suspense*, from 1913. As Stamp says, it's a variation on what was a popular formula, "the last-minute rescue"—the Liam Neeson movie before there was any Liam Neeson. A young mother (played by Weber), left at home, is threatened by an intruder while her husband is away. (The intruder here is an actor made up to look swarthy, presumably as an Italian—cinema's go-to villain of the day.) But what distinguishes *Suspense* from other versions of this old scenario is, in the critic Richard Brody's words, the director's "extraordinarily agile and expressive use of the camera, with jolting angles and shifts in perspective." Weber cuts between the three characters—the woman, the husband, the intruder—to heighten the tension. And her use of the split screen inaugurated a technique that has become part of every film student's tool kit.

In 1915, Weber broke new ground in a different way. Her film *Hypocrites* is sometimes credited as featuring the first full-frontal nude scene, with an actress portraying a character called, fittingly, "The Naked Truth." Weber was able to break this taboo, though, by making the nudity part of a moral allegory: in the movie, a group of wealthy holier-than-thou churchgoers

*"But in the Hollywood of a hundred years ago,
one of the most respected and highest-paid directors
was named Lois Weber. Not <u>Louis</u> Weber. <u>Lois</u>."*

reveal their true natures—and lust for power, sex, and money—when they come into contact with "The Naked Truth."

Throughout her career, Weber maintained a persona that Stamp describes as a "dignified, married white middle-class woman." There was nothing stereotypically "Hollywood" about her. Her conservative image matched her perspective on the role of film as she saw it: "It's a medium where I can preach to my heart's content."

Weber's evangelical impulses (earlier in life she'd preached on street corners in New York City) drove her to confront the volatile social issues of her day, including abortion and birth control. In 1916 Margaret Sanger opened the first birth control clinic in America. That same year, Weber directed *Where Are My Children?* The movie is about a district attorney who prosecutes a doctor for performing illegal abortions, before discovering that his wife and her well-to-do friends are enlisting the doctor's services. The movie was so controversial that Universal prefaced the film with a full-screen warning to parents not to let their children watch the film unsupervised.

Weber favored contraception, but in the service of eugenics. She believed that immigrants, women of color, and women in poverty should, for the social good, be restricted in how many children they bring into the world. Conversely, she believed privileged white women should be having *more* children. (The wealthier women who seek abortions in *Where Are My Children?* are indeed portrayed as selfish.) While the film's point of view has not aged well, Weber's views were not uncommon in her day. Even Teddy Roosevelt warned American women against "race suicide" in a 1905 speech. Like TR, Weber believed that white middle-class American women had a moral obligation to propagate.

So why don't we know Lois Weber's name today? In part, tastes shifted during the twenties, and Weber's brand of storytelling became less popular. But there were also structural changes taking place. As Hollywood grew more profitable, power was consolidated, and the many little players were absorbed into the major studios. And that's when Wall Street took charge. Imagine a bunch of cigar-chompers, guys like the Monopoly man, waltzing into Hollywood saying, "All right, all right, ladies, step aside . . . This is getting serious, there's big money here, this is a man's job." That's pretty much what happened.

In the following decades, women directors became the exception to the rule. There was Dorothy Arzner in the 1930s and '40s. (She was the first woman to join the Directors Guild.) In the 1950s, Hollywood actress Ida Lupino—you know her from crossword puzzles—moved on to directing films and later, television. (She was the only woman to direct an episode of the original *Twilight Zone* series.) And then there was Barbra with *Yentl* (underrated!) and *The Prince of Tides*. But not until 2010 did a woman win the Best Director Oscar—Kathryn Bigelow for *The Hurt Locker*.

Lois Weber did make it to the era of talkies, barely. She made one sound picture in 1934, the first film shot on location on the Hawaiian island of Kauai. From then until her death in 1939 she remained active, writing, working to set up pictures, trying to gain back the ground that female directors had won but then lost.

Famed gossip columnist Hedda Hopper wrote the obituary of Lois Weber in the *Los Angeles Times*: "I don't know of any woman who has had a greater influence upon the motion-picture business than Lois or anyone who has helped so many climb the ladder of fame asking nothing but friendship in return." It's likely that neither Hopper nor Weber knew how high a climb that would end up being.

DEATH OF
MEDIEVAL
SCIENCE

{800–1928}

If you're wondering about the death date assigned here for medieval science, it's not a typo. In 1928 a Scottish physician and scientist named Alexander Fleming found mold growing in an uncovered petri dish. As Fleming himself would later say:

When I woke up just after dawn on September 28, 1928, I certainly didn't plan to revolutionize all medicine by discovering the world's first antibiotic, or bacteria killer. But I suppose that was exactly what I did.

Fleming had discovered penicillin, which would begin to be used in 1942 and subsequently save millions of lives. Until the onset of antibiotics, though, people still treated infections with bloodletting, a standard treatment of medieval times.

We all know our health-care system is stuck in the Dark Ages. Likewise the science itself that rules our lives is not as far removed from medieval times as we may think.

Alchemy

At the center of medieval science was alchemy. You might know about alchemy from those enchanting Harry Potter books, through which an underemployed J. K. Rowling magically transformed 4,224 pages of prose into eight movies, two theme parks, a smash Broadway show, and $650 million in profit.

The word itself comes from the Arabic *al-kimiya*. No surprise. Modern math and science still owe enormous debts to the Arab and Persian civilizations of the

Islamic Golden Age. Consider all the math and science words that derive from Arabic—not only *alchemy* but also *algebra*, *algorithm*, *alkaline*—and of course *alka-seltzer*, which helps to neutralize the effects of too much *al-cohol*.

Alchemists sought to transform base metals like lead into "noble" ones like gold. In both the Muslim and Christian worlds, alchemists sought a mineral or substance, the Philosopher's Stone (thought to be red sulfur in Arabic lands or cinnabar in China), that could effect this magical change. That's why the first book of the Harry Potter series was originally called *Harry Potter and the Philosopher's Stone*. American publishers changed the name to *Harry Potter and the Sorcerer's Stone* because they worried that a book with the word *philosopher* in the title would scare away children.

Alchemy was also believed to possess the secret to life. The Philosopher's Stone was believed to be an "elixir" (meaning magical potion) to heal the sick, rejuvenate the body, or even bestow immortality. Today, of course, we no longer believe that concoctions of red sulfur will make us live for centuries; instead we buy big jars of turmeric at our neighborhood supplement store and juice our own celery.

While no one ever seems to have transformed iron or lead into gold, the medieval alchemists discovered many important chemical compounds, including hydrochloric acid and nitric acid. The sixteenth-century Swiss alchemist Paracelsus (1493–1541), also known as "the father of Toxicology," pioneered the use of opium derivatives for pain relief, and look how well that's worked out. The search for new compounds had another unexpected benefit, too—the discovery of all kinds of brilliant colors that were used in creating inks, dyes, and paints for illustrated manuscripts and Renaissance paintings.

I should add that I was once an aspiring alchemist. As a small child I would accompany my father to the local Giant Food supermarket. I would observe in wonder as he commanded the cashier to transform one bill into more bills. "Can you make change for a ten?" he'd ask. Then, like magic, the cashier would take his one bill and hand him six different bills! At around the age of seven the sorcerer's apprentice was ready. I asked my father if I could ask for "change." He handed me a bill.

"Can you change this five for a hundred?" I asked. In return I unintentionally got my first big laugh.

Astrology

Astrology, the belief that the relative positions of stars and planets influence the natural world and human affairs, has been in retrograde for a while, reduced today to a sad husk of its former self. I've often wondered how fortune-tellers in New York City storefronts meet their rent. Alchemy?

But astrology in the medieval world was no joke. If a secret, divine order lay behind both matter and spirit, then understanding the motions of the stars could unlock the secrets of human destiny. The big theological question was whether the forces of astrology contradicted the Christian belief in free will. It was Albertus Magnus (1200–1280) who solved that problem, explaining that astrology could help people understand and master the adverse forces that might lead them away from God—just as predicting a coming storm might help you judge whether to embark on a dangerous journey. Medieval physicians based much of their medical practice on the movement of the stars, and carried almanacs that they would consult in making diagnoses. In fact, in the later Middle Ages, doctors were often required by law to determine the position of celestial bodies before undertaking major medical treatments, such as surgery or bloodletting. Which brings us to our next topic . . .

Bloodletting

Feeling feverish? Achy? Just having a bad day? Open a vein and get rid of all that blood that's clogging your system! That's the basic logic behind the medical concept of bloodletting. The science behind bloodletting rested on the ancient Greeks' theory of the "Four Humors." This idea, which was taken as scientific fact for a good 1,500 years, posited that four bodily fluids—blood, phlegm, bile (or "choler"), and black bile (or "melancholy")—regulated human health and created basic personality types. Sanguine (bloody) people were optimistic; phlegmatic people, even-keeled; choleric people, angry; melancholic people, depressed. (I've long thought there should be a comedy tour called the Four Humors. Here's how I'd cast it: Sanguine—Sarah Silverman; Phlegmatic—Dave Chappelle; Choleric—Lewis Black; Melancholic—Richard Lewis.)

When the mixture of these fluids was out of balance, however, you became ill, and getting rid of the problematic humor was necessary to restore health. In the case of fever, headache, and apoplexy, that meant it was time for a bleeding. In the Middle Ages, when the Church forbid priests from letting blood, barbers took up the trade—they already owned all the sharp tools, after all—and the red stripe on the barber's pole is sometimes (though probably falsely) traced to their function as bloodletters.

Bloodletting lasted well past the end of the Middle Ages. When George Washington woke up early on December 14, 1799, with what doctors now believe was a severe case of strep throat, three different doctors spent the day bleeding him of eighty ounces, about 40 percent of his blood supply. Needless to say, the treatment didn't help.

It's unclear how exactly most of his blood was drawn, but it may have involved leeches—a widespread ancient practice described in early Sanskrit, Egyptian, and Chinese writings. Probably because it created a much more controlled loss of blood, leeching eventually became the favored method of bloodletting, and persisted well into the nineteenth century, at which point people finally realized that it was disgusting. Today leeches are actually making a comeback in medicine because they've been discovered to release chemicals that have vasodilating (I had to look it up, too: it means decreasing blood pressure) and anticoagulant properties that facilitate blood flow and prevent clotting. Research has shown their value in certain surgeries such as the reattachment of ears or fingers.

Scrying

ME: Mirror, Mirror on the Wall, is there a name for what I'm doing right now?
BATHROOM MIRROR: Most people call it talking to yourself. But that friend of yours with the crystal ball knows it's called scrying.

Many ancient cultures have tales of scrying—looking into crystal balls, magic mirrors, or pools of water to gain an image of the past, present, or future. I'm pretty sure it's in Harry Potter a few times. Of course it was in *The Wizard of Oz*. But it was during the Middle Ages and early Renaissance that scrying seems to have peaked. It was in sixteenth-century France, for example, that the physician and practitioner of scrying Nostradamus made his reputation via vaguely worded predictions that could be retrofitted to pretty much every major world event. (Smart cookie, that Nostradamus.)

Cornelius Agrippa (1486–1535) was supposedly a champion of scrying. For Agrippa, scrying, like alchemy and astrology, had natural causes. He insisted that scrying was not a demonic power but simply the use of one's imagination to control the perceptual world. Legend has it that in the early 1500s in Italy, Agrippa met up with the English nobleman and poet Henry Howard, Earl of Surrey—best known today as one of the first great writers of sonnets. Surrey was desperately missing his beloved mistress, Geraldine, the subject of many of those lovely sonnets. At that point, it is related, "Agrippa accordingly exhibited his magic glass, in which the noble poet saw his beautiful dame, weeping upon her bed, and inconsolable for the absence of her admirer." Agrippa supposedly also used his magic glass with some of the greatest scholars of the early Renaissance: he summoned the image of the ancient Roman orator Cicero for the Dutch scholar Erasmus, and he presented Sir Thomas More with an image of the fall of Troy, sort of like a sixteenth-century GIF.

> ME: Mirror, Mirror on the Wall, how will people one hundred years from now look back on our medical practices?
>
> BATHROOM MIRROR: They'll be horrified by the barbarism of what you call cancer treatment. They'll gasp at the insanity of the anti-vaccine cult. Most of all, they'll wonder why you just didn't do everything decreed by Gwyneth Paltrow's Goop. After all, it's so much more than a lifestyle brand!

The medieval scientists may have been a little short on the science, but their willingness to ask questions and to experiment, as well as their extraordinary imaginations, paved the way for the famous men—Copernicus, Kepler, Galileo, Newton—who brought about the Scientific Revolution. We wouldn't be here without them.

The practice survived into recorded history, so we know that by medieval times trepanning was frequently used as a cure for what was seen as deviant behavior. The idea was to release evil spirits, and the hole was generally made by drilling or scraping. Have you heard enough? Whether or not it was an effective treatment, the surprising fact is that most people lived through the procedure.

Spontaneous Combustion Unlike our other bygone "sciences," the theory of spontaneous human combustion still burns on. Most recently, in 2010 the burned body of seventy-six-year-old Michael Faherty was found on the floor of his home in County Galway, Ireland, with no other fire damage in the room, prompting the coroner to, um, chalk it up to "spontaneous human combustion, for which there is no adequate explanation." In fact, since its first recorded flare-up in 1641, scientists have tried in vain to find explanations for spontaneous human combustion, ranging from people becoming flammable due to excessive alcohol consumption to only slightly less reasonable theories involving poltergeists. (Phlogiston, anyone?) Serious scientists now have a more convincing theory: it *doesn't* happen. They point out that the most frequent victims—elderly people and alcoholics—are also the most likely to become careless around open flames.

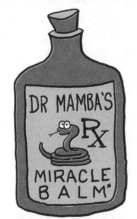

DR MAMBA'S Rx MIRACLE BALM*

*May cause spontaneous combustion

DEATH OF A
SPORTS TEAM

LOS DRAGONES DE
CIUDAD TRUJILLO
{1937–1937}

I f you don't think of me as a sports guy, I get it. (See the Mobit for my short-lived baseball career at the end of this chapter.) I'm not obviously athletic, although I can do a one-handed cartwheel with a glass of water in my free hand without spilling a drop.

But I love drama. And sports is guaranteed drama. The sides are always clear. You've got winners, you've got losers, heroes, and villains. I was eleven years old when the Americans (yay!) defeated the Soviets (boo!) in ice hockey at the Lake Placid Olympics. I've heard that the movie *Miracle*, which depicts that event, is terrific. I'm sure it is, but I don't need to see it. I can remember the thrill of the "Miracle on Ice" as it happened. (Actually it was on tape delay. And if you happened to grow up in the DC area, as I did, you may remember that our local news anchor actually announced the final score during a commercial break *in the middle of the game*. I'm pretty sure she had to go into the witness protection program after that.)

Even better, I like drama with big personalities. So a story about one of baseball's all-time great pitchers and a bloodthirsty Latin American dictator set in the 1930s on an island nation? I'm in.

Leroy "Satchel" Paige was born on July 7, 1906, one of eleven children born to a poor African American family in Alabama. He started work at a young age, carrying bags at the Mobile train station for a dime apiece. He realized he could make a lot more money if he strung all the satchels on a pole and carried them in a single trip, and that's how he earned his famous nickname.

Black players were barred from major-league baseball starting in 1884, shortly after Toledo's Moses Fleetwood Walker became the first African American to play pro ball. (You'll read about him later.) The ban wouldn't be lifted until 1947, the year Jackie Robinson became a Brooklyn Dodger. So in 1926, at the age of nineteen, the tall and sinewy Paige tried out for the all-black Chattanooga White Sox, reportedly throwing with such accuracy that he could, from the mound, knock over soda bottles lined up on home plate.

Paige became known not just as the hardest thrower around but also the most creative. He was a showman on the mound with his high leg kicks. And off the mound he became known for his homespun wit. (His later "Six Rules for Staying Young" included "Avoid fried meats which angry up the blood." Makes sense to me.) Over a forty-year career, he would become one of history's most beloved players, one of the few Negro League players known to white fans during baseball's long segregated era.

Paige knew how good he was. He would tell his fielders to sit down on the grass behind him while he struck out the opposing team. Joe DiMaggio, who batted against Paige in an exhibition game in 1936, called him the best he'd ever faced.

In 1931 he signed with the Pittsburgh Crawfords, one of the greatest Negro League teams assembled—arguably one of the greatest baseball teams ever. Paige's teammates eventually included Cool Papa Bell, the fastest man in baseball. Paige once said that Bell could turn off the lights and jump into bed before the room got dark. And the great catcher Josh Gibson, "the black Babe Ruth," who was estimated to have hit more than eight hundred home runs in his career.

The team's owner, Gus Greenlee, was a larger-than-life figure. A machine gunner in the trenches of France during World War I, the 6'2", mixed-race Greenlee came back with shrapnel in his left leg. But that didn't stop him from running bootleg whiskey to speakeasies. His sprawling numbers racket (basically an illegal lottery) earned, at its height, $25,000 a day. Naturally he opened his own nightclub—and used the profits to buy off police and politicians and provide loans to black people who had been rejected by white-owned banks. With his outsized personality, wealth, and charm, he dominated Pittsburgh politics, music, business—and sports.

Greenlee financed the first stadium built exclusively for a black ball club, Greenlee Field (what else would he call it?), even installing lights. For six years the Pittsburgh Crawfords dominated the Negro National League.

But the end was in sight. The Depression was eroding the Negro Leagues' financial foundation and state attorneys general were cracking down on numbers running. Greenlee faced a handful of indictments, and he could not be as free with the salaries as he had been. In such a climate the Craws—with a roster for the ages assembled by raiding other Negro League teams—were themselves raided. The man who stole their talent? Generalissimo Rafael Trujillo, the brutal strongman who had taken control of the Dominican Republic in 1930.

If there were a hall of fame for bloodthirsty dictators, Trujillo would be voted in unanimously on the first ballot. As a boy he had collected shiny metal bottle caps to pin on his shirt in imitation of a military leader. He began his rise to power by serving in a street gang, and then worked as the paid muscle for the wealthy owners of sugar plantations. After he forced Horacio Vasquez from power, Trujillo, then a general, won the election of 1930 with an impressively high 99.2 percent of the vote—although the numbers are somewhat less impressive once you learn that all the other candidates withdrew because of death threats from Trujillo's goons. Once in power, he renamed the country's capital city of Santo Domingo "Ciudad Trujillo." He renamed the country's tallest mountain "Pico Trujillo." He renamed the province of San Cristobal "Trujillo Province." He made his three-year-old son, Ramfis, a colonel. (To be clear, a three-year-old in military uniform is kind of cute *on Halloween.*) Trujillo later did allow an opposition party to organize. Such a policy, he believed, made it much easier to identify and murder his political enemies.

The story of how Paige came to play for Trujillo is told in Averell "Ace" Smith's terrific book, *The Pitcher and the Dictator.* Trujillo himself was not much of a baseball fan, but he knew that the Dominican people loved the game, and he thought a successful team would be good for public relations during the upcoming pseudo-election of 1937. He directed a diminutive dentist named Enrique Aybar to form

Los Dragones de Ciudad Trujillo (the Trujillo City Dragons). The goal was to defeat the reigning island champs, Las Estrellas Orientales of San Pedro (the San Pedro Eastern Stars). With Trujillo bankrolling him, Aybar traveled to New Orleans in the winter of 1936, where Paige was training. Aybar offered Paige a contract of $30,000, a ridiculous sum to a player who was receiving a few hundred a month from Greenlee. Paige knew he was underpaid in the Negro Leagues. "That bunch would hold onto a dollar bill until old George screamed in pain," he said of the Negro League owners. What's more, he was tired of the segregation he faced when playing in the South, where it could be hard to find a restaurant, or hotel, or even a gas station that would serve black people. Paige took the money with one condition. He insisted on bringing his catcher, Cy Perkins.

The two became the toast of Ciudad Trujillo, and were soon joined by other Negro League stars. The American players were thrilled with the music, the food, the beer, and what Ace Smith discreetly calls "las casas de chicas." (Paige was not one for monogamy. The story goes that he was once served with divorce papers on the mound at Wrigley Field. "Never be unfaithful to a lover, except with your wife," he quipped.) Satchel and Cy had the money to enjoy it all. And not a single establishment was closed to them because of the color of their skin. In Trujillo's dictatorship they had more freedom than they'd had at home in the States.

But Paige's first outing was rougher than expected; he gave up six runs in five innings. Soon enough a pseudonymous newspaper column suggested that stricter off-the-field control of the high-paid players was needed. The late nights and sleepy mornings were catching up with the American stars. At the same time, the two other Dominican clubs—there were just three teams on the island—were bringing in their own ringers from stateside. (The president of one of those clubs flew to Pittsburgh to court Greenlee's remaining stars. Greenlee—already in a rage over the defection of Satchel—had the visitors arrested by his friends in the Pittsburgh police force. Alas, unlike Trujillo, he lacked the power to imprison people who hadn't committed any crime, and the Dominicans were released.)

Back in the DR, Satchel's performance improved, but his team was still struggling. Another article in Trujillo's state-sanctioned newspaper called for a curb on the "licentiousness" of the American players, whose reckless lifestyle was undermining the team's success. The head of Trujillo's death squads was put in charge of discipline, and armed thugs became constant companions of Satchel and the Americans, shadowing them wherever they went. Bars and nightclubs were off-limits. No store owner would sell them whiskey. As for the casas de chicas, no chance. Evenings were spent playing long games of cards at the hotel. Even team practices lost their casual, playful air. "I started wishing I was home when all those soldiers started following us around everywhere we went and even stood out in front of our rooms at night," wrote Paige in his autobiography.

The new regimen of chastity and sobriety may have been less fun but it worked wonders on the field. By the time the playoffs came around, Paige was sporting a 6-1 record. Los Dragones defeated Las Estrellas for the championship, 8–6. Paige really couldn't afford to let the team down: as he later recalled, he was terrified of failure, thinking the whole time about the line of Trujillo's soldiers arrayed on the edges of the field, knives and guns tucked into their belts, clearly visible. The championship trophy was presented to Trujillo's son, Colonel Rafael L. Trujillo Martínez, now all of eight years old.

This remarkable season, however, rang the death knell for the Dragones. The Dominican clubs, for all the excitement of the season, had essentially bankrupted themselves with their spending sprees, and the entire league was disbanded. Satchel and the other American players collected their winnings and moved on. Banned from the Negro Leagues for defecting and unable to play for Major League Baseball, Paige and the others had no option but to barnstorm the nation sporting the pinstripes of Los Dragones, billing themselves as "Trujillo's All-Stars," even defeating the National Negro League All-Stars at Yankee Stadium in September 1937.

Eventually the NNL rescinded its lifetime bans of Satchel and the other defectors. He continued to pitch, despite age and some injuries. With the death of MLB commissioner Kenesaw Landis in 1944, the time was right for integration of the major leagues, and Jackie Robinson broke the color line in 1947. The next year Paige signed with the Cleveland Indians, helping them to win the World Series. (They haven't won since.) The forty-two-year-old was the oldest "rookie" in major-league history. He played for five years in the majors, was twice named an all-star, and even made a return appearance, pitching three scoreless innings for the 1965 Kansas City A's, at age fifty-nine. Yes, that's right, *at age fifty-nine.*

It's great to watch Paige in TV appearances from the 1960s and '70s, adored by the panelists on *What's My Line?* and tossing a ball with host Steve Allen on *I've Got a Secret.* Dick Cavett invited him on in 1971, shortly after Paige became the first Negro Leaguer to be voted into baseball's Hall of Fame. Paige is funny and gracious, even pretending to be charmed by fellow guest Salvador Dalí, who brought along his pet anteater. When Cavett asks Paige how good the players in the Negro Leagues were, he answers: "Back in those days they had a lot of Satchell Paiges. There wasn't just one. I just pitched more than everybody else back then."

"I'm as old as Methuselah," he says, as if to suggest that his longevity, rather than his great talent, is the main reason he's remembered.

In the last of his Six Rules for Staying Young he wrote: "Don't look back. Something might be gaining on you." Paige had outlasted Greenlee (who died in 1952) and the tyrant Trujillo (who was assassinated in 1961) and the fabulous if short-lived teams on which he had starred. The owners, the teams, and the leagues themselves passed on, but Paige himself seemed to just keep going.

The Philadelphia Sphas (1917–1959)

The letters stand for South Philadelphia Hebrew Association. Founded by Eddie "the Mogul" Gottlieb in 1918, the Sphas dominated basketball back when it was referred to as "the Jewish Game" because it required, in the words of one *New York Post* writer, "an alert, scheming mind and flashy trickiness." The Sphas dominated the American Basketball League in the 1930s and '40s, winning seven titles in thirteen years. Stars included household names such as Harry Litwack, Cy Kaselman, Moe Goldman, Irv Torgoff, Red Wolfe, Max Posnack, and perennial MVP candidate Shikey Gotthoffer. But the demographics of basketball—always an urban game at heart—were already changing. The Great Migration was bringing millions of African Americans to the cities of the North, while Jews were moving their families to the suburbs. Gottlieb sold the Sphas to Red Klotz, a former player, who refashioned them the Washington Generals, a traveling opponent for Abe Saperstein's Harlem Globetrotters. For the next forty-four years they served as stooges for the world's most famous exhibition club. Gottlieb, meanwhile, founded the Philadelphia Warriors of the NBA, signed a kid named Wilt Chamberlain, and never looked back.

The New Jersey Generals (1983–1985)

In 1983, the upstart United States Football League put the formidable National Football League on notice, paying big salaries for high-profile stars including Heisman Trophy winner Herschel Walker and future Hall of Famer Jim Kelly. The next year a New York real estate baron named Donald J. Trump joined the league, buying the New Jersey Generals for about $9 million. "I could have bought an NFL team," he said to the *New York Times*'s Ira Berkow at the time. "I feel sorry for the poor guy who is going to buy the Dallas Cowboys," he continued. "It's a no-win situation for him, because if he wins, well, so what? They've won through the years. And if he loses, which seems likely because they're having troubles, he'll be known to the world as a loser." Within two years the USFL collapsed, and Trump ended up $22 million in the red. The Cowboys are currently worth $5 billion.

The Washington Senators (1891–1971)

The Washington Senators baseball team died three times. The first Washington Senators played from 1891 to 1899. We know little about them except that they were awful. In 1900, the team folded. But when the American League was founded in 1901, the Senators were reborn. They were awful, too, losing so much that in 1904 sportswriter Charles Dryden quipped, "Washington: First in war, first in peace, and last in the American League." On the bright side, their historic ineptitude inspired the musical *Damn Yankees*, in which a Senators fan sells his soul to the devil in exchange for a World Series victory. That's the show where Bob Fosse and Gwen Verdon met. (Now *that's* a team.) In the 1950s, as franchises began moving westward, owner Calvin Griffith vowed the team would remain in Washington "forever." He decamped with the team for Minnesota two years later. Senators 3.0, hastily assembled at the behest of President Eisenhower, lasted only a decade. Their last game was a riot. On September 30, 1971, the Senators were leading in the top of the ninth when irate fans stormed the field and stole home. They also stole first, second, and third, grabbed handfuls of the infield grass, and ran off with the bat boys' chairs. When the umpires couldn't clear the field, the game was ruled a forfeit.

Maurice Rocca's Little League Career (1979–1979)

As reported by my older brother, Lawrence Rocca:

I don't remember if the opponent was Blessed Sacrament or Saint Camillus or Our Lady of Lourdes. What matters is the 1979 Little Flower Midget B baseball team was being humiliated once again, this time in its final game, another blowout in a last-place and soon to be mercifully completed Catholic Youth Organization season.

The culprit this time was the hulking fourth-grader batting cleanup for the other team; he'd already crushed two titanic homers before coming to bat with the bases loaded in the top of the seventh. Sitting on the hill with the rest of the tiny crowd at Bethesda, Maryland's, Westmoreland Park, my parents and I leaned forward in nervous anticipation. The infielders retreated to the edge of the outfield grass in panicked self-defense. Maurice, who was usually on the bench, betrayed no feelings in center field, where he was safe, at least, from decapitation.

A head taller than the rest of the players, Slugger swung violently, sending a towering fly to left, eliciting oohs and aahs before it hooked and landed harmlessly foul, just beyond the left fielder's stumbling, tumbling reach. Again and again this happened, the oohs and aahs turning to laughs. A fourth time. Then a fifth. Another soaring fly ball. Another round of expectant laughter building toward crescendo— suddenly stifled by a blur, a near collision, and the longest split second of silence in CYO history.

It was Maurice, running full speed from center, past left. At the last possible instant, he thrust his gloved left hand to the absolute limit of his reach, his body at a perfect 45-degree angle to the ground, just the tippy toes of his right foot touching, like Mercury with a Paul Blair–autographed Wilson. The ball stuck to his palm like Velcro, as his momentum nearly sent him into a cartwheel. And it stayed in his glove, as the crowd erupted in wild cheers and the entire last-place 1979 Little Flower Midget B baseball team ran out and mobbed him on the spot. It took three minutes for the umpire to restore order and send everyone back to their positions.

My brother was not a great baseball player, nor a particularly enthusiastic one. He knew early on that his first season of CYO baseball would be his last. But what he lacked in love and skill for the game, he made up in fidelity to two foundational rules: always hustle, and always back up your teammates. As far as improbable defensive heroics go, you can have the big-money stakes of Derek Jeter's playoff flip or the perfect cinematography of Lupus's *Bad News Bears* miracle. I'll take the one that jumped right off the pages of Joseph Campbell that day at Westmoreland Park.

The Byronic Woman

ADA LOVELACE
{1815–1852}

The world of high tech is dominated by men. The workforces of Silicon Valley giants like Google and Apple are about 70 percent male. Only around 15 to 18 percent of undergraduate computer science degrees go to women. So when we think about the pioneers behind the digital revolution that's shaped every corner of our lives, we usually think of men—like Steve Jobs and Bill Gates, or maybe Alan Turing. (He's the English mathematician who broke the Nazis' Enigma code during World War II. Benedict Cumberbatch played him in a movie.) But these men were latecomers, since the origins of the modern computer go back to the early nineteenth century. In fact, the first computer programmer, in the judgment of many, was a female mathematician, Ada Lovelace, who also happened to be the daughter of the poet Lord Byron. (You'll read about him and his fight for Greek independence later.)

In England, the middle of the nineteenth century witnessed a technological revolution far more transformative and "disruptive" than the recent changes brought about by the internet and the smartphone. Industry, urbanization, and innovations in transportation and communication radically altered daily life for most people.

Whether you were an engineer or an architect, an actuary or an astronomer, you increasingly depended on complicated mathematics to do your work. And to do that math, you relied on enormous preprinted tables of numerical calculations. (I'm not talking about those multiplication tables we were supposed to memorize in the fourth grade. Think more about the kind of table you look at when you try to calculate your withholding on an IRS form, then put a few thousand of those together in a book.)

These tables, though, were invariably rife with errors committed by the flesh-and-blood "computers"—aka human beings—who compiled them. As Kristen Gallerneaux, the curator of communication and information technology at the Henry Ford Museum, told me, those errors "could be problematic—and even dangerous—for a supply ship trying to calculate its course, or an engineer trying to build a piece of industrial equipment." And so the more society relied on technology and industry, the more it needed accurate math.

A young mathematician named Charles Babbage thought he had the solution. If a steam engine could power a loom or a train, he wondered, why not a steam-powered machine that does math? (After all, steam engines were changing everything, powering ships and locomotives, replacing human and animal labor in manufacturing and industry.) Such a machine, he reasoned, would be able to calculate much faster than humans, and without all the costly, inefficient mistakes. After securing funding from the British government, Babbage got to work on what he called a "Difference Engine." As Gallerneaux describes it, this was "a hand-cranked mechanical calculator that was meant to calculate the series of numbers needed to populate numerical tables."

But the massive project—25,000 parts, with a projected weight of four tons—ground to a halt in 1833 when Babbage fell out with his chief tool-maker and lost his government funding. Yet it was not a total failure. He had completed a model, a functioning automatic calculator. Babbage assembled the cream of London's social and intellectual worlds at his home in the fashionable Marylebone neighborhood. There he demonstrated his miraculous invention.

This is where Ada Lovelace comes in. Born Augusta Ada Byron, in 1815, the only child of Lord Byron and the heiress Annabella Milbanke, Ada was, by virtue of her celebrity parents, famous from birth. Annabella reported being mobbed by locals when she took her baby out and about in the town of Ely. But the power marriage was short-lived, thanks in part to Byron's affair with his half-sister. Soon after Ada's birth, Byron and Annabella separated permanently and Byron left England for good. He died in Greece when his daughter was only eight.

Although her father was a great man of letters, Ada was much more into numbers. Her mad mathematical skills were inherited from and encouraged by her mother, who had shown talent in math and astronomy. (Back before the divorce, Byron called Annabella his Princess of Parallelograms.) Annabella, stung by the dissolution of her marriage and the sexual scandal that surrounded her ex-husband, believed that training in math would prevent her daughter from succumbing to the volatile throes of passion that afflicted her ex. So she made sure that math and science were part of the girl's education.

And Ada showed promise. At age twelve, she undertook a major engineering project, attempting to design a flying machine whose specifications were based on her study of the anatomy of birds, including dead ones she found on the grounds of the manor. She imagined it as a kind of artificial Pegasus: "I have got a scheme," she wrote to her mother, "to make a thing in the form of a horse with a steam engine in the inside so contrived as to move an immense pair of wings, fixed on the outside of the horse, in such a manner as to carry it up into the air while a person sits on its back." (For my fourth-grade science fair I made a pulley.)

Despite their shared interest in mathematics, Ada did not get along with her mother. (She would choose to be buried next to the father she never knew.) Annabella resented the product of her ill-fated marriage and often consigned the girl to her grandmother's care. Not surprisingly, as soon as Ada could get out from under her mother's thumb, she did, running off at age seventeen with a tutor named William Turner. Ada was, however, caught and returned home before the relationship was consummated. To keep the girl's passions in check, Annabella prescribed more math, and Ada resumed her studies under the instruction of a different tutor.

Another of Ada Lovelace's teachers was a mathematician named Mary Somerville, one of the first two women admitted to the Royal Astronomical Society, and it was Somerville who, in 1833, introduced Lovelace to Charles Babbage. Babbage was taken with this brilliant young woman, and he soon invited her back to a "scientific salon" at his place to show her his Difference Engine. When Lovelace saw Babbage's remarkable machine, she was, as Gallerneaux says, "drawn to it like a moth to a flame." But unlike most of the guests, she did not simply stare at it slack-jawed. She was able to grasp how it worked. A friendship was born. Babbage encouraged her studies at the University of London and took to calling her "the Enchantress of Numbers."

Although his Difference Engine remained incomplete, Babbage continued to imagine new possibilities for mechanical computing. He conceived an even grander project, an "Analytical Engine," a machine that would perform much more complex mathematical tasks than his Difference Engine. His extensive plans for the Analytical Engine (five thousand pages of notes survive) drew on technology that had already been developed in, of all places, the textile industry.

In 1804, a Frenchman named Joseph-Marie Jacquard had invented a mechanical loom that could weave textiles with highly complex patterns. The key innovation was the use of a chain of connected punch cards—stiff pieces of paper with a pattern of holes punched out. Those cards were instructions for creating intricate designs. Where there was a hole, the thread passed through; where there was no hole, it didn't. In other words, it translated complicated patterns into a series of ones and zeroes—what mathematicians call a binary code. Babbage realized that if the information for weaving textiles could be translated into a long series of ones and zeroes, then so could complicated mathematical problems. As Lovelace herself said about Babbage's invention, "We may say most aptly that the Analytical Engine weaves algebraic patterns just as the Jacquard loom weaves flowers and leaves."

Ada, meanwhile, ended up marrying a nobleman named William King. King soon inherited the title of the Earl of Lovelace; Ada became the Countess of Lovelace. They had three children, the oldest a boy named Byron. But after some time, Lovelace, who had maintained her friendship with Babbage, returned to her mathematical pursuits—and made history.

In 1843, at the age of twenty-seven, she completed a translation from the Italian of an article by an engineer about Babbage's proposed Analytical Engine. It might seem like a minor accomplishment, but Lovelace added her own original notes, three times as long as the original essay. The notes contain step-by-step instructions on how the Analytical Engine could be used to calculate a series of numbers called the Bernoulli Sequence. In effect, she created an algorithm.

I know, this is making my head hurt, too. An algorithm is just a fixed, step-by-step sequence of rules for a computer to follow when it makes complex calculations. So the main takeaway is this: Lovelace's instructions—which would have worked, had the machine been built—are now generally recognized as the first computer program ever written.

In her notes, Lovelace also speculates on other possible applications of Babbage's machine, including the composition of music. Doron Swade, of Mountain View, California's, Computer History Museum, suggests that Lovelace's insights marked a breakthrough in the very notion of what a computer could be: "The idea of a machine that could manipulate symbols in accordance with rules and that numbers could represent entities other than quantity marks the fundamental transition from calculation to computation. Lovelace was the first to explicitly articulate this notion and in this she appears to have seen further than Babbage." In other words Lovelace was a visionary.

Lovelace was still a young woman at this point, and she continued to engage with various mathematical and scientific ideas. But her mathematical skills seem to have failed her in the world of gambling, and she accumulated crippling debt. In 1851 she was diagnosed with uterine cancer, and died the next year at the age of thirty-six, the same age at which her famous father had passed away.

As Ada Lovelace is a forgotten forerunner, we should also remember those who came before her, such as the Muslim engineer Ismail Al-Jazari (1136–1206), born in Mesopotamia, whose *Book of Knowledge of Ingenious Mechanical Devices* describes a hundred different machines and inventions. Among Al-Jazari's innovations were the cam shaft, the crankshaft, various water and candle clocks, a robot waiter who could serve tea, and a band of automata-musicians who played actual music and may very well have been programmable using pegs and levers.

DEATH OF A COUNTRY

PRUSSIA

{1525–1947}

I f places had obituaries, then the first paragraph of Prussia's might go something like this:

25 February 1947. Prussia, the once sprawling European power best known for its spiky helmets, extravagantly mustachioed Kaisers named Wilhelm, and its confusing geographical classification, died today. It was four hundred twenty-one years old. Prussia is survived by Russia, East Germany, Poland, and Lithuania, who will inherit its territory.

I've always been a bit of a geographical show-off. I know the capital of every country in the world. I can freestyle-draw a map of all the lower forty-eight states. I once did this while I was serving as a judge, live on the air, for the Miss USA pageant. (It was during the interview portion of the competition. I already knew I was voting for Miss Connecticut.) And if I meet you at a party, there's a better than even chance that I'll brag to you that I've been to a T.G.I. Friday's on five different continents. (You'll be charmed . . . I hope.)

But I've always been ashamed that I didn't know what Prussia was, exactly. (And there are only so many times I can deflect with the whole T.G.I. Friday's bit.) At first I assumed it was a combination of Poland and Russia, kind of like "Brangelina" or "Jessicro" (well, what's *your* nickname for Jessica Tandy and Hume Cronyn?). Then again, Prussia was always coming up in the context of wanton militarism, which made me think . . . *I'm pretty sure it must be German.* Fortunately, writing this Mobituary gave me the perfect excuse to learn what the hell Prussia was.

James Charles Roy, who wrote a whole book about Prussia, notes that indeed for most people the name conjures up images of "spiked helmets, jackboots, goose steps, eagles, blood, and destruction." Those nasty-looking helmets (properly known as *picklehauben*) really are statement-making: just put your head down, charge directly at your enemy, and ram him through the sternum. (If that image isn't scary enough, check out the creepy black-feathered, sword-wielding eagle on the Prussian coat of arms. It's got a tongue longer than Gene Simmons's. This is not the creature you want to meet in hand-to-hand combat on the fields of central Europe.)

But there's so much more to Prussia's story than blood and destruction.

As for what it was, exactly, Prussia was by turns a province, a duchy, a kingdom, and the leading state within the German Empire. Because Prussia was regularly engaged in one war or another, the boundaries of Prussia were always changing (mostly expanding). It was kind of like Hell's Kitchen: New Yorkers know roughly where it is, but don't ask them to tell you whether it ends at Forty-Second Street, or Thirty-Ninth, or Thirty-Fourth.

As for how it came to be, Albert of Hohenzollern, a brand-new convert to the brand-new religion of Lutheranism, established the Duchy of Prussia on the Baltic Sea as the first officially Protestant state in history in 1525. From that point on he became known as Albert of Prussia, a much better-sounding name. Flash forward through a bunch of wars, plagues, royal marriages, the invention of modern science, the plays of Shakespeare, the paintings of Rembrandt, the growth of global trade, and some major land grabs, and Albert's great-great-great-great-great-grandson, Frederick the Great, comes to the throne. He's king of Prussia. (If you live in the greater Philadelphia area you've definitely heard of his mall, the largest in America. If Minnesota's Mall of America wants to argue that point, be my guest. But be prepared and wear a spiky helmet.)

Frederick enjoyed acquiring territory as much as the next king, and he earned a reputation as a great military leader in the Seven Years' War (which sounds awful until you consider the Thirty Years' War, the Eighty Years' War or worse yet the Second Hundred Years' War, which actually lasted about 125 years). During his reign, Prussia stretched from Berlin to the edge of Lithuania. But Frederick may be equally important to history as a great cultural leader, too. He modeled himself on the Roman philosopher-emperor Marcus Aurelius. He loved French literature and philosophy. He put Berlin on the map as a center of the arts, building its opera. He was an accomplished flautist . . . and less accomplished writer of erotic poetry. (For the curious, "La Jouissance," loosely translated as "The Orgasm," is out there on the internet. You've been warned.)

Frederick was for freedom of the press and literature and promoted limited religious freedom and toleration for Catholics and Jews. (He himself was likely an atheist.) He was also known for what contemporaries referred to as his "Grecian taste in love," and had a long-term affair with his valet, a man named Fredersdorf, which is a rough German approximation for "Jeeves." He probably also had a fling with the French writer-philosopher Voltaire. To please his tyrannical father, Frederick married. He and the Prussian queen lived in separate castles and never consummated the marriage. Not surprisingly, they had no children.

The throne passed eventually to his great-great-nephew, Wilhelm I. Along with his chancellor, Otto von Bismarck, Wilhelm waged wars against Denmark, Austria, France, Ukraine, Ural, and pretty much all the blue territories on the *Risk* board. At this point Prussia extended all the way west past the Rhine. Then, in 1871, Bismarck united Prussia with other German-speaking states to form the German Empire. (Now's when you start to hear the scary music playing in the background.) At this point Wilhelm assumed the title Kaiser. ("Kaiser" is another word for emperor or hard roll.)

Wilhelm's son, Frederick, occupied the throne just long enough to have a cup of kaffee and a linzer cookie, dying young and leaving the empire to his son, the grandson of Kaiser Wilhelm I, imaginatively named . . . Kaiser Wilhelm II. (Genealogy buffs will be interested to know that Wilhelm II was the oldest grandson of England's Queen Victoria and thus a first cousin to England's King George V. George V, meanwhile, was first cousin to Tsar Nicholas II of Russia. All three monarchs were also fifth cousins, great-great-great-great-grandsons of George II of England. The way these European royals intermarried, it's a wonder they weren't all born with flippers and gills.)

By many accounts, it was the militarism of Germany arriving late to the game of jockeying for power in Europe and Africa that precipitated World War I. (By other accounts, Wilhelm II's failed efforts at diplomacy were responsible for the escalation of hostilities after the assassination of Archduke Franz Ferdinand of Austria. That's a story too long to tell here.) In the end, Germany lost the war, and, in the aftermath, handed over pieces of Prussia to neighboring states. Wilhelm II abdicated and fled to the Netherlands, and Prussia, once the most important state inside Germany, became greatly diminished in political importance. After the Second World War the Allies put the centuries-old former kingdom out of its misery—its government abolished, its borders erased, its territory absorbed by its neighbors.

Prussia's life is the story of the transformation of an insignificant medieval territory into a major European power. Its rise was all the more remarkable, the historian Christopher Clark tells us, because there was really very little that held it together as a nation: "it was an assemblage of disparate territorial fragments lacking natural boundaries or a distinct national culture, dialect, or cuisine." For a couple of centuries it was a central player in European politics and culture. Then it vanished, as the project of reorganizing Europe after World War II began. No great Empire—Roman, Ottoman, or Lee Daniels–produced—lasts forever. Today Prussia exists only in the history books, causing us to ask whether its fate—to dominate international politics and then to disappear, a victim of its own expansionism—might serve as a warning to all great nations.

But those helmets sure were cool.

Königsberg (1255–1945)

I've long been intrigued by geographical oddities like the township of Northwest Angle, Minnesota, which, because of a surveying error, sits above the 49th parallel, on the wrong side of the long border between Canada and the United States, separated from the rest of Minnesota by a big lake. Or the Mississippi River town of Kaskaskia, Illinois. When the river jumped course during the Great Flood of 1881, the village ended up on the Missouri side but still has an Illinois address. Or Königsberg, the deceased capital of Prussia.

It was located on the Baltic Sea in the easternmost part of Prussia, the area in which the name Prussia first took hold. Wedged between what's now Poland and Lithuania, the city grew to be a crucial shipping port for all of northern and eastern Europe; its harbor, deep and ice-free all year, could accommodate the largest of freighters. It blossomed into a cosmopolitan center where French Huguenots, English, Scotsmen, and Dutch mixed with Poles and Lithuanians, a home to merchants, artisans, and intellectuals. (If everyone on the planet lived in a port city there'd be no wars. People would be too busy having way too good a time, although the clinics would be jam packed.)

During the Enlightenment years of Frederick the Great, Königsberg's university boasted alumni that included Immanuel Kant, the father of modern philosophy. Kant, in fact, never left the city during his seventy-nine years. He was so consistent in his daily walks around his hometown that the good people of K-berg were said to set their watches when he passed their doors. Walking through Königsberg was also the basis for a famous puzzle in eighteenth-century mathematics, "the Seven Bridges of Königsberg," which asked whether it was possible to cross all of the town's bridges without crossing any bridge twice. In 1735 the Swiss mathematician Leonhard Euler proved that it's impossible, laying the foundation for modern graph theory and topology.

Between the bombing by the Royal Air Force and the tanks of the Soviet Army, most of Königsberg was destroyed in World War II. The communist Soviet Union claimed the city and deported its German residents—a bunch ended up in Kazakhstan, which still boasts a sizable German population. The city was renamed Kaliningrad after a former Stalin lackey whose CV included such accomplishments as sending his own wife to the gulag. (On the bright side, they also renamed Königsberg's Adolf Hitler Platz.) The Soviets closed the city to foreign visitors for security reasons. The medieval Königsberg castle, already damaged in the war, was dynamited by Leonid Brezhnev and replaced with "the House of Soviets," an enormous and still-unfinished brutalist concrete structure that locals call "the buried robot" because it looks like the head of Optimus Prime bursting out of the earth. (It's one of those things that's so ugly that if you stare at it long enough it starts to captivate.)

After the breakup of the Soviet Union, some hoped that control of Kaliningrad, née Königsberg, would revert to Germany but Russia held on to it for its access to the Baltic. Yet the independence of the nations around it has essentially orphaned it; Königsberg shares no border with Mother Russia. And so the city is often left off national weather maps on Russian television. Residents, when they travel to Moscow, talk about "going to Russia," as if it were a foreign country. In 1993 the Israeli journalist Amos Elon dubbed it "the Nowhere City," lamenting "the barren monotony of Communist urban planning" that rendered the once-verdant port, the onetime European capital where Frederick the Great crowned himself the first king of Prussia, "possibly one of the ugliest places in the world." The region was in such bad economic shape, he reported, that every night graves were raided by criminals scavenging the dead for jewelry and gold teeth.

If you do plan on vacationing there, just beware: don't call it Königsberg. An employee of Russia's national airline was recently fired for calling it that.

...and Other Places You Won't Find on a Map

PRUSSIA *is only one dead country. From antique biblical lands like the Land of Nod (just East of Eden) to once-vast empires like the Golden Horde and the Abassid Caliphate to a few "I'm not dead yet" nations that are beginning to twitch with signs of life (Catalonia, the Republic of Texas), there are enough former cities, states, and kingdoms to fill an atlas. Here are just a few:*

Assyria (2600 BC–600 BC)

You thought the Russia/Prussia thing was confusing? I'd like to tell you that the ancient kingdom of Assyria was located in the area of present-day Syria. But it was actually centered in northern Iraq, spilling over into parts of what are now Iran and Syria. Just add a slice of Turkey, and you have the basic outline. Assyria's origins date to 2600 BC. In the ninth century BC, thanks to their mastery of iron weaponry, the Assyrians ran roughshod across the Middle East, extending their borders from Egypt to the Persian Gulf up to Turkey and even out to Cyprus, becoming the largest empire in the world *up until that time.* But then the Persians, Greeks, and Romans showed up. Think of Assyria as the Roger Connor of empires. He's the guy who held the all-time home run record *before* Babe Ruth came along and broke it. In other words, the Assyrians were the heavy hitters until those even bigger boys came along. But don't cry for Assyria. It left its mark on the region—most notably in its language, Aramaic, the language that Jesus spoke.

Republic of West Florida (September 1810–December 1810)

From 1836 to 1846, Texas was an independent country. And for twenty-five days in 1846 the California Republic was an unrecognized nation, located in what is now Sonoma County. But it turns out Florida started the trend. For two and a half months in late 1810 the Republic of West Florida was an independent entity. The most interesting thing about this vanished country may be that it wasn't even located in present-day Florida.

Back before the American Revolution, Spain, France, and Britain were all trying to stake claims to a strip of coastland along the Gulf of Mexico west of what's now Florida. Britain took control of it from France and Spain during the Seven Years' War. Spain got it back at the end of the American War of Independence but traded it to France in exchange for a chunk of Tuscany, Marvin Gardens, Water Works, and a Get Out of Jail Free card. Then the United States bought the Louisiana Territory from France, believing that West Florida was part of the deal. But then Spain insisted they had never given up this part of the Gulf Coast. Restless American settlers sensed an opportunity, however, and rushed in with a wink and a nod from their own government. In September 1810, they stormed Fort San Carlos in Baton Rouge and raised their flag, a lone

white star set against a "bonnie blue" field. They established the Free and Independent Republic of West Florida under the rule of Governor Fulwar Skipwith, a name that really does not roll off the tongue. By the end of the year, the US Army had taken the territory. This pattern of conquest became, says historian William C. Davis, the "template for Manifest Destiny"—showing American settlers how they could occupy land, claim independence, then have the US government move in and secure it.

Tannu-Tuva (1921–1944)

Tucked away in southern Siberia, on the border dividing Russia and Mongolia, Tuva is located at the exact geographical center of the Asian continent, a spot now marked by a monument that uncannily resembles an enormous Prussian *picklehaube*. Its remarkable variety of ecosystems includes taiga, tundra, mountains, steppes, evergreen forests, wetlands, and even rain forests. Today Tuva is part of Russia, but for a short time after the Bolshevik Revolution it was an independent state known as Tannu-Tuva, although no one but the Soviet Union and Mongolia formally recognized its existence. But as this young nation started to acknowledge traditional beliefs like shamanism and Buddhism, Stalin said довольно is довольно ("enough is enough") and annexed it.

Still, in its short life, Tannu-Tuva attained a few significant distinctions. It was the first country in the history of the world to elect a woman as head of state: Khertek Anchimaa-Toka, who died in 2008 at the age of ninety-six. And philatelists worldwide go gaga over Tannu-Tuva's exquisite stamps, with their delicate, colorful drawings of reindeer and Bactrian camels. Tuva today is most famous for its tradition of "throat-singing," a vocal art that has been described as creating multiple tones at once by manipulating the mouth, pharynx, and larynx, essentially transforming the human throat into a set of bagpipes. (Currently searching YouTube for "Tuva's Got Talent.")

Sodom and Gomorrah (Dates Unknown) Fans of Genesis (the book of, not the band) know the story of Sodom and Gomorrah, the two cities destroyed by God's decree after things got a little rowdy. Here's what happened: Abraham's nephew Lot invites two angels to lodge with him in Sodom. The angels, in the form of men, accept. Soon after they arrive, a mob of townsmen (er, Sodomites?) surrounds the house and demands that the angels come outside so that they can "know" the new arrivals. Lot instead offers his two virgin daughters. (Thanks, Dad.) Hard pass from the mob. They then try breaking the door down, but the angels strike the townsmen with blindness and spirit Lot and his family out of the city, before destroying it with brimstone and fire. The angels warn Lot's family not to look back, but Lot's rubbernecking wife can't resist, and she turns to a pillar of salt. (The Old Testament punishments are much more creative.)

It's a story that's been used to condemn homosexuality, though biblical scholars argue over what the supposed sin is: sexual immorality or inhospitableness toward strangers. One thing that's always perplexed me: Both Sodom and Gomorrah get destroyed, but all the action up to that point takes place in Sodom. Why don't we know more about Gomorrah?

Could it be that Gomorrah's great crime is that it's just kind of boring? I mean, let's face it: there's no sex act named after Gomorrah (at least none that I know of). Not that there's anything wrong with boring. I've always imagined Gomorrah as the St. Paul to Sodom's Minneapolis. Clean, livable, a good place to raise a family. The schools are excellent. But make no mistake, when folks are looking for fun, they ride that light rail over to Sodom!

The Hanging Gardens of Babylon (600 BC–100) I don't

know where I first read about the Seven Wonders of the Ancient World but the only one I had any interest in was the Hanging Gardens of Babylon. (The Lighthouse of Alexandria? I've spent a lot of time on Cape Cod. I know lighthouses.)

According to one legend, the gardens were built by King Nebuchadnezzar II near his royal palace in Babylon, a city in Mesopotamia (modern Iraq), as a gift to his wife, Queen Amytis, who missed the mountains of her Persian homeland. Indeed they were said to resemble a man-made mountain of tiered gardens, with an inventive irrigation system pumping water from the Euphrates River below up into paradise: Flowers and trees of every variety, succulent fruits of every color, ripe for the picking. Burbling waterfalls. Drinks in curvy glasses with umbrellas, served by attendants with perfect teeth. Free Wi-Fi. Alas, it is believed the gardens were destroyed by an earthquake sometime after the first century. If the Green New Deal includes a provision to re-create the Hanging Gardens of Babylon in, say, Newark, count me in.

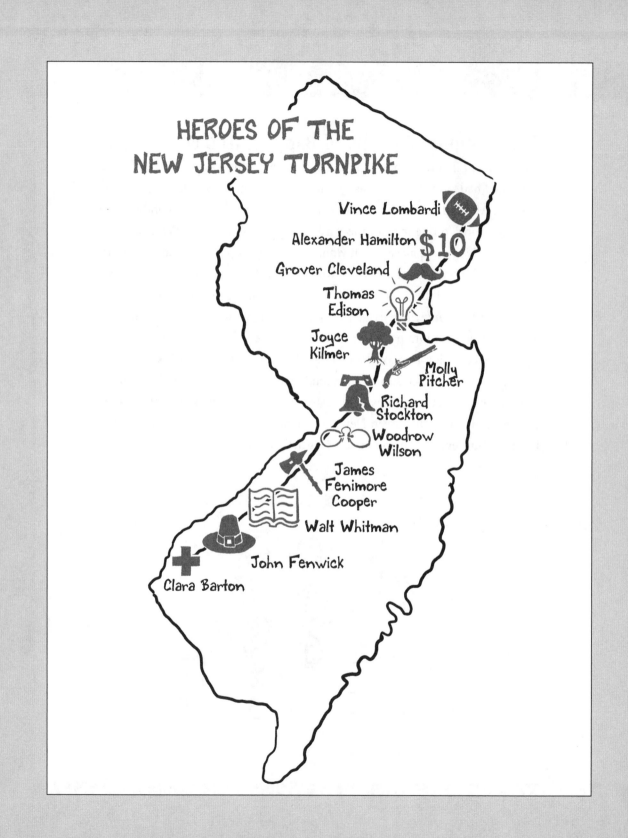

Historic Figures Memorialized by Rest Stops on the New Jersey Turnpike

New Jersey has many things to recommend it: It has the most scientists and engineers per square mile of any state. It grows the best tomatoes and blueberries in America. It has more diners than any other state. But millions of people only pass through New Jersey—via the 117-mile-long turnpike. If they know nothing else about the state, they should at least learn about the twelve historic figures for whom the turnpike's service areas are named.

Clara Barton (1821–1912) Clara Barton was the founder of the American Red Cross. As a young woman, she opened a school in Bordentown, New Jersey, but was passed over for the job of head of school in favor of a man. She went on to volunteer for the (mainly) male job of nurse on the battlefields of the Civil War. (Walt Whitman, inspired by her example, did the same. His service area is just twenty-five miles up the turnpike on the southbound side.) For the rest of her life Barton fought for the humane treatment of wounded and captured soldiers. At age eighty-two, she was forced out as president of the American Red Cross and replaced by an all-male leadership team. (I'm sensing a pattern.) Please note that in case of medical emergency, this service area does *not* have a defibrillator. The closest one is at the John Fenwick service area.

John Fenwick (1618-1683) Fenwick founded the first Quaker colony in the Americas in 1665, a worthy accomplishment no doubt. But his service area is forever fated to be confused with the James Fenimore Cooper Service Area, 34.1 miles away. How many potential love connections have been missed because, in the heat of a turnpike Tinder exchange, you and your intended got confused and ended up at *different* Auntie Anne's? Since Fenimore Cooper (more on him below) is much better known, may I humbly suggest that this service area be renamed for Summit, New Jersey's, own Meryl Streep? One day she could very well win an Oscar *playing* Auntie Anne.

Walt Whitman (1819–1892) In honor of Whitman's 1855 poem "Song of Myself" I give you . . .

"Song of My Service Area"

O Nathan's! O Roy Rogers, Carvel, and Cinnabon!
I celebrate you and sing you! My jaw hangs slack in wonder at the Caramel
Pecanbon,
with its lush sugary icing, its marvelous 1,080 calories!
Service Area, I love you!
You are large, you contain multitudes.
Your bathrooms contain multitudes too.
Yet they are surprisingly clean!
No sooner do I place my hands before the electronic sensor than the warm
water runs, bathing them, cleansing them, absolving them . . .
Absolving them as it absolves you, O my soul.

James Fenimore Cooper (1789–1851) *The Last of the Mohicans* was the first of the country's best-sellers. Cooper's adventure novel used to be one of the staples of early American literature. The friendship between its main characters, the white man Natty "Hawk-eye" Bumppo and the Native American Chingachgook, has been credited as the first in a series of great American novels, including *Moby-Dick* and *Huckleberry Finn*, that explore the theme of interracial male friendship. Cooper, a precocious student, was admitted to Yale at age thirteen but was later expelled, for reasons unclear. One story has it that he set off a bomb in chapel, another that he trained a donkey to sit in a professor's chair.

Richard Stockton (1730–1781) Stockton, a lower-tier Founding Father and signer of the Declaration of Independence, was seized from his home by the British during the Revolutionary War, dragged naked along the road, placed in leg irons, then imprisoned, starved, and tortured. While a prisoner, he signed an oath of loyalty to Britain, under duress. When he finally returned home to his estate in Princeton, his possessions had been taken and his library burned. This service area features a Quiznos.

Woodrow Wilson (1856–1924) Among our twenty-eighth president's distinctions: He's the only one to be buried in Washington, DC. He's the only one to hold a doctorate. And he's the only president who hosted a screening of the virulently racist epic film *The Birth of a Nation* at the White House. Wilson, the first southern Democrat elected president after the Civil War, also segregated the federal government—which is why his image has taken a beating in the last few years. (Princeton briefly considered renaming its vaunted Woodrow Wilson School of Public and International Affairs.) If his service station is ever renamed, I nominate New Jersey's Thomas Mundy Peterson, an ex-slave and the very first African American in the country to cast a vote. A vote on whether to revise his town's charter happened to be the first held anywhere in the country after the enactment of the Fifteenth Amendment. Who ever said local elections don't matter?

Molly Pitcher (1754?–1832) Molly Pitcher is the name of a maybe-mythical, maybe-real woman who fought in the Revolutionary War. She was probably more real than Paul Bunyan, but less real than Betsy Ross. While it is often assumed that she is a composite figure to whom many different women's deeds are attributed, there are some actual candidates for the "real" Molly. The most commonly cited is Mary Ludwig Hayes, described by the men in her company as a pregnant woman who liked to smoke and swear, and who earned her nickname by tirelessly bringing water to wounded soldiers during the scorchingly hot Battle of Monmouth.

Joyce Kilmer (1886–1918) In honor of Kilmer's 1913 poem "Trees," I give you . . .

"Trees: Part II"

Joyce Kilmer's famous poem "Trees"
Always leaves me ill at ease.
You know the verse I'm speaking of,
The one where Joyce professes love
For every tree that's ever been,
Deciduous or evergreen.
The couplets jangle every time
With singsong meter, obvious rhyme.
The sentiment, it seems, well . . . false,
A bit too thick with grandma's schmaltz.
So as you'll gather, I'm no fan.
And by the way—he was a man.

Grover Cleveland (1837–1908) Cleveland's main distinctions are presidential trivia night staples: he is the only president elected to nonconsecutive terms; he was the first president to marry while in office (at age forty-eight, to a twenty-one-year-old who had been his legal ward); his baby daughter, Ruth, had a candy bar named for her. (Nope, Baby Ruth is *not* named after baseball's Sultan of Swat.) The service area is thirty-three miles from Cleveland's Caldwell, New Jersey, birthplace—which happens to be the first presidential site I visited as an adult. I highly recommend a trip. Docent Sharon Farrell gave me a terrific tour. And get this: she raised her family on the top floor of the Grover Cleveland House. How is there not a sitcom about a docent who raises her family inside a presidential historic site?

Thomas Edison (1847–1931) Thomas Edison set up his laboratory in Menlo Park, New Jersey. It was there that he invented the phonograph and

developed the incandescent lightbulb, among other epochal innovations. Without him, this service area might very well not have lights. But Edison isn't beloved by all. You may have read about the 1880s "War of the Currents" between Edison's direct-current (DC) electrical system and Nicola Tesla's alternating-current (AC) electrical system. Well, to this day science nerds battle fiercely over which system was more important. All to say, if you're driving a Tesla, you may not want to stop here.

Alexander Hamilton (1755–1804)

Ever since 2015, when *Hamilton* debuted on Broadway, this has been by far the hottest service area on the turnpike, with Nathan's hot dogs rumored to be selling for thirty times their value. Founding Father Alexander Hamilton studied and worked for a time in New Jersey but his chief association with the state is with the town of Weehawken, where he was killed in a duel. Meanwhile the man who "won" the duel, Aaron Burr, was actually born in and buried in New Jersey.

Vince Lombardi (1913–1970)

The five-time-championship Green Bay football coach is the guy they named the Super Bowl trophy after. For a generation he embodied the virtues of hard work, discipline, and sacrifice of the individual for the greater good of the team. Yet he should also be remembered for his kindness and compassion. A devout Catholic, he became a committed, if behind-the-scenes, supporter of gay rights—in part because of his love for his gay brother, Hal. When coaching for Washington, Lombardi knew that tight end Jerry Smith and running back Ray McDonald were gay, and actively protected them from discrimination. He died from colon cancer at age fifty-seven. Wrote biographer David Maraniss, "Other great coaches have receded with their passing, confined to the narrow world of football, but Lombardi alone seems to live on, larger than his sport."

Vince Lombardi is not to be confused with Guy Lombardo (1902–1977), aka "Mr. New Year's Eve," the big bandleader who for almost half a century helped America ring in the New Year on radio, then on television.

DEATH OF A
FUNNY GIRL

FANNY BRICE
{1891–1951}

The only real downside to the premise of this book is that I can't write about Barbra Streisand. Because, as we all know, she's immortal.

I have loved Streisand ever since a Saturday afternoon in the summer of 1981 when I was twelve years old. I was sitting in the back seat of our Chrysler K-Car when this *voice* came over the radio. What I heard gripped me, thrilled me, *injected* itself into me, and sent me nearly over the edge. It was the voice of someone who wanted something, no, *needed* something, who through sheer force of will—and that glorious voice—was going to find her way, come what may. By the time the song ended I'm pretty sure I'd gone into spasms. (This is why I've never done hard drugs. That moment was a high that could never be topped.)

"That was Barbra Streisand singing 'People' from the musical *Funny Girl*," the adult contemporary deejay intoned afterward. He sounded like he was just coming down from something himself, taking a drag from a cigarette.

I used to imagine that there were boys like me all over who heard her sing for the first time that very same day, their parents' cars all tuned to that same station. And that we all had the same reaction. (Kind of like the "Twilight Bark" scene in *101 Dalmatians*, when the lead dog, Pongo, howls and dogs all over London respond to his call.) We were all hooked into each other at that moment. All of us—and no one else—on the same frequency.

I started collecting Barbra's records and listening to them constantly. For Christmas my parents gave me the cassette of her album *ButterFly*. (Later on I read that it was Barbra's least favorite album. I didn't know how to feel about that.) And this is a great point of pride for me: from that day in the K-car until now, I've never once stopped playing a Barbra song in the middle. Back in the days when I listened to Barbra on the stereo in my bedroom, I used to think, if the house is burning down and I'm in the middle of a Barbra song, I'll just have to risk it and stay until the end. (When the Walkman was invented and Barbra became portable, the world became a much safer place for me.)

By the time I saw *Funny Girl* on VHS I knew the score backward and forward. I didn't love that the movie dropped a few of the big numbers from the Broadway version. (Well, I was more than fine with the movie dropping the songs *other* characters sang.) But Streisand's legendary performance of the song "My Man"—added for the movie's finale—made up for it.

The whole performance is so exciting it's impossible to imagine anyone else playing it. After all, *Funny Girl* is the Barbra Streisand story, right? Of course it isn't. It's a biopic about the pioneering Jewish comedienne Fanny Brice. (And we'll get to her in just a moment.)

There have been at least a few instances when an actor's portrayal of a real person is so powerful, it supplants the memory of the film's subject: Hear the name of World War II general George S. Patton and you'll likely picture George C. Scott in his Oscar-winning turn in the movie *Patton*. Read about the British adventurer T. E. Lawrence and it's virtually impossible *not* to picture Peter O'Toole in *Lawrence of Arabia*. But with both those movies, you're never *not* aware of whose story you're watching. Something altogether different transpires with Streisand and *Funny Girl*: Streisand is *so* electric that you forget it's a story about Fanny Brice. You have to *remind* yourself you're watching a portrayal of a historical figure rather than a story about the ascendancy of the actual actress on the screen. She doesn't so much merge with the character as consume it. Her talent is that volcanic.

But that, it turns out, is a bit of a shame. Because Fanny Brice had a great story all her own. And I promise we will talk about her. But first . . .

Barbra played Fanny twice, first on Broadway in the 1964 musical, then four years later in William Wyler's film adaptation. The casting was so perfect that today it seems inevitable. But it wasn't. Fanny Brice's own daughter—whose husband, Ray Stark, produced both the musical and the film—felt that Streisand wasn't right for the part. Many felt otherwise. In 1964, Streisand, only twenty-one, was an up-and-coming star fresh off her Broadway debut as the put-upon secretary Miss Marmelstein in the musical *I Can Get It for You Wholesale.* According to the critic Neil Gabler, she "looked like Brice, had some of Brice's mannerisms, and shared her outsized kooky stage personality." Like Fanny, Streisand had been raised by a single mother: Fanny's mother had left her father, while Barbra's father died suddenly when she was a baby. Like Fanny, too, she had her first professional breakthrough as an amateur: Fanny at Keeney's Theater on Fulton Street in Brooklyn, Barbra at the gay nightclub the Lion in Greenwich Village.

But while the Jewish looks, the Brooklyn accent, even the life story pointed to a destiny at work in the casting, it was Streisand herself, enormously savvy about shaping her own career, who actually wrote the narrative that turned Fanny's story into her own. "This play is really about me," she told the Associated Press during a publicity interview. "It simply happened to happen before to Fanny Brice." Later she told *Playboy*: "I read conversations [of Brice's] that have never been published, and it was very peculiar, we were very much alike in a very deep area, in spirit. . . . Her essence and my essence were very similar." Make no mistake, this was deliberate image-crafting. In the words of biographer William J. Mann, "Barbra wasn't about to share top billing with the woman she was playing."

Well, maybe it's time that Fanny, who died thirteen years before Barbra played her, once again gets her name at the top of the marquee. (See, I told you we'd get to Fanny's story.)

Unlike Barbra, Fanny did change her name—and her nose. Fanny was born Fania Borach on the Lower East Side in 1891, fifty-one years before the woman who would play her. When she was three, her middle-class parents (not poor as in the movie) moved the family to Newark. Her mother, Rose, ran a saloon. Her father, a charming Frenchman nicknamed "Pinochle Charlie," mostly drank and played cards. Eventually Rose took her children to Brooklyn; the cast-off Charlie tagged along, living in his own apartment. At fifteen, after her successes at various amateur nights, Fanny landed a job as a chorus girl in a musical by George M. Cohan (considered the "father of musical theater," he's the guy who wrote "Give My Regards to Broadway"), but she was fired before it opened because she couldn't dance. Undeterred, she found work for the Columbia Amusement Company and its touring productions.

In the movie *Funny Girl*, it was a slapstick dance on roller skates that was Fanny's breakthrough, but in real life it was a role in a 1908 burlesque revue called *The College Girls*. Fanny had been told she needed a signature act and had appealed to a friend, a young songwriter named Irving Berlin (born Israel Beilin). Berlin had put together a number called "Sadie Salome, Go Home," which he sang with a Yiddish accent, about a Jewish girl who wants to reach stardom by performing Salome's racy "Dance of the Seven Veils." The dance had gained notoriety when the opera in which it was featured, Richard Strauss's *Salome*, had come to New York the previous year. We don't know exactly what the dance looked like, but it was scandalously risqué; women in the audience were reported to have "covered their eyes with their programs." After a single performance, in fact, the opera was shut down by J. P. Morgan, who sat on the board of the Metropolitan Opera, and whose outraged daughter had complained to him. But the scandal only amplified the buzz. The envelope-pushing "Queen of Vaudeville" Eva Tanguay was soon earning $2,500 a week doing a version of the dance about which she quipped, "I can fit the entire costume in my closed fist." It was Fanny's genius to turn this craze into comedy by playing up her own awkwardness and her own Jewishness instead of hiding them. She made herself into just the kind of girl who wasn't suited for such a performance, transforming the act into outrageous parody.

Another thing never mentioned in *Funny Girl*: during the tour of *The College Girls*, Fanny met a barber from Albany named Frank White. Infatuated with Fanny's stage performance, White followed the show to Boston, and, treating Fanny to dinner night after night, implored the seventeen-year-old girl to marry him. Fanny, worried about the effect of marriage on her career, demurred, but finally capitulated to her persistent suitor. She did insist that they postpone the consummation until the run of the show had ended. Eventually, however, she capitulated on that score, too, but after three apparently unsatisfactory nights with Frank in a Philadelphia hotel room, she left, never setting eyes on him again. A divorce followed two years later.

Her professional life was more successful. Back in New York she received a telegram from Florenz Ziegfeld, impresario of the *Ziegfeld Follies*, the leading musical revue on Broadway. ("What kind of mother names her son Florence?" asks Fanny's mother in *Funny Girl*.) In 1910, a job with the *Follies* was like a place in the cast of *Saturday Night Live*. The annual revue featured lavish budgets, the best talent on Broadway, and beautiful dancing girls. An offer from the Great Ziegfeld meant a chance at true stardom. (The 1917 cast was a comedic dream team, featuring not only Fanny but legendary entertainers Eddie Cantor, Bert Williams, W. C. Fields, and Will Rogers.) When Fanny first saw Ziegfeld's telegram, she was convinced it was a prank, but it wasn't. Ziegfeld, hoping to amp up the comedy in his revue, needed someone of Fanny's talents.

As a member of the Follies for much of the next two decades, Fanny succeeded by making herself into what one critic called the "anti-Ziegfeld Girl." While the dancing girls were gorgeous and conventionally sexy—Josephine Baker, Barbara Stanwyck, and Gypsy Rose Lee all spent time in the revue—Fanny was not. Instead, as she had done with Sadie Salome, she would spoof the great female performers of the era such as screen vamp Theda Bara and the avant-garde dancer Martha Graham.

Fanny's stardom and her paycheck grew (to as much as $3,000 a week), but her love life remained tumultuous. In 1918 she married Jules "Nick" Arnstein, a gambler and con man, whom she had been seeing since 1912 but could not marry until he secured a divorce, which he didn't obtain until Fanny was seven months pregnant with their daughter Frances. Fans of *Funny Girl* recall Arnstein, as played by Omar Sharif, as a charming and debonair rascal whose greatest weakness is that he is ashamed to live off his wife's earnings. But in real life, Arnstein consorted with mobsters and shamelessly leeched off his wealthy wife to finance his lifestyle and his business schemes. According to Eddie Cantor, Arnstein was "the best actor Fanny ever saw. The performance never faltered and the curtain never fell." In the film he is arrested only once, and turns himself in; in reality he did time twice, once in Sing Sing from 1915 to 1917 for wiretapping, and then again in Leavenworth from 1924 to 1927 for bank theft. And that doesn't include the criminal record he had in Europe.

But Fanny's troubled love life was also the source of what became her signature number, the torch song "My Man," which she began to sing in 1921 for the *Follies.* (No, it wasn't written for *Funny Girl.*) Fanny sang in a torn dress, holding a lamppost, looking forlorn—and without the exaggerated ethnic accent she ordinarily used for comic effect. Although Fanny claimed that she never intended it to be autobiographical, audiences sensed that the pain Fanny expressed was real. It was another breakthrough for her as a performer, and, noted biographer Herbert Goldman, "her rendition made it the greatest ballad ever in the Follies." The reviewers agreed, and Fanny began to entertain thoughts of branching out beyond comedy.

That desire to move beyond comedy may have prompted one of the most prominent episodes of Fanny's public life—also omitted entirely from *Funny Girl*: her 1923 rhinoplasty, performed by an unlicensed doctor in rooms Fanny was renting at the Ritz. Fanny didn't just get a nose job; she summoned the press corps to profile the change in her profile. The reporters, playing on the campaign slogan of then president Warren G. Harding, joked about a "return to normalcy" for the famous schnozz. Fanny wasn't aiming to "pass" as a non-Jew; by 1923, all the world knew she was Jewish. And far from concealing the surgery, Fanny gave interviews with reporters before and after.

So why did she do it? Her biographer Barbara Grossman suggests that "she seemed to have decided that her Yiddish-accented routines had become too limiting, and sought acceptance from a broader audience for which, as she saw it, her Jewish mannerisms and appearance were inappropriate." Herbert Goldman offers a different theory, the demise of her marriage: "The nose job was, in part, a breaking of her old bonds with Nick Arnstein. Fanny always made substantial changes in her life when she felt that things were just not working." Fanny's own explanation was simpler: "In noses as in life, one wearies of the too familiar. Charm lies in the unexpected. Besides, I am tired of having to fit my hats to the curve of my nose rather than the needs of my temperament." The most famous explanation of all came from Dorothy Parker (née Rothschild), who quipped, "She cut off her nose to spite her race."

But the new nose didn't bring Fanny success in serious roles. There are plenty of reasons why this might have been the case. Broad ethnic comedy that had thrived on vaudeville was taking a back seat to the more refined and sophisticated wit of more assimilated Jews like Dorothy Parker. The anti-immigrant sentiment of the twenties and the overt anti-Semitism of the thirties may have also led to a "de-Semitizing" of culture. Then there was the difference between film and stage. A show playing in New York to a multicultural crowd could be assured that its audience would warm to the varied ethnic types onstage, but a motion picture that played to the whole nation needed to play down those Jewish faces, accents, and styles. Or at least that's what the studio bosses, many of them Jewish themselves, seemed to believe. Whatever the reason, Fanny was seeing the beginnings of a kind of blackout in which the explicit representation of Jews in popular culture began to fade.

In 1937, Fanny, divorced from Arnstein, moved to Beverly Hills. She married and divorced a third time, then in the 1940s found success with her own radio show, playing an impish little girl of three or four named Baby Snooks. The show offered broad appeal and the character required no Yiddish accent. This was the final act of her career. Fanny Brice died in 1951.

In 1952, a critic named Henry Popkin wrote an essay about "The Vanishing Jew of Our Popular Culture." He quotes the great writer Ben Hecht on "the almost complete disappearance of the Jew from American fiction, stage, radio, and movies." Of course, Jews were as present in the entertainment industry as ever, but they were no longer emphasizing their Jewishness. For example, Hecht's own 1928 play, *The Front Page*, featured a character named Irving Pincus, who appears in the 1931 film version. By 1940, when the film was remade as *His Girl Friday*, the character was changed to Joe Pettibone. So too with Jerome Weidman's 1937 novel *I Can Get It for You Wholesale*. When Avon books reprinted it in 1949, it changed many names, substituting Michael Babbin for Meyer Babushkin. Interestingly, Popkin doesn't attribute the vanishing Jew to anti-Semitism but rather, in the wake of the Holocaust, to anti-anti-Semitism, the fear of being seen as anti-Semitic. The best way to avoid stereotyping is not to represent something at all.

By the time *I Can Get It for You Wholesale* became a Broadway musical in 1962, the original Jewish names had been restored. A young unknown Barbra Streisand was cast as Miss Marmelstein—and her ascent into the stratosphere began.

The different eras in which they lived go a good way toward explaining why Fanny never achieved the superstar status that Barbra would. But there's another, bigger factor at play in the difference in their fortunes. To put it bluntly, Barbra is simply more talented than Fanny was. Listen to both their versions of "My Man." There's no comparison.

Also, it must be said that Fanny was never sexy in the way that Barbra has been in so many performances. In the 1972 screwball comedy *What's Up Doc?*, Barbra's hair and skin positively glow, and she's so at ease in the role of the troublemaking seductress. Funny *and* sexy. It makes perfect sense that Ryan O'Neal—no slouch in the sex appeal department—would fall for her. There's a scene where O'Neal discovers her lying across the top of a piano. He plucks out "As Time Goes By" as she sings, slowly working her way onto the bench next to him, the San Francisco skyline behind them. The notes are as golden as her looks and the view, as she turns toward O'Neal going into *full profile*. They're not trying to hide her nose. It's being glorified. (I asked director Peter Bogdanovich about this "radical shot," as I described it. He had no idea what I was talking about and thought I was nuts. But I don't care. I'm right!)

In 2009 I profiled Arthur Laurents, just a couple of years before he died. His own remarkable career as a writer and director on Broadway and in Hollywood included credits ranging from *Rope* to *West Side Story* to *La Cage aux Folles*. He also directed Barbra in *I Can Get It for You Wholesale*. "I gave her her first role on Broadway," he told me. "And I also think it's wonderful that she has never pulled back about being Jewish."

Now that the Barbra box had been opened—and it's pretty shameless the way I've hijacked interviews over the years to talk about her—I wanted to talk about the Streisand-Redford classic *The Way We Were*, which Laurents had written, drawing on his own experience on the Hollywood blacklist. I said to him, "You gotta be proud that you have this love story that's a box-office blockbuster, and the lead female character is a Jewish communist." "Yes," he answered. "I'm proud that . . ." He paused, then added thoughtfully, "Well, she's the first Jewish star, Barbra."

Laurents (born Arthur Levine) was absolutely right that Streisand never pulled back about being Jewish, in her choice of material or her public persona. She's told many interviewers about her decision not to have a nose job, and, unlike other stars of her generation, she kept her birth name, smoothing it out only slightly with a minor alphadectomy. (Whenever I see young people spell her name "Barbara" I want to explain that for gay men over a certain age, the extra *a* is the equivalent of a hate crime.) She broke ground.

But Barbra wasn't "the first Jewish star." That honor goes to the original "Funny Girl," Fanny Brice. Fanny, every bit as ambitious and determined as her spiritual daughter Barbra, had pioneered comedy for women by making an asset of her culture and her ethnicity. Without her, and her generation of Jewish performers, one can hardly imagine American popular culture.

Really, one day someone should make a movie about Fanny Brice.

Calamity Jane (1852–1903)

Film: *Calamity Jane.* Eclipsed by: *Doris Day.*

Calamity Jane is one of those people you may actually think are fictional. Born Martha Jane Cannary, she was real enough—a frontierswoman who dressed as a man, rode horses, shot rifles, drank whiskey, and maybe worked as a prostitute. She claimed legendary gunfighter Wild Bill Hickok was her lover, but between her own possibly tall tales and the dime novels written about her, no one really knows. Doris Day eclipses the image of the real Calamity Jane through the sheer sunniness of her performance. She begins the 1953 movie-musical riding into Deadwood City on a stagecoach with a smile so broad and a voice so bright, it's hard to believe the real Calamity Jane wouldn't surrender to her before the end of the opening number.

T. E. Lawrence (1888–1935)

Film: *Lawrence of Arabia.* Eclipsed by: *Peter O'Toole.*

The real-life Lawrence of Arabia (born Thomas Edward Lawrence), celebrated as he was, simply can't compete with the movie *Lawrence of Arabia*. For three reasons: 1) The whole film, directed by David Lean in 1962, is just too beautiful looking. Shot on a wide-screen format, the desert has never looked so inviting; 2) The epic theme music, by Maurice Jarre, is just too beautiful sounding. (True story: I asked *Mobituaries* podcast theme composer Daniel Hart to listen to *Lawrence of Arabia* when he was coming up with our theme.); and 3) Peter O'Toole's eyes are just too beautiful. There's an undercurrent of insanity running through his performance. Crazy wide-eyed zeal is one thing. But when the crazy wide eyes are that blue, it's next level.

George S. Patton (1885–1945)

Film: *Patton* (duh). Eclipsed by: *George C. Scott.*

The eclipse takes place in the very first scene of the 1970 film. George C. Scott as World War II general George "Old Blood and Guts" Patton walks out alone before a giant American flag. For six minutes he addresses unseen soldiers of the US Third Army as

Actors Who Played Them

they prepare for battle: "Now, I want you to remember that no bastard ever won a war by dying for his country. He won it by making the other poor dumb bastard die for his country." Even if you've never seen the movie, you've seen the images—iconography, really—from this scene in countless film montages. I particularly like the close-ups on Scott's eyebrows, which deserved their own Oscars. (Fun fact: The real Patton had a much higher voice. Said George C. Scott: "People are used to my gravel voice and if I tried to use a high little voice it would be silly.")

George M. Cohan (1878–1942)

Film: *Yankee Doodle Dandy*. Eclipsed by: *James Cagney*.

Audiences were overjoyed when Irishman Cagney, known for his tough-guy roles, played Irishman Cohan, the greatest entertainer of his day. (You may remember Cohan from a few pages ago when he came up in Fanny Brice's story.) But this eclipse owes a good deal to the timing of the film's release. Cohan had written the patriotic standards "Over There," "The Yankee Doodle Boy," and "You're a Grand Old Flag" and the movie came out just months after the 1941 attack on Pearl Harbor. It captured the national mood and became the highest-grossing film in Warner Bros. history up to that point. Cohan saw the film shortly before his death, and, Cagney said, "gave it his blessing." Jimmy Cagney, who made it safe for boys to ask for dancing lessons, described his own performance as "one song-and-dance man saluting another, the greatest of our calling."

Eva Perón (1919–1952)

Musical: *Evita*. Eclipsed by: *Patti LuPone*.

The real Eva Perón may have been part of Argentina's corrupt regime but she was a folk hero to her country's working class. After her husband—general and fascist sympathizer Juan Perón—was elected president, the woman known as "Evita" fought for women's suffrage and workers' rights. The Argentine Congress gave her the title "Spiritual Leader of the Nation" shortly before she died from cancer at age thirty-three. (That Jesus also died at thirty-three only added to her hagiography.) Twenty-six years later, in 1978, *Evita* the musical premiered. Next to *Jesus Christ Superstar*, it has Andrew Lloyd Webber's best score. But it was star Patti LuPone's ferocious performance that was responsible for this eclipse. Specifically her outstretched arms as she sings "Don't Cry for Me, Argentina." (Yup, you're doing the arms right now.) Madonna was the perfect person to play the role on film. Clearly Madonna could relate to Eva's story, especially the early part, and not just because she had a phase where she was really into Latin guys. But the role belongs to Patti. If you disagree, I would advise you not to tell her.

Marlene Dietrich (1901–1992)

Film: *Blazing Saddles.* Eclipsed by: *Madeline Kahn.*

When Kahn, as "the Bavarian Bombshell" Lili Von Shtupp, sang "I'm Tired," she not only stole the 1974 movie—she all but erased the memory of Marlene Dietrich's performance of "See What the Boys in the Back Room Will Have," the song from *Destry Rides Again* (1939) that Kahn was spoofing. Director Mel Brooks said that Kahn "had the pipes to sing at the Met," yet she trained her virtuosic talent on comedy. Critic Richard Corliss spoke for many when he confessed to a preference for Madeline over Marlene: "Her singing moans are perfectly off-pitch, her smile wan and used-up, her speech a generous parody of Dietrich's slightly impaired diction." He also noted Kahn's legs "are slimmer and shapelier than Dietrich's ever were." To which one can only add, "It's twue! It's twue!"

Maria von Trapp (1905–1987)

Film: *The Sound of Music.* Eclipsed by: *Julie Andrews.*

The real Maria, orphaned as a child, had indeed planned on a life as a nun until Georg von Trapp hired her as a tutor and then proposed. She married him out of love for his children. Nice story, but add a score by Rodgers and Hammerstein and a performance by Julie Andrews coming off an Oscar win as Mary Poppins, and the memory of the real Maria was toast. How good is Julie Andrews in the role? She makes "brown paper packages tied up with strings" sound delightful. There's a reason that when we gave my grandmother a VCR she used it to watch *The Sound of Music* over and over and over again. (By the way, the real von Trapp family didn't escape on foot. They took a train and eventually ended up running a Vermont ski lodge where they made their own cheese.)

Jake LaMotta (1922–2017)

Film: *Raging Bull.* Eclipsed by: *Robert De Niro.*

When former middleweight champ LaMotta died, the boxing writer Carlo Rotella wrote that "the character has so eclipsed the man that by now it's hard to see around De Niro's LaMotta to the guy who died." Partly that's because LaMotta was champion for only a year, and lost five of his six bouts to Sugar Ray Robinson. It's also because De Niro didn't hold back on portraying LaMotta's unsavory side. LaMotta heaped praise on the Oscar-winning performance: "When I saw the film I was upset. I kind of look bad in it. Then I realized it was true. That's the way it was. I was a no-good bastard." (The 1981 Oscars were the first I was allowed to stay up and watch. I remember how cool it was to watch De Niro thank the real-life LaMotta, who was sitting right there.)

Spartacus (111–71 BC)

Film: *You really have to ask?* Eclipsed by: *Kirk Douglas.*

Spartacus, a Roman slave from Thrace (that's northeast of Greece), trained as a gladiator, then escaped and led a slave revolt known as the Third Servile War. Stanley Kubrick's movie, released during the US civil rights movement, took great liberties with the ancient accounts, often in ways that strengthened the parallels between slavery in ancient Rome and slavery in the United States. The epic toga fest, produced by Douglas himself, also caused controversy because it employed blacklisted screenwriter Dalton Trumbo, and spurred a boycott from the American Legion. JFK himself crossed picket lines to view it. (Douglas's boldness in openly acknowledging Trumbo has been credited with helping to end the blacklist.) But the movie belongs to Kirk Douglas and his chin. If you happen to have a picture of the real Spartacus and he *doesn't* have a dimple in his chin, don't show me.

BEFORE AND AFTER

HERBERT HOOVER
(1874–1964)

AND

JOHN QUINCY ADAMS
(1767–1848)

The Pre-Presidency of Herbert Hoover

I love rankings—whether they're for the weekend box office, the Westminster Kennel Club Dog Show, or Olympic gymnastics. As far as I'm concerned, everything should be ranked. When my high school Latin teacher, Father Nicola, started ranking us on every quiz and test, I couldn't have been more thrilled. I began memorizing those conjugations and declensions as if my life depended on it.

I also love presidential history. So presidential rankings are right up my alley. Historians are remarkably in sync on who deserves top-tier status. Usually it's Washington, Lincoln, FDR, and maybe his fifth cousin Teddy Roosevelt. Basically it's Mount Rushmore if you swap out Jefferson for FDR. (Occasionally some smarty-pants will lobby for James K. Polk as first-tier: "He had four goals and accomplished them all. So there!" Someone should remind said smarty-pants that the Polk-initiated Mexican-American War was called "our most evil war" by no less a person than General Ulysses S. Grant. So THERE!)

All the major presidential rankings evaluate the individuals based on their performance in office. But no one is anointed president at birth. (Except Jeb, which is why George W. taking his slot must still burn.) All of America's chief executives led lives before entering the White House—some of them lives of great achievement that would have stood the test of time . . . had their failures in the White House not erased the memory of all the good they'd done before they got there. Alas, as far as history is concerned, life before the White House is preseason ball. It doesn't count.

That doesn't seem entirely fair, judging a president entirely on his (and one day her) presidency. And that's why I'm proposing a Mount Rushmore for pre-presidencies. The first three honorees on this hypothetical monument won't surprise you. The first spot goes to George Washington. Duh. He led the Continental Army in the American Revolution and he presided over the Constitutional Convention before serving as our first president. He could have made himself king and he didn't. However long this country lasts, we owe him.

I'm giving the second slot to . . . James Madison, father of the Constitution and author of the Bill of Rights. Simmer down, Jefferson groupies. TJ only got a slot on the actual Mount Rushmore because the Declaration of Independence is a much more romantic piece of writing. Seriously, imagine walking into a pub in the 1790s and saying you wrote the Declaration of Independence . . . or saying you wrote the Constitution. See which one gets you more play. But Thomas Jefferson wasn't that great a president. (I love the Louisiana Purchase, too, but it doesn't take a genius to know a bargain when you see it.) So time to give some love to the always overshadowed Madison, who was in fact our shortest president at five foot four.

The third slot on the pre-presidential Mount Rushmore goes to . . . Ulysses S. Grant. No amount of revisionism will turn him into a first-tier president. But before he entered the White House he led the Union in the Civil War. He quite literally kept this country together. (Remember how I just said an unsuccessful presidency wipes out the memory of a glorious pre-presidency? Grant is the big exception to that rule.) Plus he just seems like a terrific guy. Mark Twain had to convince him his story was worth telling as an autobiography, that's how self-effacing Grant was. (His memoir is generally regarded as the best of any president's.) One of my favorite pieces I've done for *CBS Sunday Morning* was about Grant and the painful and poignant end of his life from throat cancer. (I highly recommend a visit to the house in Saratoga Springs, New York, where he died. They've still got the glass container of "cocaine water" he gargled with to ease the pain.)

As for the fourth wild-card slot on the Mount Rushmore of pre-presidents, I'm giving it to . . . drumroll . . . Herbert Hoover! (Okay, if you read the title of this chapter it's maybe not a shocker.)

If you're like me, you first learned about Herbert Hoover through the musical *Annie*, in which an ensemble of homeless people in three-part harmony lay the blame for the Great Depression at the feet of President Hoover. (*Annie* is also where I first heard about Beau Brummell.) The defining event of Hoover's presidency was the Wall Street Crash of 1929, which ushered in a decade of economic hardship. The man himself, thanks in part to *Annie*, is generally remembered as a coldhearted business mogul, aloof from the sufferings of the ordinary people. Now, whether or not Hoover deserves much of any blame for the economy's collapse—historians will tell you it's a complicated story—our focus on the Crash has obscured an extraordinary career that would be noteworthy even if the man had never been elected president. As his great-granddaughter, the political commentator Margaret Hoover, told me, "This man lived for ninety years, and he is judged for four of them."

In fact, Hoover's pre-presidential career may be the most remarkable of any president's. The problem, of course, in telling Hoover's story before 1929 is you can never erase the knowledge that this story doesn't end well. There's that Great Crash looming, the big jagged line on the graph that drops off the bottom of the page. It's like watching *Titanic*. No matter how much you get caught up in the romance, you know what's coming. This Ship Is Going Down.

Still, let's try to imagine a life of Herbert Hoover without the Crash. If we can, we might be able to recapture the improbable rise and spectacular successes of a man who deserves *also* to be remembered as an innovative engineer, a mining tycoon, an internationally celebrated humanitarian, and one of the most influential cabinet secretaries in American history.

Hoover was born in the village of West Branch, Iowa. (Book a trip today—the entire village is preserved.) The son of a blacksmith, he was orphaned at age nine and shipped west to rural Oregon, where he suffered a miserable childhood in the care of distant relatives. Indeed it was a hard-knock life for him. (Final *Annie* reference.) At age seventeen he entered Stanford, a member of its very first class. It was here that he started demonstrating his toughness and drive, as historian Ken

Whyte relates in his engrossing biography of Hoover. As treasurer of Stanford's student activities committee, Hoover prided himself on his thrift and his ability to say no. When former US president Benjamin Harrison attended a student baseball game without having purchased an admission ticket, the young future president confronted Harrison and quietly insisted that he pay just like everyone else.

At Stanford he studied geology, working summers for the US Geological Survey. How determined was he to make something of himself? While visiting Yosemite National Park with friends, he received an invitation to join an expedition led by renowned geologist Waldemar Lindgren. Too poor to travel by stagecoach, Hoover instead walked eighty miles in three days.

He would travel much farther after graduation. By 1897 the twenty-three-year-old was off to Australia with the British mining firm of Bewick, Moreing & Company, inspecting and evaluating potential sites for the company to acquire.

Hoover thrived in the outback and within a year was promoted to junior partner. At that point he cabled a marriage proposal back home to his Stanford sweetheart, a young woman named Lou Henry. (Her father had wanted a boy.) Lou was one of the first women in America to earn a degree in geology. She and Bert were a perfect match: While he wrote several textbooks on mining—one of which became the standard for most of the twentieth century—together they translated the 1556 mining text *De Re Metallica* from its original Latin. It was a labor of love that took five years as they sat on opposite sides of a desk, reference works piling up around them. (Now that's what I call a classics love story.)

The newlyweds spent a year in China, where Herbert essentially ran the nation's coalfields. A few years later, he struck out on his own as a consultant, becoming known as the "Doctor of Mines." He would restore failing businesses to health in exchange for a stake in the ownership. Among his ventures was a highly profitable silver mine in Burma. By 1914 he was very rich.

The early twentieth century was the great age of engineering. (Engineering was to its day as Silicon Valley is to today.) Feats like the Brooklyn Bridge and the

Panama Canal promised that technology, wedded to human ingenuity, could obliterate all limits to what society could accomplish. Engineering was a great force for human progress, and Hoover saw the future itself as something to be engineered—imagined, planned, and executed. (Think of that famous palindrome "A man, a plan, a canal: Panama.") And as an engineer, an innovator, and an apostle of the future, Hoover represented the spirit of progress.

If Hoover's obit had been written in 1914, he would have been remembered as a talented engineer turned business magnate. Not bad. But the next chapter in his life made him into something greater, a kind of human dynamo, virtually a modern superman.

When World War I broke out in August 1914, 120,000 Americans found themselves stranded in Europe, trapped in the middle of a war zone. It was Hoover—and remember, he was still just a private citizen—who solved the crisis. He mustered all the logistical and operational know-how he'd developed in business and engineering to assemble the ships to get the Americans home. And as remarkable as this accomplishment was, a much greater one was in the offing. Germany had cut off Belgium's food supply, and millions of innocent people were starving. The United States, still neutral in the conflict, was reluctant to get involved. The British, including a young Winston Churchill, sat on their hands, insisting that the Germans bear responsibility for what they'd wrought. Yet when confronted with the Belgian crisis, Hoover didn't waffle. As Ken Whyte told me, "Everyone was arguing that they didn't have responsibility to feed the Belgians. Hoover said, 'I'll feed them. Let me through.' And pretty much bullied his way through both lines." Driven by an idealism rooted in his Quaker childhood, he raised billions of dollars; found food supplies in Canada, the United States, and Argentina; mobilized the ships he needed; and got them past a British blockade and through German lines. The delivery of 11 million metric tons of food was not only an operational triumph but a diplomatic one, too, given the warring governments involved: "He was dealing as though he were his own state department," said Whyte. All this, again, as a private citizen.

When America did enter the war in 1917, President Wilson needed someone to coordinate American food production. There was only one possible choice. The Doctor of Mines was anointed Food Czar. Hoover led the US Food Administration, organizing rationing systems and public communications. Then, when the war ended, he took up the task of feeding the war-ravaged population of Europe, bringing food to millions of hungry children. Some have estimated that in Hoover's career as a humanitarian he may have saved a hundred million lives.

Tom Schwartz, the director of the Herbert Hoover Presidential Library and Museum in West Branch, told me: "I still get these e-mails and letters, and now, we're talking about grandchildren and great-grandchildren of people who Hoover fed, and they realize that the Hoover legacy allowed for them to be here on earth and contribute."

Hoover's celebrity at the time made him popular with Democrats and Republicans alike. He became known as "the Great Humanitarian." The combination of humanitarian idealism and technocratic competence was hard to resist. Hoover's own politics were roughly aligned with Teddy Roosevelt's progressive wing of the Republican Party. Of course, he had hardly been a saint as a businessman, extracting great wealth from Asian nations while using foreign labor to depress wages. But engineering had given him a set of political principles; neither laissez-faire nor socialist, he believed that centralized planning, organization, and smart management of any enterprise would result in efficiency, success, and benefits for the whole of society. It was in this spirit that in 1919 he founded the Hoover Library (now the Hoover Institute at Stanford) for the study of war and peace. Hoover believed in research, in expertise, and in applying the human mind to solving human problems. He was a technocrat, not an ideologue, in many ways similar to JFK—who was in fact a great admirer.

By 1920, Hoover was being courted by Republicans to run for president. But because of his past support for Wilson's internationalism, the party went with Warren Harding. When Harding won, though, Hoover served the new Republican president just as he had served his Democratic predecessor. As secretary of commerce for both Harding and Calvin Coolidge, Hoover took what had been a dead-end post and revolutionized it. "He took a sleepy backwater office and he used it to benefit the American consumer," said Tom Schwartz. "He had industries sit down and instead of each making proprietary products where the parts weren't interchangeable, he had them set standards."

Now, standardization may not sound terribly exciting. But consider that before Hoover was in charge, there were sixty-six different sizes of paving bricks on the market. Hoover's Commerce Department set a single standard. The dairy industry, meanwhile, had had forty-two different-sized containers for milk. (Can you imagine what a nightmare that would be, calling home from the supermarket? "Sorry, honey, did you want the seventeen-ounce? Or the seventeen-and-a-half-ounce?") Hoover got them to do it by pint, quart, half gallon, gallon. The standard size of an electric light socket was set under Hoover. It's not a stretch to say that Hoover standardized much of American life in and outside the home, saving costs for manufacturers and consumers—and saving lives. It was under his tenure that three-colored traffic signals (red, green, and what was then called "amber") were made uniform across the country.

Never before and never since has there been a secretary of commerce who made such an impact.

He embraced the new technologies of the young century, including aviation and broadcasting. On April 7, 1927, in the very first successful long-distance demonstration of television, an audience in New York saw an image of Secretary of Commerce Herbert Hoover speaking from Washington, DC. That's right, Hoover was the first person to appear on TV. (Actually the broadcast began with a close-up of Hoover's forehead, because he was sitting too close to the camera.)

Hoover's most prominent feat came in 1927, when the Great Mississippi Flood ravaged ten states on the banks of the river, displacing over 600,000 people. Fourteen percent of the state of Arkansas was underwater. Hoover coordinated the relief and rescue, organizing ships and supplies, supervising the construction of refugee camps, using the radio to appeal directly to the American people for donations to the Red Cross. He called the relief effort a triumph of American "mass organization and . . . mass production." It catapulted Hoover to the Republican nomination. Billed as "Herbert Hoover, Master of Emergencies," he coasted to victory in 1928 over Al Smith, winning every state except the stubbornly Democratic South and the heavily Catholic states of Massachusetts and Rhode Island. (Smith was the first Catholic major party candidate in American history.)

Hoover was sworn in on March 4, 1929. In his inaugural address, he promised to reduce crime, enforce Prohibition, improve education, avoid imperialistic adventures abroad, and regulate business. (In fact, he had regularly warned that an economic panic could hit and urged government oversight of markets to stabilize volatile business cycles.) He concluded his address on an optimistic note, in which he affirmed his belief in American know-how: "I have no fears for the future of our country. It is bright with hope." Hoover had taken the helm of the ship of state. And then . . . Mayday! Mayday!

The Post-Presidency of John Quincy Adams

If all goes as planned, there is life after the White House. And while a pre-presidency is ideally preparation for the highest office in the land, a post-presidency is often reparation for a job less than well done. A chance at redemption. Which brings me to the Mount Rushmore of Post-Presidents, the hypothetical memorial to those chief executives who finally found their groove in retirement.

The first position is being saved for Jimmy Carter. At this point the first line of his obit could conceivably put his work on behalf of human rights and with Habitat for Humanity *before* his single term in office, slathered as it was in "malaise."

William Howard Taft gets a spot. The poor guy never even wanted the job; his friend and predecessor Teddy Roosevelt pushed him into it, expecting Taft to be Roosevelt's puppet. (I've always imagined TR and Taft as Timon and Pumbaa from *The Lion King*.) When President Taft, elected in 1908, dared to do his own thing in office, an aghast Roosevelt challenged his reelection, running as an Independent in 1912. Roosevelt got more votes than Taft, but Democrat Woodrow Wilson beat them both. It was a humiliating defeat for Taft. But then in 1921, Taft got his real dream job when he was appointed chief justice of the Supreme Court! I think Americans were all relieved to finally see Taft happy.

The third slot is a little harder to decide. John Tyler, our tenth president, sure as hell isn't taking it. He was elected to the *Confederate* House of Representatives after his time as president, though he died before the first meeting. (I did interview his grandson. Yes, the grandson of a man born in 1790 is alive. The men in that family sire children well into their old age with younger second wives. That's how you end up with three generations that span the history of the United States. At ninety-two, as of this writing, Harrison Tyler is a total delight, and yes, I hope he finds a young second wife so that we can keep this thing going.)

Andrew Johnson is the only president to return to the Senate after the White House. That *sounds* interesting—a nice factoid to bust out at a party. But Johnson spoke only once in this office, in opposition to the post–Civil War measures that protected former slaves. And then he died.

Let's give the third slot to Rutherford B. Hayes. Even though his election in 1876 precipitated the Compromise of 1877, which as you'll remember ended Reconstruction, he spent his post-presidency advocating for free public education for the masses. (If you happen to be in northwest Ohio, may I suggest you pay a visit to Hayes's estate, Spiegel Grove, in Fremont? It's the *first* presidential library. And the thirty-one-room mansion has a wraparound porch that's eighty feet in length and twelve feet deep. And the trees! When I visited in 1998 I was so taken I wanted to pack my bags and move there.)

And so we come to the fourth recipient of this just-invented honor—another president whose record in the Oval Office, like those of Carter, Taft, and Hayes, is regarded by scholars as meh, yet who distinguished himself in surprising ways after leaving the White House: John Quincy Adams.

Quincy Adams, in fact, had an accomplished pre-presidency, too, as a lawyer, professor, and diplomat. The son of President John Adams, he was raised for a career in public affairs. As a boy, he traveled with his father on missions to Europe on behalf of the fledgling republic, and as a young man he scored brilliant diplomatic successes while serving in the administrations of every president from Washington through Monroe. He negotiated the Treaty of Ghent ending the War of 1812, and as Monroe's secretary of state formulated the doctrine opposing European involvement in the Americas, aka the Monroe Doctrine. (Yes, the boss always gets the credit.) In all this, he was driven by a need to please his sometimes cruelly demanding father, who had his son translating Thucydides from the original Greek at age ten and sent him to Russia at fourteen to serve as secretary for the diplomat Francis Dana. (When I was fourteen my father was sending me off to the drugstore with quarters to play *Ms. Pac-Man*.) While his brothers suffered from depression and alcoholism, the dutiful John Jr. devoted himself to winning his dad's love. "The first and deepest of all my wishes is to give satisfaction to my parents," he wrote.

In fact, according to biographer Paul C. Nagel, one of Quincy Adams's motives in running for president in 1824 was to complete what he saw as the unfinished work of his father, who had been voted out after one term. Quincy Adams wanted to make good on his father's goal of rising above partisan politics—then seen as a real threat to the republic—and to redeem the elder Adams's own disappointed hopes. During the 1824 election itself, Quincy Adams often sought his father's counsel. And when he notified his father of his victory, the aging and normally reserved ex-president responded movingly: "Never did I feel so much solemnity as upon this occasion. The multitude of my thoughts, and the intensity of my feelings are too much for a mind like mine, in its ninetieth year." The son continued to draw on his father's wisdom and experience as he assumed the office.

Yet as chief executive, Quincy Adams struggled. He had won a divisive four-way election over Andrew Jackson without a popular majority, and throughout his four years in the White House he battled an entrenched opposition. To make things worse, while Jackson was cultivating his base and forging cross-regional alliances with northerners like Martin Van Buren, Quincy Adams held aloof from politicking. (In keeping with his reputation for aloofness, he refused to wear a powdered wig to his inauguration. We know Beau Brummell would have approved.) Then came his father's death—famously, on July 4, 1826, the very same day Jefferson died, and on the fiftieth birthday of the nation. (That sound you just heard is lightning.) To make things even harder, November's midterm elections returned a Congress sympathetic to Jackson. In the 1828 presidential election, a dispirited Adams was trounced by the former general. He returned to Massachusetts an unsuccessful one-termer—the only one-term president, at that time, since his father.

Previous presidents had retired to private life, and Adams, already sixty-one, expected to do the same. He had lost his appetite for public service. The 1828 campaign had been ugly. Jackson himself blamed Adams's supporters for his wife's death after their very personal attacks on her. (She had married Jackson with the understanding that her divorce from her first husband had been finalized. Years later she found out it had not, making her an unwitting bigamist for a time.) And Jackson's campaign had spread a rumor that Adams had, as ambassador to Russia, acted as a pimp, obtaining an American prostitute for Tsar Alexander. Adams, disgusted with Jackson politically and personally, did not deign to attend the inauguration of his populist successor.

Adams was dealt another blow the next spring when his son George—suffering under a failed law practice, mounting debt, and the shame of having fathered an illegitimate child with a chambermaid—committed suicide by throwing himself from a ferry into Long Island Sound. John Quincy Adams, like his father before him, was a demanding father, and it may have been an imminent confrontation with the old man that pushed George to suicide. For Adams, retreat into private life now seemed inevitable. He wrote in his diary, "My life for the public is closed, and it only remains for me to use my endeavors to make the remainder of it useful to my family and my neighbors, if possible." Among the projects he planned for his retirement was the organization of his late father's papers in preparation for writing a biography that would shape the man's legacy. He was still a dutiful son.

But in September 1830, his friend Edward Everett approached him, suggesting that he stand for Congress in Massachusetts's 12th District. Adams hesitated. What gave him pause was not the idea of serving, but his distaste for campaigning. His wife, worn out by Washington politics, opposed the idea; his son Charles thought it beneath the dignity of a former president. But supporters continued to encourage him, and he agreed. He saw political unrest in Europe and South America, and sensed that the same turbulence might soon be roiling the United States. After his disappointing presidency, service in Congress meant a chance at redemption.

Adams easily won the seat with nearly 75 percent of the vote. On his election, he wrote in his diary: "My election as President of the United States was not half so gratifying to my inmost soul. No election or appointment conferred upon me ever gave me so much pleasure." It was of course a relatively minor position for an ex-president, one that no other man who had run the nation has ever humbled himself to seek. But at sixty-four years old, Quincy Adams found himself "launched again upon the faithless wave of politics."

For the next eighteen years in Congress, Adams fought for freedom of speech, national infrastructure, and universal education. Though generally opposed to Jackson and the Democrats, he was true to his (and his late father's) belief in transcending party, and sided with his old enemy when principle compelled him. Surprised by his occasional support, Democrats gave him the moniker "Old Man Eloquent" for—well, for his old-man eloquence. And indeed he proved a skilled speaker, debater, and strategist on the floor of the House.

The issue that now came to dominate American politics was slavery. Adams had never favored slavery, but in his early career had pragmatically supported a policy of compromise in the interest of national harmony. But in the late phase of his career, he found a new passion. (He had, as the kids say, no f—s left to give.)

Congress had established something called the gag rule. It was basically a prohibition on even debating slavery. Adams took up the fight against the gag rule under the banner of freedom of speech. He exploited every loophole to discuss slavery and to call the gag rule into question. This won him a great following among abolitionists. He further won their hearts when he opposed the inclusion of Texas as a new state in the union—it would mean the expansion of slavery and more power for the "slavocracy." Adams's commitment to these causes made him a hero to many, giving him, in the words of one biographer, "a degree of popularity that had eluded him his entire life."

And then came the event that would define John Quincy Adams's post-presidency. In Connecticut, a group of Africans had been taken into custody after seizing control of a slave ship, the schooner *Amistad*. (If you've seen Steven Spielberg's *Amistad*, you know the story. And hopefully you've forgiven Matthew McConaughey for that accent.) In July 1839, fifty-three Africans of the Mende people, having been captured in West Africa and sold into slavery in Cuba, took command of the slavers' ship, killing the captain and demanding that the Spanish crew return them home. But the Spaniards secretly navigated northward, and a United States patrol boat seized the ship. As the Mende were being held in a Connecticut jail for murder and mutiny, their case split the country politically. Abolitionists argued that the Mende, captured illegally, must go free, while slaveholding interests saw their release as a dangerous precedent. Eventually, a federal judge declared that the Mende were legally free, and ordered the United States to return them to their homeland. But President Martin Van Buren (Jackson's old ally) feared alienating the South. He instructed the US attorney to appeal the case. It soon reached the Supreme Court.

The seventy-two-year-old Adams, who had always loathed Van Buren, volunteered to help. He had not argued a case in court in thirty years, and his hands now sometimes shook involuntarily. He thought he might be of use in shaping the defense, but the abolitionists insisted that he speak before the court. His stature as a former president and the son of a Founding Father meant that he could not be easily dismissed. His eloquence, honed over years of congressional debate, would be an asset. Adams consented, and delivered a full-throated condemnation of Van Buren's position. The real criminals, he argued, were the Spanish slave traders. Invoking the Declaration of Independence, he called for the Africans' inalienable rights of life and liberty to be restored.

The court agreed and ruled for the Mende. It was a great triumph for Adams—perhaps the most significant of his long career.

Abolitionists and the freed Mende themselves raised money for their passage back to Africa. But before they left, they presented Adams with the gift of a Bible, along with a letter that read in part:

> *Mr Adams, Dear Friend we write this to you because you plead with the Great Court to make us free and now we are free and joyful we thank the Great God. I hope God will bless you dear friend. Mendi people will remember you when we go to our own country & we will tell our friends about you and we will say to them Mr Adams is a great man and he plead for us and how very glad we be and our friends will love you very much because you was a very good man and oh how joyful we shall be.*

In his final years, John Quincy Adams redoubled his opposition to the growth of slavery, opposing the Mexican War, which he saw as another vehicle to expand slavery westward. The final vote he cast on the floor of the House was to oppose a tribute to the veterans of that war. Immediately after casting his vote, he suffered a cerebral hemorrhage and collapsed on the floor of the House. He died two days later, having found as a congressman a passion and a following that had eluded him as president.

THE MOUNT RUSHMORE OF TERRIBLE PRESIDENTS

I've long loved visiting presidential homes and gravesites. And I have a special appreciation for the docents who serve at the homes of our worst chief executives. They endure all sorts of loaded or flat-out insulting questions. ("Did he do *anything* good?" "Did he ever stop beating his wife?" "Where's the bathroom? Honestly that's why we stopped here.") But for the most part they stand by their men—their awful, dissolute, cretinous commanders-in-chief. And so I dedicate to those docents this final alternative Mount Rushmore, honoring our most terrible presidents.

First slot goes to Andrew Johnson. Being dirt-poor and illiterate till adulthood doesn't get him any sympathy points here. He was drunk at his vice presidential inauguration. When he took over for Lincoln after the assassination, he could have at least tried to honor the Great Emancipator's legacy. Instead Johnson—thin-skinned, racist to the bone, mean, and miserable—did everything he could to block aid to the newly freed slaves. (Fun fact about me: My very first piece for *The Daily Show* was a visit to the home of Andrew Johnson in Greeneville, Tennessee. Twenty years later I returned to do a piece on Johnson for *CBS Sunday Morning*. See you in 2038, Greeneville!)

Warren Harding gets the second spot. At best he was oblivious to the doings of the most corrupt administration (of the twentieth century). Before Watergate, Harding's Teapot Dome scandal was the most sensational in American history. Harding does deserve credit for popularizing the word *normalcy*. (His campaign slogan was "A Return to Normalcy.") His only other distinction is that he had the largest feet of any president, size 14½.

Speaking of Watergate, I'm giving the third spot to Nixon, though it feels a little too easy. Yes, the lies, the corruption, the bigotry were bad. But he was also pretty innovative and forward-thinking (see the opening of China and the establishment of the EPA). Plus I suspect a lot of the dislike for Nixon had to do with his less than sparkling personality and his propensity to sweat. But we should include at least one bad president from the modern era and . . . well, let's leave it right there.

The last spot goes to the very worst. James Buchanan was just a disaster. The last president to serve a full term before the outbreak of the Civil War, he kicked off his term by publicly backing the Supreme Court's *Dred Scott* decision, which you read about in the Reconstruction chapter. Along with *Plessy v. Ferguson* ("Separate but equal") and *Korematsu v. United States* (which upheld the legality of the World War II internment of Japanese Americans), it's the court's most disgraceful ruling. Buchanan aggravated the situation by stuffing his cabinet with southern pro-slavery guys. He locked in his place as the worst of the worst after he lost his bid for reelection. During these crucial months, while he was still president, *seven states* seceded, while Buchanan did nothing. Talk about a lame duck. It kills me that Buchanan (our only bachelor president) was probably gay. Talk about NOT representing. (I do love his Lancaster, Pennsylvania, estate, named Wheatland. Docent Betty Nauman gives a marvelous tour. Make sure to see the outhouse built for five!)

"IT'S AN HONOR *just to be nominated" is not something you'll hear from a failed presidential candidate. But even if they bombed at the ballot box, some of these people had lives well worth remembering.*

William Jennings Bryan (1860–1925) William Jennings Bryan was just thirty-six—the youngest major-party nominee in history—when he beat Congressman Richard Bland for the Democratic Party nomination in 1896. (Yes, Democrats almost picked a guy named Bland.) Bryan went on to lose that year and again in 1904 and again in 1908. You could say he failed to evolve. Indeed in the last year of his life, 1925, he and his anti-evolution views lost in court to the great lawyer Clarence Darrow during the landmark Scopes "Monkey" Trial. Bryan, nicknamed "the Fundamentalist Pope" by journalist H. L. Mencken, believed "the contest between Christianity and evolution is a duel to the death."

Pat Paulsen (1927–1997) I'd like to think that deadpan political satire on TV started with *The Daily Show.* But Pat Paulsen was doing it about eight election cycles earlier. The writer-performer on *The Smothers Brothers Comedy Hour,* known for his bone-dry delivery (I don't know if he ever broke on camera), first ran for president in 1968, with a campaign built on the premise of continually denying that he was running for office. "I'd rather remain as I am today—a calm, ordinary, simple savior of America's destiny." A remarkable amount of his material still lands, from the simply absurd—"The number one cause of forest fires is trees"—to the much more biting—"All of the problems we face in the United States today can be traced to an unenlightened immigration policy on the part of the American Indian."

Pigasus the Pig (dates of birth and death unknown) Chicago 1968 is remembered for the six days of violent clashes between antiwar protesters and police during the Democratic National Convention. Many people watching at home wondered

if the country itself was unraveling. But there was also some pretty good guerilla street theater going on that week. On August 23, the Yippies—the Youth International Party founded by Jerry Rubin and Abbie Hoffman—introduced a 145-pound black-and-brown pig named Pigasus as their nominee to an enthusiastic crowd. (That cartoonists had long depicted corrupt politicians and police as pigs was probably no coincidence.) Supporters held signs reading "Live High on the Hog." The rally, however, was quickly broken up by Chicago police, who arrested Pigasus and his human associates for public nuisance and breach of the peace.

Eugene V. Debs (1855–1926)

The great labor leader Debs ran five times as a Socialist candidate, and his campaigns were among the most influential third-party runs in American electoral history. In 1912, he garnered 6 percent of the national vote. In 1920, his total dropped to 3.4 percent. But the tally of almost a million votes was perhaps more impressive than his previous total since he was running from inside a prison cell in the Atlanta Federal Penitentiary, where he was serving time for sedition. (He had urged Americans to resist the draft in 1918.)

Victoria Woodhull (1838–1927)

Woodhull was the first woman to mount a serious campaign for president, selecting Frederick Douglass as her running mate in 1872 on the ticket of the Equal Rights Party. (Never mind that Douglass never acknowledged the selection and instead supported Republican Ulysses S. Grant. Or that Woodhull herself was too young to legally run.) Before that she had been the first woman to own her own Wall Street brokerage firm and the first woman to launch a weekly newspaper. Before *that* she had made a small fortune as a fraudulent spiritualist and clairvoyant. Oh, and she was a vocal proponent of "free love," living at one point with her ex-husband, her husband, and her lover. No wonder her life was made into a Broadway musical. But even with a song in which Woodhull rhapsodizes about clergyman Henry Ward Beecher's physical endowment—yes, really—audiences were left unexcited. *Onward Victoria* ran for just one performance in 1980.

John Anderson (1922–2017) Before the third-party candidacies of Jill Stein and Ralph Nader, there was John Anderson, a liberal Republican congressman who ran as an Independent against Carter and Reagan in 1980. Anderson polled as high as 24 percent over the summer, but his final tally dwindled to 6.6 percent of the vote. I'll always have a soft spot for John Anderson. He lived right up the street from us in a split-level and early in the morning would hit tennis balls against the wall at Western Junior High. (In the Maryland suburbs outside DC that counts as a celebrity sighting.)

Alfred E. Smith (1873–1944) No, you're thinking of Alfred E. Neuman, the gap-toothed freckled face of *Mad* magazine (1952–2019). Al Smith was America's first Catholic major-party nominee, a four-term New York governor who lost to Herbert Hoover in 1928 in a landslide. Although Smith's religion and his opposition to Prohibition contributed to his loss, historians credit him for mobilizing urban wage-earners and Catholics as part of a new Democratic coalition that would launch FDR to power four years later. Perhaps most importantly, Smith, who lived his whole life in the New York City working-class neighborhood in which he was raised, gets name-checked by the slum dwellers in the musical *Annie*.

Alf Landon (1887–1987) No, you're thinking of the furry brown cat-eating extra-terrestrial sitcom star of the late 1980s with the rippled snout and razor-like wit. Wrong Alf, though the GOP might've been better off running an alien life-form for president in 1936. Alf Landon, the governor of Kansas and republican nominee, lost to FDR by the largest electoral margin in modern history. (He won only the eight electoral votes of Vermont and Maine.) Years later, George McGovern and Walter Mondale almost broke his record, but, thanks to the Twenty-Third Amendment, managed to eke out enough extra electoral votes from Washington, DC, to save them from this dubious honor. Landon also has the distinction of being the only major-party candidate to live past one hundred—meaning he was old enough, at his death, to have seen the debut season of *Alf*.

Gracie Allen (1895–1964)

Before there was Pat Paulsen, there was Gracie Allen, the radio star who performed as a ditzy innocent opposite her husband and straight man, George Burns. In 1940, as part of a publicity stunt for their show, Allen declared her candidacy as the nominee of the Surprise Party. The announcement went something like this:

GRACIE: "George, I'll let you in on a secret. I'm running for president."

GEORGE: "Gracie, how long has this been going on?"

GRACIE: "Well, 150 years. George Washington started it."

Henry Clay (1777–1852)

While too young to be a first-tier Founding Father, Henry Clay is most famous as a three-time Speaker of the House, an influential senator from Kentucky, and a five-time presidential candidate. Another distinction: he managed to lose as the nominee for three different parties: as a Democratic-Republican in 1824, a National Republican in 1832, and a Whig in 1840. As a young lawyer, Clay successfully defended Aaron Burr from charges of treason, when the latter was accused of planning to start his own country out west after killing Alexander Hamilton. (Sequel anyone?) One more distinction: widely regarded as one of the most influential politicians *not* to have served in the White House, Clay was the first person to lie in state in the US Capitol rotunda.

Margaret Chase Smith (1897–1995)

In 1964 Smith, a Republican and the first woman to be elected to both houses of Congress, became the first woman to have her name placed in nomination at a major-party convention. (Barry Goldwater ended up winning the party's nomination.) But she should be remembered for her "Declaration of Conscience," a speech she gave in 1950 as a freshman senator calling out her fellow Republican Joe McCarthy's politics of "hate and character assassination." Statesman and philanthropist Bernard Baruch said that if a man had given the same speech "he would be the next President."

Aaron Burr (1756–1836) Before gaining fame on Broadway as the man who shot his former law partner, Burr had an illustrious political career in the early years of the republic. The grandson of Puritan mega-preacher Jonathan Edwards, he served gallantly under Benedict Arnold in the Revolutionary War. (Burr and Arnold: both of them heroes before they were villains.) In 1800, as Thomas Jefferson's running mate, he ended up tying Jefferson for president. (Back then electors cast two votes without designating which was for prez and which was for veep. A constitutional oops that soon got fixed.) When they sorted it all out, Jefferson was president, and Burr was vice president. In 1804 came the fateful duel with Hamilton, the last time a sitting vice president shot another human being until 2006, when Dick Cheney shot fellow quail hunter Harry Whittington.

Dr. Spock (1903–1998) No, you're thinking of the child of a Vulcan named Sarek and a human named Amanda Grayson. Dr. Benjamin Spock was born to a wealthy Connecticut family, won a gold medal as part of the 1924 US Olympic men's crew team, and went on to become a best-selling author and pediatrician, dispensing the most influential advice on child-rearing since King Solomon. But although he taught millions of parents to be more kind and loving to their babies, he didn't persuade many people to vote for him in 1972 when he ran as the nominee of the People's Party. His platform advocated the legalization of abortion, homosexuality, and marijuana. Other controversial views included ending the Vietnam War and providing free health care for American citizens. Nineteen seventy-two was also the year of the first *Star Trek* convention.

Before Jackie

MOSES FLEETWOOD WALKER
{1857–1924}

Jackie Robinson is an American hero. When he broke Major League Baseball's color line in 1947, it changed professional sports and the nation forever. Every team in the major leagues, in fact, has retired Robinson's number, 42, including teams that didn't even exist in 1947. No one, not Babe Ruth or Willie Mays or Hank Aaron, has been so honored. But sports fans might be surprised to know that, technically speaking, Jackie Robinson wasn't the first black ballplayer in the major leagues.

That honor belongs to Moses Fleetwood ("Fleet") Walker. As you can read on a plaque outside Fifth Third Field in Toledo, Ohio, "In 1883, Walker joined the newly formed Toledo Blue Stockings and became the first African American Major League ballplayer when Toledo joined the Major League–sanctioned American Association the following year." Now this deserves a "Holy Toledo!"

The current minor league team in the city is the Toledo Mud Hens. (Fans of the TV show *M*A*S*H* may remember that Jamie Farr's Corporal

Klinger, a Toledo native, wore a Mud Hens jersey from time to time.) Rob Wiercinski, the communications guy for the Mud Hens, points out that "in order for a color barrier to be broken, one had to be set up in the first place." In other words, Walker wasn't only the first black big-league base-ball player—he was one of the men whose mere presence on the diamond provoked the backlash that would bar black players from baseball for decades to come.

Walker was born on October 7, 1857, in Ohio and played baseball at Oberlin College and at the University of Michigan. Before long he was playing for the Minor League Toledo Blue Stockings as the team's catcher, barehanded in those days. Soon after, in 1884, Toledo's team got promoted to the American Association. In the days before the modern National and American Leagues, the American Association was the big time. While there were other black players who joined team rosters, including Walker's own brother, Walker was the first. But there were no celebrations around this milestone. And just like Robinson would later on, Walker faced intense racial bigotry. There were even threats of lynching. Future Hall of Famer and Chicago player Cap Anson—a white man and one of the biggest stars of his era—unsuccessfully protested Walker's participation in the game.

Walker's time in the majors was short, less than a season. During this period, he batted .263 with only 152 at bats. He suffered from a few injuries and he was eventually dropped from the team. He scraped out a career for a few years in other leagues. While catching for Newark, New Jersey's, Little Giants, he was paired with an African American pitcher named George Washington Stovey. In 1887, they were set to play against Chicago . . . and Cap Anson. This time Anson flat-out refused to play if the black team members were put on the field. Newark gave in to Anson's demands. Soon after, baseball officials across the board decided not to sign any more black players. The color line had been drawn.

Post-baseball, Walker held a variety of jobs but eventually got in trouble with the law. After stabbing a man to death during a drunken racial altercation—he was being harassed by a white man—he was acquitted. He did end up in jail later on, for mail fraud. Not every pioneer is a saint, after all. At the same time, the injustices he'd experienced inspired him to get angry and political. He more or less gave up hope for a truly integrated society, and in 1908 wrote a short book, *Our Home Colony*, advocating black emigration to Africa. In it he claimed, "It is contrary to everything in the nature of man, and almost criminal to attempt to harmonize these two divergent peoples while living under the same government."

Late in life Walker had some success in business, but when he died in 1924 at the age of sixty-six, there was barely any public acknowledgment. Baseball was then run by a stern Kentucky-born judge named Kenesaw Landis, the game's first commissioner, who firmly rejected the idea of integration. In 1943, the great African American actor, singer, and civil rights activist Paul Robeson addressed the baseball owners at their winter meetings. But all of them, on orders from Landis, ignored his pleas, not even venturing a polite question or remark. It wasn't until after Landis's death the next year that Branch Rickey, general manager of the Brooklyn Dodgers, was able to sign Jackie Robinson. (You may remember that soon after that, Satchel Paige was signed to the Majors.)

Today more people are learning Walker's story. A new state law will honor Walker on his birthday every year. Toledo is doing its part to keep his name alive, too. Just across from the Mud Hens' ballpark is Fleetwood's Tap Room. It features forty-eight different beers on tap and displays a big picture of this forgotten forerunner. And at the ballpark you can now get a Moses Fleetwood Walker bobblehead—the true marker of stardom in today's sports world. The vendors place it for display right next to the Mud Hens' most famous fan, Jamie Farr.

For black ballplayers, Fleet Walker and Jackie Robinson are bookends to a sixty-three-year-long journey in the wilderness. Baseball researcher Larry Lester may have put it best when he wrote: "While Walker failed to lead his people to the Promised Land, Robinson delivered his people. Both men wrestled with Jim Crow. 'Fleet' bruised his knuckles and lost the early rounds. However, Jackie later bloodied his nose and won the fight."

A final thought: baseball isn't the only sport that has a lost history of African Americans. As mentioned, before color lines were broken, they had to be drawn, and they were usually drawn in response to the early participation of black athletes. The first Kentucky Derby was won by a black jockey, Oliver Lewis, in 1875—and he beat a field that contained twelve other African Americans. Black jockeys, in fact, won fifteen of the first twenty-eight Kentucky Derbies. Perhaps the most successful was Isaac Murphy, the son of a former slave, who won the race three times and was the first to win in consecutive years. Tennis legend Arthur Ashe once compared the dominance of early black jockeys to the modern-day dominance of black basketball players. But African American participation in horse racing dropped off sharply in 1904, mainly in response to the behavior of white jockeys, who often threatened black jockeys, boxed them in, or rode them into the rails. Owners and trainers, emboldened perhaps by the Supreme Court's 1896 *Plessy v. Ferguson* decision endorsing segregation, allowed this to happen, and black people disappeared from the sport for nearly a century. Not a single African American competed in the Kentucky Derby between 1921 and 2000, when Marlon St. Julien rode Curule to a seventh-place finish.

DEATH OF A DIAGNOSIS

HOMOSEXUALITY AS A MENTAL ILLNESS

{1952–1973}

Until 1973, homosexuality was considered a mental illness by the American Psychiatric Association. This diagnosis helped justify harsh antigay laws. (Homosexuality was illegal in forty-two states and the District of Columbia at the time.) The APA classification also gave medical authority to barbaric treatments—as late as the 1940s, some psychoanalysts had approved lobotomies to "cure" homosexuality.

But in December 1973, in a landmark decision, the APA's leadership reversed itself, voting to remove homosexuality from the *Diagnostic and Statistical Manual*, its catalog of mental illnesses. In 1974 the full membership ratified the decision.

This would have a major impact on the lives of gay people. But how would I know? I was only five years old at the time. The big news in the Rocca house that year was the arrival of the twenty-two-volume set of the *World Book Encyclopedia*.

Oh how I loved our 1974 *World Book Encyclopedia* set growing up. On so many afternoons, after coming home from elementary school, I'd lie on my stomach on the red carpet in the family room paging through the volumes. I would pore over the "Facts in Brief" for different countries—the capital city, the official language, the basic unit of money—and commit them to memory. And I loved how it captured the drama of the Cold War. The entry for "Germany" included a picture of West Berlin—a man in sunglasses lounging at a bustling outdoor café, surrounded by brightly colored shops . . . right next to a picture of East Berlin—a pile of rubble on a deserted street on an overcast day.

Never mind that I was reading this same set well into the 1980s. A few years ago, after my mother sold the house I grew up in, I laid claim to the full set. It lines the wall in my bedroom now. That's how close the 1974 *World Book* is to my heart.

No volume got pulled off the shelf more than the "H." Even today it opens to page 275, which begins with a short entry on **HOMONYM** and ends with a paragraph on the Syrian city of **HOMS**. But fascinated as I was with linguistics and Middle Eastern trading centers, my real interest was the entry in the middle of the page: *HOMOSEXUALITY*.

My God, I'm looking at it now and I remember that electric combination of curiosity, excitement, and most of all terror that shot through my body when I even saw the word.

As a child, I only dared to read this article when I knew I was home alone. I had a secret to keep. I must have read it over a hundred times, that's how hungry I was for information. If I was defective, I wanted to know if I could be fixed. The answers had to be in here somewhere. After all, this was the encyclopedia.

"Most homosexuals appear no different from other members of their own sex." Note to self: Be like those homosexuals.

"But some behave, dress, and talk like members of the opposite sex." Note to self: Don't be like *those* homosexuals.

"Sometimes two homosexuals establish a long-term relationship that is similar in some ways to marriage." Yeah, right.

"According to the most widely accepted theory, a child can learn to be attracted to either of the sexes . . ." Okay, I'm a quick learner. Tell me what to do.

"Some people may try to change their homosexual preference through psychiatric treatment. The younger the person—and the stronger his motive for changing his preference—the more likely he is to be able to change." I'm smart and I'm motivated. So this is on me. Once again, tell me what to do!

The short paragraph on the history of homosexuality included this tantalizing morsel: "Some ancient Greeks not only accepted homosexuality but considered it an ideal relationship. . . . Such men believed that only men could fulfill the role of true friend and lover." If I had a time machine, I knew where I was headed.

But the end of that paragraph brought the end of the reverie: "Still others have forbidden it, and some have punished it harshly."

I wanted the measly entry to go on longer but it never did. I think I thought that if I read the 1974 *World Book* entry enough times a new sentence would magically appear, offering what, I don't know. Reassurance?

That homosexuality was ever a psychiatric diagnosis may seem strange to people today. Trust me, I know a lot of crazy gay people, but they're not crazy because they're gay.

Homosexuality first became a subject of psychological study in the nineteenth century, just as modern psychology was coming into being. Doctors and researchers began to study and classify all varieties of human sexuality. Loads of fancy words entered the dictionary: *sadism, masochism, nymphomania, copromania, undinism, pagism, picacism, satyriasis* . . . Happy googling! Two of these novel classifications were *homosexuality* and *heterosexuality*, terms coined in 1868. Of course same-sex sexual activity is as old as life itself. (I am a complete sucker for any news item about gay animals. Gay penguin stories seriously make me squeal.) But the sexologists' view was new in that it saw homosexuality not in religious terms as a sinful behavior, or in legal terms as a criminal act, but as an inborn trait of the whole person. In other words, it wasn't just something you did. It was something you were.

Some sexologists, like the German physician Richard von Krafft-Ebing, viewed the condition as pathological—that is, as a mental illness. In his major work, *Psychopathia Sexualis* ("Mental Illness of Sex"), he compiled more than two hundred case studies of various sexual practices, including instances of shoe fetishism, whipping, the "violation of corpses," and along with them, homosexuality. For many, it was the first time they read about homosexuality. Bear in mind that Krafft-Ebing also thought that excessive masturbation could turn you into a murderer, so we should take his views with a grain of salt.

Then came Sigmund Freud. He viewed homosexuality much more compassionately. In 1935 he wrote to a mother seeking therapy for her gay son, assuring her that homosexuality was neither a "vice" nor a "degradation" nor an "illness." He noted that Plato, Michelangelo, and Leonardo da Vinci had been gay, and called the persecution of homosexuals "a great injustice." He wrote that he would not aim to change her son's orientation but rather would strive to "bring him harmony [and] peace of mind."

In the United States, however, later generations of psychiatrists departed from Freud, adopting the views of a Hungarian émigré named Sandor Rado. Rado viewed homosexuality as a mental illness produced by bad parenting. (Typically the "blame" was laid on an overbearing mother and a distant father.) Edmund Bergler, a leading psychoanalyst of the 1950s, wrote this about homosexuals:

> *I have no bias against homosexuals; for me they are sick people requiring medical help. . . . Still, though I have no bias, I would say: Homosexuals are essentially disagreeable people, regardless of their pleasant or unpleasant outward manner . . . [their] shell is a mixture of superciliousness, fake aggression, and whimpering.*

No bias there!

When, in 1952, the APA published the first *Diagnostic and Statistical Manual*, they classified homosexuality as a "sociopathic personality disturbance." To be sure, some researchers disagreed. Among these were psychologist Elizabeth Hooker and the Czech physician Kurt Freund, known to posterity as the inventor of a machine that measures male arousal called the penile plethysmograph. (If I weren't such a grown-up, I'd call it a "bonerometer.") But as long as the APA was committed to the belief that homosexuality was a mental illness, the chances of wide-scale acceptance and equality for gay people remained bleak. When lobotomies went out of fashion in the mid-1950s, in came *A Clockwork Orange*–style behavioral treatments, involving nausea-inducing drugs and electric shocks to the brain or the genitals. Forced institutionalization was common, and hysterectomies and castration were deemed legitimate medical "remedies."

The fight against the pathologizing of homosexuality was led by two activists, Barbara Gittings and Frank Kameny. Gittings, raised in a religious Catholic home, had found herself struggling to come to grips with her attraction to women while a student at Northwestern University in the late 1940s, eventually spending so much time researching homosexuality in the campus library that she neglected her classwork and failed out. A trip to San Francisco introduced her to a "homophile" organization called Daughters of Bilitis, the first lesbian civil rights group in America. She soon started a New York chapter, became editor of its journal, and began to organize public demonstrations for gay rights.

Kameny, meanwhile, had been born to a Jewish family in Queens, New York. He attended college at sixteen, served in the army during World War II, and earned a PhD in astronomy from Harvard. Soon after getting his doctorate, however, he was arrested in a police sting operation in a men's room in San Francisco. (Because California was the first state where gay bars were legal, local police departments frequently sought to entrap gay men there in the 1950s.) When the arrest came to light, Kameny was fired from the United States Army Map Service; President Eisenhower had barred gays from federal employment. Kameny's dismissal roused him to activism, and he founded a Washington, DC, chapter of a gay rights group called the Mattachine Society. (Gay rights organizations had such great names back then.) He fought against DC sodomy laws and became a leader in the 1960s gay liberation movement.

Kameny recognized that as long as doctors pathologized homosexuality, changing wider social attitudes would be difficult. When Gittings heard Kameny talk at a 1963 convention of gay rights groups, she was fired up by his rejection of the medical establishment and his insistence that he and other homosexuals were perfectly healthy. Appearing on David Susskind's popular talk show in 1971, Gittings challenged the host when he invoked "a great body of medical research" that regarded homosexuality as an illness. For her, the real sickness was not homosexuality but the hatred of it. As she said to Susskind: "Your attitudes toward us are the problem. There's nothing wrong with homosexuality. The only thing wrong with it is that you people are upset about it. Why are you upset?" As she put it, it was the supposed science that had to be questioned.

In 1970 gay and lesbian rights groups picketed the annual American Psychiatric Association conference in San Francisco. The next year, Gittings, Kameny, and other activists infiltrated the meetings themselves. During a public lecture, Kameny grabbed the microphone and declared: "Psychiatry is the enemy incarnate. Psychiatry has waged a relentless war of extermination against us. You may take this as a declaration of war against you." This bold call to arms prompted soul-searching among the psychiatrists, many of whom were startled to find themselves cast as oppressors of the people they thought they were helping.

Sympathetic elements within the APA helped Gittings and Kameny organize a panel, "Psychiatry: Friend or Foe to the Homosexual?," at the next year's meetings in Dallas. But Gittings and Kameny needed a psychiatrist on the panel to give them legitimacy. Gittings invited a gay, untenured Temple University psychiatry professor named John E. Fryer to attend. Fryer had been fired from the University of Pennsylvania a few years before after being outed by his own cousins. He was nervous about speaking: "I was not feeling very secure. . . . But I thought about it and realized it was something that had to be done. I had been thrown out of a residency because I was gay; I had lost a job because I was gay. That perspective needed to be heard from a gay psychiatrist." But coming out could mean the end of his career.

Fryer's solution? A disguise. "I told Barbara that I would participate on the panel but I could not do it as me," he later recalled. Fryer stood six foot four inches tall and weighed close to 300 pounds; he would not be easy to disguise. But his boyfriend at the time had been a drama major in college and helped him design an effective costume. Wearing a wig, a baggy tuxedo, and a stretched-out Richard

Nixon mask, and speaking through a voice modulator, Frye addressed a ballroom full of curious shrinks in Dallas.

Identified to the 1972 audience as "Dr. Anonymous," Fryer spoke about the closeted life he led as a member of the "Gay PA"—that group of gay APA members who knew of each other's existence. He told the audience that he was forced to keep his two lives separate, and compared his situation to that of a black man passing as white, having to live in constant fear of being exposed. And he stressed that it was perfectly possible to be both "healthy and homosexual." In a moving conclusion, Fryer acknowledged that coming out was a big risk for one's career and livelihood. But hiding one's identity, he said, meant "an even bigger risk," the risk of "not accepting fully our own humanity." He pressed his fellow psychiatrists to help others become more open-minded: "We must use our skills and wisdom to help them—and us—grow to be comfortable with that little piece of humanity called homosexuality."

Fryer's talk—and the entire panel—made an impact. The APA did what any self-respecting professional organization would do: it formed a committee to investigate the question. That committee found no scientific evidence to support the continued inclusion of homosexuality in the *DSM*, and the next year the APA Board voted to remove the diagnosis, urging that "homosexuals be given all protections now guaranteed other citizens." Kameny cheekily called it the day "we were cured en masse." The "Gay PA" eventually became an official subgroup of the APA, and today the Association of Gay and Lesbian Psychiatrists (AGLP) is, by its own account, the oldest professional LGBTQ organization in America.

Still, the change was not complete. Homosexuality was removed from the *DSM* but a new diagnosis, "sexual orientation disturbance," replaced it, said to afflict people "in conflict with" their sexual orientation. Not until 1987 did homosexuality completely disappear from the *DSM*. The World Health Organization did not remove homosexuality from its International Classification of Diseases until 1992. Today the horrifying malpractice known as "conversion therapy," though discredited in the mental health professions, remains legal in thirty-four states.

Diagnoses are meant to help identify what ails people, and to help make these people better. But in the case of homosexuality, a diagnosis did the opposite. It gave credence to deep-seated prejudices. It made an untold number of gay people believe they were defective. And who knows how many gay people who had real problems *didn't* seek psychiatric counseling because they viewed psychiatry as the enemy?

Barbara Gittings, Frank Kameny, and John Fryer had the self-knowledge and the courage to challenge accepted wisdom, to stand up to the experts. They were willing to tell the leading body of psychiatrists in America that when it came to gay people . . . it was wrong on psychiatry. They were right.

That article on **Homosexuality** in the 1974 *World Book* was written by a man named Carlfred Broderick. At the time I thought the name might be made up. (Who would dare attach a name to the topic?) It turns out Broderick was a University of Southern California sociology professor and marriage counselor (and a Mormon bishop) who made six appearances on *The Tonight Show* with Johnny Carson in the mid-1970s. Since then I've watched all those appearances. He's a tall rangy guy—looks a little like Ray Bolger—and he's funny, not a prude or scold, at ease talking about infidelity and "sexual problems." He even makes a crack about being known as a "licensed" sexologist. I'm not sure why but when I was watching those appearances on my laptop in 2019 I was really hoping he'd mention homosexuality, even just hint at it. But he doesn't. I guess it really was unspeakable back then, even on a late-night show.

Looking back, I feel lucky to have been born when I was. A friend of mine who's twenty years older than I am used to go to his high school library to sneak looks at Krafft-Ebing's book. That was his only resource. The word *aberrant*, which he learned from the book and which was used to describe homosexuals, has stayed with him. Gay people of my and future generations owe a lot to the activism of Barbara Gittings (1932–2007), Franklin Kameny (1925–2011), and John Fryer (1937–2003).

Wandering Womb / The Vapours

For centuries women who exhibited symptoms ranging from insomnia to indigestion to a strong interest in sex were given the vague diagnosis of "hysteria." The ancient Greeks called it "wandering womb," in the wacky-even-for-three-thousand-years-ago belief that the uterus could meander around inside a woman's body, wreaking havoc. Prescribed treatments included frequent intercourse and aromatherapy. By the eighteenth century the name was "the Vapours," referring to gases thought to emanate from the womb. In the late nineteenth century, some doctors decided it could be relieved by a "uterine massage" that would induce a tension-relieving "paroxysm." "Some doctors" were of course all male. Women were systematically excluded from medical schools until the 1970s . . . which probably explains why it took until 1980 for the diagnosis of hysteria to be removed from the *Diagnostic and Statistical Manual of Mental Disorders*.

Consumption, Ague, The Grippe

Chances are you know these terms from some old novel in which a character melodramatically suffers for days on the brink of death. These illnesses haven't disappeared—they've just changed names, the way Byzantium became Constantinople and then Istanbul. Simply another name for tuberculosis, consumption was conspicuous with nineteenth-century-opera heroines. While it's not easy to catch, it *is* contagious and the principal reason I won't eat from a buffet without a sneeze guard, although I do think I'd make a decent Mimi in *La Bohème*. Ague, meanwhile, was malaria, although it also described other conditions that brought on fevers and chills. And the grippe? That's now what we call the flu. (You may remember *Guys and Dolls*'s Adelaide lamenting "la grippe, la postnasal drip. . . .") If you're a fan of these old-fashioned terms, there's also dropsy (edema), lockjaw (tetanus), and St. Vitus's dance (chorea).

You thought two left
feet was tough.

Left-Handedness The 10 percent of human beings who are left-handed have long been considered unlucky, deceptive, or even evil in cultures the world over. During the Spanish Inquisition the Catholic Church condemned those who used their left hand. Zulu tribesmen of the 1800s placed the left hands of children into holes filled with boiling water to discourage their use. The nineteenth-century criminologist and white supremacist Cesare Lombroso lent dangerous authority to the long-standing social stigma, claiming a scientific connection between left-handedness, moral degeneracy, and the "savage races." No wonder schoolteachers continued discouraging it in students, often through physical abuse. J. W. Conway's 1935 *On Curing the Disability and Disease of Left-Handedness* argued that being a lefty was a handicap in a world that was industrializing and standardizing. Handicap? Turns out being a southpaw is a fast lane to the West Wing. Seven of our last fifteen presidents—that's a whopping 47 percent—have been left-handed. I'm not sure what that means but I'm sure a CNN panel will eventually sort it out.

Red Hair Judas was a ginger. At least that's the way the apostle who betrayed Jesus was portrayed in medieval Christian art. That may have simply been a way for artists to distinguish the bad guy, but it only helped justify the persecution of redheads for centuries. In 1928, the English scholar and believer in the occult, Montague Summers, wrote that "Those whose hair is red . . . are unmistakably vampires." Irish writers including Jonathan Swift and James Joyce made jokes about the reputed sexual appetites of redheaded women, while Cesare Lombroso, the same genius who thought left-handedness was a sign of degeneracy, associated red hair with criminality. All of this, of course, is insane. I will concede that I've always been a little freaked out by Raggedy Ann's and Andy's hair. Not because it's red, but because it's *yarn*.

Drapetomania If you ever need proof that medical diagnoses reflect cultural beliefs and biases, just consider the condition once called drapetomania. Writing in 1851, the Louisiana physician Samuel Cartwright used this term to describe a mysterious disease that caused African American slaves to run away from their owners. Cartwright said that drapetomania (from the Greek *drapetes*, meaning a runaway slave) was "a disease of the mind," but it was also one that was "curable." The condition, he asserted, was caused by indulgent slave owners who treated slaves too gently. (Yes, that was actually a diagnosis.)

REPUTATION ASSASSINATION: A STORY OF THREE KILLINGS

GIACOMO MEYERBEER
{1791–1864}

ARNOLD BENNETT
{1867–1931}

AND

DISCO
{1970–1979}

#CancelFredRogers #CancelYoYoMa #CancelJanePowell

Remember when it was only things that got canceled? When school was canceled you were happy. When your favorite sitcom was canceled you were sad. Then, once Twitter began, *people* started getting canceled. But unless you're General Pinochet in 1980s Chile, you don't have the power to disappear anybody. And so your #CancelBobVila campaign is likely to backfire.

But while more and more of today's #Cancel campaigns are #Fails (#CancelCicelyTyson?), history shows us some hit jobs can stick. Herewith three Reputation Assassinations.

(By the way, all those hashtagged cancel examples above are made up—at least they were when this book went to press. I expect all those people will be canceled by the time we go to paperback.)

Giacomo Meyerbeer (1791–1864)

Who do you think was the most successful opera composer of the nineteenth century? Are you thinking Puccini, whose *La Bohème* remains a staple of opera houses to this day? Or maybe Rossini, whose *Barber of Seville* inspired Bugs Bunny's *Rabbit of Seville*, which was a staple of my childhood? Or perhaps you're an aficionado of Doritos and chose Verdi, whose music has been featured in *two* of the snack food's Super Bowl ads. If so, I'm afraid you're mistaken. The answer, which you should have guessed from the title of this essay, is Giacomo Meyerbeer.

Now, unless you're a serious opera person—and owning an old CD of the Three Tenors doesn't qualify—you probably are thinking that Meyerbeer sounds like a craft brew, one with a strong hoppy taste and distinctive citric notes. But Meyerbeer was a towering figure in his day, admired by fellow composers, adored by the public. In the words of music critic Zachary Woolfe, he "was a uniquely powerful hitmaker, as well as an innovator who brought opera to new levels of orchestral color, dramatic scale, choral mass, historical richness and theatrical dazzle." In fact, he ruled the world of European opera until he fell victim to . . . Reputation Assassination.

Jacob Beer was born in 1791 to a well-off assimilated Prussian-Jewish family in Berlin. He added "Meyer" to his last name to honor his beloved maternal grandfather, and changed "Jacob" to "Giacomo" as a young man when he lived in Italy. As a child, Jacob was recognized for his virtuosity at the piano. He studied with the best teachers available, including Antonio Salieri. (Quick digression: If you're picturing actor F. Murray Abraham, that's because he played Salieri in the movie *Amadeus* and was depicted as Mozart's jealous rival. Ironically, Salieri is only *remembered* today because of *Amadeus*—and the most likely false rumor that he poisoned Mozart. That makes him a *beneficiary* of Reputation Assassination. But back to Meyerbeer . . .) Although young Jacob was fast developing a reputation as one of the leading pianists in Europe, he opted instead to pursue a career as a composer, and left for Italy to study opera.

Meyerbeer's breakout hit didn't come until many years later, in 1831. That year saw the production of *Robert le Diable* ("Robert the Devil"), an opera based on the medieval legend of Robert, Duke of Normandy, who happened to be the spawn of Satan. This would have been a great elevator pitch, if only elevators had been invented. The success of the opera, however, stemmed less from the story line than from Meyerbeer's decision to create one of the first "grand operas"—spectacles featuring over-the-top scenery, large casts of characters, big orchestras and choruses, and sweeping five-act plots. Of course, the melodrama of a nobleman fighting off the maleficent influence of his father, the Prince of Darkness, didn't hurt, and the third-act erotic ballet of ghostly nuns added a little spice. Need I tell you—*Robert le Diable*, produced for the Paris Opera, did monster box office.

This megahit put Meyerbeer in the enviable position of retaining total command of his career. Meyerbeer was already wealthy, thanks to his father's financial success. He had the freedom to take the time he needed to complete his ambitious works, and the leverage to bargain when it came to matters of production; he refused, for example, to let a director cast his own mistress as the lead in his opera *La Prophète*. Meyerbeer followed the success of *Robert le Diable* with another grand opera, *Les Huguenots*. It told the story of the notorious St. Bartholomew's Day massacre of 1572, in which the assassinations of prominent French Protestant families spilled over into Catholic mob violence that killed thousands. *Les Huguenots* ran in Paris for over 1,000 performances. From then on, everything Meyerbeer touched turned to gold. And his success allowed him, like a nineteenth-century George Lucas or James Cameron, to advance the technology of opera production, as he pushed for innovations in lighting, scenery, and other aspects of staging to enhance the impact of his work. *La Prophète* used an electric spotlight to create the effect of sunrise. *L'Africaine* used the first-ever fully revolving set. By the 1840s, Meyerbeer stood at the pinnacle of the opera world.

Not for long. Meyerbeer's reversal in fortune began in 1850 with an anonymously published essay called "Jewishness in Music." The author, who revealed himself only after Meyerbeer's death, was the composer Richard Wagner. Now, while Meyerbeer may be new to you, I'm guessing you may have heard about Wagner. Even if you think the Ring Cycle is a setting on your washing machine—I know, I know, that's an old joke—you're probably familiar with Wagner's "Ride of the Valkyries." You may have heard Elmer Fudd's rendition ("Kill the Wabbit . . . Kill the Wabbit . . .") in the Warner Bros. cartoon classic *What's Opera, Doc?* Or in that scene from *Apocalypse Now* where Robert Duvall blasts it from his helicopter as he bombs the Vietnamese.

"Jewishness in Music" is anti-Semitism masquerading as music criticism, and while it doesn't actually name Meyerbeer, the target is clear. (Wagner did name Meyerbeer when he republished the essay in 1869.) The essay begins by assuming that all people experience a basic "involuntary repellence" from "the nature and personality of the Jews." It then criticizes the Jewish way of speaking as "quite out-landish and unpleasant," calling it "a creaking, squeaking, buzzing snuffle." Because Jews are foreigners, says Wagner, they will never master European speech. And since music is a kind of heightened speech, passionate music will always be beyond their reach. Finally, since Jews only enter society by buying their way in, they have no "connection with the natural soil" or "the genuine spirit of the Folk." They can only imitate great music, "just as parrots reel off human words and phrases, but also with just as little real feeling and expression as these foolish birds."

There had been anti-Semitic digs in the past about Meyerbeer's religion, but the odd thing about this attack is that Wagner had been an admirer and something of a friend. Meyerbeer had even been personally generous to Wagner, helping him financially and working to bring about premieres of Wagner's operas *Rienzi* and *The Flying Dutchman.*

So why did Wagner turn on Meyerbeer so viciously? The most charitable ex-planation is that Wagner, whose own early work was influenced by Meyerbeer, was moving in a new, very different artistic direction with his operas *Tannhäuser* and *Lohengrin* and had simply lost respect for Meyerbeer's work. Another theory is that Wagner was resentful that Meyerbeer had refused to give him a loan. At the time he wrote the essay, Wagner was financially strapped and living in exile in Switzerland as a result of his participation in a political uprising. The simplest reason, however, might be that the down-on-his-luck Wagner was envious of Meyerbeer's success and stoking deeply rooted anti-Semitic beliefs was a powerful way to tear him down.

Whatever motive lay behind the essay, after it was published, Wagner's reputation began to rise, and Meyerbeer's to fall. It wasn't instantaneous, and Meyerbeer's work was performed for decades after his death in 1869, but it was steady. Wagner's friends and followers kept up the attacks. After Wagner's own death in 1883, the campaign was carried on by, among others, George Bernard Shaw (who was a pretty outspoken anti-Semite himself). The final straw came when the Nazis took power in Germany in 1933 and banned Meyerbeer's music. Yet it wasn't only in Germany that opera companies stopped performing his works. As the *Washington Post*'s Philip Kennicott points out, through the 1920s, New York's Metropolitan Opera staged twenty-nine performances of Meyerbeer's *L'Africaine*, but since 1934 has never done so again. It hasn't put on *Les Huguenots* since 1915. And while supporters occasionally mount a new production or predict a revival, Meyerbeer's work remains largely forgotten.

"We are speaking of a monumental fall," writes critic Ethan Mordden, "as if Puccini, today, suddenly lost his popularity and, ten years from now, had vanished from sight except for sporadic, generally unsuccessful revivals of *La Bohème* and *Tosca*."

Now, I'd be remiss if I didn't point out that there's another big reason why modern audiences don't know Meyerbeer: His music frankly hasn't aged well. My friend Erick Neher, culture editor at the *Hudson Review*, is my go-to person on all things operatic. Here's his take:

"There's definitely a reason, in this day and age of constant excavation—with composer after composer having their works re-enter the repertory after long absences and scholars constantly unearthing neglected works, *especially* works that were victim to political/social/racial discrimination—that Meyerbeer just can't seem to become hip again. And I really think that it's because when musicians and audiences actually spend time with his music, they're usually disappointed. It's just not that interesting."

In fact it kind of sucks. Believe me, I wanted to love it.

Composer Felix Mendelssohn could well have spoken for the other leading composers of the day when he said of Meyerbeer's work: "Something for everybody, but there's no heart in it." When theater critics have called Andrew Lloyd Webber the "Meyerbeer of his day," it hasn't been meant as a compliment. (Maybe not so coincidentally *Phantom of the Opera*, Andrew Lloyd Webber's biggest hit, pokes fun at the kind of grand opera Meyerbeer revolutionized. *Robert le Diable* is even mentioned in one scene. That may be a case of Webber trying to own the joke.)

But none of that mitigates the treachery of the attacks on him from peers who had indeed spent years watching and listening and learning from him. "No one, not even Wagner, failed to profit from Meyerbeer," writes Mordden. "They looted him for decades. By 1900, what had been good in Meyerbeer was better in everyone else. . . . Moreover these later operas were easier to stage and sing. So Meyerbeer faded away."

Yes, there's a perverse irony in all this: Wagner, the assassin, owes an artistic debt to Meyerbeer, his victim. Wagner aimed in his opera to produce a "total artwork." His opera tried to integrate all performance elements—not only the orchestra, voice, and story, but also dance, production, even special effects. Where did Wagner get this idea? Probably from Meyerbeer's "grand opera," the large-scale spectacles with their choral music, their bold emotional range, and their incorporation of elements from popular theater and song. And Wagner's signature innovation of the leitmotif—a short phrase of music associated with a particular character; think of that little riff that plays every time Darth Vader walks on-screen—can also be found in Meyerbeer, who used recurring bits of melody, harmony, and rhythm to establish thematic patterns.

After World War II, Wagner himself took some lumps; it was hard for people to excuse his anti-Semitism when Hitler had considered him a favorite composer. But his legacy remains in a way that Meyerbeer's doesn't. Yet today, Wagner's work, with its celebration of Teutonic myth and ethnic identity, seems—even for some admirers—to possess uncomfortable reactionary, nationalistic themes. Meanwhile, Meyerbeer, the cosmopolitan figure who integrated German, Italian, and French elements, wrote his most successful work, *Les Huguenots*, as a kind of warning. The story of a massacre rooted in religious prejudice, the grand opera spoke powerfully to audiences across Europe about the perils of tribal hatreds.

Arnold Bennett (1867–1931)

Since you're holding this book, or e-reader, or phone, or hologram, in your hands, I'm going to assume that you are something of a reader. You probably know some of the famous writers of the early twentieth century: Virginia Woolf, James Joyce, D. H. Lawrence . . . But what about Arnold Bennett? No, not Benedict

Arnold . . . Arnold Bennett. At one time Bennett was a bigger deal than any of those others I just mentioned. He may not have dominated British literature in quite the way Meyerbeer dominated European opera, but he was, technically speaking, a serious A-lister. He was also, like Meyerbeer, a victim of Reputation Assassination. In Bennett's case, the murder weapon was a lecture delivered to a group of female college students, and the assassin was a woman now almost universally regarded as one of the twentieth century's greatest writers, Virginia Woolf.

Enoch Arnold Bennett was born in 1867 in Staffordshire, England, the son of a solicitor. (That's the kind of English lawyer who doesn't get to wear a wig in court. A barrister is the one with the wig.) As a young man, Bennett worked as a clerk for his wigless father, but his father paid him so little that at age twenty-one he left Staffordshire once and for all and moved to London, where he clerked for a more generous but equally wigless solicitor. Then, after winning a contest in a popular literary magazine, Bennett ditched the clerk's life entirely and struck out on his own as a writer, working as an editor, reviewer, self-help author, and novelist. In 1902 he cemented his reputation by publishing *Anna of the Five Towns*, the first of many popular and acclaimed works of fiction that focused on life in provincial Staffordshire, where he grew up.

Over the next twenty years or so, Bennett returned again and again in his writing to this region, known back then as "the Potteries" because it produced . . . well, you guessed it. He churned out novels at the steady rate of about one a year, along with book reviews, popular journalism, and even eight plays that were produced for the London stage. In fact, Bennett wrote so much and so steadily that, years after his death, when his biography was published, it turned out to be a very boring book. Most of his life had been spent sitting at a desk, pen in hand.

At any rate, by 1919 Bennett was, according to the scholar Samuel Hynes, "probably the best-known English novelist of the time. His name on a poster sold newspapers, and strangers recognized him on the street." He had risen from his middle-class roots to great wealth and literary celebrity. He was now known, as

Hynes says, for selling piles and piles of books, and he "kept a yacht and a mistress on the proceeds." Bennett's public stature grew so great that when he was lying on his deathbed with typhoid at his London flat in 1931, the city covered the streets in straw to muffle the noise of traffic and afford the great man some peace and quiet in his final hours.

Because of his popularity, however, Bennett became a big fat target for the younger generation of writers who were looking to take down their elders. The American poet Ezra Pound, who had moved to London in 1908, wrote a poem in which he mocked Bennett as "Mr. Nixon," a hack writer who, in "the cream gilded cabin of his steam yacht," offers advice on how to butter up reviewers. Pound's friend, the writer and painter Wyndham Lewis, later blamed Bennett for being a yes-man for publishers, ushering in "the era of puff and blurb in place of criticism." But the most famous and the most lethal attack came from Woolf.

The Bennett-Woolf brouhaha (or should I say imbroglio?) was a battle of sexes as well as a war of generations. It seems to have begun in 1919 when Woolf published an unsigned essay called "Modern Novels" in the *Times Literary Supplement*. In the essay, Woolf complains about three of the most successful writers in England—H. G. Wells, John Galsworthy, and Bennett. Her gripe: these older male novelists are "materialists." They do a great job describing the physical world, she says, but they forget the spiritual world. Their books are well made but ultimately soulless. All of Bennett's "enormous labor" of painstakingly re-creating the world of the Staffordshire Potteries leaves the reader asking, "What is the point of it all?"

Given how literary circles worked in London, Bennett probably saw the front-page essay, and probably also figured out who had written it. But it wasn't until 1923—four years later—that he got revenge, with an essay called "Is the Novel Decaying?" Bennett started off praising Woolf. He said that her latest novel, *Jacob's Room*, her most experimental work to date, was extremely clever. The problem, however, was that it was so obsessed with being clever that it didn't bother to create convincing characters that the reader could believe in. Woolf, he said, was all bark and no bite.

That threw down the gauntlet. Woolf responded with another attack, called "Mr. Bennett and Mrs. Brown," which she delivered as a lecture at Girton College, Cambridge University's all-female college, in 1924. She later published it as an essay in her friend T. S. Eliot's magazine, *The Criterion*, and it's now a staple of college English anthologies. In the most famous line from the essay, Woolf wrote that "in or about December, 1910, human character changed." Whole dissertations have been written about that sentence.

Woolf saw all around her a rapidly changing world—in art, in literature, in women's roles in society, in marriages, in sexuality, in the way people dressed, in the way people talked, in world politics, in everything. Human nature itself was coming to be seen as something more complicated, mysterious, and elusive than it had been in the past. So what might look to Bennett to be a solid, well-drawn character was to Woolf just "a sack stuffed with straw, a dummy." The writers of the past—like Bennett—relied comfortably on old familiar conventions and tools to create these characters, but for the writers of the future, Woolf says, "those conventions are ruin, those tools are death." Writers like Woolf—the ones we now call modernists—don't just describe the external appearances and behavior of characters, but turn their attention inward, to the mind, even the soul. Just as Impressionist painters like Claude Monet tried to catch the changing light of a sunset on haystacks, Woolf and the modernist writers tried to catch the ever-changing thoughts, feelings, and impressions that rush through the human mind on an ordinary day—what was called stream of consciousness.

Woolf tells a little story about an old woman on a train, whom she names Mrs. Brown. She says that the Mr. Bennetts of the world don't know what to make of Mrs. Brown. In fact, these self-important men are not really interested in her character at all. They're so focused on the outside world that they don't pause to imagine what her experience might be. Bennett's books, she says, might make readers want to "join a society" or "write a cheque" for a good cause, but they don't make anyone want to go back and read the book again, to understand the mystery of a character like Mrs. Brown.

Bennett, the heavyweight, had so far taken Woolf's punches pretty well. He was by all accounts a relatively affable man, perhaps a bit shy, and suffered from a stammer. But after this attack from Woolf, it was no more Mr. Nice Guy for Mr. Bennett. In the last years of his life, he gave Woolf's novels an unbroken string of bad reviews. Describing her experimental stream-of-consciousness method, he said things like, "I regard her alleged form as the absence of form, and her psychology as an uncoordinated mass of interesting details, none of which is truly original." Ouch. They met occasionally at literary events and dinner parties, but seem mostly to have deliberately avoided each other.

Every five or ten years, some critic or book reviewer or blogger will write something—usually in a kind of highbrow English outlet like the *TLS*—about how Bennett got a raw deal. Sometimes they accuse Woolf of snobbery toward the middle-class Bennett. But really, that's just kind of a reverse snobbery. You know, "Look how cool I am. I like the uncool Arnold Bennett instead of the great Virginia Woolf." The truth is that Woolf won the dustup because, even if human character didn't change around 1910, tastes in literature did. For the rest of the century, serious "literary" writers were much more likely to follow the path of Woolf and her fellow modernists exploring the obscure corners of human nature than that of the ponderous Arnold Bennett, with his reliable but predictable plots and characters. There's a parallel here to the shift that took place in opera: the psychological depth of Wagner's operas prevailed over the focus on external spectacle in Meyerbeer's work.

People can argue in the pages of the *TLS* about whether they prefer Bennett's old-fashioned realism or Woolf's experimental stream of consciousness, but today they both take a back seat to the greatest English novelist of them all . . . J. K. Rowling.

Disco (1970–1979)

The final victim of Reputation Assassination wasn't a writer, or composer, or even a person. It was a whole culture. Disco, born out of the New York underground club scene in the early seventies, went from the margins to the mainstream in 1977 with the release of the movie *Saturday Night Fever*. The movie's soundtrack, featuring the Bee Gees, became the best-selling of all time up to that point. But the dominance of disco was short-lived. By the 1980s it was as much of a historical artifact as the lava lamp and the waterbed. So what happened?

The usual culprit here is "Disco Demolition Night," the July 12, 1979, culmination of the "Disco Sucks" campaign orchestrated by Chicago radio shock jock Steve Dahl. The underperforming Chicago White Sox baseball team had hired Dahl for a promotion between games of a doubleheader. Dahl invited fans of rock—and haters of disco—to bring disco records to destroy between the games. About 20,000 attendees were expected, but more than 50,000 ended up packing Comiskey Park to chant "Disco Sucks" and blow up a crate stuffed with vinyl in the outfield. But then the promotion turned into a riot, as about 7,000 attendees rushed the field, leading to the forfeiture of the evening's second scheduled game. Nile Rodgers, of the great disco band Chic, later said, "It felt to us like Nazi book-burning. This is America, the home of jazz and rock, and people were now afraid even to say the word 'disco.'" Record companies began relabeling disco recordings "dance music" and the genre, already past its peak, went into rapid retreat.

Even at the time, some critics viewed what had happened that night as a white, male, conservative backlash against a music that drew its creative energy and its initial popularity from black, gay, and Latino subcultures. Steve Dahl has defended what happened as a more innocent rebellion of mostly blue-collar midwestern kids who loved their rock and roll and had no use for the poseurs and phoneys they associated with disco. "They had their t-shirts and their ripped jeans, their long hair and their long neck beers," he later wrote about the crowd turned mob. "Their music heroes played rough and loud."

Whatever their motives—the effects of copious amounts of Schlitz and weed can't be discounted—it was a remarkable expression of anger and a sign of just how far disco had come in less than a decade.

According to Stanford professor Richard Powers, "Disco was born on Valentine's Day 1970, when David Mancuso opened The Loft in New York City," a "club" that was actually his own apartment on the corner of Broadway and Bleecker. Mancuso was a sometime acolyte of sixties psychedelic drug guru Timothy Leary, and titled his Valentine's Day party "Love Saves the Day." (You figure out the acronym.) Mancuso was soon hosting regular private underground parties that he would DJ himself, and a gay underground club scene sprang up. Other DJs, black and white, gay and straight, including Larry Levan, Nicky Siano, and Frankie Knuckles, presided over parties at places like Paradise Garage and the Gallery. (No, I wasn't invited.) This was the hothouse that nurtured the early growth of disco.

The music itself drew on various influences—soul, funk, gospel, R&B, even going all the way back to doo-wop. Probably the most important direct precursor, however, was the so-called Sound of Philadelphia, developed by songwriter-producers Kenny Gamble and Leon Huff, whose Philadelphia International Records came to supplant Motown Records as the dominant label for black popular music in the early seventies. There's a good case to be made for the O'Jays' 1972 "Love Train" as the first disco hit (a year before the Hues Corporation put out "Rock the Boat"). The fundamentals of the disco sound were a fast tempo of around 120 beats per minute and a rhythm called "four on the floor"—a bass drum hit on every beat with offbeat hi-hat openings. Add a driving, syncopated bassline, a horn section, and, eventually, lush orchestral strings, and you've got disco. The gender-bending use of the male falsetto (a trademark of the Bee Gees) became a distinctive feature, too, as did the release of extended 12-inch EPs, designed for uninterrupted dancing, not the three-and-a-half-minute rock single meant for radio play. Finally, thanks to Donna Summer's collaboration with the Italian producer Giorgio Moroder, came a full-on embrace of electronic instruments. Listen to "I Feel Love" from 1977 and you get the idea.

So the club scene was originally gay, and the music was originally black. The dancing, meanwhile, was in many ways originally Latino. Sometime in the 1950s or early '60s, American kids dancing to rock and R&B stopped holding each other as ballroom dancers had, breaking out to find their own individual space on the floor. But New York City's Puerto Rican and Cuban communities had never abandoned the tradition of dancing in pairs. This kind of dancing resumed in the disco era and became as much a part of disco's appeal as the music itself. (There were mini-fads like the bus stop, that line dance at wedding receptions that you've mistakenly called the hustle all these years. The actual hustle, which I had to learn for a *CBS Sunday Morning* piece, is a couples dance and it's not easy.)

Through the midseventies, disco produced lots of chart-busting hits (yes, I just wrote chart-busting): Thelma Houston's "Don't Leave Me This Way," Gloria Gaynor's "I Will Survive," Chic's "Le Freak" and "Good Times." And then came *Saturday Night Fever*, starring John Travolta of the sitcom *Welcome Back, Kotter* as a working-class kid from Brooklyn who escapes his drab life by donning a white polyester three-piece suit and transforming into a superhero of the dance floor. The script was based on a 1976 profile by British journalist Nik Cohn in *New York* magazine called "The Tribal Rites of the New Saturday Night" that, incidentally, turned out to be made up, with the main character, Vincent, modeled not on any real resident of Bay Ridge, but on a British guy Cohn had known in London a decade earlier. Yet John Travolta's performance coupled with the music by the Bee Gees—then a moderately successful Australian band brought on board by the producer Robert Stigwood—created a phenomenon. In early 1978 the movie's soundtrack knocked Fleetwood Mac's *Rumours* out of the number one spot on the *Billboard* chart, and reigned atop the charts for six months. Today it ranks as the second-best-selling soundtrack of all time (*The Bodyguard* with Whitney Houston now holds the top spot) and it remains the only disco recording to win a Grammy for Album of the Year.

But the impact of disco can't be measured in just record sales. In the wake of

Saturday Night Fever, the number of discotheques around the United States "exploded," writes Richard Powers, "from 1,500 to 45,000." Purists may ridicule the ordinary people who took up disco music, dancing, and fashion as latecomers, but for all kinds of Americans, disco provided not only a feeling of excitement but one of sophistication. They didn't need to be in New York's Studio 54—where Bianca Jagger famously celebrated her thirtieth birthday by riding in on a white horse—to participate. Disco allowed them to dress up, to perform, to lose themselves on the dance floor. That disco might be gay-adjacent only made it more exciting—even dangerous!—to some.

But almost immediately the success of disco brought imitation and exploitation. It was probably to be expected that rock stars like Rod Stewart and the Stones would produce their disco hits, but when KISS and Frankie Valli jumped on the bandwagon, it was a sure sign that the apocalypse was nigh. With the Village People's "Y.M.C.A." and Rick Dees's "Disco Duck," the genre had unquestionably entered the terrain of the novelty song. (Steve Dahl, the orchestrator of Disco Demolition Night, had a hit with "Do Ya Think I'm Disco?," a parody of Rod Stewart's "Da Ya Think I'm Sexy?," which itself sounds like a parody.) For kids, there was now "Sesame Street Fever," featuring a handsome Grover in a dazzling white suit, standing boldly in Travolta's iconic pose beneath a glittering mirror ball. ("Larry Levan's 12-inch disco mix of 'C Is for Cookie' by Cookie Monster . . . is a bona fide work of genius," claims British journalist Adam Mattera.)

Artistically, disco hit rock bottom with *The Ethel Merman Disco Album*, featuring the First Lady of Broadway, at age seventy-one, performing discofied versions of standards by Irving Berlin, George Gershwin, and Cole Porter. Merman herself hated disco, but wanting to stay relevant, laid down her renditions of "Everything's Coming Up Roses" and "Alexander's Ragtime Band" with synthetic drums added later. Promoting the album on *The Tonight Show with Johnny Carson*, she brought promotional tees emblazoned across the front with "ETHEL BOOGIES." (Booked that night alongside Angie Dickinson and Dr. Henry Heimlich, she also demonstrated that she still knew shorthand from her secretarial days. Good God, I love watching old episodes of Carson.) *The Ethel Merman Disco Album* was a flop and it deserved to be. Its only value now is as camp. (Vinyl originals sell for up to fifty dollars.)

In the end, pinning the blame for the assassination of disco's reputation isn't so simple. DJs will tell you that disco didn't die at all; it just went back underground, where it came from. The spirit of disco informed house music and EDM (that's electronic dance music, for those who don't want to google it) and even hip-hop. You can hear it in popular funk and pop from Prince to Bruno Mars. And the original disco hits have proved indestructible: "Y.M.C.A." has become about as mom-and-apple-pie as you can get, performed regularly by preschoolers and the grounds crew at Yankee Stadium. When I'm pushing my cart through Bed Bath & Beyond and "We Are Family" comes on, I feel at one with all my fellow shoppers.

Still, the *era* of disco assuredly belongs to the past. Maybe disco was equally a victim of an angry backlash *and* of its own success. So while shock jock Steve Dahl might indeed have been disco's assassin, it's about time we admit that Ethel Merman was the second gunman.

In each of these Reputation Assassinations, the takedown was brutal. The anti-Semitism surrounding the attack on Giacomo Meyerbeer was unconscionable, as were the racism and homophobia that were at least in the mix in the demise of disco. But all three victims were also particularly vulnerable targets. Arnold Bennett wasn't a very good writer. (Virginia Woolf was intolerant, all right—of bad writing.) Meyerbeer wasn't a very good composer. And by the late 1970s much of disco was just flat-out terrible—all of which may suggest that the arc of the moral universe bends not just toward justice but also toward good taste.

Eve You'd think that Eve would be celebrated as a trailblazer for, you know, being *the first woman ever*. But over the centuries she's been vilified for disobeying God, leading the human race into sin, and getting us all kicked out of Eden. Adam, meanwhile, gets a free pass even though he went along with it all. The early Christian writer Tertullian called Eve "the devil's gateway" and other nasty things, but the prime assassin of Eve's reputation was the poet John Milton. Milton's epic *Paradise Lost* (1667) was so widely read that he became the public face of Eve-shaming. Eve is described by Milton as inferior to Adam, weak and gullible. When Satan slithers his way into Eden, he persuades Eve to eat the forbidden fruit. She then persuades Adam, who sins, in Milton's words, because he is "fondly overcome with female charm."

Fatty Arbuckle (1887–1933) Silent film actor Roscoe "Fatty" Arbuckle was as big a star as Charlie Chaplin or Buster Keaton. But on September 11, 1921, he was arrested in the death of twenty-five-year-old actress Virginia Rappe, who had died at a "gin party" (this was during Prohibition) hosted by Arbuckle at San Francisco's St. Francis Hotel. The cause of death was peritonitis, brought on by a ruptured bladder, but prosecutors said it was the result of a sexual assault by Arbuckle. As the case played out in the tabloids, Arbuckle rapidly lost the battle for public opinion. Finally, in 1922, after two mistrials, a jury declared Arbuckle "entirely innocent and free from all blame." But after Rappe's death, Will Hays, a politician and Presbyterian deacon, had been brought in by Hollywood to clean up the industry's image. Despite Arbuckle's exoneration, Hays (who would soon have a censorship code named after him) banned him. Arbuckle managed to piece together directorial work under a pseudonym, but his career as an actor was over. He died of a heart attack in 1933.

Richard III (1452–1485) In Shakespeare's play, Richard is a hunchbacked tyrant who kills off all rival claimants to the throne, including—infamously—his two young nephews, Edward and Richard. Eventually Richard is himself killed in battle by his successor, the future king Henry VII. But might *Shakespeare* have been the real killer . . . the reputation assassin? Shakespeare wrote *Richard III* during the reign of Elizabeth I, a granddaughter of Henry VII. His version of history would, naturally, be slanted in favor of legitimating the accession of the reigning queen's grandfather. That's the argument of the Richard III Society, which advocates for "a more balanced assessment of the king." Dr. Phil Stone, chairman of the society, contends that Richard was a victim of Tudor propaganda. In reality, he says, Richard was an "innovative king" who made the justice system more accessible to common men and supported a nascent publishing industry. Also, after his bones were discovered underneath a parking lot in 2012, it was revealed that he wasn't hunchbacked. He just had scoliosis.

William Shakespeare (1564–1616) Over the years, Shakespeare's reputation has survived more assassination attempts than Castro or the Road Runner. Leo Tolstoy considered Shakespeare un-Christian and immoral. George Bernard Shaw was another Bard-basher, writing, "I have striven hard to open English eyes to the emptiness of Shakespeare's philosophy, to the superficiality and second-handedness of his morality, to his weakness and incoherence as a thinker, to his snobbery, his vulgar prejudices, his ignorance." Then there was Voltaire, who wrote that "Shakespeare was a savage with some imagination . . . but his plays can please only in London and Canada." Most recently, radio host Ira Glass prompted outrage in 2014 when he tweeted, "Shakespeare sucks," dismissing *King Lear* with a blithe "no stakes, not relatable." But the assassins' bullets ricochet harmlessly off the Bard's chest.

Before AA

THE WASHINGTONIAN MOVEMENT
{1840–1860}

I f you still have a phone book—and no, I'm not going to write a Mobit for the phone book—you can open it to page one and just before the American Automobile Association, you'll find AA, Alcoholics Anonymous. Since its founding in 1935 by a stock speculator and a colorectal surgeon, the organization has grown to an estimated membership of 2 million people.

But a hundred years before AA, there was the Washingtonian Temperance Society, a national organization dedicated to reforming alcoholics. The Washingtonians were not the first to push for temperance. But earlier groups had seen drinking as a sin, and drinkers, therefore, as beyond redemption. The Washingtonians were different. For them, as for AA a century later, the alcoholic—then more commonly called a dipsomaniac— was a victim who merited compassion and support.

The movement began with a group of six men who drank together at Chase's Tavern on Liberty Street in Baltimore, Maryland. In April 1840, these men—William K. Mitchell, John F. Hoss, David Anderson, George Steers, James McCurley, and Archibald Campbell—heard a preacher decrying the dangers of drink. For whatever reason, the preacher struck a chord. A few days later, the men wrote and signed a pledge:

We whose names are annexed, desirous of forming a society for our mutual benefit, and to guard against a pernicious practice which is injurious to our health, standing, and families, do pledge ourselves as gentlemen that we will not drink any spirituous or malt liquors, wine or cider.

They named their group the Washington Temperance Society after George Washington—apparently unaware that the first president lived out his retirement at Mount Vernon running a thriving rye distillery.

The Washingtonians made it their purpose to evangelize, urging each member to recruit new members. Their motto was, "Let every man be present, and every man bring with him a man." At first they continued to assemble at Chase's, but soon the tavern owner's wife pointed out that her husband was accommodating "customers" who weren't buying any alcohol. Even worse, these men were undertaking a campaign that would, if successful, drive the tavern out of business. Thrown out of the bar for being sober, the pledge-takers began to gather at private homes. Soon they had enough members to rent a hall.

As the crowds grew, Mitchell, the group's president, realized their meetings needed some entertainment. Drinking games were obviously out of the question. So Mitchell began the tradition of personal testimony—having each man stand up and recite his own story of alcohol abuse, up to the moment where he resolved to change his ways once and for all. It was a story people loved to hear, over and over.

John H. W. Hawkins, a milliner (that's a hatmaker), had turned to the bottle after being wiped out in the financial crisis known as the Panic of 1837. He became famous for winning converts to the Washingtonian movement with this heartrending testimony:

> Never shall I forget the 12th of June last. The first two weeks in June I averaged—it is a cross to acknowledge it—as much as a quart and a pint a day. That morning I was miserable beyond conception, and was hesitating whether to live or die. My little daughter came to my bed and said, "I hope you won't send me for any more whiskey today." I told her to go out of the room. She went weeping. I wounded her sorely, though I had made up my mind I would drink no more.

Confessions like this fostered compassion for the drinker and his family. As the group's handbook explained, the movement "considers the drunkard as a man—our brother—capable of being touched by kindness . . . We therefore stoop down to him in his fallen condition and kindly raise him up, and whisper hope and encouragement into his ear." Such sentimental tales of redemption were indeed perennial favorites in nineteenth-century American culture. In short, good storytelling was key to the society's growth.

And grow it did. I'm reminded of the old commercial for Fabergé Organic Shampoo from the 1970s. One model tells two friends, and they tell two friends, "and so on and so on" as the screen keeps subdividing until there's an infinity of feathery-haired blondes touting the healthy shine that only Fabergé can give your golden tresses. That's exactly what happened to the Washingtonians—not the shiny, feathery hair, but the power of word of mouth as a marketing tool. Each reformed drunkard told two friends, and they told two friends, and so on and so on . . . Within a year they had attracted 4,000 people to an open-air meeting in New York. Word sped up and down the coast. To mark their first anniversary, they held a parade in Baltimore where local membership already numbered 1,000. (While the membership seems to have been exclusively male, women did attend Washingtonian Society rallies. And alcoholic women organized themselves into separate "Martha Washington" societies.)

In the summer of 1841 Washingtonians fanned out across the country, spreading the word to Pittsburgh, Wheeling, Cincinnati. By the end of the year they had enlisted 200,000 members nationwide. In Illinois, early in 1842, a prominent young lawyer named Abraham Lincoln saluted the group in a public speech.

Lincoln's "Temperance Address," delivered in Springfield on the 110th anniversary of Washington's birth, noted that although the temperance movement had been around for decades, "it is just now being crowned with a degree of success hitherto unparalleled." Rather than enduring the hellfire-and-damnation approach of the old preachers, the public was hearing from men who themselves had been "victim[s] of intemperance." These men, Lincoln said, could testify to their own suffering and redemption "with tears of joy trembling in [their] eyes." This movement was changing the nation.

By 1843 membership by one estimate reached a million. Yet only a few years later, enthusiasm waned. One factor might have been that the movement was often at odds with the church-based temperance movement, which emphasized the sinfulness of drink and scorned the Washingtonians' attitude of treating the drunkard with compassion and love. And although the philosophy of the Washingtonians was, broadly speaking, religious—they believed they needed God's help to achieve sobriety—certain Protestant denominations looked down on the group with a class bias—that is, like they were a bunch of bums.

It's also quite possible that the Washingtonians' success was never as great as reported. The eye-popping numbers they tallied were those who signed their names to the pledge. But it's impossible to know how many of those who signed their names came home from the meeting and poured themselves a drink.

The last local Washingtonian Temperance Society, based in Boston, seems to have stopped its weekly meetings in 1860, marking an end to the movement. But the Washingtonians stand out in the history of the temperance movement as the first to create a community of reformed alcoholics, and the first to cultivate a support network for the drinkers dedicated to helping them stay sober. Like AA, they established a routine of weekly meetings, and a confessional style of sharing personal struggles. Like AA, too, they insisted on total abstinence (a practice that may not be necessary for all alcoholics). Finally, like AA, they were not affiliated with a particular church, but still based their program on a faith in God or a Higher Power. So while the Washingtonians faded from public memory, their basic message of compassion for the alcoholic has triumphed.

DEATH OF A
BROTHER

BILLY CARTER
{1937–1988}

Has there ever been another presidential family as colorful as Jimmy Carter's?

Jimmy, the oldest of four siblings, seemed to come out of nowhere during the presidential campaign of 1976. The peanut farmer from the small town of Plains, Georgia, seemed to be just what the country doctor ordered after the trauma of the Watergate scandal.

His mother, Lillian, was the folksy, feisty matriarch, somehow both grand and down-to-earth. She had joined the Peace Corps when she was sixty-eight, traveling to India to work with the poor. Equally at ease on her porch or on Johnny Carson, she epitomized the word *authentic* long before that word became leeched of its meaning through overuse. (My mother was a big fan of "Miss Lillian," as she was known.)

Next in line after Jimmy came sister Gloria. She was named Most Outstanding Female Motorcyclist in 1978. She was one of the first women inducted into the Harley-Davidson 100,000 mile club. Then came sister Ruth, a faith healer who was credited with helping her born-again brother Jimmy find Jesus.

And pulling up the rear, thirteen years younger than Jimmy, was brother Billy. "I have one sister that's a holy-roller preacher. I've got one that's a motorcycle rider, and I've got a brother that's running for President," he once said. "And I feel sure I'm the only sane one in the family." *Sane* is not the first word I'd use to describe Billy.

As a presidential history buff, I've long been fascinated with the prodigious number of black sheep presidential brothers. They go way back to John Quincy Adams's brother Charles. Their father, John Adams, who was also president, had once called his dissolute son Charles a "mad man possessed by the devil." Ulysses

S. Grant's brother Orville was investigated by Congress for accepting kickbacks. Lyndon Johnson's hard-drinking brother Sam Houston Johnson embarrassed LBJ with a tell-all book. George W. Bush's brother Neil was a key player in a failed savings and loan that cost taxpayers $1.3 billion. And remember Bill Clinton's half-brother, Roger? His secret service code name was "Headache." He was accused of lobbying for presidential pardons in exchange for cash and a gold Rolex. I have one of Roger Clinton's CDs. (It's not bad. Think Phil Collins by way of the Ozarks.) But no presidential sibling has ever grabbed headlines the way Jimmy Carter's brother, Billy, did.

You could tell that Jimmy and Billy were brothers. They had the same big toothy grin. But otherwise they were a study in opposites: If Jimmy represented that "city on a hill" that Puritan John Winthrop long ago envisioned as a moral beacon and that America yearned for post-Watergate, then Billy was that dive bar that, let's face it, we all need to hit up once in a while. Billy smoked. Billy drank. In fact, Billy held court with the press from a Plains filling station that he'd turned into a bar.

It's where he once told CBS News reporter Dan Rather what he thought of reporters, right to his face: "About ninety-five percent of the television reporters get the information from producers. They don't know what in hell goes on. And in fact, I've come to the conclusion the only reason anybody's a television reporter is because they can't read and write at all."

Billy was real.

During the 1976 campaign, Billy did for Jimmy what an ideal vice presidential candidate does: he balanced the ticket. Many voters *admired* Jimmy. But they *liked* Billy. Billy was that other side of ourselves: the one who didn't monitor the White House thermostat the way micromanaging Jimmy would. (Walter Mondale was Carter's running mate. Yes, I had to look it up, too.)

When America met Billy during the campaign, he was married with six children and helping to run the family's peanut business. (In fact, the business was substantial. Peanuts were the focus but the company sold seeds and services to area farmers for a variety of crops.) It was what he'd expected to do growing up.

Because of the age difference between Billy and his older siblings, he had been raised, in effect, as an only child, working alongside his father, Earl Sr., whom he idolized. Jimmy had left for the US Naval Academy when Billy was just six years old. But when Billy was sixteen, his father died. Billy's life was turned upside down.

"He was going to follow in granddaddy's footsteps," Billy's son Buddy told me. "But when he died everything suddenly changed. That future wasn't there anymore. Jimmy had to come back."

Jimmy, whom Billy didn't really know, came home and took over the business. And so Billy drifted for a while. He served in the Marines, then worked some odd jobs. He moved to Atlanta, where he enrolled in college but dropped out. Then in 1962 when Jimmy went into state politics and Billy was needed at home, he returned to Plains and assumed his rightful place managing the family business. "This was the shot in the arm I needed," he later wrote. "I threw myself into the job." By most accounts he was happy.

Fourteen years later, the night Jimmy won the Democratic nomination for president, he gave special thanks to his younger brother: "Without you, it couldn't have happened. You stayed home and kept everything going." But after Jimmy was elected president, control of the business went into a blind trust. Billy tried to buy it but was refused, so he quit in frustration. (When the attorney who managed the trust asked him to stay on as an employee, Billy told him "I'd rather fry in hell.") At that point his profession became "Being Billy Carter."

There he was on Merv Griffin talking with Zsa Zsa Gabor. "Billy Carter, I think you're vonderful!" she gushed. "I am dying to once see a peanut farm. Does a peanut grow on a tree or where does it grow?" There he was popping up in a fake cornfield on TV's *Hee Haw*, surrounded by a bevy of blondes. There he was judging the World Cannon Ball and Belly Flop Contest in Vancouver for five thousand dollars. (He couldn't resist competing and gave himself a 9.)

And there he was on the cover of *Newsweek*, holding a can of Billy Beer. Yes, Billy lent his name to a beer. I own a six-pack of it, with the old-style pull tabs intact. Not that I'd ever consider drinking it. (Dan Rather described the taste of it to me this way: "Told me something when the dogs wouldn't drink it.") But truth in advertising wasn't about to stop Billy. "It's the best beer I've ever tasted," Billy said in commercials. "And I've tasted a lot."

That second line couldn't be truer. I had a vague recollection of Billy being kind of funny, an all-in-good-fun good ol' boy. But looking at those old TV appearances today, it's pretty clear Billy was drunk through most of them. It's hard to understand what he's saying a lot of the time, he slurs that much. And there's something else going on with his speech, which he wrote about later: "I think one of the reasons I was shy was that I had this persistent stutter, which I've tried hard to overcome. I still lapse into a stutter when I'm real tired, or nervous, or when I'm around somebody else who stutters."

He does seem ill at ease in these appearances, different from the Billy that sparred with Dan Rather back in Plains.

By the summer of 1980 Billy had become a liability for his brother, who was in enough trouble of his own. In the midst of a tanking economy, the Iran hostage crisis, and a challenge to his own renomination from Senator Ted Kennedy, Jimmy had to answer questions for a full hour during a special prime-time news conference about Billy's mysterious business dealings in Libya. The details are complicated but suffice it to say, the optics weren't good. Jimmy Carter won renomination but was walloped by Reagan in the general election. The blame can't be placed on Billy, but he certainly didn't help.

For most people that's where the story ends. Jimmy went on to a distinguished post-presidency and Billy, the misfit younger brother, was forgotten. But Billy's next chapter was his finest. Even before the 1980 election, Billy had gone into treatment for his alcoholism.

His widow, Sybil Carter, recounted for me the moment Billy told the family he had a drinking problem: "He turned and he looked at the children and he said 'I want you to know I'm an alcoholic and I have to go away because I have to do something about this.' And the kids looked at him and said 'Daddy, are you just realizing this? We've known it for a long time.'"

Billy devoted the rest of his life to being a better—and sober—husband and father. Sybil and their six children—and I loved spending time with each and every one of them during a trip to Plains—have made peace with their time in the public eye and Billy's antics.

"Looking back, things got out of hand," Sybil said. "I think he was trying to be what the press had tried to turn him out to be, a redneck brother."

They've come to cherish the memory of a man whom they remember as kind and decent. Daughter Mandy told me about the time in the mid-1980s when she and Billy were walking through Los Angeles International Airport. They saw a man carrying a six-pack of Billy Beer. Billy tapped the man on the shoulder. "And the guy was just floored and Daddy signed it for him," she said. "He didn't do it because he thought he was a celebrity. He did it because he knew it would make the person feel good."

But the most surprising insight for me came from Billy and Sybil's youngest son, Earl. Earl was just a baby when his uncle Jimmy became president, so he doesn't remember when his father was a late-night comedy staple. He knows a very different Billy Carter: "The strangest thing is I'm a recovering alcoholic and being in AA meetings, I don't tell people who I am," says Earl. "And people bring up my dad saying if he got sober then I can, too. My father is alive and well within the AA community." (About his work speaking to other recovering alcoholics, Billy wrote this: "Who's some good ol' boy going to relate to when he winds up in jail drunk and can't remember what he did to get there? Elizabeth Taylor? Betty Ford? A psychiatrist? Or me?")

Three months before Billy Carter died in 1988 from pancreatic cancer—the disease that took his father and both his sisters—he gave an interview to CBS News. He'd lost almost fifty pounds. He looked like his brother Jimmy does now. But what startled me the most was that he was only fifty-one years old at the time, just a little older than I am now. That means he hadn't yet hit forty when the media circus came to Plains back in 1976. No, he wasn't a kid then, but I know I couldn't have handled that kind of spotlight at that age, let alone with six kids.

In the interview, Billy was reflective, more at ease with himself. He spoke more deliberately and was easier to understand. But he was still Billy Carter. When he was asked to reflect on his behavior during his brother's Oval Office years he said this: "There are some things I shouldn't have done. There are things I should have done. If I had to do it over again, I'd probably screw it up worse than I did the first time. Hindsight ain't worth a damn."

When he was asked if he was losing hope in his battle with cancer, he repeated what he'd told his doctor: "On my dying breath, I want you to give me a shot in the ass of something trying to get me well. That's how far I want to go with it."

Come to think of it, *sane* is a pretty good word to describe Billy.

Branwell Brontë (1817–1848) Those Brontë sisters sure knew how to write. Charlotte Brontë gave us *Jane Eyre*. Younger sister Emily wrote *Wuthering Heights*. Anne, no slouch herself, penned *The Tenant of Wildfell Hall*, which in recent years has come to be regarded as the first feminist novel. And then there's their little brother, Branwell. The only boy in the Brontë clan was a likable, redheaded . . . deadbeat. Unlike his three famous sisters, young Branwell never got his act together. Though well educated, he managed to get fired from all four of his early careers: first as an unsuccessful portrait painter, then as a family tutor (he was sacked within a year), and then as a railway clerk (he was canned when the books didn't add up). His last job, once again as a family tutor, ended when he seduced his boss's wife, a woman fifteen years his senior named, appropriately enough, Mrs. Robinson. Bran's most notable work is the only known portrait of the Brontë sisters. Bran is actually *in* the painting, too, but somehow ended up being covered up by a column in the background. Yes, really.

Seth Brothers Cain and Abel were history's first tabloid sensation, but there was another member of that famous biblical family that you never hear about—Seth. "Seth who?" you ask. Well I don't know his last name, since back then apparently no one had a last name. But we do know this from the book of Genesis: after Cain killed Abel, their parents Adam (still a spry 150 years old) and Eve got busy . . . and had a third son. Seth kept his head down throughout the Old Testament—raising his family and *not* killing people—so not much is remembered about him. Other than the fact that he's a direct ancestor of a few people you may have heard of—like Noah. And Jesus. And, I guess, almost everybody else, come to think of it. According to Genesis, Seth had lots of kids and lived to the age of 912. Adam lived to be 930, so imagine being in your 700s and still being told by your dad, "Meh, you're no Abel."

Magda Gabor (1915–1997)

The three Gabor sisters were proto-Kardashians: famous for being famous, these glamour-pusses from Hungary took the country by storm in the 1950s. But only two managed to stay famous. While Eva became known for the TV series *Green Acres* and Zsa Zsa became known for slapping a cop, eldest sister Magda became known for being Eva and Zsa Zsa's sister. It's not that she wasn't fabulous and beautiful—she was. And it's not that she didn't rack up a large number of rich and very temporary husbands—she did. (While Zsa Zsa had nine, Eva only had five. Magda tallied up a respectable six.) And it's not that she didn't have that lavish Hungarian accent—of course she did, dahling. But while she dabbled in Hollywood, her true calling turned out to be as a socialite, mostly in Palm Springs and the Hamptons. Also, Magda suffered a stroke in 1966 that seriously impacted her ability to speak. According to one source, the only word she could say was *superb*. The "dahling" was implied. (Back to the marriages for a moment: One of Magda's husbands, actor George Sanders, had previously been married to Zsa Zsa. That's right, Magda accepted a hand-me-down husband *from her younger sister.*)

Gummo Marx (1893–1977)

Think it's awkward being known as "the other Marx Brother"? Now imagine being the one people called "No, the *other* other Marx Brother." That would be Gummo, or as I like to think of him, "Zeppo's Zeppo." Milton "Gummo" Marx was the fourth of the five brothers, but he was, along with Groucho, the first of the brothers to perform onstage. Gummo didn't much like performing, though, in part because he had a stammer. So during World War I he enlisted in the military. Gummo was replaced in the act by his younger brother Zeppo, and he went on to enjoy much success as his brothers' manager and a well-respected talent agent and producer. But clearly he never lost his sense of humor. "I attribute their success entirely to me," Gummo said once about his brothers. "I quit the act."

Donald Nixon (1914–1987)

Sure, Billy Carter wasn't always helpful to his brother, Jimmy, but there's no evidence that he cost him an election. Donald Nixon, on the other hand, may have done just that. Back in the 1950s, while Richard Nixon was serving as vice president, his little brother ran Nixon's, a small chain of burger joints in California. It featured the famous(ish) "Nixon-burger with cheese" for a mere 20 cents. But in 1957, Don found himself broke, and he accepted a $205,000 bailout loan from none other than the shadowy billionaire Howard Hughes. Suspicions immediately arose that Hughes was trying to buy influence. The "Nixonburger scandal"—which today would be called . . . "Nixonburgergate"?—dogged Richard throughout his 1960 campaign for president as well as his later campaign for California governor, both of which he lost. As for the business, well, Nixon's went belly-up just a year after receiving that loan. As Donald Nixon himself might have said, "I am not a cook."

DEATH OF THE ENTERTAINER

SAMMY DAVIS JR.

{1925–1990}

I came to appreciate Sammy Davis's supernova talent fairly late in life. It was the late 1990s, before you could just call up any clip on YouTube, and I paid a visit to the Museum of Television and Radio in New York for a screening of a recently unearthed concert performance of the Rat Pack from 1965. Frank Sinatra, Dean Martin, and Sammy were backed by the Count Basie Orchestra (and directed by a young Quincy Jones). They were performing for a black-tie audience in St. Louis. The special, which aired back in 1965 on closed-circuit television, was hosted by Johnny Carson and titled *The Frank Sinatra Spectacular*. After all, Frank's nickname was "Chairman of the Board" for a reason. There was no one bigger in entertainment at the time.

But it's Sammy who dazzles here. At one point, accompanied only by a drum, he sings a medley that goes from Cole Porter's "I've Got You Under My Skin" (scatting part of it) to Ray Charles's R&B classic "What I Say" (complete with screams that sound more James Brown) to the country-western standard "You Are My Sunshine" and points in between. Like the world's most expensive sports car, he shifts gears seamlessly, his dance moves as smooth as his transitions between the songs. At one point in the medley he "interrupts" himself to demonstrate for "some of the older folks" in the crowd the latest dances sweeping the nation. He does the mashed potato, the jerk, and the frug—all of them delightfully. The audience eats it up hook, line, and sinker. He's at one with them, with the drummer who's been playing behind him the whole time—and with himself. He's absolutely comfortable onstage—which is no small thing.

Remember, it's the middle of the country and it's 1965. Sammy is a black man performing for an all-white audience. Yet he manages to negotiate the situation without sacrificing his dignity. When he's onstage with the other performers he's treated like a kid brother, yes. (Is that because of his race? Or because of his five-foot-five height? Probably both.) Dean Martin carries him around at one point. But it's Johnny Carson who seems like the odd man out. When the group sings "Birth of the Blues" Sinatra pushes Carson aside at one point. Sammy ribs Johnny: "How does it feel to sit at the back of the bus?"

All of the men onstage are great talents. But it's Sammy who is having the most fun, so much fun that he genuinely doubles over with laughter at moments. It's a boyish enthusiasm that we all wish we had for . . . anything. A pure love for performing that had already seen him through many lifetimes' worth of drama—and a near-death experience almost a decade before.

In the wee small hours of November 19, 1954, Sammy Davis Jr., a then twenty-eight-year-old fast-rising nightclub performer, was driving through the night from a show in Vegas to a recording gig in Los Angeles. His 1953 Cadillac Eldorado convertible sports car was the height of luxury—a symbol of how far he'd already come—with a wraparound windshield, real leather seats . . . and a serious design flaw. The chrome hub of the steering wheel protruded, stuck out almost like a missile, aimed straight at the driver's face. This being the 1950s, the car had no seat belts.

In San Bernardino, Sammy's car collided with another car . . . and the left side of his face collided with that steering wheel. His left eye was knocked out of its socket.

The late Dr. Frederick Hull, a surgeon, rushed to the hospital to work on Sammy. I spoke to his daughter, Nancy, who was thirteen years old at the time. Nancy told me that her father's first priority was to save Sammy's other eye. But the first question that Sammy asked her father was whether his legs were okay. Sammy was at the time primarily known as a dancer.

This traumatic event opens Sammy's autobiography *Yes I Can*, which he wrote with Burt Boyar:

As I ran my hand over my cheek I felt my eye hanging there by a string. Frantically I tried to stuff it back in, like if I could do that it would stay there and nobody would know. The ground went out from under me, and I was on my knees. Don't let me go blind. Please, God, don't take it all away.

When Sammy said "don't take it all away," I don't think he was praying for his life. At least not the way that you or I might. He was talking about his showbiz life. As he put it, "All the beautiful things, all the plans, the laughs—they were lying out there, smashed just like the car."

Sammy spent almost two weeks in the San Bernardino hospital recovering—later on he'd famously be fitted for a glass eye—and the outpouring of love was almost like a memorial service. Marilyn Monroe, Eddie Cantor, Jackie Robinson, Ella Fitzgerald—they all sent telegrams. Even the waiters at the Hollywood nightclub Ciro's, where he'd become an "overnight sensation" just three years before, sent their good wishes. The admiration of his friends and peers mattered. But in a life of dramatic ups and downs, it was the adulation of audiences that sustained him—in the words of one friend, "nourished" him. And he gave those audiences everything he had.

Of this horrendous accident, Sammy later reflected, "I think it's probably the best thing that ever happened to me." He knew that was "an odd thing to say," but at that moment, he said, "My friends rallied around me and convinced me there was still a lot to be done."

Now, if you didn't grow up with Sammy Davis Jr., or if you only know him from Billy Crystal's *Saturday Night Live* impression, or from a trivia buff's list of famous African American Jews, then you may not appreciate his singular talent. Over my ten-plus years as a correspondent on *CBS Sunday Morning*, Sammy's is the name that's come up the most frequently in interviews. Former San Francisco mayor Willie Brown, a good friend of his, told me about Sammy's command over an audience. "Easily the greatest," he declared. Kim Novak and Nancy Sinatra both talked about what a joy he was to be around, how playful and childlike (not child-ish) he was. LeVar Burton, who did a guest spot with Sammy on *Fantasy Island*, and Ben Vereen both revered Sammy as a role model. Vereen recalled watching him as a kid, at a time when black performers were a rare sight on television: "If there was a black actor on TV in those days, we'd watch. Sammy would come on *The Ed Sullivan Show* and do everything. And I mean everything." Broadway legend Chita Rivera echoed that assessment: "He was everything," she said. "He could play any instrument, he could sing, he could dance like a maniac." The inscription on his tombstone in Hollywood's Forest Lawn sums it up: "The Entertainer: He Did It All." And he did: Singing, Dancing, Acting, Comedy. He was at least a quadruple threat—quintuple if you count his inimitable gun-spinning routine.

It helped that he started early. Sammy was born in Harlem in 1925 to parents who both knew showbiz. His mother, Elvera Sanchez, was a dancer. She was Cuban American, though Sammy, worried about anti-Cuban sentiment in the sixties, always said she was Puerto Rican. His father, Sam Sr., was also a hoofer. When the younger Sammy was just three and a half years old, he won an amateur contest at the Stanley Theater in Philadelphia, singing "I'll Be Glad When You're Dead, You Rascal You." (He'd sing that same song in a film short when he was seven years old.) His parents split up early and just when most kids start school, Sammy hit the road—the vaudeville circuit—with his father and Will Mastin, a family friend he always called his uncle. They were billed as the Will Mastin Trio.

While Sammy was said to be self-conscious about his lack of formal education—he never spent a single day in a classroom—he never said he regretted his early life on the road. Sam Sr. said the young boy only cared about one thing, the world of entertainment. He affectionately recalled little Sammy pronouncing with a lisp, "I'm gonna be in th'ow business."

The Will Mastin Trio was a success, but it was the diminutive Sammy Davis Jr. who stood out. Many years later, Shirley MacLaine remembered Dean Martin and Frank Sinatra sneaking her into Ciro's to see this singing-and-dancing dynamo: "I could not believe my eyes and my ears. Never had so much come out of something so small for so long." It's a common refrain among his admirers: there was something—an inner *light*—that came out of Sammy that made it impossible *not* to look at him, that made him more than the sum of his mad individual talents.

Consider his impressions. His Humphrey Bogart was perfect, his Jimmy Cagney spot-on. As for his marvelously muttering Marlon Brando, well, you're really going to need to dial up the *Mobituaries* podcast for the full effect. Sammy's friend the Oscar-winning songwriter Leslie Bricusse told me that Sammy learned to imitate others so well because he'd spent so much time in movie theaters growing up. That was his school.

One time, appearing on a Julie Andrews variety show in 1973 (don't you love the sound of that, Julie Andrews variety show?), Sammy put his skills to the test against the famous impressionist Rich Little. Sammy sang as Nat King Cole . . . then Rich did Liberace . . . then Sammy did his Jerry Lewis to Rich's Dean Martin. What struck me watching this was that while Rich Little may have been technically better, it was Sammy I couldn't stop watching. I asked Laurence Maslon, the writer of the 2019 *American Masters* documentary on Davis, about this. "The genius of Sammy is when he imitated someone he imitated them from the inside out. . . . Sammy gets to the essence of that person."

Meanwhile, Sammy's talent as a singer was always, well, undersung. As in all things, when he sang, he showed total commitment. He never looked down at the material, even when he could have. (Yes, I'm talking about you, Candy Man.) And while other vocalists might have been more powerful or more technically accomplished, Sammy knew how to tell a story with a song.

Exhibit A is "I've Gotta Be Me." The song wasn't just a Sammy hit. It was a statement of purpose for Sammy, maybe even a mantra. Written by Walter Marks, it was actually first performed by Steve Lawrence in the 1968 Broadway musical *Golden Rainbow*, about a single dad raising his son in Las Vegas. (The musical co-starred Steve's wife, Eydie Gormé, one of the greatest voices of her era. Listen to her version of "When the Sun Comes Out" and be prepared to be blown away.) Steve thought "I've Gotta Be Me" would be more powerful coming from his friend. He recognized that the lyrics—"Whether I'm right, whether I'm wrong, whether I find a place in this world or never belong"—had more resonance coming from an African American during such a turbulent time. (During the course of the musical's run, Dr. Martin Luther King Jr. and Robert F. Kennedy were both slain.)

Being "me" for Sammy Davis Jr. was indeed a complicated matter. Not only was he black, he was Jewish. As he wrote in a long piece for *Ebony* magazine in February 1960, his car accident had prompted some soul-searching. And conversations with various Jews in his life, including the hospital chaplain and his old friend and mentor, the great entertainer Eddie Cantor, helped him to find common themes in the histories of blacks and Jews.

Being the entertainer he was, Sammy could always get a laugh out of his identity. "I'm colored, Jewish, and Puerto Rican," he used to say. "When I move into a neighborhood, I wipe it out!" He had a deft way of joking about his race without either offending or apologizing. Early in his career, this ability had been a means of survival. In 1943, the eighteen-year-old Sammy was drafted into service and into one of the US Army's first integrated units. Until then his father and uncle had tried as best they could to shelter him from racism. Now there was no one to protect him. The other soldiers did horrendous things to him—painting him white, pouring urine in his beer. And remember, Sammy was not a physically imposing man. Trips to the infirmary were regular—that's how many fights he was getting into. He got his nose broken three times.

When he was transferred to an entertainment unit, things got better for him. He once told his daughter, "Talent was my only weapon." Indeed, it was his talent that eventually helped him not just to survive the army but to excel once he left the service. Those impressions he did? They weren't just funny; they were bold. Back in the late 1940s black performers didn't do impressions of white performers in front of white audiences. That is, until Sammy did. His father and his partner Will Mastin, with whom he re-teamed post-army, were nervous when Sammy first started imitating white celebrities. But one night, while Sammy was doing his Jimmy Cagney, he heard a white man in the audience marvel, "My God, he sounds just like him!"

Now, imitating white performers was one thing; dating a white woman was another. A dalliance with screen siren Kim Novak—they met at a party—was considered scandalous in 1957. Not long ago I talked to Kim, during a visit to her horse farm in Oregon. She told me that their relationship ended when Harry Cohn, the much-feared head of Columbia Pictures, threatened to take Sammy's other eye out. The interracial romance was verboten for the time. In 1960, after a short marriage to African American actress Loray White, Sammy married the white Swedish model and actress May Britt. His union with Britt created such an uproar—marriage between blacks and whites was still illegal in many states—that he was disinvited from performing at the JFK inaugural. Not even his great friend Frank Sinatra, who headlined the entertainment for it, could get him back on the program.

This was not the behavior of a man overly eager to please a mainstream audience. Sammy's politics were even more controversial. In 1972, he embraced President Richard Nixon during his reelection campaign. Quite literally, Sammy hugged Nixon. And let's just say much of the public did not hug back. In the wake of the civil rights movement, African Americans were shifting heavily into the Democratic Party column, and many of them were dismayed to see such a prominent black man supporting the president who had run on a "southern strategy" of courting aggrieved white voters. (Former mayor Willie Brown believes that the outrage came more from white liberals than from African Americans, many of whom were still Republicans.) Of course Sammy's embrace of Nixon might have had something to do with the way JFK had treated him back in 1961. Regardless, Sammy appeared at Jesse Jackson's PUSH conference—a gathering of social justice activists—where he addressed his critics and affirmed his black identity: "Disagree, if you will, with my politics. But I will not allow anyone to take away the fact that I am black."

He ended his appearance by singing—what else?—"I've Gotta Be Me."

But if Sammy defined who he was with "I've Gotta Be Me," his love life was, unfortunately, better defined by a different song—"What Kind of Fool Am I?" The song was written by Anthony Newley and Leslie Bricusse for the British musical *Stop the World—I Want to Get Off*. The character who sings it is a striver who fritters away the love of his wife and daughter in favor of a life of philandering and fame. In old age he realizes what he's lost.

Sammy often felt, looking back, that he'd behaved foolishly. Touring as much as he did, he always struggled to sustain a relationship. Leslie Bricusse suggested that there's "maybe a little bit of autobiography" in Sammy's rendition. It's truly plaintive, almost anguished. Performing the song on *The Andy Williams Show* in 1962, he tears into lyrics like "Why can't I cast away this mask of play and live my life?"

He ended up having two kids with May Britt. But when they split up, he didn't fight for a share of custody. As he later told CBS, "I lost every ounce of what was valuable. I made the wrong choices." Later, he dated Chita Rivera. She said that as a lover, "he was just as talented in that area as he was otherwise." But they fought, and the relationship didn't last. During one evening out at a club, they got into an argument and Sammy pulled his glass eye out and held it in front of Chita. "Is this what you want from me?" he shouted at her. (How is Sammy's life not an Oscar-winning biopic and how is this detail not a scene?!)

Sammy's deepest—certainly most enduring—relationship may have been with his audience. "That was his domain," his friend the singer Dionne Warwick told me. "You had to see this man just own a stage and the audience. I mean he actually owned you. He brought you *into* him." Leslie Bricusse told me the story of how, on New Year's Eve 1977, Sammy and Liza Minnelli performed for three hours. When they finished, they brought a small group of their friends up to Sammy's suite . . . and then did the entire show all over again. Performing was everything.

Lest anyone think that Sammy didn't enjoy his material success, well, "What Kind of Fool Am I?" could also describe Sammy Davis Jr.'s relationship with money. His former agent Larry Auerbach told me he "was one of the worst people I ever saw with any kind of money. He had no idea what money was and what it was worth." Almost everyone I talked to for the *Mobituaries* podcast episode on Sammy had a story of him giving them ridiculously expensive presents. When he died, Larry Maslon said, he owed more money to the IRS than any single individual in history up to that point.

After Sammy was diagnosed with cancer of the throat in 1989, his doctors told him he needed surgery. But the surgery would involve removing his voice box. As far as Sammy was concerned, that wasn't an option. In November of that year, six months before he died, his best friends—no surprise, they included some of the greatest living performers—rushed to organize a tribute show. A very gaunt Sammy sat in the front row. He was sixty-three, marking his sixtieth anniversary in showbiz. Frank Sinatra took the microphone and told Sammy he loved him: "I can't say it any more than that. You're my brother." Michael Jackson, who from a young age had studied Sammy from the wings, sang an originally written song called "You Were There." It paid tribute to Sammy as a trailblazer. Then, halfway through the show, the great tap dancer Gregory Hines came on. Hines danced, and the crowd went wild.

If you watch the old footage, you can see what happens next. Hines approaches Sammy, who isn't scheduled to perform—he looks so weak sitting in the front row. Then Altovise Gore, Sammy's third wife, pulls out Sammy's tap shoes. Sammy can't resist. He puts them on and gets up onstage. Sammy comes alive in that sequence. When you watch this, you forget how sick he is. The light is still there. Dionne Warwick said that he once told her he wanted to die onstage. In this final performance, he came close, basking in the love that only an audience could give him.

Wiley Post (1898–1935)

Wiley Post was a famous aviator way back when there was such a thing as "famous aviators." The 1926 oilfield accident that took his left eye didn't slow him down at all, and in 1933 he became the first man to fly solo around the world. He went on to help develop the first pressure suit, which allowed pilots to fly in high altitudes. And he's credited by many with discovering the jet stream. (That's the fast-moving air current that you want your pilot to ride when you're on a long flight.) Still, everyone said Post was crazy when he dismissed safety concerns and built his dream aircraft

using parts from two different existing airplanes. Post headed for Alaska with his good friend humorist Will Rogers aboard the plane—and the two died in a catastrophic crash a couple of days later, probably due to the plane's poor balance.

Andre DeToth (1913–2002)

It's challenging enough for a one-eyed Hungarian to come to America and make it as a movie director. DeToth did that *and* married screen siren Veronica Lake. But what's extra special about Andre DeToth is that he managed to score one of his biggest hits with *House of Wax*, a horror movie that was also the first *3-D color feature film*. That's right, Andre directed a movie full of bats and skeletons popping out at the audience using the most cutting-edge 3-D effects that he himself could not see. DeToth experienced his own real-life horror movie when he was kidnapped, pistol-whipped, and almost murdered while scouting locations in Egypt in the 1970s. Due to his black eye patch, he'd been mistaken for one-eyed Israeli defense minister Moshe Dayan. His captors only relented after examining his, um, groin and discovering in 3-D that he was not Jewish.

Polyphemus Shepherd, lover, giant, wine enthusiast, and perhaps the world's least gracious host, the Cyclops Polyphemus, son of the god Poseidon, is featured in one of the most memorable chapters of Homer's *Odyssey*. Coming home from a long day of shepherding, Polyphemus finds Odysseus and his men occupying his cave. He responds by sealing them *in* the cave and then, even more impolitely, eating two of them. The next morn-  ing he proves that this was no fluke by eating two more for breakfast. Odysseus extricates his men by serving the Cyclops extremely strong wine and stabbing him in his one eye with a sharpened stick, turning him quite literally "blind drunk."

Peter Falk (1927–2011) Thirty-five years spent inhabiting the character of "Columbo," TV's most famous rumpled detective, made Peter Falk a favorite to audiences worldwide (and practically a religion to my friend and *Wait Wait . . . Don't Tell Me!* co-panelist Paula Poundstone). But Falk's famous squint (his right eye was removed due to a rare form of cancer when he was three) was already renowned before he ever donned the trench coat. In 1961, ten years before he played Detective Columbo, Falk became the first actor ever nominated for an Oscar and an Emmy in the same year. He pulled off the same feat the very next year. Falk also had an eye for art (the left one, obviously), and was an accomplished painter and sketch artist.

Hannibal (247 BC–181 BC)

Before *Silence of the Lambs*, the most famous Hannibal was the great military commander of ancient Carthage, Hannibal Barca. Born in 247 BC to a renowned military commander in what is now Tunisia, young Hannibal quickly became a brilliant military tactician in his own right—and a major thorn in the side of Rome, against whom he lost an eye during an early battle. It's Hannibal's arsenal of nutty battlefield tactics that make him my favorite ancient conqueror. He intimidated foes by riding into enemy territory on an elephant. He once won a fight by tying wood to the horns of oxen, setting the wood on fire, then sending the oxen into "battle." The Romans fell for the diversion, while Hannibal's army snuck around back and ambushed them.  But wait, there's more: he once won a naval battle by lobbing clay pots full of venomous snakes onto the deck of his opponent's ship. The opposing sailors laughed at the pots at first, and then—quite quickly—it became a *lot* less funny.

Tex Avery (1908–1980)

Legendary animator Tex Avery lost his eye in a moment of office horseplay when a colleague launched a paper clip off a rubber band, and Avery turned into the line of fire. But even before the accident there was something wonderfully skewed about Avery's vision. Working under director Friz Freleng—not to be confused with Fritz "German director of *Metropolis*" Lang—and supervising artists Bob Clampett and Chuck Jones, Avery more than anyone deserves credit for creating Bugs Bunny, Daffy Duck, and Porky Pig.  Avery could do it all—visual gags, verbal quips, breaking the fourth wall. And pretty much defy every law of physics. In the words of animator Debra Solomon, "he created a world in which anything was possible." (P.S.: Tex Avery should not be confused with Tex Ritter, the singing cowboy and father of *Three's Company* actor John Ritter.)

Elle Driver SPOILER ALERT! Honestly, there's no way I can talk about Daryl Hannah's character from Quentin Tarantino's epic *Kill Bill* movies—*especially* how she became one-eyed—without a spoiler or two. So . . . long after Elle Driver almost poisons her former colleague the Bride (Uma Thurman) while she's in a coma after being shot by their boss, Bill (David Carradine), and shortly after Elle kills her colleague (and Bill's brother) Budd with a strategically placed black mamba, Elle and the Bride find themselves in a climactic battle. It is during this struggle that Elle reveals her eye was plucked out by the Bride's mentor, their (purportedly) thousand-year-old sensei, Pai Mei, after she, well, *sassed* him during a training session. In response, Elle poisons him. In order to leave some mystery here, let me just say that by the fight's end, Elle Driver is no longer one-eyed.

DEATH OF A SQUARE

LAWRENCE WELK
(1903–1992)

To say I watched a lot of TV growing up would be an understatement. When my brother Lawrence told Mrs. Barnett across the street that he had a younger brother, she didn't believe him. That's how little I went outside. My skin took on a bluish hue, sort of the color of skim milk.

When I was nine years old I memorized the *TV Guide*. Granted that wasn't the greatest feat back Before Cable—an era that yes, millennials, did exist. (And no, that's not what BC stands for.) Back then there were five, six channels tops. Our TV didn't have a remote control, so I did get some exercise.

My parents were strict about what I could watch. Nothing "risqué." (On an episode of *Fantasy Island*, someone's fantasy was a hookup outside of marriage— well, that was bound to come up—so that was it for me and *Fantasy Island*.) I was allowed *one hour* of "inappropriate" TV a week. It was a no-brainer; I chose *Dallas* . . . then switched over to *Dynasty*. (Not long ago, when I told my friend Faith about my weekly "inappropriate" TV allowance, she called it—perfectly—my "TV Rumspringa.") Mainly my television diet consisted of sitcoms like *Three's Company* (come to think of it, how did *that* escape the ban?). In the summers and when I was home sick during the school year it was soap operas (*All My Children* and *Ryan's Hope*) and game shows. I liked the bad ones like *Sale of the Century*.

But when we went to my grandmother's apartment on Sundays, we had limited control over the TV. Momma liked the old movies on channel 5. (That's when I fell in love with Hitchcock's *The Birds*. Remember the know-it-all old lady in the beret—the one who blows smoke in Tippi Hedren's face while telling her that birds

225

have never been known to attack humans? I remember my grandmother scowling at her.) And at 8 p.m., on that same channel, was another program she liked: *The Lawrence Welk Show*.

The Lawrence Welk Show was an hour-long musical variety show hosted by bandleader and accordion player Lawrence Welk. He and his orchestra served up a soothing stream of waltzes, polkas, and ballads. Welk had a pretty strong German accent and approached his job with a kind of Germanic discipline. Once one song ended it was on to the next. His patter in between was brief: "Isn't she nice?" he'd say about one of his singers. "Aren't they great?" he'd say about two of the show's dancers. "And now in honor of Stephen Foster Memorial Week, here's 'I Dream of Jeannie with the Light Brown Hair,'" he'd say to tee up the next number.

He called his genre "champagne music" because early in his career a dancer had said that it was light and bubbly. The show was sponsored by the vitamin supplement Geritol, which tells you all you need to know about the demographics of its audience. This was old people TV and as a kid, I couldn't wait for it to end. (I was holding out for *The Jeffersons* at 9:30 p.m.)

Indeed the show had an almost sedative effect—not just the sound but also the look: a polyester and chiffon fantasia of powder blues, peaches, and cream tones as the singers and dancers glided in and out of numbers. (These performers—members of the show's "Musical Family"—seemed to exist only in Welk's world. And it was extremely rare for anyone famous from outside the show to appear.) The musicians were always in matching suit and tie, Welk himself more elegantly turned out, usually with a pocket square. Floating bubbles filled the stage. Chandeliers hung overhead. It was hard to tell where all of this was taking place. A reception hall on another planet?

Welk wasn't edgy. He wasn't surprising. He was aggressively *uncool*. And he was a phenomenal success. By the end of his life, he had become the second-richest performer in all of show business, right behind Bob Hope. And his show was hailed by the *Los Angeles Times* as "the longest-running prime-time musical program in television history." (It was eventually surpassed by *Soul Train*.) Lawrence Welk did it by working hard, trusting his instincts, and sticking to his guns, critics be damned.

He was born in 1903 to a large family of Catholic German immigrants in Strasburg, North Dakota, a German-speaking enclave. (Welk didn't learn to speak English until his twenties.) When he was born, the family was living in a sod house—basically a house made of dirt and grass. As a boy Welk had dropped out of grade school to work on the family farm. But he longed for a career playing the accordion, and his father agreed to sell a cow and lend young Lawrence the four-hundred-dollar profit. (I know, it sounds like a fairy tale.) Welk paid his parents off through four years of what amounted to indentured servitude on the farm, after which he took to the road, accordion in tow, to pursue his musical dreams.

It was the 1920s and jazz was the music of the day. But even as a young man, Welk, though he always enjoyed Dixieland, leaned toward the more conservative style of "sweet" jazz with its emphasis on melody, its minimal improvisation, its strong sense of orchestration. Soon he was leading a ten-piece band called the Hotsy-Totsy Boys (that name is about as racy as he ever got) and steadily gained a name across the upper Midwest. When TV arrived, Welk moved to Los Angeles and landed his own show in 1951 on the local station KTLA. By 1955 he was offered a national audience on Saturday night on ABC.

Even by the standards of the 1950s, Welk was a square. His only aim, from the start, was to please his viewers, whom he referred to as "very nice people." But the suits at ABC in New York City and the moneymen at Dodge-Chrysler in Detroit (they were an early sponsor) fretted that Welk's middlebrow shtick would fall flat on national prime time. They urged changes that would make it younger and sexier, whether in the form of a chorus line, more comedy, or high-profile guest stars. They were also looking to eliminate what they saw as the show's quirky regionalism.

(Welk was fond of pointing out where songs and singers hailed from, especially if they hailed from North Dakota.) But Welk was already in his fifties and confident of the show's appeal—and his own.

His accent, a source of self-consciousness when he was younger, had become a trademark as distinctive as Groucho Marx's eyebrows or the gap in David Letterman's front teeth. The satirist Stan Freberg would mimic Welk's favorite phrase, "Wunnerful, wunnerful!," in parody. But Welk himself understood that the accent—a connection to his immigrant parents—was part of his charm, and he took the phrase for the title of his autobiography.

"He wasn't trying to hide his accent, and that was great," comedian Fred Armisen told me. He imitated Welk on *Saturday Night Live* as part of a sketch built around the fictional Maharelle Sisters. (*The Lawrence Welk Show* had lots of sister acts.) The Maharelles included three lovely blondes . . . and their deformed sister Dooneese, played by Kristen Wiig. It was absolutely hilarious—and I'm pretty sure something Welk would've hated.

Like me, Fred grew up watching Lawrence Welk. "My parents used to watch him, which meant I used to watch him in the seventies," he told me. "It was just sort of on and it was *pleasant.*" Fred means that as a compliment. "Visually it was so soothing. The colors, the staging." He compares it to the modern-day HGTV show *House Hunters*: "Nothing dramatic or shocking happens. There's enough ugliness in the world. [It's] a show where you're allowed to . . . sit down for a minute." In order words, a refuge. And that's increasingly what *The Lawrence Welk Show* became.

During the early sixties, when the charts were dominated by Elvis and Ray Charles and—starting in 1964—the Beatles and the Rolling Stones, Welk's show began to seem more and more like a world apart for viewers who felt alienated or put off by the angry, rebellious, and threatening postures of rock. It was the ultimate in counterprogramming. When the orchestra did cover popular songs, they adapted them to the Champagne Music sound. (One adaptation that may not have connected with the core audience: Welk singers Gail Ferrell and Dick Dale performing "One Toke Over the Line." The story goes that Welk had no idea what the song was about. But he liked that it included the words "Sweet Jesus.")

But mostly the show stuck to old-time standards. This was a safe space. When the show featured cutaway shots of bald men and blue-haired ladies from the audience dancing in pairs, that wasn't inept editing or clumsy camerawork. It was intentional. (Those couples weren't just old. They were overwhelmingly white, as was the makeup of the Musical Family—and TV in general in the 1960s. Welk dancer Arthur Duncan became the first African American regular on any TV variety series when he joined the show in 1964.)

Welk assumed the role of father—often a strict one—with his Musical Family. He fired a clarinetist for improvising a jazzy solo during a Christmas carol. He dismissed singer Alice Lon, many believe, for wearing too short a skirt. He would not accept advertising for cigarettes or alcohol, refused to play Vegas, and generally steered clear of stand-up comedians, who might sneak in racy material.

He was well aware of what youth culture thought of him. In one memorable episode from 1969, an old hippie in sunglasses and a sheepskin vest ambled out onstage and silenced the orchestra. "Don't you cats know this polka jazz is strictly from Squaresville?" he asked, before launching into a cover of Wilson Pickett's R&B classic "She's Lookin' Good." As dancers began removing the hippie's wig and garb, they revealed the suited bandleader underneath. Welk turned and stared right into the camera, declaring, "We're not going to change our style, folks, and that's a promise. We wouldn't do that to you nice people."

In 1971, what's known as the "Rural Purge" radically altered what people watched. The broadcast networks, seeking a more sophisticated demographic, canceled a slew of still-popular but older-skewing shows with rural settings that had dominated the airwaves throughout the sixties. *Green Acres, The Beverly Hillbillies, Lassie, Hee-Haw,* and *Mayberry R.F.D.* were put out to pasture, making room for a new generation of smarter, more socially conscious shows like *M*A*S*H, All in* *the Family*, and *The Mary Tyler Moore Show*. (The rural sitcoms were set in worlds completely insulated from current events like the Vietnam War and the civil rights movement.) Out with the old sitcoms went many popular variety shows that, while not set in small towns, appealed to the people who lived there. Jim Nabors, Johnny Cash, Andy Williams, and even the great Ed Sullivan were cut. So was Welk.

But Welk wasn't done by a long shot. He took his show to syndication, where he was soon aired on 250 local stations nationwide, reaching 30 million viewers—more than ever before—and extending the run of his show for another eleven years. It was an extraordinary third act. What's more, he was able to use his television fame to launch a business empire that would include millions of dollars in music publishing rights (some twenty thousand songs) and real estate assets, including Lawrence Welk Village, a resort catering to retirees, and the Lawrence Welk Museum, which features the world's largest champagne glass. Welk himself, though he lived in Santa Monica, kept a mobile home in the "Champagne Village" trailer park (part of Lawrence Welk Village) and would frequently visit to mix with the guests, taking out his accordion and playing for them.

I admire Lawrence Welk. Not because he became rich. That was just a by-product. I admire him because he knew what he liked. And he knew that his audience liked what he liked. Nothing else mattered. He didn't allow shifting trends or nervous executives to interfere with the bond he'd developed with all those millions of "nice people."

That toughness, that conviction, is usually associated with young rebels, not aging polka-playing squares. But Lawrence Welk was kind of a bad-ass. His traditionalism was in its own way subversive.

As for the music itself, I've come around to it. (At this point you shouldn't be surprised that I'm the audience for a Stephen Foster medley.) Maybe it's because I've hit fifty. But now I understand why Momma liked it. It's pleasant, as Fred Armisen said. And pleasant can be very nice indeed.

. . . and Other Victims of the "Rural Purge"

CBS HAD LONG BEEN KNOWN *as the Tiffany Network for its high-quality programming. But by 1971 it had so many sitcoms featuring rural characters, it had been nicknamed "the Hillbilly Network." A young, hard-charging executive named Fred Silverman sought to change that. In search of a younger, more upscale audience, he persuaded the network to "whack the hell out of that schedule." Of the subsequent purge, Pat Buttram—known to posterity as Mr. Haney on* Green Acres—*remarked, "CBS canceled everything with a tree, including* Lassie." *A few representative victims:*

The Beverly Hillbillies (1962–1971)
As fans of this show's theme song know, Jed Clampett struck it rich when, back in the Ozarks, he was shooting at some food and up through the ground came a-bubblin' crude—oil, that is. And so he moved his whole family to Beverly—Hills, that is. But there's no way the Clampetts were as rich as Paul Henning, the creator of *The Beverly Hillbillies*, one of the most successful sitcoms of all time. Viewership reached upwards of 57 million during its nine seasons. (Consider that the *finale* of *The Big Bang Theory* had 23 million viewers.) The series inspired "country cousin" sitcoms *Petticoat Junction* (also created by Henning) and *Green Acres*, both of which took place in the fictional town of Hooterville. As ratings softened, crossover episodes became more frequent, reaching peak country with the Thanksgiving 1968 episode of *The Beverly Hillbillies*, which featured characters from the other two shows. But after falling out of the top thirty, the series bought the farm.

The Ed Sullivan Show (1948–1971)
First, let's clear something up: Mr. Ed Sullivan was the variety show host. Mr. Ed was the talking horse. Both were TV stars in the early 1960s, and though they looked similar, there's no evidence they were related. Sullivan's show was one of the longest-running casualties of the purge, having debuted in 1948. He had tried to preserve American decency by refusing to allow Elvis on his show in 1956, but gave in after rival Steve Allen—no fan of rock

and roll himself—hosted the King and demolished Sullivan in the ratings. (The King, forced to wear a tuxedo and croon "Hound Dog" to an actual basset hound, regretted performing on Allen's show.) By 1964 Sullivan had learned his lesson and featured the Beatles for three consecutive weeks, drawing 73 million viewers. But whatever street cred he had built up with the youth was long gone by 1971.

The Andy Griffith Show (1960–1968)

The original beloved *Andy Griffith Show* ended in 1968, when Griffith decided to leave Mayberry in search of greener pastures. (So I guess he, um, purged himself?) His CBS comeback vehicle was a misbegotten dramedy called *Headmaster*, starring Griffith as the head of a tony Southern California prep school. The series took on story lines including teen drug use, miniskirts, and romantic relationships between teachers and students. It lasted only fourteen episodes, getting its lunch eaten by *The Partridge Family*. CBS pulled the plug in favor of *The New Andy Griffith Show*, with Andy as the mayor of Greenwood, North Carolina. But that show fared even worse, lasting only ten episodes before giving way to reruns of *Headmaster*.

Bonanza (1959–1973) and *Gunsmoke* (1955–1975) The Rural Purge

was also the last stand for the TV western. In the 1958–59 season, seven of the top ten highest-rated shows were westerns, including the top four: *Gunsmoke, Wagon Train, Have Gun—Will Travel,* and *The Rifleman.* Put some kind of gun in your title, and Americans tuned in. The Emmys even created a special award for the genre. TV critic Brandon Nowalk points out that TV westerns gave a start to creative talent like *Star Trek* creator Gene Roddenberry. But by the seventies, it was time for the genre to be moseying along. *Bonanza* held on until 1973. *Gunsmoke* had looked like a goner back in 1967 when it fell out of the top thirty. But CBS chairman William Paley's wife, Babe, rode in to save the day (it was her favorite show) and it was the more highly rated *Gilligan's Island* that was sunk. After twenty seasons and 635 episodes of *Gunsmoke* there was hardly another significant western on TV until HBO's *Deadwood* in 2004.

A final word: These shows did not die in vain. They made way for sophisticated groundbreaking comedies like *The Mary Tyler Moore Show* and Norman Lear's *All in the Family* and *Maude.* In other words, *Green Acres* died so that *Good Times* could live. We thank the Rural Comedies for their service.

DEATH OF
AN ICON

AUDREY HEPBURN
{1929–1993}

It was my first job after I arrived in New York as a wide-eyed twenty-three-year-old in 1992. Macy's department store . . . and I mean *the* Macy's, the flagship store, on Thirty-Fourth Street in New York, in Herald Square. I worked behind the counter as a ladies' fragrance specialist for Chanel. I was not, mind you, a spritzer. Spritzers are the male models *in front* of the counter, the bait I'd cast out to lure customers so that once I'd reeled them in I could dazzle them with my knowledge of the product line. I still remember the pitch lines I came up with for each fragrance:

Chanel N°19 if you were a businesswoman who was equal parts "business" and "woman." Chanel N°22 if you wanted to smell like the Queen Mother. (I was a huge Queen Mother fan.) Cristalle if you wanted to smell like a sporty society girl who didn't break a sweat on the tennis court. Coco if you were a divorcée looking to get her groove back. And of course the classic Chanel N°5 if you wanted to smell like your high school French teacher. (To more than a few male customers, I had to explain that *eau de toilette* is not actually toilet water.)

One of the perks of the job was that occasionally celebrities would walk through. My former colleague Raymond Ramirez—who is still at Macy's—still gets excited about the times he got to see Cher and Lena Horne. Our old boss Javan Bunch remembers when Elizabeth Taylor came through. But for me, the one truly magical moment took place in April 1992, during the annual flower show. That day I came face-to-face with bona fide old-time Hollywood stardom. Well, sort of face-to-face.

I was right behind the counter when Audrey Hepburn walked by. Actually, that's wrong. She floated by. I'm not just talking about her impossibly perfect posture, which indeed made it seem like she was being pulled by a string from above.

It was more than that. I've met a lot of stars and most of them, frankly, kind of disappoint. She didn't. More than gracefulness, she exuded grace.

My old Macy's colleagues remember that day, too. How could they not? There was a buzz of excitement. Yet at the same time, when Audrey Hepburn floated through, the whole floor became very quiet, as though the world itself momentarily came to a stop. Even if selfies and smartphones had existed then, you never would have tried to do something like wrap your arm around her and shove your hand in front of her face. That would've been unthinkable.

Now, before I get too deep into her story, I should make something clear. While of course there was only one Audrey Hepburn, there was, however, another very famous "Hepburn"—Katharine. So for all my younger readers—and by "younger" I mean anyone who hears the phrase "old movies" and thinks the first Star Wars movie—let's take a moment to disambiguate: Audrey Hepburn is NOT Katharine Hepburn.

Some basic facts:

Are they related? NO. They are not sisters. They are not even third cousins.

Who was older? Katharine, by twenty-two years.

Which one wore the pants? Well, they both did. And quite well, I should add.

Which one had the very distinctive speech pattern? Again, they both did. Katharine's accent is called mid-Atlantic, not because that's how people from Delaware talk, but because it's a mash-up of British and American pronunciations. It was standard for Hollywood stars of the 1940s to adopt it. Audrey's accent, however, is harder to place. I guess it was a British/Dutch/American blend, reflecting the different countries she lived in. Wherever it comes from, though, it was unique, just like the woman herself. (I believe it was the great drag performer Charles Busch who said that the way to approximate an Audrey Hepburn accent when saying someone's name is to flip the beginning consonant sounds for the first and last names. So "Cary Grant" becomes "Gary Crant." Try it!)

No one else sounded like her. No one was like her at all, which explains why more than a quarter century after her passing—yes, it's been that long—the image of her in a black dress and sunglasses, having breakfast outside Tiffany's, is as identifiable as Marilyn Monroe standing above a subway grate or James Dean in his red jacket. But while those stars are iconic and somehow larger than life, our attachment to Audrey feels different . . . more intimate.

Her son Sean Ferrer thinks he understands why. As he said to me, "Audrey Hepburn is not the movie star from Hollywood. Audrey Hepburn is the young girl from across the landing who puts on a little black dress and goes out into the world. . . . She represents us, not them. And we're rooting for her." We *do* root for her. Whether she's the chauffeur's daughter who dazzles the industry tycoon and his brother in *Sabrina*, or Eliza Doolittle in *My Fair Lady*, or, my personal favorite, the bohemian bookworm turned fashion model in *Funny Face*, she somehow manages to be both aspirational and totally accessible—someone we feel we understand, and who understands us.

It's typical that her character in *Funny Face*, Jo Stockton, can't see her own beauty. She thinks her face is funny. But while Hepburn wasn't a bombshell like Marilyn Monroe or Elizabeth Taylor, the face that seemed funny to Jo Stockton was considered an ideal to many. The late, great writer-director Nora Ephron—the creative force behind movies such as *When Harry Met Sally* and *Sleepless in Seattle*—recalled to me once how she always wished she looked like Audrey. She told me a terrific story. When Nora was sixteen she visited Edith Head, the great costume designer of Hollywood's Golden Age. As Nora remembered it:

> *Edith Head then took me to see her famous dressing room, which had thirty-six panels of mirror, one for every ten degrees. It was a completely circular room. And she said that there was only one person who could stand in that room and look good in all thirty-six mirrors, and it was Audrey Hepburn.*

The perfection that Edith Head saw in Hepburn wasn't simply a physical feature. It was a kind of aura that she exuded.

If you ever watched Johnny Carson, you know that he was positively unflappable. Nothing could ever throw him off his stride. Audrey appeared on *The Tonight Show* in 1976 and it's kind of wild watching Carson and his sidekick Ed McMahon reduced to anxious schoolboys as they get ready to welcome her on the show. Johnny confesses to Ed that he feels "a little nervous," and Ed understands. He tries to explain it. "She's kind of . . . very, very . . . special," he says, and finally describes her as "delicate." Her son Sean Ferrer said that he "never saw anyone misbehave in front of her." It's like she was a kind of royalty. But although she exuded a kind of vulnerability, Ferrer points out that anyone who knew what Hepburn lived through could never consider her truly delicate.

And Audrey Hepburn lived through a lot. In fact, I think that may be the reason she pulled off all those Cinderella roles so beautifully. Her own early life was something of a fairy tale . . . and I don't mean the Disney kind. I'm talking Grimm. She told CBS back in 1991 that despite appearances, she had never led a life of glamour. She grew up in war-ravaged Europe, surrounded by suffering, and was profoundly shaped by a childhood that saw hunger, cruelty, and death.

She was born in Brussels, Belgium, on May 4, 1929. Her father was an English banker and her mother a Dutch aristocrat. She spent some of her youth in the United Kingdom, where she trained as a dancer, and where her parents were supporters of the British Union of Fascists, a pro-Hitler political party. Her father abandoned the family in 1935, and in 1939 Audrey moved with her mother to neutral Holland. (Audrey's father, who remained in England, would spend the war years in a British detention camp.) In 1940 came the Nazi blitzkrieg, in which the German military completely swamped the underprepared forces of nation after nation. Holland came under German occupation.

In spite of her mother's earlier political sympathies, the horrors of the Nazis soon became apparent to Audrey. The German invaders executed a favorite uncle, ostensibly for participation in a resistance plot. Her half-brother Ian was sent to a German labor camp. A young teenager, Audrey did what she could to help the resistance, raising funds through secret dance performances.

The war was a lasting trauma for her. Her hometown of Arnhem became a battlefield. Hepburn talked about her wartime experience during her American television debut in 1951 on a show called *We the People*. She was just twenty-two years old, new to Broadway, and starring in a play called *Gigi*, the precursor to the musical and movie. On camera, Hepburn's evident excitement and her budding stardom quickly modulate into poignancy as she begins to reexperience what happened to her during the war. (The format of the show apparently called for interviewees to reenact moments from their lives. It makes for a strange and, in this case, affecting viewing experience.) Hepburn recalls her Christmas from seven years earlier, in Arnhem, after her uncle had been executed. The Nazis had blocked the food supply and her family was living on the edge of starvation during what became known as the Dutch Famine: "It was the morning of December twenty-fourth, when, finally, my aunt told us there wasn't a scrap of food left in the house. Well, I'd heard one could sleep and forget hunger. Perhaps I could sleep all through Christmas. I'd try."

But then comes a Christmas miracle—the resistance sends a delivery, ten potatoes, which Hepburn recalls as "the most wonderful and most beautiful thing I ever saw."

Audrey's son Luca Dotti described this period of his mother's life as "a long torture." Dotti is Hepburn's son from her second marriage, to Italian psychiatrist Andrea Dotti. He lives in Rome now, and heads the Audrey Hepburn Children's Fund. Dotti told me that during the war, Audrey and her family were so desperate for food, they had to make flour out of tulip bulbs. By the time Holland was liberated, she weighed only eighty-eight pounds. That trauma and stress affected her for the rest of her life. As a result, Dotti said, "All her life was a search for stability." A solid home life became crucially important to her; she enjoyed cooking, and, despite her svelte appearance, enjoyed eating, too—particularly chocolate, which she associated with the Allied liberation of Holland.

By the end of the war, Dotti said, his mother was "a survivor." And as a survivor, he said, "you always have this duality. You are happy to be alive but you have this sense of guilt because the person next door didn't make it." (Don't forget his father was a psychiatrist.) And for Hepburn, one of those people who "didn't make it," while not a literal next-door neighbor, was another Dutch girl. Audrey Hepburn felt a special connection to someone you wouldn't necessarily expect—Anne Frank.

As she told CBS's Kathleen Sullivan in 1989, "We both lived through the same war. Exactly the same age—I was born the same year Anne Frank was born." She even read Frank's famous diary in Dutch, in galleys, before it had been published:

And it was one of the most devastating experiences I've ever had. Because more than just reading a book, it was like having the whole war played back to me. She, obviously, was locked up, inside. I was outside . . . and here was somebody . . . who had been able to put on paper everything I'd felt during those years. And it destroyed me, I must say. And it has stayed an extremely emotional experience for me.

As Hepburn understood, she was free, while Frank had been imprisoned; she lived, while Frank perished. Yet Hepburn had lived under the Nazi occupation and with her own eyes seen Dutch Jews being taking off to the camps. As Dotti told me, she imagined herself as a kind of soul sister to Anne Frank.

After the war, Otto Frank, Anne's father, actually wanted Hepburn to play his daughter on-screen. He visited her home in Switzerland to try to persuade her. But she said no to the role. Sean Ferrer said that "it was much too close to what she lived through," that the memories and experiences—and perhaps the survivor's guilt— that she would re-experience terrified her.

Both of Hepburn's sons talked to me about the lifelong impact of the war on their mother. She resolved, they said, never to complain about hardships, since nothing could compare to the horror of the war. And in her late fifties she became a goodwill ambassador for UNICEF, motivated in part by gratitude to the organization that once fed her. Yes, long before Angelina, there was Audrey, traveling the globe, in the 1980s and '90s, raising awareness about the world's poorest, actively lobbying governments to help children in need. While she appeared in a few films here and there, it was her charitable work that defined her later years. She never forgot the relief that came at the end of the war.

She told CBS's Harry Smith in 1991 that she had confidence that the springs of human compassion would never run dry: "Giving is like living. I mean if you stop wanting to give, I think there's nothing more to live for." Coming from almost anyone else, this would seem hopelessly clichéd. But not from Audrey.

The darkness of Hepburn's wartime experience may seem like the polar opposite of the light she emits on-screen. And yet . . . I can't help but wonder if this combination of yearning and gratitude is what still draws us to her today. Those experiences really seem to show up on-screen. It's worth rewatching the movies in light of all that Hepburn went through during the war years. I'm pretty sure I can see her story in those performances—as the wounded Holly Golightly looking for a better life, or as Princess Ann, who feels the genuine joy of freedom on her Roman holiday. It's no coincidence that in the screen test that launched her—and you can watch it yourself on YouTube—she's talking about the war. And then—I wasn't about to leave this out—there's her performance in the 1967 film *Wait Until Dark*. Hepburn plays a blind woman who is terrorized inside her home. Co-star Alan Arkin plays her tormentor and supposedly hated doing the tormenting. I mean, who wants to be mean to Audrey Hepburn? The scenes were intense. Audrey, quite possibly channeling her wartime experience, endures the struggle and survives.

Listen—there were plenty of other talented actresses in the 1950s and '60s, and they were beautiful, too. Some of them were supposed to be the "next" Audrey Hepburn: Millie Perkins, Maggie McNamara, Susan Strasberg. But they hadn't lived through what Audrey lived through. Peter Bogdanovich, who directed Hepburn, summed it up perfectly when he called her an "iron butterfly."

There's one group of fans that seems to understand this rare combination of exquisite delicacy and steely strength—the Japanese. How do I know this? Just before my stint working at Macy's I was living in Japan, where I studied Kabuki. Yes, really. I taught English on the side because it was the early 1990s, I had no other income, and a cup of coffee in Tokyo cost about twelve dollars. One of my students, a very nice woman named Ritsuko, asked me out to a movie. It may have been a date; I still don't know. We ended up going to an Audrey Hepburn film festival, where we saw *How to Steal a Million*, co-starring Peter O'Toole. A life-sized cardboard cutout of Audrey greeted us at the festival entrance. Fans posed for pictures next to it.

Now, I've talked about the personal attachment a lot of fans have for her. Well, in Japan the Audrey-love is deep. There's a famous all-female theater troupe called Takarazuka. They staged a musical version of *Roman Holiday*. Hepburn was even ranked above Gandhi in a Japanese poll on the most well-liked historical figures.

Luca Dotti told me it was through Japanese fan mail and small tokens like origami that he first began to grasp the scope of his mother's fame. During his childhood in Rome, he would watch Japanese tourists trying to follow in his mother's film-star footsteps. They would come to Rome to reenact every scene from *Roman Holiday*, down to the Vespa rides and the ice cream and tossing coins into the Trevi Fountain.

In case you haven't seen *Roman Holiday*, it's the movie that won her an Oscar. She plays Princess Ann, who's visiting Rome on a royal tour and ends up playing hooky for the day. While pretending to be a commoner, she falls in love with an American journalist, played by Gregory Peck. When the Japanese saw *Roman Holiday* it was love at first sight. That was 1953. The war was still a recent memory and American culture was really just starting to take root in Japan.

The Japanese connection to the film may have something to do with the importance of duty. You see, SPOILER ALERT, Princess Ann tearfully leaves her true love to return to her royal world. Not a Hollywood ending. But for the Japanese, this ending made sense.

There was something else about Hepburn that appealed to her Japanese fans: her cuteness. Apparently the Japanese found Hepburn's pixie haircut cuter than Hello

Kitty. Hepburn talked about it in a Dutch TV interview in 1988. In Japan, in the fifties, Hepburn said, "all girls had very long hair and it was all part of the tradition. And they all cut off their hair and I was held responsible." Taki Katoh, a former show business coordinator in Japan, confirms this is the case. She worked with Hepburn back in the seventies. At the time, Hepburn had, in a surprise move, left Hollywood, when she was still very much in demand, to live abroad and focus on motherhood. But in 1971, when she felt it was time to get back in front of the camera, it was Taki who helped her get work—for Japanese commercials. It's that *Lost in Translation* thing where Americans appeared in ads that were never broadcast in the United States. (I remember when I first arrived at Narita Airport outside Tokyo back in 1991 seeing a giant billboard of Jodie Foster lying seductively across the hood of a car.) Audrey caused a great sensation doing Japanese TV commercials for high-end wigs.

But it wasn't until 1983 that Audrey Hepburn actually went to Japan. The occasion: a fashion show for her designer and dear friend Hubert de Givenchy. When Hepburn landed in Tokyo, it was like Princess Ann from *Roman Holiday* herself had finally arrived.

Hepburn was naturally exhausted after a very long flight and she worried she might disappoint fans who were accustomed to seeing her as a young woman onscreen. At the time, she told Taki that she was worried, saying, "If the Japanese fans look at me in that tired face, they may not like me anymore." Taki recalls how she reassured her friend the movie star that Japanese fans would always love her.

Taki and Audrey remained friends for years. Taki has a file of letters from Audrey, in which the actress expresses her feelings for Japan, speculating a little playfully that in a past life she might have been Japanese.

When I caught a glimpse of Audrey Hepburn in Macy's back in 1992, I had no way of knowing how little time she had left. In November of that year she underwent surgery for cancer of the appendix. She died on January 20, 1993. You would have thought it would have been front-page news. Front page, even above the fold. (Yes, I still think in newspaper terms.)

But someone else was front and center that day. It was the first inauguration of President William Jefferson Clinton. Yup, Bill Clinton kinda stole her spotlight.

When I interviewed President Clinton recently, I asked him if he was aware that Audrey Hepburn died on the day he was sworn in to office. He had no idea. "It was a fairly busy time," he said. But he remembered her with the affection that so many of his generation felt for her, running through his favorite moments from *Roman Holiday*, *Funny Face*, *Breakfast at Tiffany's*, and *Sabrina*.

At the same time that President Clinton was busy with the inauguration, my friend Caryn James was writing Hepburn's obituary for the *New York Times*. The obit is very well done. It talks, naturally, about Audrey's elegance and grace, her Oscar for *Roman Holiday*, the "string of films" in which she played "the lithe young thing with stars in her eyes and the ability to make Cinderella transformations." All true. Yet there's a whole other story behind this obituary.

Caryn was in the newsroom the day of the inauguration. As she told me, it was about 5 p.m. as the editors were deciding which articles should go on the front page. Suddenly the editor of the culture section rushed over to her, saying, "Thank goodness you're here. Katharine Hepburn is dead and we have a ten-year-old obituary. Can you rewrite it?" Alas, someone had failed to disambiguate.

At any rate, Caryn says, the editors started "tearing apart page one, because they thought Katharine Hepburn was dead." Well, as they set about verifying the news, someone at the news desk mentioned that the information had come from the United Nations. The UN, as in UNICEF, where Audrey Hepburn had been a goodwill ambassador. At that point, said Caryn, "it was like one of those cartoon moments where you saw the lightbulbs go on over everyone's head." It was Audrey who had died, not Katharine.

Caryn, working on short notice, wrote Audrey's obituary, not Katharine's, and since Audrey was only sixty-three (not eighty-five), she was starting from scratch. To review her career is to be struck by how brief her heyday was—her major films were all made between 1953 and 1967. Caryn thinks that part of the reason for this is that Audrey never needed to act in the way that other performers do: "She had a family. She had her UN work. She really didn't feel as driven to do things that she wasn't really passionately interested in doing."

I can remember as a kid how special it felt to watch the Oscars. (The first one I was allowed to stay up for, I watched on the little black-and-white TV in my parents' bedroom. They were dozing off so I kept the volume low and crouched close to the set.) In those days, the broadcast had a magic that it just doesn't have anymore. It was an event when Audrey Hepburn would show up and float across the stage to deliver, say, the best costume award. Because she wasn't on-screen 24/7, or all over the internet, or on a reality show, when she did appear it truly was a special moment. (Actually she *is* all over Instagram, a real tribute to her staying power.)

Maybe it's weird to feel nostalgic for a time you didn't live through. I wasn't around during Audrey Hepburn's prime. But one day not too long ago, I was feeling especially reflective and so I tweeted—because what's the point of thoughtful introspection if you don't share it with hundreds of thousands of followers? I went ahead and tweeted: "How did we drift so far from Audrey Hepburn? Can we ever get back?" I got quite the response. One person answered "No way. There is no comparison." Another wrote: "She was not of this world."

There's a yearning for her, or for what she represents. Not delicacy—that's really not the word that captures her—but *grace*, in not just manner and bearing but in spirit. There's a reason she's still very much with us. On days when the news is particularly dreary, and people are being especially awful, and I'm flipping through the channels and I land on an Audrey Hepburn movie, I can't help but wonder: "How did we drift so far from Audrey Hepburn? Can we ever get back?" One can only hope.

SO YOU'RE AT A PARTY *and someone mentions Eugene McCarthy and you think, "Wait, was he the beloved ventriloquist dummy of the 1940s or the Republican senator from Wisconsin who set off the Red Scare in the 1950s?" Neither. He was the liberal Minnesota senator of the 1960s who scared LBJ off from running for reelection.*

George Gobel or Joseph Goebbels: Which one was on Hollywood Squares? *(Gobel)*

Elsa Maxwell or Elsa Lanchester: Which one was the Bride of Frankenstein? (Lanchester)

John Paul Jones: Was he the father of the American Navy or the bassist for Led Zeppelin? (Both. Two different men. Same name.)

Now that I've cleared up any potential confusion surrounding Audrey Hepburn and Katharine Hepburn, here are some other pairs that might otherwise have you running to the bathroom to search your phone for answers.

Davy Crockett & Daniel Boone
The confusion stems from actor Fess Parker, who donned buckskins and a coonskin hat to play both men on TV. But it was Davy, a Tennessee frontiersman who died at the Alamo, who wore the hat. Pioneer Daniel was born much earlier, helped settle the future state of Kentucky, and was celebrated in Lord Byron's epic poem *Don Juan.* It's not clear what he wore on his head.

Molly Pitcher & Molly Hatchet
Molly Pitcher was a legendary figure who brought aid to American soldiers in the Revolutionary War. (You remember her from the New Jersey Turnpike.) Molly Hatchet was a legendary band that brought comfort to insecure adolescent boys with mullets.

Andrew Johnson, Andrew Jackson & Stonewall Jackson
Both Jacksons were generals; both Andrews were president. Andrew Jackson is on the $20; Stonewall was on the Confederate $500. None of them was really great on civil rights.

Attila the Hun & Genghis Khan
Many confuse these two Asia-based warlord/emperors. Attila was way back in the fifth century and farther west. Think "*Hun*gary," which was named for Attila's people. Thirteenth-century Genghis is considered the founding father of Mongolia. Both were known for their wrath, neither for being a hon.

Hubert Humphrey, Herbert Hoover & J. Edgar Hoover
Herbert was a president, Hubert was a vice president, and J. Edgar had a lot of vices. Herbert helped J. Edgar get his job as director of the FBI, even though they weren't related. In death all three lay in state in the US Capitol; J. Edgar Hoover was the only civil servant in history afforded that honor.

Dom DeLuise & Paul Prudhomme
Two jolly men, alike in size, shape, disposition, facial hair, and a predilection for berets. Prudhomme's the TV chef on spice bottles. DeLuise is the one in a bunch of Mel Brooks movies and palled around with Burt Reynolds. That Dom also wrote two successful cookbooks only makes this more confusing.

Alan Hale & Nathan Hale
Although both men were famous for dangling from ropes, Alan "the Skipper" Hale's hammock on *Gilligan's Island* was considerably more comfortable than Nathan Hale's hangman's noose, from which he swung during the Revolutionary War. Nathan coulda used a "little buddy" that day.

Joan of Arc & Joan Van Ark
Joan of Arc was a prominent figure in the Hundred Years' War, while Joan Van Ark (still alive!) was a prominent figure during thirteen seasons of the 1980s prime-time soap opera *Knots Landing*. In her role leading the French army during the Siege of Orleans, Joan of Arc saw a lot of action. In her role as Valene Ewing (who plowed through five marriages), Van Ark also saw a lot of action.

Torquemada & Savonarola & Casanova

Torquemada and Savonarola were both Dominican friars with a repressive streak, but Savonarola staged bonfires of the vanities (objects that might tempt one to sin) while Torquemada staged bonfires of actual *people* during the Spanish Inquisition. Both would've gladly burned the great lover Casanova, who had more fun than the other two combined.

Norman Fell & Norman Conquest

TV's "Mr. Roper" had nothing to do with William the Conqueror's invasion of England in 1066. But *Three's Company* was based on the English series *Man About the House*. So both Norman and William benefited hugely from grabbing some British property.

Gore Vidal & Vidal Sassoon

Gore was the prose stylist; Sassoon was the hairstylist. Both died in 2012, and neither had anything to do with Sasson designer jeans. (Fun fact: It was while watching Vidal Sassoon's short-lived daytime show in 1980 that I learned the word *pizzazz*.)

Alvin Ailey & Beetle Bailey

Ailey is the giant of modern dance whose eponymous company is known as the "Cultural Ambassador to the World." Beetle is a cartoon GI created by Mort Walker. So . . . not very similar. But both *Beetle Bailey* and the Alvin Ailey American Dance Theater continue to thrive long after their creators' demise.

Nostradamus & Nosferatu

Although both hail from Europe somewhere around 1500, these two had wildly divergent careers. Nostradamus was a real-life French astrologer and seer who made cryptic predictions, while Nosferatu—a synonym for *vampire* and the title of the classic 1922 horror film—famously emerged from crypts.

The Aviatrix

BESSIE COLEMAN
{1892–1926}

alled "Brave Bessie," "Queen Bess," and "The Only Race Aviatrix in the World," Bessie Coleman was the first African American woman *and* the first Native American woman to hold a pilot's license. In the early 1920s, she was known for performing dangerous stunts—"death-defying" was the favored epithet—that thrilled thousands. According to Matt Anderson, curator of transportation at the Henry Ford Museum, she "may be the single most inspirational pilot from aviation's first decades," a woman who "overcame prejudices against her race *and* her sex." Sadly, like many who took up this exciting but perilous profession, Bessie Coleman died in an aviation accident—though not before soaring to her place in history.

Born in East Texas in 1892, Bessie was one of thirteen children of a Native American sharecropper and an African American maid. As a young woman, she studied briefly at the Colored Agricultural and Normal University in Langston, Oklahoma, but lacked the money to complete her degree, and in 1912 moved to Chicago to live with some older brothers. (A "normal" school was one that trained graduates to become teachers.)

The airplane at this time was fairly new. (It was only in 1903 that the Wright Brothers had made the first powered flight of a heavier-than-air machine in Kitty Hawk, North Carolina.) Yet flying had already taken hold of the popular imagination, and a slew of aerial adventurers were following Orville and Wilbur in taking to the skies. By 1909, the city of Reims, France, was hosting an international air "meet," drawing nearly half a million spectators to watch pilots race each other and perform tricks. Los Angeles followed in January 1910, with the first American air show. As these shows began to catch on, stunt pilots became star performers.

When World War I broke out in 1914, planes began to be used for military purposes—first reconnaissance, then bombing, and eventually to take out the enemy's aircraft, using biplanes equipped with mounted machine guns. Flying aces—those who shot down five or more enemy aircraft in dogfights—became national heroes. (Quick digression: You may remember that Snoopy used to daydream that he was a Flying Ace. In his leather helmet, scarf, and goggles, his doghouse became his biplane, a Sopwith Camel, and he'd ascend into the bright blue sky battling Germany's Manfred von Richthofen, aka "the Red Baron," arguably the greatest fighter pilot of all time. Whenever the Red Baron would get the better of Snoopy, he'd shake a fist and yell, "Curse you, Red Baron!" Fortunately, Snoopy always survived to fight another day. The real von Richthofen—whose nickname indeed was "Red Baron"—wasn't so lucky. After eighty victories, he was shot down over France in 1918.)

Bessie Coleman was captivated by the exploits of the military pilots of the First World War. Like so many Americans, she had seen newsreel footage of World War I pilots and admired their abilities. Her older brother John had fought in the war and used to tease his sister by telling her that in

France aspiring female pilots were admitted to flight schools. (A French-woman named Raymonde de Laroche had been the first woman in the world licensed to fly in 1909.) Coleman also knew of the story of Harriet Quimby (nicknamed "the Dresden China Aviatrix" because of her fair skin), an American who became the first woman pilot to cross the English Channel solo. Quimby dazzled crowds flying in her purple satin flying suit—but was killed in a 1911 flying accident. There were other pioneering female pilots: in 1915 American Katherine Stinson, dubbed "the Flying Schoolgirl" for her youthful appearance, became the first woman to fly in Asia. And the very colorful Elinor Smith ("the Flying Flapper of Freeport") became at sixteen the youngest licensed pilot in America. In 1928, Smith stunned New York City by flying underneath four of the city's East River bridges. (If I had been a pioneering stunt pilot, I might have called myself "the Witty Wingman of the West Village." You got something better? Tweet me your suggestions.)

The thrill of flying appealed to Coleman more than the risk of dying scared her, and she applied to flight schools in the United States. But, as both a woman and a person of color, she faced open discrimination, and no American school would accept her. Yet she was undeterred. Instead of giving up, she just changed plans. With the backing of Robert S. Abbott, a wealthy African American Chicagoan and publisher of the *Chicago Defender*, a prominent black newspaper, she applied to French flight schools. Just to write the application she had to learn French, so she did. She was accepted, and she trained in France from 1921 to 1922, learning to do loop-de-loops and other tricks, and earning a license from the Fédération Aéronautique Internationale. (Amelia Earhart didn't earn her license till 1923, the sixteenth woman to do so.)

By this time, flying had become a major entertainment in the United States and Europe. When the war had ended in 1918, there was suddenly an abundance of trained pilots looking for ways to make a living, and also an abundance of unused Curtis JN-4 "Jenny" biplanes. So pilots undertook "barnstorming" tours across America, moving from farm to farm, where people would gather from miles around to watch them perform. They performed dangerous stunts that included spins, dives, loops, barrel rolls, wing-walking, parachuting, even midair plane transfers. Their "flying circuses" dazzled the crowds, and the way they courted death evoked a morbid fascination. Often they gave passengers rides as part of the festivities. Charles Lindbergh worked as a barnstormer for a while. There was even an all-black flying circus that called itself "the Five Blackbirds."

When Coleman came back to the United States with her license, the decision to become a barnstorming stunt pilot was easy. Her ultimate goal was to open a flight school that would serve African Americans. Stunt-flying was the most logical way to raise funds for the school. With Abbott's support, and the publicity provided by his newspaper, she began giving air shows.

It was a dangerous business. In 1924, she broke her left leg and some ribs in a plane crash. Yet she began touring again as soon as she was healthy. And when she wasn't giving exhibitions, she was giving talks about aviation and her experiences.

Coleman was steadfast in associating her flying with her efforts to achieve equal rights. Explaining her decision to pursue aviation, she said, "I knew we had no aviators, neither men nor women, and I knew the race needed to be represented along this most important line, so I thought it my duty to risk my life to learn aviation and to encourage flying among men and women of our race." While in flight school back in France, she even attended the Second Pan-African Congress in Paris, an early effort to redress the effects of European colonialism and promote racial equality, organized by the great African American writer and activist W. E. B. Du Bois.

Her first domestic air show, held on Labor Day, 1922, was dedicated to the African American Fifteenth Infantry Regiment, which fought in World War I. She rejected a film project that would have provided publicity because she thought it promulgated degrading stereotypes. One time, in 1925, she agreed to an air show in Waxahachie, Texas, where she had lived as a girl. But when the organizers decided on separate entrances to the stadium for black and white spectators, Coleman refused to fly. Eventually the organizers capitulated on the segregated entrances, although Coleman could not get them to allow integrated seating. Throughout her career she saw her exhibitions and talks as a way of promoting aviation among African Americans and fighting stereotypes about her people's limitations.

On April 30, 1926, Coleman was in Florida, rehearsing for a show she had agreed to do for the Jacksonville Negro Welfare League. She was speeding through the skies at 110 miles per hour, about 3,500 feet up. She was supposed to nosedive, plummeting earthward in a way that would thrill the crowd. But instead of leveling off, the plane turned over—later it was discovered that there was, literally, a wrench in the engine. Coleman, who was wearing neither seat belt nor parachute, fell from the open plane to her death. Her mechanic, William D. Wills, died in the crash as well.

Coleman's body was conveyed to Chicago in a coffin draped with an American flag, and accompanied by veterans of the Eighth Infantry, the all-black regiment. Ida B. Wells-Barnett, the pioneering journalist and co-founder of the NAACP, presided at the funeral in Chicago's Pilgrim Baptist Church, where more than five thousand people assembled to pay their respects. For years, aviators would drop flowers on her gravesite. In 1929, black pilots founded the Bessie Coleman Aero Club in Los Angeles. Many African American pilots who followed Coleman were doubtless inspired by her credo: "The air is the only place free from prejudices."

DEATH OF A CAREER

VAUGHN MEADER
{1936–2004}

In the late fall of 1962, one of President John F. Kennedy's closest advisors, Arthur Schlesinger Jr., was driving in his car when all of a sudden he heard the following question come over the airwaves: "Now that you're in office, what do you think the chances for a Jewish president are?" The voice that answered was familiar to Schlesinger; in fact, its distinctive upper-class Boston accent was unmistakable: "Well, I think they're pretty good. Let me say, I don't see why a person of the Jewish faith can't be president of the United States." He paused, then said: "I know as a Catholic *I* could never vote for him, but other than that—" A burst of raucous laughter followed.

Schlesinger was bewildered at the president's flip response, but his confusion was soon cleared up when he learned the voice belonged not to his boss but to Kennedy impersonator Vaughn Meader. Yet Schlesinger was concerned enough that when he returned to the White House, he drafted a memorandum to the president that read: "This raises the question of what in hell a president of the United States ought to do about mimicry."

I'm guessing many of you have never heard of Vaughn Meader, but for one brief shining moment—okay, a twelve-month period between late 1962 and late 1963—he was a really big deal. He had a popular parody album called *The First Family*, a spoof of the Kennedys. In old video clips, he looks like a distant Kennedy cousin: young, clean-cut, with a thick head of hair. And his JFK impression is uncanny. To hear it, you'll have to listen to the podcast . . . unless you happen to have a copy of the album in an old collection of vinyl somewhere. And that's not so unlikely: in 1963, the album was not only number one on the charts, it was in its day the best-selling record of all time, music or comedy.

The parody was, for the most part, pretty gentle. To get the feel of it, you're going to have to imagine Meader doing Kennedy's voice; if you're under thirty, think of Mayor Quimby on *The Simpsons*. Mostly, the comedy worked by bringing the larger-than-life president down to scale, hearing him engaged in everyday activities. For example, in one bit he addresses a room of world leaders: "Under discussion today will be nuclear disarmament followed by the UN bond issue and a matter of the trade agreements. Now, first there is a most important matter to settle. Mr. de Gaulle: yours was the chicken salad and coffee. That's a dollar forty . . ."

In 1962 and '63, Meader was just about everywhere—radio, TV appearances, your family's living room as everyone gathered to listen to the LP. Then, all of a sudden, he wasn't. On November 22, 1963, President Kennedy was murdered while riding in a motorcade through Dallas, Texas. That horrible day ended the president's life and changed the life of the nation. That's what my high school history teacher Mr. Ochs taught us: there was America before the assassination . . . and America after.

The same is true of Vaughn Meader. Before the assassination, Meader was a household name. After, he was an entertainer without an act.

Abbott Vaughn Meader was born in 1936 in Waterville, Maine, and by all accounts had a harrowing childhood. His father drowned when he was one, and his young mother moved from Maine to Boston to work as a cocktail waitress. Meader had to shuttle between Maine and Massachusetts for much of his youth, spending some of that time in children's homes. He says he started entertaining people to avoid punishment when he got into trouble. Near the end of high school, his mother was institutionalized. Meader ran away to the army.

He ultimately was stationed in Germany, where he met the first of his four wives and played in a band. It would be entertainment, not military service, that turned his life around. After he was discharged, he did a risqué piano act around the New York City area and then moved on to Greenwich Village, where he honed a politically themed comedy routine. It was at this point that he dropped his first name, Abbott. He became Vaughn Meader.

Then one fateful night, during his performance, a voice came out of Meader. It was the president of the United States, John F. Kennedy. Meader got laughs. So he started to reserve the last ten minutes of his routine for an impression of Kennedy's live television press conferences. A typical exchange had the comedian interacting with straight men playing reporters who asked setup questions:

JFK: Yes, the gentleman over there.
REPORTER: Sir, when are we going to send a man to the moon?
JFK: Whenever Mr. Goldwater wants to go.

It was a winning formula.

At this point, Meader was still, for the most part, playing small clubs. Meanwhile, a disc jockey named Bob Booker, along with his partner Earle Doud, wanted to capitalize on America's fascination with its new president, as well as the surging popularity of comedy albums. The comedy album was a new phenomenon . . . even the musical LP had been in existence for only about a decade. At first comedians like Shelley Berman resisted the new medium. Why put all your best material on one record that cost only a few dollars? Why would anyone pay to come see you perform live when they could listen to a recording at home? But soon enough they saw what an album could mean for a comedian's career. In 1960, *The Buttoned-Down Mind of Bob Newhart* became the first comedy album to top the charts, outselling Elvis, Sinatra, and the Kingston Trio. When Newhart won Album of the Year at the Grammys, it was another first for comedy.

Booker and Doud had thought that an album about the president—who, with his youth and good looks, his beautiful wife, and adorable children, was a bona fide celebrity—would be a hit. As Booker said to me, "You've got this giant star. He's a movie star, he's a political star, he's a world star, my God, and such a good-looking man with this beautiful wife, right? We said if you take this character and the family and put them in everyday situations, that's funny."

This was the beginning of what would become the *First Family* album. The only problem was Booker and Doud had no idea who could play the head of this First Family—that is, until they turned on the TV the evening of July 3, 1962. On the air was an inexpensive CBS summer replacement show called *Talent Scouts*, featuring Meader doing his JFK on TV for the first time. Some of Meader's material was hit-and-miss, but, according to Booker, "When he did Kennedy it was perfect— absolutely perfect." The producers had found their man.

In addition to the uncanny nature of Meader's impersonation, there was something else striking about his *Talent Scouts* performance, a kind of disclaimer he made at the end of his star-making routine. It's the kind of statement I can't imagine any comic making today:

> *I'd like to make one final statement at this time. And I would like to make that final statement as myself, Vaughn Meader. And that is to say, thank you to the United States, a country where it is possible for a young comedian like myself to come out on television before millions of people and kid its leading citizen. Thank you. Good night.*

Before the performance aired, Meader wrote a telegram to the president himself. "Dear Mr. President," it read, "I respectfully call your attention to the 'Talent Scouts' show which we taped last night for viewing on CBS television Tuesday night, July 3rd at 10:00 p.m. I impersonated you but I did it with great affection and respect. Hope it meets with your approval. Respectfully, Vaughn Meader." This seems odd today, downright bizarre. (Can you imagine Alec Baldwin sending a note to President Trump asking if his cold opening on *Saturday Night Live* was acceptable?) Meader's material was hardly controversial by today's standards.

In 1962, however, not everyone was ready for entertainers to be mimicking a president. It took Booker and Doud about a dozen pitches before they found a label willing to produce the album. People told them it was an insult, even a piece of pro-communist propaganda. But Booker believed in his product, and eventually, he and Doud sold the record to a label called Cadence. To promote it, Booker gave the thirty-five-minute album to a DJ friend at WINS radio in New York, who heard a cut or two just before going on the air. He was laughing hard. According to Booker, the DJ went on and for three straight hours played *First Family* virtually without a break. Success was immediate and overwhelming. As Booker recalls, "Every light in the place lit up. I mean, it was crazy. The phone calls from the other stations were coming in. Television bookings for Vaughn all in three hours. Broke it wide open, one disc jockey."

The *First Family* album took off like a rocket and Vaughn Meader was in for the ride of his life.

While his act was going viral, Vaughn Meader was playing a gig in Detroit and didn't really grasp the scope of his success. He didn't fully believe the reports of the album's popularity until he returned to New York and heard his voice being broadcast as he walked down the street. Suddenly everyone in TV wanted Vaughn Meader to appear on their show, including beloved singer Andy Williams, who was hosting a popular new variety series on NBC. Meader, who had been earning $7.50 a night performing in small-time Village clubs, would soon command a $5,000 fee for New Year's Eve 1962.

I listened to *First Family* and I have to say—it's a total blast. It's not a hard-edged satire. It's parody, the kind of fun, zany takeoff that I used to love reading in *Mad* magazine when I was a kid. Like when they turned "CHiPS" into "CHiMPS" or "The Godfather" into "The Odd Father." That kind of thing. It's not really meant to make you think; it's meant to make you laugh. As the writer Vladimir Nabokov once said, "Satire is a lesson. Parody is a game." And who doesn't love a good game?

Okay, so some references may not play for today's audiences, like JFK playing *Monopoly* with Republican Senate minority leader Everett Dirksen. But a surprising amount of it really holds up, like gags about the First Lady's famous televised tour of the White House in 1962. On the comedy album, Jackie, played by Naomi Brossart, points out absurdities like "the Dolly Madison Pinochle Room" and "the Richard Nixon dumbwaiter." I squealed when she randomly started speaking French.

One of the biggest laughs comes when the president divvies up Caroline and John John's bath toys:

> *Nine of the PT boats, two of the Yogi Bear beach balls, the ball of Silly Putty belong to Caroline. Nine of the PT boats, one of the Yogi Bear beach balls, and the two Howdy Doody plastic bouncing clowns are baby John's. The rubber swan is mine.*

The "rubber swan" line became the big water-cooler moment—the one people kept repeating to each other.

Now, while jokes about the president getting attached to a bath toy seem very safe from today's vantage point, the very idea of imitating the president was, in 1962, pushing the limits of comedy. Jack Paar, the former host of *The Tonight Show*, was hosting his own prime-time show and admitted to having some misgivings about inviting Meader on, but eventually decided that some mild irreverence was okay. After all, as the famed anthropologist Margaret Mead told *Life* magazine about the album, "This making fun of people in authority is very healthy. It is the difference between democracy and tyranny. . . . When you have people who cannot laugh at people in power—then is when you're in trouble."

But others were not so sure. Presidential advisor Arthur Schlesinger, the one who was so concerned about that voice on the radio that he wrote a memo about the dangers of impersonating the president, feared that the public wouldn't know the difference between the real JFK and the fake. He compared Meader's act to Orson Welles's 1938 radio broadcast of *The War of the Worlds*, during which the fictional account of a Martian invasion raised a panic among many confused listeners.

Some in the president's circle tried to get the Federal Communications Commission to stop the album.

This wasn't a new anxiety. Years before, Franklin Roosevelt's press secretary Stephen Early had directly asked media outlets not to give airtime to Roosevelt impersonators. Yet JFK responded to the parody with his characteristic coolness and dry wit. "Actually I listened to Mr. Meader's record," he told reporters, adding, "but I thought it sounded more like Teddy than it did me." The press corps loved it. (Jackie was more thin-skinned; she found the impersonation mean-spirited and resented the fact that her kids were part of the sketches.)

Vaughn Meader went on to win a Grammy for Best Comedy Performance. *The First Family* won Album of the Year, beating out the likes of Tony Bennett and Ray Charles. The comedian had found his act, right?

Well, not exactly. Meader didn't want to do the same act over and over. While Booker and Doud were developing fresh material for a second volume of the *First Family* album, Meader announced to the men that he was tired of doing Kennedy. He'd begun his career as a musician. He wanted to sing, to play music, to branch out. But he was under contract to Booker and Doud, and the producing team wasn't about to let the prospect of a second hit album get away. Booker and Meader had a fight. Meader wanted out; Booker wouldn't let him go. Meader insisted he had other talents—and Booker told him he didn't. Without his Kennedy impression, Booker bluntly told him, Meader was nothing special. Meader recorded volume two and it was released in the spring of 1963. It sold fairly well but nowhere near the original album.

As Meader said in a 1998 interview, "Once I was in, I couldn't find the way out." But he kept looking.

On the morning of November 22, 1963, the Associated Press published a story by veteran Hollywood columnist Bob Thomas that started as follows: "It's always a bit surprising to find a new star in show business trying to run away from the thing that made him famous. Today's example is Vaughn Meader." Thomas then went on to write: "He also is searching for ways to destroy his image as a JFK imitator."

That afternoon the president was assassinated.

Meader learned of the news from a cabbie in Milwaukee. He'd just arrived for a live show. At first he thought the cabbie was joking, because just about everyone who recognized Meader made some kind of bad joke about JFK. But when the radio news report confirmed the terrible truth, he went to his hotel and, in his words, "got drunk, got the next plane out, went back to New York, and I guess I stayed drunk." Booker, Doud, and Cadence Records decided to destroy the remaining albums. And just like that, Vaughn Meader's meteoric rise to fame was over.

One week after the assassination, comedian Lenny Bruce was back onstage in New York. If you don't know Lenny Bruce, he was, along with Mort Sahl and maybe one or two others, the comedian who really transformed American stand-up in the fifties with his irreverence, his honesty, his anger—and his use of four-letter words. Bob Booker saw Bruce perform that night and remembered a moment that has since become legendary. Bruce came onstage, grabbed the mic, and said, "Boy, did Vaughn Meader get fucked." Booker said he'd never heard an audience laugh so hard in his life. Bruce had said what many people were thinking.

For Meader, as he himself said, "It was over. Over, over." He had wanted to move on from the Kennedy impersonation before the assassination. But now he was worse than pigeonholed. He was a living reminder of a national tragedy. He recalled a winter afternoon in New York City:

As cold as it is, I'm walking down Second Avenue and a steel riveter, a riveter with a hard hat, sees me and stops his rivet and walks over and squeezes my hand and says: "Oh, so sorry, man." And like, you know, I was getting that, you know, like almost pity. And I think I had to go to a great extent, I know I did, I stayed drunk. And then after that, I stayed drugged, to get away from pity, feeling sorry for me, you know.

Vaughn Meader was only twenty-seven years old, the age at which most careers are just getting started. *He* hadn't died. But he was collateral damage. Another line attributed to Lenny Bruce was that they should put two graves in Arlington Cemetery: one for Kennedy and one for Meader.

In the year after the assassination, Meader didn't disappear completely. He popped up on television a few times in 1964, but never again as JFK. That same year he put out his own album called *Have Some Nuts*. Another later one was called *If the Shoe Fits*. While they received some nice reviews, they just didn't sell. He traveled the country for the next decade. But as his widow, Sheila Meader, recalled, the man she called by his birth name, Abbott, never found that second act:

> *He insisted on writing his own stuff and he needed a writer. You know . . . he would never have succeeded in something like* The First Family *if there hadn't been an Earle Doud and a Bob Booker to write it. He was a delivery man. Abbott delivered. Abbott spoke. Abbott had a voice that felt like warm oil was being rubbed into your skin. It was beautiful.*

But being a "delivery man," as Sheila put it, wasn't enough for Meader. Whether it was his own limitations as an artist, or the public's perception of him—probably both—he never caught on again. He fell into substance abuse—alcohol, marijuana, cocaine, LSD, psychedelic mushrooms. Under the influence of these substances, he tried to find a way forward. In 1972 he recorded a Jesus comedy album called—wait for it—*The Second Coming*. He pursued his passion for honky-tonk music and even appeared in a few movies in the 1970s, including the commercial flop *Linda Lovelace for President*. Eventually he moved back to his home state of Maine.

It was there, in the early 1980s, that he met Sheila, who heard him playing piano at a local inn—a far cry from Carnegie Hall in 1963. They would remain together for twenty years. Sheila described for me a relationship with highs and lows and a man deeply conflicted by the thing that had once made him so famous—a man haunted, you might say. Meader was haunted not by the ghost of Kennedy, but by the ghost of who he, Vaughn Meader, had been as an entertainer. "He wanted to be known as Vaughn Meader but on the other hand he didn't want anything to do with Vaughn Meader. He was Abbott. And he wrote his music and he entertained people and he played the piano. And that's what he wanted."

In the last years of his life, Meader got a call, out of the blue, from CBS. Producers wanted to profile him for a new cable show hosted by Paula Zahn. Meader, for all he had been through, was excited to get one more moment in the spotlight. But when CBS sent a young producer named Kevin Huffman to do the interview instead of Zahn herself, he was crushed, reminded once again of his status as an also-ran. It's downright painful today to listen to the tape of the sixty-two-year-old Meader as he's asked to do the Kennedy voice one more time. For me, more than anywhere else, this is where I can hear what a struggle it was just being Vaughn Meader.

"Why do the voice?" Meader asks Huffman. Why do the voice if you don't have a punch line to bring down the house? But then Meader did do the voice—not for laughs but to reflect on the meaning of Kennedy's assassination, the spirit of the nation, and maybe, indirectly, his own difficult and remarkable life story. He began haltingly, almost certainly making up the words as he went along:

> Two hundred years ago in Concord, Massachusetts, a shot was fired that was heard around the world. Thirty-something years ago in Dallas, Texas, another shot was fired that was heard around the world. The first bullet, fired from the Concord Bridge, signaled the birth of the American spirit. The second bullet, fired from the Texas Book Depository, attempted to end that spirit. And we've seen in the last thirty-something years, how nearly successful that second bullet was. But in the final analysis, there is no bullet, there is no bomb, there is no power on the face of this earth that can destroy the American spirit.

This is a totally different JFK impersonation from what you hear listening to Meader divide up the bath toys between Caroline and John John.

That CBS interview from 1998 was the last the public would hear from Vaughn Meader. He died six years later on October 29, 2004, just one day after my own father died.

Pop always talked about the time before Kennedy was shot as a more innocent time. He heard the news on the car radio and pulled the light blue VW Bug he was driving—the first car my parents ever owned—over to the side of the road and wept. It *was* a different time . . . a time when the presidency was held in such regard that Vaughn Meader would end his routine with the assurance that it was all in good fun.

We're never going back to that time. We can't, and I'm not saying we should try. But that doesn't mean we shouldn't pay our respects . . . not just to Vaughn Meader but also to that time before that horrible day. To hear Vaughn Meader in his prime, to hear that clever and charming—if hardly radical—comedy album, is to travel back to an era that today feels sweet, disarmingly innocent, and yes, funny.

The Story of Melba Moore's
Ill-Fated Sitcom (1986–1986)

Of course, Vaughn Meader isn't the only performer whose career was derailed by world events. By the mid-1980s, Melba Moore was a household name. She'd performed with Diane Keaton in the original cast of *Hair* and eventually became the musical's first black leading lady. Soon after, her performance in the 1970 Broadway musical *Purlie* won her a Tony. (Luckily, the show was filmed for TV. Her performance of the song "I Got Love" is simply smashing.) She went on to star in her own TV variety show, record hit records, and receive Grammy nominations. All that remained was to conquer prime-time TV with her own sitcom. And in 1986, she got just that—*Melba* was greenlighted by CBS, and it was packed with the key ingredients for eighties TV success. And by "key ingredients" I mean a terrible premise (Melba and her "white sister" Susan raise Melba's nine-year-old daughter), a terrible theme song ("We're Sisters"), and terrible clothes (shoulder pads!). What could go wrong?

Well, one thing went very wrong. On the morning of January 28, 1986, the space shuttle *Challenger* broke apart shortly after launch, killing all seven crew members, including a schoolteacher who'd been selected to become the "first teacher in space." The nation was devastated.

That day was also scheduled to be the premiere of *Melba*, and for some reason lost to history, CBS decided to go ahead and air the show, just in case a shocked, mourning nation was hungry for a fun, brassy new sitcom that night.

It wasn't.

Melba scored historically low ratings, and the network immediately pulled it from the schedule. To add to the indignity, they aired the remaining episodes that summer—the second episode scored the lowest ratings in CBS's history.

Melba herself continues her successful recording and stage career to this day, but she has never returned to the world of sitcoms. Though here in the age of "peak television," I'm still holding out hope for a reboot.

Where's Chuck? The Graveyard of Disappeared and Dead Sitcom Characters

FROM AN EARLY AGE *I learned that the television universe is divided into hour-long dramas and half-hour sitcoms. On dramas, death is a fact of life. Consider that over the course of six seasons of* The Sopranos, *ninety-two characters died—many of them gruesomely. On* Game of Thrones *it was even grislier. In its eight seasons, 70 percent of the characters were killed off—all of them gruesomely. (Fun fact: I played a gossip columnist in a 2008 episode of* Law & Order: Criminal Intent *and got blown up in a car.)*

But ever since my childhood basement-dwelling days of nonstop TV watching, I've been haunted by the phenomenon of sitcom characters who die or simply disappear. This rare occurrence even has a name. "The Chuck Cunningham Syndrome" is named for the older brother of Ron Howard's character, Richie Cunningham, on the hit 1970s–'80s series Happy Days. *Chuck appeared for two seasons, usually bouncing a basketball or eating a sandwich. And then he vanished, his existence in the family's history erased from the memory banks of the sitcom universe. Like a thought criminal in Orwell's 1984, Chuck became an "unperson." Like a victim of East Germany's Sitcom Stasi, he simply disappeared. Or as Led Zeppelin might have put it, Chuck climbed that stairway to Sitcom Heaven. (You get my point.) Henry Winkler explained to me that the character became superfluous when Winkler's own character, Fonzie, became a fan favorite and took on the role of de facto older brother to Richie. In other words, for Fonzie to live, Chuck had to die.*

I explored this topic on the first season of the Mobituaries *podcast. After that episode aired, I was struck by the outpouring of grief for the beloved characters lost over the television decades. But there was also anger about the cases we didn't cite. (Yes, Sharon in Fort Wayne, I loved Colonel Blake on M*A*S*H, too!) I hope that in these next few pages the healing can continue.*

Judy Winslow, *Family Matters* Jaimee Foxworth played youngest sibling Judy Winslow on the 1990s sitcom about a working-class Chicago family. A pint-sized spitfire with a quick wit, Judy got her share of laugh lines for four seasons. But when Jaleel White's neighbor character Steve Urkel, in suspenders and thick glasses, marched into the scene, audiences surrendered to his charms—and Judy started getting less and less sass to throw. As fans well remember, in February 1993, Grandma Winslow got married. Judy was a flower girl. She walked down the aisle and was never seen or heard from again. The character of Judy was survived by her older brother and sister, her mother and father . . . and Urkel.

Chico Rodriguez, *Chico and the Man* Comedian Freddie Prinze (father of Freddie Prinze Jr.) was just nineteen when he made an explosively funny debut on *The Tonight Show*, becoming the first stand-up comic to get welcomed to the couch by Johnny Carson after a debut appearance. The following year, 1974, he was starring in his own sitcom opposite Jack Albertson. But the young actor battled depression, and in 1977, with his marriage falling apart, he shot himself. The producers rejected the idea of recasting and instead stalled for time. Other characters referred to Chico being "in Mexicali with his father." Ratings plummeted and fans demanded an explanation for the character's disappearance. NBC finally aired an hour-long special to address the death, but it came off as an exploitive ratings grab. The show soon met its own demise.

Martin, *Love, Sidney* In 1981 Tony Randall played Sidney Shorr, the first gay central character on an American television series. (No, *The Odd Couple*'s Felix Unger was *not* gay.) Think of this show as a sad-sacky proto–*Will & Grace*. The depressive Sidney, usually in a sweater vest, lived in a cramped New York apartment with his friend Laurie, played by Swoosie Kurtz, and her daughter. The only clear indication that Sidney was gay happened during one episode when the camera panned slowly to a picture of Sidney's dead lover, Martin. The series was canceled soon after. (I did love the theme song as sung by Gladys and Bubba Knight!)

Susan Ross, *Seinfeld* In 2015, Jason Alexander, in an interview with Howard Stern, revealed that George Costanza's fiancée, Susan—who famously died from licking toxic glue on the envelopes for their wedding invitations after George insisted on the cheapest possible envelopes—was killed because the actress, Heidi Swedberg, was "f---ing impossible to work with." It was a perfect Seinfeldian irony: George is too cowardly to break the engagement directly, but is saved by his own cheapness. It turned out to be, Alexander said, "the single coldest moment in the history of television."

The cast of *Bewitched* On the podcast I explored the Case of the Two Darrins. (Dick York replaced Dick Sargent in the lead role of Darrin without any explanation and the show's ratings sank. Turns out, you never forget your first Darrin.) Perhaps there was a curse on the series. *Bewitched* also had two actresses play nosy neighbor Mrs. Kravitz. (When Alice Pearce died of ovarian cancer, she was replaced by Sandra Gould.) *And* there were two Mrs. Tates. (Irene Vernon left the series to pursue a career in real estate in Florida and was replaced by Kasey Rogers.) But there could never be two Aunt Claras. When actress Marion Lorne died, her character was retired and the actress was posthumously awarded an Emmy.

Mr. Hooper, *Sesame Street* I was always more of an *Electric Company* person (Rita Moreno shouting "Hey, you guuuuuuys" was what hooked me on TV in the first place), but only *Sesame Street* could have handled the death of a beloved cast member with such a balance of sensitivity and candor. Character actor Will Lee played the elderly Mr. Hooper, the goodhearted curmudgeon who made birdseed milk shakes for Big Bird at his corner store. When Lee died of a heart attack in 1982, the producers rejected a bogus plot line about retirement in Florida, and instead had the other grown-up characters gently but forthrightly explain Mr. Hooper's death to his feathery friend. "It won't be the same," says Big Bird. "You're right, Big Bird, it'll never be the same without him," replies grown-up Bob, his voice breaking. "But you know something? We can all be very happy that we had a chance to be with him and to know him and to love him a lot when he was here."

Becky Conner, *Roseanne*

The case of "the Two Beckys" is often studied in conjunction with "the Two Darrins." In 1992 Lecy Goranson left *Roseanne* to attend Vassar College. The following season the producers cast Sarah Chalke in the role. But since Goranson's contract allowed her to play Becky if she was available, she returned two years later. To confuse things even more, Chalke filled in when Goranson wasn't available. The revolving door situation became a running gag on the show. (At one point the Conner family sits around watching an old episode of *Bewitched*. "I cannot believe that they replaced that Darrin," says Roseanne. "Well, I like the second Darrin much better," replies second Becky actress Sarah Chalke.) The two actresses seem to have gotten along well and remained on friendly terms throughout. Twenty-plus years later, Roseanne's character was killed off from the reboot of her own sitcom after a racist tweet about Obama advisor Valerie Jarrett.

Chuckles the Clown, *The Mary Tyler Moore Show*

Chuckles was an occasional character on the series, a Bozo-like TV clown who hosted kids' programming at the same local station where Mary worked as a news producer. In 1975, CBS aired "Chuckles Bites the Dust," in which the TV clown, having been named as grand marshal in a local parade, is killed. As Mary's boss, Lou Grant, explains, "He went to the parade dressed as Peter Peanut and a rogue elephant tried to shell him." The episode, written by David Lloyd, was a masterful blend of black humor and tender sentiment. For most of the episode, Mary is aghast as her coworkers make jokes about the clown's death. But once they get to the funeral, it's

Mary who's unable to stifle her laughter during the eulogy for Chuckles. She falls apart—and so did the audience.

Opie's Mother, *The Andy Griffith Show* Growing up in Mayberry, Opie Taylor (played by young Ronnie Howard) went fishing with his Pa (Sheriff Andy, played by Andy Griffith). But where, may I ask, was *Opie's mother*? We know from the episode of *The Danny Thomas Show* in which Sheriff Andy Taylor was first introduced that Opie's mother died when "he was the least little speck of a baby." But it's not clear in the series if Opie understands that. In one episode, when he accidentally kills a bird with his slingshot, Andy asks him to listen. "Do you hear that?" he asks. "That's those young birds chirping for their mama that's never coming back. Now you just listen to that for a while." Clearly Opie could have benefited from the counseling being offered on *Sesame Street*.

Lieutenant Colonel Henry Blake, *M*A*S*H* *(This one's for you, Sharon!)* Colonel Blake, played masterfully by McLean Stevenson, was a surgeon and the commanding officer of the 4077th. "I loved playing Henry," the late actor once said, "because I was really playing my dad, a good and simple man but an inept administrator." (Stevenson, just like his character, was from a well-to-do Illinois family. He was a second cousin of presidential candidate Adlai Stevenson.) By the end of the smash series' third season, Stevenson was tired of playing a supporting character, so his character was killed off flying home to America. (Even in repeats—and we watched them at home over and over—this episode put a lump in my throat.) Stevenson went on to star in a string of flop sitcoms, including *Hello, Larry*. "The biggest mistake I made," he said in 1991, "was I thought everybody loved McLean Stevenson. It was Henry Blake that people loved."

DIED THE SAME DAY

FARRAH FAWCETT

{1947–2009}

AND

MICHAEL JACKSON

{1958–2009}

Farrah Fawcett and Michael Jackson died on the same day, but you can be forgiven for not knowing that. "King of Pop Is dead at 50" read the banner headline in the *Los Angeles Times.* Farrah was below the fold. The *Chicago Tribune*'s entire front page was Michael. Farrah was in the little "refer" box at the bottom, her full obit inside.

It's understandable that Farrah was overshadowed at the time—Farrah had been living very publicly with cancer for three years; Michael's death was a major shock. And while Farrah was an icon, Michael was a phenomenon, a constant pop culture presence for forty years up to that point. He was eleven years old when the Jackson 5 had their first number one hit with "I Want You Back." He began a solo career in 1971 and became a supernova when *Thriller* became the best-selling album of all time within a year of its 1982 release. His death was a story not just about music but also about race, business, fashion, and celebrity justice. (Jackson had first been accused of child molestation in 1993 and acquitted at trial in 2005.)

But since Jackson's death, even more serious allegations of sex abuse against him have been raised, complicating (to say the least) his legacy. He wasn't mentioned at all during 2019's *Motown 60* anniversary special. Quite the contrast with the *Motown 25* special, when he sang "Billie Jean" and debuted his moonwalk and pretty much everyone on the planet lost their minds. And so during the recent tenth anniversary of Michael's and Farrah's deaths, in a posthumous reversal of fortunes, it was Farrah who got the love. Two big TV specials and her own *Time* magazine commemorative issue.

It's about time.

The mid-1970s were a sluggish period in America, but then Farrah came along, motivating us to move past our malaise. She captured the mood we *wanted* to be in—healthy (that glow!), happy (that smile!), ready to get up and go. And of course she had that amazing hair, which seemed to have a life of its own, as dynamic and exciting as she was. (Yes, I'm well aware that straight guys might have a different take on the appeal of Farrah, but this is my book.)

She became world famous with that poster of her in the red one-piece. The story goes that she rushed through the shoot because she wanted to go play tennis. I believe it. There was never the sense that Farrah spent a lot of time cultivating an image as a sex symbol. The poster sold 12 million, still a record. It was everywhere, including on the bedroom wall of Tony Manero, John Travolta's working-class character in the blockbuster *Saturday Night Fever*. Of course it was.

Months after the poster came out, *Charlie's Angels* premiered. It was a total sensation: three women who were beautiful *and* fought crime. Sure, it was a little weird that they did so at the behest of a man they never saw and only heard through a speakerphone. (John Forsythe, who later starred on *Dynasty*, was cast as the voice after the originally cast actor Gig Young showed up to his first voice-over session drunk.)

But *Charlie's Angels* managed to connect with women and men. It was sexy and preposterous (where did they keep the guns?) and new: an all-women-led action series. And there was tons of action. They drove stock cars, motorcycles, skateboards—whatever conveyance was required to catch the bad guys. "Angels in Chains" is my favorite episode and the highest rated of the series. The Angels get themselves arrested so they can investigate a women's prison in fictitious Pine Parish, Louisiana, where the inmates have been incarcerated on trumped-up charges. Forced into fancy cocktail dresses by a sadistic prison guard named Maxine—"Drop the towels and get to it"—they soon discover that the warden is running a prostitution ring. Yes, this big house is actually a cathouse. The Angels, of course, expose it all. Criminal justice reform, Aaron Spelling–style!

When we were little my best friend Mario and I would force his little brother Rodger to play Charlie's Angels with us. Rodger wanted to play soccer but sorry, we needed a third. We were so into the series that Mario drew a poster of the show's logo—a silhouette of the Angels in fight poses against a fiery background—and hung it in his, um, closet. The girl who lived next door to Mario had a whole set of *Charlie's Angels* dolls. This girl—let's just call her Helga—wouldn't allow Mario to touch the dolls. He was only allowed to watch. "It was a rule she made and I'm still not over it," he told me recently.

I loved all the Angels. But Farrah was in a class all her own: she radiated friendliness, fun, big dreams, and a great American can-do spirit. (For the record, I had great respect for Kate Jackson's character—aka the STEM Angel—but it should be said that they were *all* smart.)

Farrah Fawcett was born on February 2, 1947, in Corpus Christi, Texas. Her father was an oilfield contractor and her mother was a homemaker. In high school she was a cheerleader and voted "most beautiful" by her classmates all four years. But this is crucial: She was the type of popular girl who was nice to everyone, not a mean bone in her body. She knew she was a knockout but she never preened, she had a sense of humor about herself, and she stood up for kids who were picked on. I have no firsthand source for this but I don't need one. I instinctively know this to be true and I won't be told otherwise!

Soon after moving to Hollywood she appeared on *The Dating Game.* She chose Bachelor #2. It was the right choice. Seriously, the other two guys looked sketchy. She and the winning bachelor won a trip to an Austrian ski resort. (I've always wondered if the couples actually went on those trips. How awkward would that be?)

Early on she played a bunch of bit roles, including in *Myra Breckenridge,* the X-rated critical and box-office flop based on the Gore Vidal novel. Critic Rex Reed starred in it and told me that Farrah was a total sweetheart. (That's saying something because he hates everyone.)

Not surprisingly, Farrah was cast in a lot of TV commercials. A Head & Shoulders shampoo spot she did with Penny Marshall—post–*Odd Couple*, pre–*Laverne & Shirley*—is funny. Farrah shows off a talent for light comedy. But it must be established that there has never been another ad as sexy as the Noxema shaving cream spot that ran during Super Bowl VII in 1973. Farrah lathers superstar quarterback Joe Namath's face while singing, "Let Noxema cool your face." "I'm so excited," chirps Namath. "I'm gonna get creamed." Hot stuff but more corny than porny.

Farrah was only on *Charlie's Angels* for one season. She was such a breakout that it's not surprising she thought she belonged in movies. (She probably got a lot of bad advice.) In 1978 she starred opposite Jeff Bridges in the comedy-mystery *Somebody Killed Her Husband*. Critics nicknamed it "Somebody Killed Her Career." Her career languished.

Then, in 1983, Farrah did something that has since become a cliché. But when she did it, it was bold. She took off her makeup and took over the lead role from Susan Sarandon in the off-Broadway play *Extremities*, playing a victim of an attempted rape who turns the tables on her attacker. She earned good reviews, then even better ones when she played a woman fighting back against her physically abusive husband in the TV movie *The Burning Bed*. At the time, Fred Blau, her makeup artist on *The Burning Bed*, said "To disfigure her face is difficult for me. It's like putting your foot through a Rembrandt."

As the *New York Times*'s Alessandra Stanley put it in a posthumous appreciation of Farrah: "Long before Charlize Theron gained weight to make 'Monster' and Nicole Kidman put on a fake nose to play Virginia Woolf, Ms. Fawcett scrubbed off her tawny good looks to play battered—and battering—women in 'The Burning Bed' and 'Extremities.'"

That lack of vanity would be central to Farrah's final, most important act. "Her greatest legacy will be how she documented her cancer," her friend Sherry Lansing, cofounder of Stand Up to Cancer, told me. Lansing met Farrah when they were both models, long before Lansing became the first woman to run a major Hollywood studio.

Farrah was diagnosed with anal cancer in 2006. It was caused by the HPV virus, which is sexually transmitted. "Up until Farrah people didn't mention anal cancer," Lansing said. "She destigmatized it." Farrah threw herself into treatment and for the sake of awareness, documented it all. That included her decision to cut off her own hair before chemo took it from her—proving to everyone that she was way more than her looks before she died at the age of sixty-two. As Lansing put it, "She didn't care that that would be the last image of her. In fact she wanted it to be."

There's a reason we all cared about Farrah long after her 1970s heyday. Pretty faces—female and male—are a dime a dozen in Hollywood. But the audience is smart. It can sniff out a phony. Eventually it sees inside a person, into who that person is. With Farrah it wasn't the hair, the tan, or those perfect teeth that people loved over the long run. The memory of all that was sweet, but the sense that she was a thoroughly decent person was even sweeter. You can't fake that.

Mahatma Gandhi / Orville Wright (January 30, 1948)

Gandhi, who led the movement for Indian independence through nonviolent civil dis-obedience, was slain just six months after British rule over the subcontinent had ended. So naturally he took the lead headline above the fold in the *New York Times*. Wright also made the front page. After all, he did co-invent the airplane. But it had been forty-five years since that first successful flight so he's below the fold. (Orville Wright should not be confused with Orville Redenbacher, the beloved bow-tied popcorn pitchman. Wright died in a hospital. Redenbacher died in a jacuzzi.)

John Adams / Thomas Jefferson (July 4, 1826) These two Founding

Fathers didn't just die on the same day. They died on the fiftieth anniversary of the sign-ing of the Declaration of Independence. Their relationship was complicated. After a nasty election in 1800, where Jefferson defeated the incumbent Adams, the two didn't speak for twelve years. But in 1809 their mutual friend Dr. Benjamin Rush had a dream prophesying their eerie connection, which he described in a letter to Adams. "These gentlemen sunk into the grave nearly at the same time, full of years and rich in the gratitude and praises of their country." When that day came, it's been said that Adams's very last words were "Jefferson . . . lives." In fact, Jefferson had died a few hours earlier.

Ingmar Bergman / Michelangelo Antonioni (July 30, 2007)

Call this one the Day the Art House Died. You'd think that this pair of hugely influential European art film directors would've loved the irony of passing away on the very same day. But I'm pretty sure Bergman would've hated sharing the spotlight with Antonioni. The Swede was very public about his distaste for the Italian, saying that Antonioni "had never properly learnt his craft," and "sure, there are some brilliant bits in his films . . . but I can't understand why Antonioni is held in such high esteem." Then again, that was the same interview in which Bergman called Jean-Luc Godard's films "affected . . . self-obsessed, and dull," and Alfred Hitchcock "completely infantile." All proving my point: art house directors are WAY worse than Real Housewives!

Same Day

Sammy Davis Jr. / Jim Henson (May 16, 1990)

Sammy Davis Jr. and Jim Henson were to Entertainment what Adams and Jefferson were to Independence. (I'm imagining Sammy on his deathbed, his final utterance "Kermit . . . lives.") Both of them died too young. Davis was sixty-four and had been sick for a while. (See his Mobit on page 210.) Henson was the visionary creator of the Muppets. He was just fifty-three when he died suddenly of pneumonia. That we lost both in the same day was a shock—but not quite as shocking as the fact that Sammy Davis Jr. *never guest starred on the Muppets*. Especially when you consider that the only human as funny and lovable as the Muppets was Sammy Davis Jr.

Dick Sargent / Kim Il Sung (July 8, 1994)

It couldn't have been easy for *Bewitched* actor Dick Sargent to be known as the "Second Darrin," following as he did in the footsteps of Dick York, who was simply better in the role of the flustered husband on the classic sitcom. The final insult: being overshadowed on the day he died by a totalitarian mass murderer. North Korea's founder and grandfather to incumbent madman Kim Jong Un killed up to 3.2 million of his own citizens. Sargent, on the other hand, advocated for gay rights after coming out late in life. I know which one I'd call "Great Leader."

Orson Welles / Yul Brynner (October 10, 1985)

When they died, legendary actor Yul Brynner stole the spotlight from legendary actor/writer/director Orson Welles. That's because Brynner, dying of lung cancer, had prerecorded an antismoking commercial that aired on every major America network and all around the world just days after his passing. Welles hadn't been seen on TV for at least a couple of years, when he stopped doing ads for Paul Masson wines, Sandeman's port, Domecq sherry, Jim Beam bourbon, Nikka whiskey—the list goes on. In their prime, both were known for eponymous roles—Brynner for *The King and I*, and Welles for *Citizen Kane*. Both were nominated for Best Actor for those films, but only Brynner took home an acting Oscar. Then again, he had every reason to be great as King Mongkut, having performed the role onstage a whopping 4,625 times.

William Shakespeare / Miguel de Cervantes + those 11 days

(April 23, 1616) These two masters died on the same date—eleven days apart. Catholic Spain had been on the Gregorian calendar, by edict of Pope Gregory XIII, since 1582. Meanwhile, Protestant England stayed on the Julian calendar until 1752, when the British government decreed that September 3–13 of that year would be skipped altogether. So this Mobit isn't only for the greatest writers in their respective languages, but also for those lost eleven days. Here's hoping J. J. Abrams will investigate.

Margaret Thatcher / Annette Funicello (April 8, 2013)

Although there is no evidence that they ever met, I like to think of the Iron Lady and the Mouseketeer as spiritual sisters. Hear me out: they both had distinguished early careers—Funicello on *The Mickey Mouse Club*, and Thatcher in the House of Commons. And although their achievements surpassed expectations for women of their generation (expectations set by, well, men), both chose to reach higher, and both succeeded. Thatcher became the first-ever female prime minister of the United Kingdom, and Funicello defied the odds by becoming that rare child star who continued to work in Hollywood, starring with Frankie Avalon in hit films like *Beach Blanket Bingo* and *How to Stuff a Wild Bikini*. After being diagnosed with multiple sclerosis, she became an intrepid advocate for those suffering from neurological disorders.

River Phoenix / Federico Fellini (October 31, 1993)

The great Italian director's quiet passing at the age of seventy-three was overshadowed by the sudden and tragic death of River Phoenix in 1993. That they both died on Halloween seems darkly appropriate—in Fellini's case because of the outsized and grotesque nature of his imagery, and for Phoenix because of the ghastly nature of his passing. (Not known as a partier, he nonetheless OD'd and collapsed, convulsing, on the sidewalk outside Hollywood's Viper Room.) While Fellini devoted his life to probing the possibilities of cinema as a writer and director, Phoenix, fifty years his junior, had a range of interests that belied his age. He was a singer, a songwriter, a guitarist, an accomplished tap dancer, and was also a political and environmental activist. Fellini, for his part, disliked politics. That might have had something to do with growing up in Mussolini's Italy.

Dudley Moore/Milton Berle/Billy Wilder (March 27, 2002)

Call it the Day the Laughter Died. Shockingly, even though all three comedic dynamos were involved in dozens of movies in the middle of the twentieth century, I couldn't find a single instance of any of them working together. Although known for their comedies, all three had range: Wilder, a brilliant writer/director, was equally at ease with a comedy like *Some Like It Hot* and a film noir like *Sunset Boulevard*. Moore enjoyed a second career as a jazz pianist and composer. And Berle also proved to be greatly endowed . . . with talent as a dramatic actor.

Cecil B. DeMille/Carl "Alfalfa" Switzer (January 21, 1959)

What I love about these two is the dramatic reversal of fortune they've experienced since they passed away. DeMille was one of the most celebrated filmmakers in history, a founding father of American cinema, with an epic career spanning every genre, bridging the silent and sound eras. Child actor Switzer, on the other hand, played Alfalfa in the *Our Gang* series. He was the "Little Rascal" with the off-key singing voice and the jet-black hair parted down the middle with a signature cowlick. (Full disclosure: I was always a Spanky person.) Switzer faded from view after he left the series, taking bit parts and training hunting dogs on the side. In fact, one of his final gigs was as an uncredited Hebrew slave in DeMille's final project, the towering, award-winning blockbuster *The Ten Commandments*. Both men died soon afterward, Carl at the age of thirty-one, shot during a dispute over a fifty-dollar reward for a lost dog. But today I'd bet more people treasure Switzer's work than DeMille's. Although their one collaboration still gets pretty good ratings every Easter.

DEATH OF A
LEVIATHAN

THE STATION WAGON
{1949–2011}

My family had a station wagon for a couple of years in the early 1970s. But I was only three or four at the time so I can barely remember it. It was yellow, I think, or maybe it was cream colored. Was it a Chevy? What I do know is that one afternoon my mother put my brother in the back seat after a doctor's appointment and the car started rolling backward in the parking lot. À la Angie Dickinson in *Police Woman* she had to jump into the front seat and pull the emergency brake. This was reason enough for my father to trade in the station wagon for an Impala sedan soon after. And just like that, the one thing that made us like TV's Brady family—and who were more all-American than the Bradys?—was gone.

For a few decades, from the midfifties to the mideighties, station wagons like the Oldsmobile Vista Cruiser, the Chrysler Town and Country, and the Ford Country Squire were as central to the American Dream as the white picket fence and the basketball hoop in the driveway. These were the quintessential family cars. (FYI, the Bradys had at least two different station wagons, both of them Plymouth Satellites.) And the bigger the wagon, the cooler the family. By the 1970s the Ford Country Squire was a nearly nineteen-foot-long behemoth and got a whopping eight to ten miles to the gallon. You could cram four or five kids into the back seat, but that's not where I wanted to be.

Anytime I was lucky enough to ride in one (and I'm sure I befriended some kids *because* their families had station wagons) I headed straight for the *way* back. With the seats folded *down*. The freedom. The danger! I loved being thrown against the side when the car turned, all the better when other kids were back there, all of us ricocheting off each other after a pizza party at Shakey's. Riding in the way back gave me the same out-of-control thrill I got from roller coasters. Related: I used to fantasize about climbing into the dryer so I could just spin and spin. It's probably a good thing I didn't figure out how to turn the dryer on from the inside.

What gave these cars an extra flair was the vinyl appliqué wood-grain paneling. It made it feel like a house on wheels. The paneling was a throwback to the earliest station wagons, which were made mostly of wood. These wagons were DIY affairs. The customer would buy the chassis of, say, a Model T, then order the wood body from a coachbuilder or hire a carpenter to make it and bolt it on. "It was just much lighter and easier to build the body out of wood," says my friend Matt Anderson, curator of transportation at the Henry Ford Museum. "The technology just didn't exist at that time to build a large body out of steel." By the 1930s these vehicles—and many were beauties—were known as "Woodies."

The earliest station wagons were used on farms or as delivery vehicles, and to transport passengers between railroad stations and hotels. That's how the vehicle got the name "station wagon." (This is the kind of factoid I love.) By the time the baby boom hit, the station wagon had caught on with families. "The first real modern station wagon is the 1949 Plymouth Suburban," says Matt. "It's got an all-steel body. The name itself tells you how that vehicle was marketed. The rise of the suburbs was a big factor in the adoption of the station wagon."

Now, it's true that station wagons were an absolute nightmare for any teenager learning to parallel park. They were larger than the standard parking space, the sight lines were miserable, and I'm pretty sure that rear defrosters hadn't been invented yet. And of course they were dangerous. The way back was a death chamber. (For the more safety-conscious there was a rear-facing fold-up seat, introduced by Chrysler in 1957. It had seat belts, not that you could ever find them. It also had the benefit that someone sitting back there could call out whenever luggage strapped to the roof rack came free and tumbled out onto the highway.)

By the early 1980s the family station wagon was already beginning to acquire value as kitsch. We know this for a fact because in 1983 Warner Bros. released

Harold Ramis's *National Lampoon's Vacation*. The true star of that movie is not the bumbling Chevy Chase but the "Wagon Queen Family Truckster," an enormous hearse-like vehicle that is gradually gutted over the course of the film due to a combination of vandalism and incompetent driving.

But as *Vacation* was "celebrating" the station wagon, its demise was looming. There were warning signs. The oil crisis of 1973 made fuel efficiency a priority for consumers. The ingenuity of Japanese engineering was making it harder and harder to stay loyal to American cars that handled poorly and seemed in constant need of repair. Then came what car journalist Amos Kwon has called "the testosterone-robbing minivan," which Lee Iacocca introduced at Chrysler in 1983. With better fuel economy, more headroom, and, best of all, a sliding side door, the minivan was a hit among practical-minded carpooling soccer moms. Mandatory car seats rang the death knell of the "way back."

The station wagon belonged to the Golden Age of the highway, the new system of interstates built by Eisenhower and Kennedy. Up through the eighties, that highway system represented nothing less than freedom itself, flight from dreary routines of city and suburb, access to all our nation's great beauty and natural attractions. But then, with traffic and suburban sprawl getting worse and worse, those endless highways were no longer our means of escape. They became another part of what we needed to escape from.

And so after the minivan, we fell in love with the four-wheel-drive SUV, the kind that—at least in the commercials—could drive right over a guardrail, plow through a rocky riverbed, and scale a craggy mountain at forty-five degrees. Maybe it was the renewed nuclear fears of the eighties, or just a vague sense of looming catastrophe, but suddenly we all needed military-grade vehicles of our own—something that could get traction on a glacier and stand up to machine-gun fire if needed. When the next blizzard, hurricane, or wildfire hit, local and state authorities weren't going to save us.

In 2011 Volvo announced that it would stop selling station wagons in the

United States. Sales had dropped from 40,000 in 1999 to 480 in 2010. Auto buffs immediately began to mourn its passing. But the truth is that by 2011 the station wagon was already long dead. The Volvo wagon of the nineties was no more a real station wagon than a barn swallow is a real dinosaur. At best, it was a stunted descendant of the magnificent monsters that roamed American highways during the Late Cretaceous period of American automotive history.

Don't get me wrong, I'm a fan of auto safety. But boy, if someone gave me the keys to a 1979 Ford Country Squire, I'd be sorely tempted to take a week off and ride that beast to the Grand Canyon.

McDonald's Collectible Drinking Glasses

Ronald McDonald has been the mascot of McDonald's ever since 1963, when he was first played in TV ads by future *Today* weatherman Willard Scott. In 1970 a lonely Ronald was joined by the Hamburglar, Officer Big Mac, and the milk-shake-loving Grimace in McDonaldland, a spectacularly imaginative concoction of ad agency Needham, Harper & Steers, which seemed awfully similar to the then popular kids' TV show *H.R. Pufnstuf*. (Google the images of Mayor McCheese and H.R. Pufnstuf himself and you'll see what I mean.) The courts agreed and ordered McDonald's to pay $1 million to the show's producers. Small fries given that the ad campaign had been so successful. The McDonaldland characters became inescapable—as a line of plastic action figures, a complete set of which goes for about six hundred dollars on eBay . . . and as collectible drinking glasses, each one brightly painted with a different character.

It's a safe bet that a good half of the liquid I consumed growing up was via those glasses. But it turns out the glasses themselves weren't so safe. In July 1977, the paint used on the exterior was discovered to contain lead content up to eighteen times the legal limit. Although the company that manufactured the glasses, Owens-Illinois of Toledo, Ohio, declared that the glasses "in no way present a health hazard," regulatory agencies weren't lovin' it. By that point McDonald's had given away as many as 60 million of these IQ-killers in various promotions over five years. Under pressure from the Food and Drug Administration, they agreed to cease distribution. Unfortunately my family missed the memo and the glasses remained in our cupboard up until three years ago, by which point the images had faded to not much more than outlines. My mother's response: "But the painting was on the *outside*!" (P.S.: Let's all raise a non-lead-painted glass to Willard Scott in the hopes that he lives to announce his own hundredth birthday.)

Quaaludes In the pilot episode of *The Brady Bunch*, just before they're married, Mike confesses to Carol that he has a case of nerves. "Why don't you take a tranquilizer?" asks Carol. "I took one," says Mike. "Well maybe you should take another one," says Carol. "Nothing doing," says America's dad. "I want to be calm for the ceremony but there's the honeymoon to consider." I have no idea how much of the Brady honeymoon was fueled by synthetic drugs, but the fact that the quintessential family show of the era was promoting double doses of tranquilizers makes you realize how mainstream these things were. Quaaludes, the brand name for methaqualone, began as an insomnia and anxiety treatment and soon became a recreational drug, easy to get from a doctor who didn't ask too many questions. It fast became a popular club drug, sometimes called a disco biscuit. Highly addictive, even lethal when taken in large doses or mixed with alcohol, Quaaludes were finally banned in the United States in 1984.

Alar An apple a day keeps the doctor away, right? Not if it's sprayed with daminozide, the plant-growth regulator manufactured from the sixties through the eighties by the Uniroyal Chemical Corporation and sold under the brand name Alar. Alar was sprayed on apples and other fruits in order to keep them on the tree longer, aiding the ripening process and—most important—cutting down on labor costs for big fruit producers. But evidence that Alar causes cancer emerged during the 1970s, and by 1984 the proof was overwhelming. A federal ban finally passed Congress in 1996. Alar is still found all over crossword puzzles.

Shag Carpeting Okay, I can't prove that shag carpeting, huge in the free love era of the 1960s and '70s, ever killed someone. But according to a 2001 piece in the British newspaper the *Telegraph*, carpets function as "toxic sponges" soaking in all kinds of pollutants that we track in from outside. Now imagine the billions of hippie microorganisms teeming inside those deep plush piles of looped yarn that make up a shag carpet—trillions if the shag carpeting was inside a van. I'm not a licensed pediatrician, but I bet that encouraging a baby to roll around a shag carpet from the 1970s would build up all sorts of immunity.

Jarts Jarts, also called lawn darts or javelin darts, were weighted metal darts, about a foot long, that you used to toss around the backyard, trying to get them to land inside a plastic ring. If you threw them high enough, they could really gather speed as they plummeted to earth. Kids loved Jarts until the government, citing several injuries and at least one death, tried to ban them in 1976. After pushback from several dangerous-toy lobbying groups, the Consumer Product Safety Commission agreed to a compromise: Jarts would be allowed only in sporting goods stores. Then in 1987, seven-year-old Michelle Snow was tragically killed by a mis-thrown Jart. Her father, David, campaigned tirelessly for an outright ban, and eventually the CPSC voted 2–1 to prohibit their sale. (Gotta wonder about that one "no" vote.)

Electric Blankets

Electric Blankets On a cold winter night during the Carter administration there was nothing like curling up under a soft cozy blanket laced with thick electrical wiring. Before safety features like an automatic shut-off became mandatory in 2001, exposed or damaged wiring made electric blankets a serious fire hazard. (We got rid of the two we owned when my father started worrying we could be electrocuted.) Even today, the American Pregnancy Association warns that the heat from an electric blanket can decrease a male user's fertility. Fun fact: In the vintage sci-fi invasion film *The Thing from Another World*, the monster is freed from the block of ice in which he is encased when an electric blanket is casually tossed aside, melting the creature's prison and loosing him upon the world.

UFFI UFFI was a kind of expanding foam insulation sprayed into walls and crawl spaces. As a kid, I thought it looked kind of pretty, like Reddi-Wip topping. The problem was that one of the *F*s in "UFFI" stands for formaldehyde, which, when sprayed into the air, poses a cancer risk. When UFFI's use became a cause of concern, manufacturers protested that symptoms of exposure were limited to watery eyes, nasal irritation, wheezing, coughing, fatigue, red or blotchy skin, severe allergic reactions, burning sensations in the eyes and throat, nausea, difficulty breathing, headache, malaise, insomnia, anorexia, loss of libido—I'm running out of room here.

The First Great Wall

HADRIAN'S WALL
{128–1746}

B efore the Berlin Wall, before the Great Wall of China, before Pink Floyd's *The Wall*, there was Hadrian's Wall, running across what is now northern England, just south of the Scottish border. Hadrian's Wall reached seventy-three miles coast to coast from the mouth of the Tyne River at the North Sea to Solway Firth in the Irish Sea. Large portions of it still stand. It was a massive engineering project, built at the command of the Roman emperor Hadrian, who visited Britannia, Rome's northernmost province, in the year 122. Beyond the unprotected northern border lay the enemy territory of Caledonia, roughly corresponding to modern-day Scotland. It took six years and fifteen thousand soldiers to construct the wall. (I'd like to think that when they finished building it, they all shouted in unison, "Yo, Hadrian! We did it!")

Made of stone, with some portions of turf, the wall was doubtless intended as a fortification at one of the outposts of the empire. Yet its purpose was probably as much political as military—to control immigration, smuggling, and trade, as well as to project a message of strength and to testify to the achievements of the emperor himself. It stood about twenty feet high, presenting a forbidding sight to anyone who approached from the north. It is the largest ancient monument in Britain.

In an interview in 2000, George R. R. Martin, the writer of *Game of Thrones*, said that Hadrian's Wall inspired the Wall in his series:

> *The Wall comes from Hadrian's Wall, which I saw while visiting Scotland. I stood on Hadrian's Wall and tried to imagine what it would be like to be a Roman soldier sent here from Italy or Antioch. To stand here, to gaze off into the distance, not knowing what might emerge from the forest.*

Of course, Martin did Hadrian one better, making his Wall approximately 300 miles long and, at its high points, 700 feet tall. When you have to keep out undead magic creatures called White Walkers rather than roving bands of angry Scotsmen, you need a little extra oomph.

For Martin, as for many others, the wall has represented a border between the known world and the unknown—a limit point of civilization from which its guardians could look out searchingly on the great mysterious beyond. Late Roman writers, in a volume of biographies called *Augustan History*, noted that Hadrian built the wall "to separate the Barbarians from the Romans." (Please note: Hadrian did not promise that the Barbarians would pay for the wall.)

As Martin mentioned, the soldiers standing watch at the wall's various forts came from all over the vast empire, which in Hadrian's day had reached its greatest expanse—about 2.2 million square miles. It included the whole Mediterranean world, stretched east to Armenia and Mesopotamia, and nearly all the way around the Black Sea. Most of the boundaries of the empire were natural barriers—rivers (the Rhine, the Danube, the Euphrates), mountain ranges (the Atlas, the Caucasus, the Carpathians), and the Sahara Desert. But the northern border of Britannia was an exception, and thus the wall was built.

The soldiers stationed at Hadrian's Wall represented diversity on the scale of an Olympic Village: some from Dacia (Romania), others from Syria, still others from as far away as North Africa. According to the archaeologist Lindsay Allason-Jones, this made northern England "as cosmopolitan as you can get," a home to people of "every colour of skin and every language." The infantrymen also kept their own customs and religious traditions, and so the province of Britannia, though unified by a common Roman culture, would have been a truly multiethnic place.

The emperor Hadrian likely appreciated this. He was born in the provinces, in Spain, near modern-day Seville, in the year 76. His full Latin name was Publius Aelius Hadrianus, and his family was actually "Hispano-Roman," meaning that it had roots in both Spain and Rome. But he was no unlettered rustic: his father was a first cousin to the emperor Trajan.

Both of Hadrian's parents died when he was a boy, and so at age ten he became a ward of the emperor. At fourteen he moved to Rome at the emperor's behest and received an education appropriate to the Roman elites. However, his relationship with Trajan appears to have been complicated and troubled, and it was Trajan's wife, Empress Plotina, who took an interest in Hadrian's future and signed the papers to make him Trajan's heir.

When Hadrian succeeded Trajan in 117, he was forty-one. As emperor, he had his share of problems. He had a miserable marriage, made for political reasons, to Trajan's grand-niece Sabina. The ruggedly handsome

Hadrian—he was the first emperor to wear a full beard—was much happier with his young Greek male lover Antinous, who was much more than a boy toy. Hadrian and Antinous dined out and vacationed together openly. After Antinous drowned, Hadrian had the younger man deified. You can still see statues of the young Greek, including a famous one at Delphi.

Things weren't much easier on the work front for Hadrian. He fought with the Roman Senate. He struggled to put down a revolt in Judea called the Bar Kochba Revolt, which he had provoked by ordering a temple to Jupiter constructed on the ruins of Solomon's Temple in Jerusalem, a site sacred to the Jews. One ancient source says that 580,000 Jews perished in the fighting.

Yet despite his troubles, Hadrian put his all into the empire, winning raves from Edward Gibbon centuries later in *Decline and Fall of the Roman Empire*. While Trajan had expanded the boundaries of the empire, Hadrian focused on retrenchment and stability. He spent twelve years of his twenty-one-year reign touring all the provinces of the empire, seeing to administrative and military matters. And he loved to build things. In Rome he put money into the Temple of Venus and restored the Pantheon (which, incidentally, is my favorite site in Rome). So when he came to the northern edge of the province of Britannia, where a Caledonian uprising had recently been put down by the Roman governor, a great, grand wall seemed to be a no-brainer. It proved to be one of his great legacies.

For a few centuries, the wall served its purpose, even if it was occasionally breached. But eventually the Roman Empire weakened, and in the early fifth century AD Rome withdrew from Britain. Over the next millennium time and nature took their toll on the wall. Stones were repurposed to build a monastery. Farmers quarried the wall for material. Then in 1746, when Scottish rebels up north were again making trouble, a system of military roads was constructed, raiding Hadrian's Wall for stone.

Then, around 1830, John Clayton, the town clerk of Newcastle-upon-Tyne, took on the preservation of what was left of the wall, a portion of which ran through his property. He bought up more land, began excavating the forts that once lined the wall, and published his findings. Clayton dedicated his life to the preservation of the wall, and he continued to unearth important discoveries into his nineties. At a fort called Chesters, he opened an archaeological site to the public. It was made into a museum in 1903. In 1987, one hundred fifty years after Clayton began his efforts, Hadrian's Wall was declared a World Heritage Site. This colossal feat of engineering, a display of might to all those who would challenge the great power of Rome, is now a ruin, a testament to the slow passage of time and the gradual erosion of empires.

CELEBRITIES WHO PUT THEIR BUTTS ON THE LINE

ELIZABETH TAYLOR
{1932–2011}

MARLENE DIETRICH
{1901–1992}

AND

LORD BYRON
{1788–1824}

y now, you may have gathered I love show business. (And presidential trivia! And geography!) But I'm well aware that some people are wary of show business, especially show business*people*. They make an easy target: they're rich, they're beautiful, and, with all due respect to *US Weekly*, they're not just like us.

But whenever I get cynical about our culture of celebrity, I remind myself that there are some superstars who have put their reputations (and sometimes their wealth) on the line in service of truly noble ideals—like freedom, charity, and love.

Elizabeth Taylor (1932–2011)

If you read the Audrey Hepburn chapter then you'll remember that back when I was twenty-three, I worked behind the Chanel fragrance counter at Macy's in Herald Square. To my right was a fancy French fragrance called Boucheron. But the real action was just to my left.

Women of all sizes, social classes, colors, and ages streamed by all day long, drawn to the giant image of a still-ravishing-at-sixty violet-eyed goddess, as if it were a shrine and the fragrance incense. This was the counter for Elizabeth Taylor's two fragrances, White Diamonds and Passion.

Has anyone else embodied *passion* quite the way Elizabeth Taylor (who hated being called Liz) did? As a kid I didn't quite understand the attachment. I just knew she liked getting married. Then I watched her 2001 sit-down with Larry King. It's one of the most riveting hours of TV I've ever watched. Taylor takes us on a grand tour of her epic life: she remembers being fifteen years old and standing up to studio boss Louis B. Mayer after he spewed profanities at her mother ("Mr. Mayer, you cannot speak to my mother like that! I don't give a damn whether I work in motion pictures or not!") . . . she recounts wrenching open a crumpled car door to save a near-death Montgomery Clift after his auto accident ("where I got the strength, I don't know") . . . she reflects on the fights she had with husband #4 and #5, Richard Burton ("Wonderful," she coos), and the making up that followed ("Oh yes," she purrs) . . . she flaunts her giant Krupp diamond ring, once owned by the wife of a Nazi munitions supplier ("And when it was up for auction, I thought how poetic that would be if a nice little Jewish girl like me ended up with it." Taylor had converted to Judaism in 1959. "So Richard got it for me.") . . . and in the best moment of the interview, she describes her afterlife encounter with husband #3, Mike Todd, when she'd briefly died herself in 1961. ("And the white light was so welcoming and warm, and I was finally happy. He had been dead three years. And I said, oh, God, Mike, I'm home, *I'm home*. And he said, no, you have so much more to do. And you have to fight. And he turned me around, and he said you must go back. And he pushed me gently.")

The first time I finished watching this interview I had to lie down. The woman deserved a third Oscar for this appearance.

That's right, she won two Oscars because she was in fact a great actress. She rode to stardom as a twelve-year-old in *National Velvet*, in which she did most of her own stunts. (More on that later.) She was twenty-three when she convincingly aged more than a quarter of a century in *Giant*. And she was thirty-two when she won an Academy Award for playing a world-weary fifty-two in *Who's Afraid of Virginia Woolf?* And yeah, I know she only got her first Oscar for *Butterfield 8* because she'd almost died from pneumonia months before. (Her friend Shirley MacLaine, nominated that same year, said "I lost to a tracheotomy.") But seriously, has anyone ever worn a slip and stood in a doorway the way Taylor did in that movie?

Part of what made her a great actress was that passion. No amount of drama school training can compete with that. I've long felt complicit in the death of Shelley Winters's character in *A Place in the Sun*. But I'm sorry, I needed her to drown so that Montgomery Clift could end up being with Elizabeth. (If you haven't seen the movie, it's in my top five.) To paraphrase Maggie the Cat, her character from *Cat on a Hot Tin Roof*, Elizabeth Taylor was *ALIVE*—on-screen and off.

"Every day she lived in the amazement of life," her friend the songwriter Carole Bayer Sager told me. "Watching her make a hot dog at Dodgers Stadium, it was like art. How she put everything on that hot dog but very carefully—the mustard, the sauerkraut, the relish. And when she took a bite, she took a *bite*."

That passion for life—that *zeal*—would power the biggest fight of her life—a battle waged on behalf of millions the world over.

In July 1981, a *New York Times* article by Dr. Lawrence K. Altman was headlined "RARE CANCER SEEN IN 41 HOMOSEXUALS." The cases were mostly in New York City and the San Francisco Bay Area. "Eight of the victims died less than 24 months after the diagnosis was made," Altman noted. Health professionals were soon calling it "GRID," or gay-related immunodeficiency. By the end of 1983, the new acronym was AIDS. The next year, researchers identified the cause of the disease as the human immunodeficiency virus, or HIV. By now the numbers were reaching epidemic proportions.

Televangelists Jerry Falwell and Pat Robertson pronounced the disease God's vengeance on a sinful lifestyle. During a now-infamous 1982 White House press briefing, Reagan press secretary Larry Speakes repeatedly mocked a reporter's questions about the disease. In the audio recording of the briefing, you can hear several men and women in the press corps laughing along. Not until 1985 did President Reagan himself publicly mention the word *AIDS* (in response to a question) and not until 1987 did he deliver a speech on the crisis. That same year education secretary William Bennett openly rejected a recommendation by Surgeon General C. Everett Koop, himself an evangelical, for widespread safe-sex education.

Throughout the eighties, public perception of AIDS and its victims was shrouded in misinformation, rumor, fear, and prejudice. Pretty much everyone was scared. I was in eighth grade in the fall of 1983 when one of my teachers raised the topic. An otherwise nice girl turned to me with a grin and said, "That's what *you're* going to get." (A few years ago she reached out to me on Facebook to apologize. Of course I accepted. Who in junior high didn't say something cartoonishly nasty to someone else?)

As this public health crisis—really, panic—was unfolding, Taylor was in her early fifties. She had gained weight, her struggles with painkillers and alcohol had taken their toll, and she was no longer the alluring screen star she had once been. Worse, she had become a favorite target for tabloids and comedians. John Belushi had played her on *Saturday Night Live*'s "Celebrity Corner," gobbling down drumsticks. ("I'm on a strict diet," says Belushi, mouth full. "Nothing but chicken.") Joan Rivers, herself an early and fierce advocate for HIV/AIDS sufferers, made Taylor a favorite target with old-fashioned punch lines: "Is Elizabeth Taylor fat? Her favorite food is seconds."

It was at this moment, when someone of lesser mettle and conscience would have receded from the public eye, that Elizabeth Taylor heard her calling. "People were talking about it," she remembered. "It was the topic at every cocktail party. 'Oh, this *dreadful* disease, darling. AIDS, oh, it's so awful. Oh, it must have been those homosexuals.' And it just irritated me so much that I— But wait a minute. I'm angry, but what am *I* doing? I'm sitting back here, getting all riled up. My blood pressure has probably gone sky-high. But what have I done? What have I done?"

And so, in January 1985, when activist Bill Misenheimer and Bill Jones, a high-end Hollywood caterer, asked her to chair the first Commitment to Life Dinner, a fund-raiser run by a local group called AIDS Project Los Angeles, she said yes. Taylor was still Hollywood royalty and retained a rare star power needed for their benefit to succeed. As Misenheimer later told *Vanity Fair*, "There are three big draws in the world: Elizabeth II, the pope, and Elizabeth Taylor." Sober after a stint in the Betty Ford Clinic, Taylor was ready for a new direction in life. She had been involved in charitable causes before—but her commitment to people living and dying from HIV was to become a mission. As she later said, "I decided that with my name I could open certain doors. . . . I could take the fame I'd resented and tried to get away from for so many years . . . and use it to do some good. I wanted to retire, but the tabloids wouldn't let me. So I thought, If you're going to screw me over, I'll use you."

Taylor immediately started asking her highest-profile friends to join in the cause, and was stunned by their refusals. At Reagan's second inauguration later that month, she even broached the cause with the First Lady (Taylor was friends with both Ronald and Nancy), but was coldly rebuffed. The job was going to be harder than she realized.

Nineteen eighty-five, it turned out, was a watershed for how the public viewed AIDS. Two big things happened: In June, Ryan White, an Indiana teenager, made headlines when his school district refused to let him attend classes because he had HIV. White had contracted the virus through treatments for hemophilia, and the story of a drug-free midwestern white kid suffering from the disease—and from public discrimination—began to move the needle on popular sentiment. Then in July, screen icon Rock Hudson was revealed to have the disease. Taylor, who had starred with Hudson in *Giant*, was shocked; she knew Hudson was gay but had assumed he was suffering from cancer.

She was with him the night before he died. "And oh, he was just skin and bones. And I thought, I am going to do everything in my living power to get at this disease and *kill* it by its throat."

Terrible as it was, Hudson's decline actually helped Taylor's work on the Commitment to Life Dinner. The film industry suddenly became aware that the disease was taking, as Taylor put it, "one of their own" and at last "Hollywood really got their shit together." The gala itself took place in September 1985 at LA's Bonaventure Hotel. Twenty-five hundred attendees watched performances by Rod Stewart, Stevie Wonder, Cher, Cyndi Lauper, and others, and took out their checkbooks for AIDS Project Los Angeles.

The benefit was only the beginning. That same summer Taylor teamed up with Mathilde Krim, a pioneering HIV/AIDS researcher. Together they founded amfAR, the American Foundation for AIDS Research, a nonprofit that would go on to raise more than half a billion dollars for AIDS research, education, and prevention. Under Taylor's leadership, amfAR soon went international. The cause became even more personal for Taylor when her own daughter-in-law, Aileen Getty, was diagnosed with the virus in 1987.

In 1991, Taylor took a new step, establishing the Elizabeth Taylor AIDS Foundation. While amfAR devoted most of its resources to research for vaccines and treatment, ETAF focused on education and prevention, through programs like needle exchanges and sex education. Taylor covered the operating costs by donating, in perpetuity, 25 percent of all royalties she received for the use of her image or likeness.

AmfAR and ETAF weren't the only organizations working to eradicate AIDS and to care for those suffering from it. ACT UP, cofounded by Larry Kramer (who'd convened the very first meeting of activists back in 1981), was devoted to political action and the urgent task of shaping public policy.

But Taylor's approach, based on fostering compassion, complemented the radical activism. Her public prominence was critical in helping AIDS advocacy go mainstream, earning it legitimacy with large corporations, donors, and foundations. In 1987, she even prevailed on her friend Ronald Reagan to make his first public speech on AIDS.

By 1991, public opinion was beginning to change. Tony Awards host Jeremy Irons wore a red ribbon to the show to call attention to the cause, and overnight it became a symbol. That same year Magic Johnson's shocking announcement of his infection was another reminder of the reach of the epidemic. After Bill Clinton's election in 1992 there was a dramatic shift in federal policy, steep increases in funding for research and treatment, and the establishment of an office dedicated to AIDS research at the National Institutes of Health. Of course, the disease continued to claim its victims, even as treatment improved and public awareness increased.

In 1993 Elizabeth Taylor received the Jean Hersholt Humanitarian Award at that year's Oscars. In her introductory remarks, Angela Lansbury lavishes Taylor with what would be meaningless clichés if said about almost anyone else: "She is more than a symbol. She is a *leader*, an activist, and a shining example of the use of celebrity for the celebration of life." She points out that "Elizabeth took up the cause when it wasn't politically correct." Then Taylor, the movie star turned missionary, speaks:

> *I accept this award in honor of all the men, women and children with AIDS who are waging incredibly valiant battles for their lives, those to whom I have given my commitment, the real heroes of the pandemic of AIDS.*

Taylor says the word *AIDS* in such a blunt, forthright way that it's almost defiant. Even in 1993 it was a word that many people whispered. And then she ends with an appeal, an exhortation that could very well be delivered from the pulpit:

> *I call upon you to draw from the depths of your being to prove that we are a human race. To prove that our love outweighs our need to hate. That our compassion is more compelling than our need to blame. That our sensitivity to those in need is stronger than our greed. That our ability to reason overcomes our fear. And that at the end of each of our lives, we can look back and be proud that we have treated others with the kindness, dignity, and respect that every human being deserves. Thank you and God bless.*

In 2011, at the age of seventy-nine, Taylor died from congestive heart failure, surrounded by her four children. Since the first Commitment to Life Dinner, great progress has been made on treatment and prevention of HIV, though to date the disease has claimed 35 million lives and roughly the same number live with the virus. Taylor's foundation continues its work around the globe with innovative

ideas like mobile health clinics in Malawi that can reach those who lack the resources to make it to clinics or hospitals.

Why did she do it? Why did she attach herself to a cause when the victims were
seen by so many as pariahs? Maybe growing up in such a singularly strange environment, wildly famous from the age of twelve, gave her a special understanding
for "the other." (A friend of Taylor's told me that "she seemed drawn to broken or
unlikely people.") Or maybe her empathy for AIDS sufferers sprang from the physical pain she lived with all her life. When she was filming *National Velvet* she had
two serious falls and sustained a spinal injury. She would endure more than forty
different surgeries over her lifetime.

Or maybe her generosity of spirit was innate. Carole Bayer Sager says she's
never met another celebrity with the bigness and openness of heart that Taylor had:
"She would open her house on Sundays. Most celebrities don't open their homes.
They just don't do that. I just found it surprising and fantastic. Some of the people
she had over were big stars. Some of them were the people who worked for her.
Family style. It wasn't unusual to have Nancy Reagan on one side of you and her
manicurist on the other side. She was never jaded, with all the living she did."

In that same Larry King interview from 2001 Elizabeth Taylor talked about one
hospital stay when she almost died:

*Even an hour is plenty of time when you don't know whether you are going
to live or not. And you think: Why did I make it? Why am I not dead? Everything indicated that I should be. There must be some reason that God wants
me to live. There must be something left for me to do. And I have to find out
what that something is and go out there and do it!*

Marlene Dietrich (1901–1992)

Marlene Dietrich was 100%.

In 1972 the German-born screen legend and internationally known cabaret artist was in London rehearsing for a concert. She was seventy years old.

As with everything related to her image, Dietrich knew exactly how she wanted to be lighted. Her trusted longtime lighting designer Joe Davis was on hand to make sure her expectations were met. Dietrich's twenty-two-year-old grandson, Peter Riva, was also there. He remembers the scene vividly: "I'm standing next to her on the London stage, with Joe Davis. And way up in the clouds, at the top of the theater, there's a guy pointing a spotlight on her face. She kept telling him, waving a hand, where to move the light. The man called down, 'I think that's perfect, Miss Dietrich.' Joe Davis called up, 'Do exactly as Miss Dietrich says.' Marlene gestured again a few times and then turned to Joe and said, 'That's fine.' So I asked Joe how she knew [it was fine]. 'When it begins to burn her eyes, she knows it is dead center.'"

Like Elizabeth Taylor, Marlene Dietrich today is remembered by many for her beauty. But Dietrich's persona—cool, husky-voiced, at times androgynous—was always more daring. As the theater critic Kenneth Tynan wrote, "Her masculinity appeals to women and her sexuality to men." In the western *Destry Rides Again* Dietrich gets into a bar fight, a real knock-down, drag-out with another woman, rolling around the floor, before Jimmy Stewart dumps a bucket of water on both of them. Then Dietrich attacks *him* with a bottle, a chair, and her fists. (Incidentally this is the movie where she sings "Boys in the Back Room," brilliantly parodied by Madeline Kahn as "I'm Tired" in *Blazing Saddles*. See page 136.)

Turns out Dietrich wasn't afraid of a good fight in real life. *Destry* came out in 1939, the year Hitler's Germany invaded Poland, commencing World War II. And Dietrich stepped right into the breach to help her new beloved homeland, the United States of America, defeat the country of her birth. "I don't think she was ever happier, more fulfilled, than when she was serving the Allied troops," Peter Riva told me. She knew well what was at stake.

Born in Berlin as Marie Magdalene Dietrich in 1901, Dietrich lost her father when she was just five. While still a girl, she came up with the name "Marlene" by fusing her first and second names. It was her first act of self-creation. She embarked on a career in entertainment, as a chorus girl in Berlin revues and then as an actress in the city's vibrant cinema scene. Her breakout performance came as a cabaret singer in Josef von Sternberg's *Blue Angel*. Immediately Paramount Studios came calling, and Dietrich moved to Hollywood to star in a series of six films in the early 1930s, all directed by Sternberg. She was usually cast in the role of a vamp or femme fatale, but fast won a reputation for breaking the rules. In 1933, while sailing from New York to France, she received a warning from Paris's chief of police that should she arrive in the city wearing men's trousers, she would be arrested. And so, naturally, she made sure to wear a white pantsuit when she disembarked. The Paris papers hailed it as a revolution in fashion, and the next day the chief of police showed up with a bracelet inscribed with an apology.

During the same years that Dietrich was conquering Hollywood, Adolf Hitler was coming to power back in Germany. Dietrich watched political developments in her home country warily. Although the German government had banned *Blue Angel* in 1933 (Sternberg was Jewish), Hitler loved the film. He wanted Dietrich to return to Germany to continue her career.

"Marlene was staunchly opposed to autocrats and fascists. When she got to that position of security and fame she took every opportunity she could to oppose the Nazis," Riva told me. "German foreign minister von Ribbentrop came to visit her [in 1937] at the Lancaster Hotel in Paris bearing a 'Mother's Cross' to woo Marlene back to Germany. It would have essentially made her 'Queen of Germany' with the promise of a carefree life. She said no then and many other times. Hitler never asked again, just labeled her a traitor to the Fatherland."

Instead she worked with Jewish émigré director Billy Wilder. Jews had been leaving Germany since the Nazis came to power in 1933, but in 1938, with Kristallnacht—a nationwide pogrom against Jewish homes, businesses, synagogues, and schools—the refugee problem became a crisis. Dietrich and Wilder started a fund to sponsor refugees, and Dietrich escrowed her entire salary from 1937's *Knight Without Armour*—at $450,000 per film, she was one of Hollywood's highest-paid stars—to support the cause.

And then in 1939 this woman, who was culturally German to the core, publicly renounced her home country and became an American citizen. She made sure the cameras were there when she was sworn in. "She wanted the oath of American citizenship to be captured on film," says Riva, "in order to send a message to the Third Reich *and* good Germans—for them to know she was taking that stand." This didn't go over well back home: the Nazi newspaper *Der Stürmer* wrote that she had been corrupted from her years spent among the Jews of Hollywood, calling her decision a betrayal of the Fatherland.

Dietrich didn't care. With the bombing of Pearl Harbor, she went further. In 1942, she traveled throughout the United States to promote the purchase of war bonds. Some estimates credit her with raising a million dollars in sales. "I am delighted to have the opportunity to help my country in any way I can," she told the *New York Times* that year. "I consider it a privilege. Not a duty." She also supported the government's wartime propaganda which used German language radio to demoralize the Nazi troops.

But Dietrich's greatest efforts were for the USO. In 1944 and 1945 she volunteered for multiple tours, entertaining troops and prisoners of war in Algeria, Italy, France, and Germany for eighteen straight months—with more time at the front, Billy Wilder said, than General Eisenhower. She earned a reputation for abiding the rough conditions—a lack of electricity, sleeping in tents—and for being willing to tour near enemy lines. The closer the better, as far as Dietrich was concerned.

Riva recalls: "Danny Thomas [who was a young comic at the time, touring with Dietrich] once said to me, 'Your grandmother,' laughing and shaking his head, 'she tried to get us killed! We were performing our act for five guys in a foxhole with howitzers firing overhead.'"

She performed for as many as half a million troops, singing and even playing the saw, which she bowed like a violin. (As a teenager she had aspired to be a concert violinist until a severe wrist injury dashed her hopes.) She did some comic bits, too; in one act, she purported to be a mind reader. She would call a serviceman up onstage and state that she would tell the audience his thoughts. After a sly look at the young man, she'd quip, "Oh, think of something else—I can't talk about that!"

"Actually I think Dietrich wanted to be a soldier and you couldn't very well be a soldier so she fought her way," said her daughter, Maria Riva (mother of Peter), in a 1996 British documentary. Maria Riva's acclaimed 1992 memoir described Dietrich as not so much a mother as a queen with her family as court. But on Dietrich's contributions to the war effort, Riva is unstinting. "She did a magnificent job. Certainly when she was finally overseas she practically was a soldier. She never said 'I was with the USO.' She was in the army."

One of her more famous paramours, the actor Douglas Fairbanks Jr., claimed that Dietrich entertained the idea of helping the Allied cause in an even grander way—by killing Hitler. Dietrich biographer Charlotte Chandler quotes Fairbanks as saying that Dietrich toyed with plans to seduce and then assassinate the German leader. Back in the thirties, when Hitler still held out hopes that Dietrich would return to Germany, Marlene suggested to Fairbanks that she might accept the offer—on the condition that she be granted a private audience with der Führer. Her plan was to "gush" about Hitler, soften him up, and then strike the fatal blow. When Fairbanks expressed skepticism about the plan—surely she would be searched before being allowed to meet privately with Hitler—she countered that she would subject herself to a strip search, and use a poisoned hairpin as the lethal weapon.

"She always felt a responsibility to do one hundred percent," says Peter Riva. "If you detest Hitler enough, you're gonna give that one hundred percent of your effort."

After the war, the United States honored its adopted citizen with the Presidential Medal of Freedom in 1947. France named her a Chevalier of the Legion of Honor, Belgium a Knight of the Order of Leopold. In 1965, she became the first

German (and the first woman) to receive the Medallion of Valor from the state of Israel; she was also honored by the Jewish Veterans of World War II. But not everyone honored her. When she returned to Germany in 1960, she encountered threats, protests, and chants of "Marlene Go Home!" from those who still felt she had betrayed the nation.

For the rest of her life she shared a bond with the young men alongside whom she'd served. "They were her boys," says Peter Riva. "She felt responsible for them. She felt grateful to them. When she sang in Vegas the first time in 1953 at the Sahara, many of her boys wore uniforms. She called [us] the next morning, crying, happy that her boys remembered and that she was able to thank them once more. Every time I saw her perform—London, Switzerland, Paris, New York, Jersey— it was always the same, she'd ask if any of her boys were in the audience. They'd whoop and holler, she'd smile, flash a leg, and sing provocatively. They were hers and she was theirs. She knew their sacrifice, never forgot."

"She loved this country," says Peter Riva. "She did, loved the spirit of 'can do.' When the first space shuttle flew in 1981 she called everyone she knew to turn on the TV and watch. It wasn't about space travel, it was about the American ability to reach out, explore, improve, *try*. She loved that Americans built their lives on trying, persevering—the real immigrant spirit. And she was an immigrant."

Lord Byron (1788–1824)

Well before Dietrich put her butt on the line for the cause of freedom, the poet Lord Byron did the same. Okay, about half of you are thinking "Lord Byron wasn't a celebrity." And the other half are asking "Who's Lord Byron?"

For those out there who weren't English majors, Byron was probably the most celebrated of the great Romantic poets, which made him a celebrity in his age, and definitely the most scandalous. He wrote in the years following the American and French Revolutions—when the promise of democracy and liberty was sweeping the globe, when figures like Toussaint L'Ouverture in Haiti and Simón Bolívar in

South America were taking up arms for the ideals that Thomas Paine had written about (remember him?). For Londoners, it was also an era of glamour and excess, when the fashionable class, represented by people like Beau Brummel (remember him?), was the object of endless attention for its parties, affairs, and scandals. Byron belonged to both these worlds: he was a revolutionary and a rogue.

Born to an aristocratic family in 1788, George Gordon Noel Byron was ten years old when a great-uncle died, making him the sixth Baron Byron. He attended Cambridge, and at nineteen took his seat in the House of Lords. (Yes, he inherited a seat in Parliament. That's why he's Lord Byron.) Yet his sympathies were, from the beginning, with the little guy. For instance, in Great Britain, Roman Catholics had long been denied basic civic rights. Byron supported Catholic emancipation to remove those restrictions. He spoke out for Irish independence and the rights of workers. The first speech he gave in Parliament was in support of the Luddites—not those weird friends of yours who don't use social media, but the original Luddites: textile workers who protested their poverty by smashing the new industrial machinery that was putting them out of work. That's what made him a revolutionary.

Now for the rogue part: Byron was reputed to have bedded hundreds of women as well as men. Not so surprising, considering he was wealthy, titled, brilliant, and strikingly handsome. His fellow poet Samuel Taylor Coleridge said of him, "His eyes the open portals of the sun—things of light, and for light." With the publication of Byron's book-length poem *Childe Harold's Pilgrimage* in 1811, with its intense, brooding hero, he became a sex symbol. After reading it, one young (and married) noblewoman, Lady Caroline Lamb, demanded to meet the poet. Never mind that Byron was married. He and Lady Lamb began a passionate affair that ended melodramatically: the jilted mistress sent young Byron a lock of her pubic hair along with a letter signed "Your Wild Antelope." (That lock of hair is still preserved in the archives of the National Library of Scotland.) Even more shocking was Byron's affair with his half-sister, Augusta Leigh, whose daughter he probably fathered.

The scandal of that affair, along with mounting debts, and the subsequent

from private donors, and even sold his northern England estate, Rochedale Manor, which had been in his family since 1638. He tried to drum up American support, too. But although President Monroe was sympathetic to Greek independence, he was not ready to meddle in European affairs.

Ultimately, Byron managed to raise a "Byron Brigade" of about two hundred Souliots, and led his men in drills over the early, rainy months of 1824. The plan now was to attack the Turkish fortress at Lepanto (today called Nafpaktos), at the mouth of the Gulf of Corinth—the site of a famous naval battle 250 years earlier, where Venice and Spain had defeated the Ottomans, and where another great writer, Miguel de Cervantes, had lost the use of his left arm. But the raid never came to pass. In February 1824, Byron was taken seriously ill, suffering epileptic seizures. Coordination among different Greek factions foundered. Then, in April, Byron caught a virus. Quite possibly bloodletting (remember bloodletting?) caused an infection. Byron fell into a high fever and eventually a coma. He died on April 19, 1824, at the age of thirty-six.

It was not until 1830 that the Greeks would triumph in their struggle for independence, when long-sought European intervention had weakened the Ottoman navy and forced a settlement, making Greece the first newly independent nation-state in Europe. In the end Byron did not make any military contribution to the struggle, but he drew worldwide attention to the cause, held fast to the noble ideals of self-governance, and helped to set Greece on a path where modernizers, rather than warlords, shaped the fate of the nation. He remains a national hero.

Before his departure for Greece, Byron wrote, "I should prefer a grey Greek stone over me to Westminster Abbey." As it turns out, his body was returned to England, but his notorious sex life kept him out of Westminster Abbey, where the great English writers Chaucer, Dickens, and Tennyson are buried, among others. Instead he was buried in a twelfth-century Nottinghamshire church, his devotion to Greek independence commemorated by a marble plaque donated in 1881 by King George I of Greece.

PEOPLE ARE LIVING LONGER *than ever before, so really there's no excuse for distinguishing yourself in just one way. Elizabeth Taylor, Marlene Dietrich, and Lord Byron managed to wear more than one hat. Here are some other notable multi-hyphenates:*

Paul Winchell (1922–2005)

Paul Winchell's voice is familiar to generations of cartoon lovers—as Dick Dastardly in *Wacky Races*, evil Gargamel in *The Smurfs*, and as Tigger the tiger in *Winnie the Pooh*. He won a 1986 Grammy for singing "The Wonderful Thing About Tiggers." But in the 1950s he also designed, built, and patented an early version of the artificial heart. I would have loved to hear him sing "The Wonderful Thing about Tickers."

William Howard Taft (1857–1930)

If you know anything about Taft, it's probably that our twenty-seventh president was also our heaviest, weighing in at 340 lbs. His presidential bathtub could fit four men. (Now that's a White House scandal just waiting to happen.) But despite losing reelection in 1912 the man had a big second act—as chief justice of the Supreme Court.

Harold Sakata (1920–1982)

Long before he endeared himself as the bowler-throwing henchman Oddjob in the first James Bond blockbuster, *Goldfinger*, Sakata himself went for the gold—and won the silver—for the United States in weight lifting in the 1948 Olympics. Between those gigs, his other "odd job" was that of a professional wrestler.

Johnny Weissmuller (1904–1984)

A six-time Olympic medalist and twelve-time Tarzan, the Hungarian immigrant (birth name "János Weissmüller") lived the American Dream. The iconic Lord of the Apes swam to five golds and one bronze in the 1920s, picking up fifty-two US national championship titles along the way.

One Thing

Hedy Lamarr (1914–2000) While her male co-stars were primping in their trailers, 1940s screen siren Hedy Lamarr was experimenting with scientific equipment provided by her friend Howard Hughes. The resulting patent for "frequency hopping" was ignored by the Hollywood press, but it fascinated geeks a generation later, when it became the backbone for Wi-Fi and Bluetooth technology.

Matthew Fontaine Maury (1806–1873) Maury, known as the "Pathfinder of the Seas," is considered one of the fathers of both oceanography and meteorology. He also served as an officer in the US Navy until he decided to join the Confederacy as an admiral, proving that sometimes meteorologists don't know which way the wind is blowing.

Carlton Cole Magee (1872–1946) You'd probably like Magee if I told you he was the newspaperman who broke the 1920s Teapot Dome scandal (Watergate before Watergate) and came up with the Scripps newspaper company motto "Give Light and the People Will Find Their Own Way." And you'll probably stop liking him when I tell you he also invented the parking meter.

Alan Thicke (1947–2016) Most people remember Alan Thicke as the dad on *Growing Pains*. But he was also an accomplished songwriter, responsible for the theme songs for multiple game shows, as well as for the sitcoms *Diff'rent Strokes* and *The Facts of Life*.

Bert Convy (1933–1991) Before he became a renowned game show host (*Tattletales*; *Win, Lose, or Draw*), Bert Convy was a renowned Broadway actor. He was the original Perchik in *Fiddler on the Roof* and the original Cliff in *Cabaret*. And before *that*, Convy was a somewhat less renowned minor-league baseball player. And might I add, Bert Convy was a very, very handsome man and died way too early.

DEATH OF A TREE

THE LIVE OAKS OF TOOMER'S CORNER

{1937–2013}

On Saturday, April 20, 2013, tens of thousands of people gathered at the corner of College Street and Magnolia Avenue in the center of Auburn, Alabama, to take part in an extraordinary ritual, a ritual that may very well perplex anthropologists of the distant future. It was a funeral of a kind—but a funeral for two trees, southern live oaks (*Quercus virginiana* in Linnaean nomenclature) that stood at the spot known to locals as Toomer's Corner. For eighty-five years these two specimens had served as silent sentries at the entrance to the Auburn University campus. And for about half of their arboreal lives, they had presided over the jubilant celebrations of students and alumni after every victory of the university's vaunted football team.

The trees were technically not yet dead, but they were most certainly dying—starving to death, unable to photosynthesize. The valiant efforts of the state's best tree doctors had failed to revive them. The town and the university, having passed through the stages of denial and anger, had reached the point of acceptance: the trees were going to be put out of their misery, cut down.

Many campuses have a spiritual center—a bell tower, a statue, a quadrangle—that takes on a special role in the communal life of the college. At Auburn, that site is Toomer's Corner, named for Sheldon Toomer, a former halfback turned drugstore owner who set up shop there in 1896 and whose business today is best known for Auburn Tigers tchotchkes and fresh-squeezed lemonade. In 1937, catty-corner from the drugstore, two trees were planted that became the heart and soul of the campus. Memories differ as to how the tradition began, but sometime in the 1970s the spirited (as in joyful, sometimes aided by spirits) young men and women of Auburn began the practice of "rolling" the trees after games—such was the lingo for draping the lordly, leafy oaks with enough toilet paper to clean up after a family of elephants ate a healthy dinner.

With the beloved oaks scheduled to meet their fate at the hands of a team of chain saw–wielding Kevorkians, one last "rolling" was planned. More than 80,000 students, alumni, families, and townspeople congregated at Toomer's Corner. Speeches were given, tears were shed, and then the Charmin, Cottonelle, White Cloud, Soft-n-Gentle, and Quilted Northern Ultra-Plush began to fly. But what made this bizarre ritual all the more poignant was that the trees that were, in their own way, being laid out for death had not fallen victim to blight or old age. They had been murdered.

When I first read about the killing of these live oaks, I found it disturbing— really more than disturbing: I found it *sinister*. What kind of a person would kill two beautiful innocent living things? I thought about how cruelty to animals is a predictor of violence against other people, sometimes horrific violence. I thought of a kid up the street from where I grew up named Kevin. He used to get a kick out of crushing little baby bird eggs he found in nests. I don't know what happened to him but I still don't like the name Kevin. I even thought about the Taliban blowing up the monumental statues of Buddha at Bamyan, Afghanistan, in 2001.

Look, you might think that comparing the killing of two trees to the torture of animals or human beings or to the destruction of a religious shrine is over the top. And maybe it is . . . But sorry, what kind of person would do this? To make sense of all this, I realized I had to visit the scene of the crime and meet the man who did it.

But first, I needed some background. I needed to understand the history of Auburn football. And to understand Auburn football, I needed to understand its rivalry with the University of Alabama. (From here on out, I'll refer to the University of Alabama and its team the Crimson Tide simply as "Alabama.") Wayne Flynt, a scholar of Alabama history, helped explain this complicated story to me.

The Auburn-Alabama rivalry has its origins in the politics of the Civil War and Reconstruction. In 1862, Congress passed the first Morrill Land Grant Act, ceding federal resources to the states for the creation of colleges dedicated to "such branches of learning as are related to agriculture and the mechanic arts." The idea behind these new universities was a radical one in higher education. Instead of organizing their curricula around scholarly book-learning along the model of Oxford and Cambridge, these new schools emphasized practical skills, training students in the technical knowledge that farmers, mechanics, and engineers would need as the United States modernized. In many states these schools now bear the name "A&M" or "State"—they're sometimes called "Aggie" schools—though the original land-grant schools also included Purdue, Cornell, and the Massachusetts Institute of Technology.

When the windfall of federal land-grant money became available, Alabama's existing universities, naturally, began to fight over it. During Reconstruction, the Alabama state legislature was controlled by Republicans, and the Republicans granted the federal money to a small private Methodist school in the town of Auburn called Eastern Alabama Male College, rather than the University of Alabama. The college was renamed the Agricultural and Mechanical College of Alabama. Since 1960 it has been known as Auburn University.

However, if you've read the Mobit for the Black Congressmen of Reconstruction—and if you haven't, why the hell not?—then you already know that Reconstruction was short-lived. Soon after the Compromise of 1877, southern white Democrats (the former Confederates) regained political control of the South. When they did, they attempted to roll back every last change that the Republican lawmakers had instituted. In Alabama, the new legislature was dominated by alumni from Alabama, and the changes they sought to undo included the establishment of the new "A&M" university. In other words, the Alabama alums tried to seize the federal resources for their own alma mater. It was an ugly political fight, but Auburn survived—and so did the hatred.

The rivalry had a socioeconomic dimension, too. Alabama, established back in 1831, was home to the state's power elite. Its traditional curriculum, its law school, its business school, even its well-connected system of fraternities functioned to help the children of the state's wealthy and prestigious families retain, for another generation, their power and status. Auburn, meanwhile, was primarily a school for farmers and engineers, a "cow college," a poor country cousin. (Today, however, Auburn alumni take pleasure in the irony that their school, with its STEM emphasis, produces the higher-paid graduates, including Tim Cook, the CEO of Apple.)

Into this economic and political rivalry came the new game of football, imported from the Northeast. Previously, manliness in Alabama had been demonstrated in farming and hunting, then in battle during the Civil War. Then the gridiron became the new battlefield. In 1893 an annual match between Auburn and Alabama was inaugurated, and over the twentieth century, the rivalry took on a fervor that even the most storied conflicts couldn't approach. As sports radio host Paul Finebaum (who will have a big role in this story) explained to me: "It's difficult to describe, particularly to someone who doesn't live here. It's really the Israelis and the Palestinians. . . . Two sides that have a long history of hate." Not surprisingly, from the first there were arguments over rules, tactics, officiating—and sometimes even violence between the opposing fans. The animosity reached such a height that the annual game was suspended in 1908. Only in 1947, at the behest of the state legislature, was the rivalry renewed.

During this long hiatus, however, the better-funded, more prestigious program at Alabama thrived, and football became a way for the whole state by proxy to gain respect on the national stage. The South had been left reeling from the Civil War, and in the nation's economic and cultural centers it was viewed as a backwater. But then, as Finebaum said: "In '26 Alabama boarded a train and went to the Rose Bowl and beat Washington. And it was one of the biggest moments for the South in decades." Both Auburn and Alabama at the time were all-white, but Alabama was the one that took up the cause of the defeated Confederacy in doing battle with the football powers of the North and West. As Wayne Flynt told me, during the years where the Auburn-Alabama rivalry was suspended, "The University of Alabama was the one that was carrying the sword into battle on behalf of white identity, southern white identity, not Auburn."

By the time the annual game between the rivals was renewed after World War II, college football had secured its place as the only sport that mattered in the state. Pro baseball, basketball, football, and hockey teams had sprouted up in the big cities of the North and Midwest, but the South never had the growth to sustain pro franchises. Until the end of the 1980s, in fact, there were, outside of Atlanta and Texas, virtually no big-league sports teams in the South.

But if Alabama lacked pro sports, it did have Bear Bryant, Alabama's legendary football coach. During the civil rights era, the national media and much of the country looked upon figures like Alabama's segregationist governor George "Stand in the Schoolhouse Door" Wallace and the brutally racist Bull Connor—the state's "Commissioner of Public Safety" who ordered fire hoses and attack dogs to be used against civil rights marchers—with derision and contempt. Bryant by contrast became a respected national icon. (Bryant's own record on civil rights has long been debated. While the Crimson Tide wouldn't integrate until 1971—yes, *1971*—Bryant had been quietly lobbying Alabama alum Wallace for years to allow him to recruit black players.)

Today everyone in Alabama roots for either Alabama or Auburn. It's just a way of life in the Yellowhammer State. (I'm sure the state has plenty of bird lovers but really they should just call it the Pigskin State.) The teams play every year at the end of the season, in a game called the Iron Bowl, which attracts more viewers on regional TV than the Oscars or the Super Bowl. Alabama has been the dominant team, with a total of seventeen national championships, most famously under Bryant in the 1960s and '70s, and for the last decade or so under Nick Saban, the only man to come anywhere near Bryant in the Crimson Tide pantheon. Auburn, in contrast, claims only two national titles (or five, depending on how you count—but that's a long story for sports geeks only). Yet in spite of that disparity, the head-to-head numbers are surprisingly even, thanks in large part to Auburn superstars like Bo Jackson and Cam Newton: Alabama holds an edge of 45–36, with one tie. And the Iron Bowl has often proved instrumental in deciding the national champion.

The 2010 Iron Bowl, held on November 26, was one for the ages. If Auburn-Alabama is the Arab-Israeli conflict, then this game was the Suez Crisis, the Six-Day War, and the Yom Kippur War all rolled into one. Auburn, led by quarterback Cam Newton, came in undefeated and ranked second in the nation behind Oregon. But Alabama, playing at home, was the reigning national champion and a three-and-a-half-point favorite. Emotions, as always, were at a fever pitch. To make things even more heated, Newton was under investigation for his father's alleged solicitation of bribes during his son's recruitment. The story was raging in the sports press, and Alabama fans had nicknamed the star athlete "Scam Newton."

Over a hundred thousand people filled the stands in Tuscaloosa, the home of the University of Alabama. During warm-ups, the Alabama public address system taunted "Scam" by playing Steve Miller's "Take the Money and Run" and Dusty Springfield's "Son of a Preacher Man," while fans threw *Monopoly* money at him. Alabama jumped out to a 24–0 lead at the end of the first half. But Newton's size, speed, and strength proved too much for the Alabama defense. He led his team back from the biggest deficit in Iron Bowl history to win by a score of 28–27. Auburn went on to defeat Oregon for the national championship, while Newton won the Heisman Trophy and became the top pick in the next year's NFL draft. (He would later lead the NFL Carolina Panthers to Super Bowl XL.) The game was immortalized in the annals of the rivalry as "The Camback."

The close losses hurt the worst, and Alabama took this one hard. One fan in particular took it very hard. In January, an Alabama supporter identifying himself only as "Al from Dadeville" called in to Paul Finebaum's radio show, the region's most popular sports talk program. He began by claiming that when Bear Bryant had died back in 1983, Auburn students had "rolled" Toomer's Oaks in celebration.

Finebaum was skeptical—there's absolutely no evidence that such a celebration took place—but the caller insisted he had a newspaper clipping to prove it. (He later said the clipping was destroyed in a fire.) He continued with a claim that sounded like both a boast and a confession: "This year I was at the Iron Bowl and I saw where they put a Scam Newton jersey on Bear Bryant's statue. . . ." There *is* evidence that this happened. He went on: "Let me tell you what I did. The weekend after the Iron Bowl, I went to Auburn, Alabama . . . and I poisoned the two Toomer's Trees . . . I put Spike 80DF in them." Spike 80DF contains tebuthiuron, a powerful herbicide that kills plants by blocking photosynthesis. Finebaum began to sound concerned:

FINEBAUM: Did they die?
CALLER: They're not dead yet but they—
FINEBAUM: They will be?
CALLER: They definitely will die.
FINEBAUM: Is that against the law to poison a tree?
CALLER: Well, do you think I care?
FINEBAUM: No.
CALLER: Okay, I really don't . . . Roll, damn Tide!
(Click.)

Led by horticulture professor Gary Keever, Auburn began to test the soil around Toomer's Oaks. Keever quickly confirmed that the trees had been poisoned with massive doses of Spike 80DF. Within a month of the phone call to the Finebaum show, the police had arrested a suspect and charged him with criminal mischief. The real name of "Al from Dadeville" was Harvey Updyke Jr.

Unlike Toomer's oak trees, Harvey Updyke Jr. is very much alive today. I arranged to meet him on a hot summer afternoon—not in Alabama, but in Texas, where he was living with his son and daughter-in-law. I wanted to hear from the man himself just what would motivate such a horrific crime.

When I meet Harvey he is sixty-nine years old and looks it. His hair is such a light blond that it seems white. He has a biker mustache—the kind that Hulk Hogan has—with a goatee. He is wearing a houndstooth Alabama cap to match his short-sleeved polo with the crimson "A" insignia.

To call him a rabid fan would be a gross understatement. Harvey named his first daughter Crimson Tyde. He named his son Bear Bryant. He wanted to name his next daughter Allie, as in "Allie Bama," but her mother vetoed the idea. He owns more than sixty Alabama hats and his truck is decorated with a decal of the cartoon boy Calvin—of *Calvin and Hobbes* fame—urinating on Auburn. He emphasizes how loyal a fan he's been for four decades, even "when they was down"—a reference to the team's uncharacteristically poor decade of performance following a scandal in the midnineties.

Like many of the most fervent fans on both sides of the Alabama-Auburn rivalry, he didn't actually attend either school. As Erin C. Tarver, a philosophy professor at Emory University and the author of a study of sports fandom, observes, "Fans of the University of Alabama's football team exhibit a borderline religious devotion to the Crimson Tide, even if they have no academic connection to the university." Many actual alumni, in fact, are a little embarrassed by the frenzy of the fans who paint their bodies with team colors, hurl insults at each other on social media, and rant madly on talk radio.

Yet for all Harvey's fervor, he doesn't strike me as a killer. I meet his son, his daughter-in-law, his young granddaughters—Harvey roots like crazy for them at their softball games. Twenty minutes into our conversation, if I have to sum him up in one word, it's not "scary" or "creepy," but . . . "grandpa." On the surface, he really seems like a regular ol' grandpa.

If anything I'm now even more baffled by what he did. I realize a lot of sports fans are crazy. Every Sunday, men across the country regress to the emotional age of eight and don expensive jerseys bearing the names of other men—athletes usually much younger and physically fitter than themselves, men whom they have never met unless they've paid money and stood patiently in line for hours for an auto-graph and a handshake. Fans in fact often care about the outcome of a game far more than the players themselves do. Psychologists who study the phenomenon will tell you the benefits of group identification, the feelings of bonding and be-longing it can produce, even among those loyal to perennial losers. But in Harvey Updyke, the causes go deeper. Lots of people cheer, scream, paint their faces, and tailgate to excess. Very few murder trees.

So, down in the heat of the Texas summer, I still don't have a handle on how this friendly grandpa character could have done what he did. But then we go grab lunch at a local surf-and-turf spot. Over catfish fingers and a mixed green salad, I hear what I can only describe as Harvey's origin story.

When Harvey was three years old, he tells me, his father, a trucker, was killed by a drunk driver. (Newspaper accounts suggest that the older Updyke fell asleep at the wheel before crashing and that no other vehicle was involved. But I believe that Harvey Jr. believes his father was killed by a drunk driver.) The only memory Harvey retains of Harvey Updyke Sr. is of being picked up to kiss his dead father's forehead as the body lay in an open casket. "It scared me to death," Harvey recalls. "It felt like marble or something. . . ." His father's sudden death became the defining event in his life. Years later, he became a police officer. He says he could be lenient on speeders, but never on drunk drivers.

Into the void left by the death of Harvey Updyke Sr. stepped Bear Bryant. When Harvey was little, Bryant had a TV show that aired statewide every Sunday after Alabama football games. (Harvey lived just over the state line in Florida, close enough to pick up the TV signal.) The revered coach would recap the previous day's game, show highlights, interview players, and impart to his viewers—really congregants—what one historian calls "platitudes, homilies, and paeans to God, country, and family." Harvey Jr., young and fatherless, watched religiously, as his mother ironed. At the age of seven or eight, Harvey says, he told his mother that he would name his own son Bear Bryant, since Bryant was everything a father should be. He remembers especially that Bryant would make his players call their parents on weekends: "And you know I just thought he was a great person. I still think he is."

I can see why the strong, proud, successful figure of Bear Bryant offered safety and security to the vulnerable, fatherless Harvey. And I can only imagine how hard it hit Harvey when Bryant died in 1983. Then twenty-seven years after that came the Auburn victory in Tuscaloosa, on Bear Bryant's home turf, on top of the outrage of seeing Bryant's statue desecrated with the jersey of the hated "Scam" Newton. Add to this Harvey's belief that Auburn students had celebrated the death of Bear Bryant.

None of this is to excuse what Harvey did. It's inexcusable. Investigators initially worried Auburn's water table had been contaminated. That's how much Spike 80 Harvey had used. But it is worth understanding his twisted rationale. Throughout my day with Harvey, I struggle to make sense of who he really is. Sometimes I see that regular grandpa, somewhat chastened and even embarrassed by the knowledge that he committed a terrible act. Harvey expresses remorse and an awareness of wrongdoing ("Them trees wasn't hurting me"), and concedes that he deserved to serve time (though be boasts that he was quite popular in prison). At Finebaum's urging, he even called in to the show again to offer a kind of apology.

Other times, however, he seems proud and defiant. He avoids the word *regret*. He tells me in one of his typically maddeningly confusing locutions: "I didn't mean it . . . yes, I did." When he reflects on what he did, he seems remorseful and defensive at the same time: "If it was any kind of living animal—any kind of dog, cat, or, you know, there's no way I would have done it. I don't even like cats and I wouldn't have done it. . . . But it's too late now."

Having confessed to killing the trees first on the radio and then to the police, Harvey Updyke had no chance in court. Moreover, he liked to talk to the media, made a terrible witness, and caused lawyer after lawyer to quit in frustration. Eventually he struck a plea bargain, agreeing to six months behind bars, a five-year probation, and a fine of $800,000 to be paid in monthly installments. To date, he has paid very little.

By the end of the final rolling of the original Toomer's Oaks on April 20, 2013, hardly a square inch of bark was visible. The toilet paper lay thick on the ground; it hung from traffic lights, shrubs, and the celebrants themselves. In some places, said Gary Keever, the paper "was so deep that you were just looking at the tops of people's heads." It was the end of a tradition that had lasted over forty years. The remains of the trees were fashioned by expert craftsmen into polished keepsakes. Inside the campus gates, a memorial walkway was planted with seedlings grown from acorns taken from the original oaks, nurtured by Auburn's own esteemed forestry faculty.

It was a cathartic day, where fans could honor and mourn the loss of two non-human living beings with whom they had formed a genuinely meaningful bond. As Keever noted at the time, the trees had created a gathering place, providing under their generous canopy a shared space where Auburnites could perpetuate a storied—if asinine—tradition. (The toilet paper, it turned out, was killing the trees before Harvey even poisoned them.) "They are just two trees, technically," Keever told me. "But the role that they played was something special in our lives."

In February 2016, almost three years after the original oaks were taken down, new trees were planted, and the tradition of rolling the oaks at Toomer's Corner resumed. But that September, as the trees were draped in paper after a fourth-quarter comeback win over LSU, a twenty-nine-year-old man named Jochen Wiest, unaffiliated with either Auburn or Alabama, set the toilet paper on fire. The tissue, alas, made for superb fuel, and the tree was engulfed in flame. Wiest was immediately apprehended and later pleaded guilty to first-degree criminal mischief. He received a suspended sentence of three years and was ordered to pay $20,000 in restitution. This second act of vandalism shocked an already shaken Auburn community, and Tiger loyalists feared that the trees might become a recurring target. New oaks were planted yet again in February 2017.

The World's First Christmas Tree

In the Old Town section of Riga, Latvia, amid the cobblestones of Town Hall Square, a stone marker commemorates the spot where the world's first Christmas tree stood—well, sort of. There in 1510, the story goes, a professional guild of unmarried merchants known as the Brotherhood of the Black Heads paraded through town carrying a fir tree decorated with candles and fruits. Their celebration included singing, dancing, drinking, and, finally, burning the tree to the ground. Today, every Christmas, a tree is decorated here, though the arson part has been discontinued. But like so many historical claims, bragging rights to the site of the first Christmas tree are fiercely disputed. Estonia, Latvia's neighbor to the immediate north, asserts that its capital, Tallinn, is the actual location of the first Christmas tree. Tallinn's claim dates back to 1441. I can't settle this one but I can tell you who holds the record for the longest-standing Christmas tree: my father loved the holiday so much, one year we kept ours up until March!

The Tree of Ténéré

The Tree of Ténéré was for many years regarded as the world's most isolated tree. An acacia tree in the Sahara Desert, it was the only tree for 250 miles in any direction. Travelers used it as a landmark. A French military officer described it as "a living lighthouse," writing, "One must see the tree to believe its existence. What is its secret? How can it still be living in spite of the multitudes of camels which trample at its sides?" The tree had acquired a kind of sacred status to the Tuareg salt traders who passed by in their caravans, yet never touched its branches for firewood. Then, in 1973, the tree was destroyed by a Libyan truck driver, probably drunk, and apparently so incompetent that he could not avoid the *only tree for 250 miles in any direction*.

Anne Frank's Chestnut Tree

Readers of Anne Frank's diary will remember how, in hiding from the Nazis in Amsterdam, she looked out her window at a white horse-chestnut tree growing in the courtyard of number 188 Keizersgracht. In the winter, the tree's bare branches, silvered with raindrops, reminded Anne of the beauty of the world she could only view from a distance. On February 23, 1944, she wrote: "As long as this exists, and it certainly always will, I know that then there will always be comfort for every sorrow, whatever the circumstances may be." The tree became a symbol of hope. In 1993, when a leaking underground fuel tank endangered its roots, the city of Amsterdam undertook soil purification. A decade later caterpillars and fungus threatened the tree. The owner of the property on which it sat wanted to take it down (I don't want to know this person), but a public protest prevented him. Yet it soon became clear that the tree's life was nearing its end. The Anne Frank House created the Sapling Project, through which it distributed saplings from the original chestnut tree to schoolyards and parks worldwide. Finally, in 2010 a storm took down the sixty-five-foot-tall tree, which had lived for roughly 170 years.

The Giving Tree If you've never read this book by Shel Silverstein—or had it read to you—it tells the story of an apple tree and a boy. The boy plays in her branches, rests in her shade, and eats her fruit. But then the boy grows up and leaves, returning only occasionally and always to ask the tree for things—her fruit, her branches, eventually even her trunk, which she willingly gives and he uses to build himself a boat. She is selfless and never says no, even when the boy acts like a brat. He finally returns as a tired old man, seeking only the stump that is left to sit on. The tree obliges, happy to give what little she has left . . . and boy, this story makes me feel like crap. Call your mother.

The Spaghetti Tree (b. April 1, 1957) In 1957, the BBC news program *Panorama* presented a newsreel-style black-and-white feature about the early arrival of Switzerland's annual spaghetti harvest. Yes, spaghetti. Over footage of young women harvesting spaghetti from trees and laying it gently in baskets, reporter Richard Dimbleby, who had earned people's trust as an acclaimed war correspondent, explained that generations of patient breeding had led to plants that yield spaghetti strands of remarkably uniform length. Spaghetti was at that time a relatively rare dish in the United Kingdom. Dimbleby's paean to "real homegrown spaghetti" elicited hundreds of inquiries by letter and telephone from Brits seeking to grow their own spaghetti trees. Orson Welles's *War of the Worlds* broadcast may rank as one of the scariest hoaxes, but the Spaghetti Tree has been called the greatest April Fool's joke ever played.

The Senator At the start of 2012, the Senator was a 3,500-year-old, 125-foot-high bald cypress tree in Longwood, Florida, thought to be the largest of its species. It had once served as a landmark for Seminoles and other Native Americans who lived in central Florida. But on the night of January 16, twenty-six-year-old aspiring model Sara Barnes visited Big Tree Park to smoke meth. In order to see in the dark, she started a fire *inside the tree.* The fire blazed out of control, and the Senator was soon reduced to little more than what the *Orlando Weekly* described as a "poor, scorched stump." Barnes was sentenced to probation and community service and ordered to pay for the removal of the tree's remains and the cost of the investigation. Luckily, clones of the tree have been planted. These should grow to the height of the original in approximately 3,500 years.

Augustine Washington's Cherry Tree

You may have heard about this one: the six-year-old future father of our nation was given a hatchet for his birthday and used it to cut down his father's favorite cherry tree. When Augustine Washington confronted his son, the lumberjack-in-training fessed up, saying, "Father, I cannot tell a lie, I cut it down with my hatchet," setting a standard of honesty that American children would for the coming centuries seek to emulate. It turns out that the episode was invented by an early biographer of Washington's, a minister named Mason Locke Weems, whose main goals were (a) to sell books and (b) to turn Washington's life into a string of simplistic moral parables. This bogus anecdote was then picked up in 1836 by another minister, William Holmes McGuffey, whose *McGuffey Readers* were a staple on nineteenth-century American reading lists. P. T. Barnum got in on the act, too. Among his performers in the 1830s was an elderly enslaved woman, Joice Heth, who Barnum claimed was 161 years old and the former nanny of George Washington. Heth would tell the cherry tree story as if she had been an eyewitness. Of course, not everyone has found the story harmless. Oscar Wilde thought that America's obsession with honesty explained everything wrong with the nation, from its "crude commercialism" to its "materializing spirit" to its "lack of imagination." As he said: "The story of George Washington and the cherry tree has done more harm, and in a shorter space of time, than any other moral tale in the whole of literature." Plus, who gives their six-year-old an ax as a birthday present?

DEDICATION

MARCEL "JACK" ROCCA
{1929–2004}

On Christmas morning 1979, while my brothers and I were ripping the wrapping paper off our presents, my father opened a box from my mother. It was actually a rectangular case and inside was a trumpet.

My father had played the trumpet as a teenager. There's a wonderful picture of him in his Boy Scout uniform blowing on the horn. He looks like a bugler summoning the troops for the day.

He'd stopped playing after a short while and regretted it enough that my mother knew what to get him that year. She and my grandmother, who was visiting from Colombia, had found it at a pawnshop in downtown DC. I remember his genuine delight when he opened the case. My father was fifty years old.

With very rare exceptions, he went down to the cellar twice each day, *every day*, to practice. A half hour of scales and other exercises in the morning. Then an hour of playing the horn, mostly Dixieland ("None of that 'cool jazz' for me," he'd say) after he came home from work.

Our house in Bethesda, Maryland—just outside of DC—was a

modest-sized split-level and noise carried so I can't say that I didn't complain sometimes about the trumpet. That's putting it mildly. My father usually put the mute in. (There was a red-and-white one.) The ticking of the metronome was the sound bed of my youth.

Sometimes I would roller skate in the cellar as he was playing in the evening. There was laundry hanging in two rows. (The dryer crapped out in the mid-1970s and until we bought a new one about fifteen years later we line-dried our clothes.) I would skate in and out between hanging towels and bedsheets. And if I worked up enough speed I'd grab the metal pole in the middle of the cellar and spin around, my version of a salchow. Or was that a lutz? All I knew was that in that moment I was at Innsbruck winning gold to "When the Saints Go Marching In." Say what you will about my routine, but my music selection was out of the box.

The trumpet brought my father so much joy in life. Even as a child I knew he was too late in life to be taking this up as a career. Of course he knew it, too. He just wanted to be good at it, to produce a beautiful sound. That's no small thing. You can pick up the clarinet and play *something* in a matter of weeks. I know. I took up the clarinet at around the same time and gave up . . . in a matter of weeks. To produce any kind of a sound with the trumpet takes constant work. (There was a series of faded xeroxed sheets taped to the wall that explained how to improve your "embouchure." That's the way the player's lips connect to the mouthpiece. It's a word I'm proud to have spelled just now without the help of autocorrect.)

He'd always had a nice singing voice. He told me that Irving Berlin's favorite singer was Fred Astaire—yes, *dancer* Fred Astaire—because even though Astaire had a thin, reedy voice, he sang with such heart. My father sang and played the trumpet with heart. As I write, I'm looking at the old sheets of yellow legal pad paper where he wrote out his song lists by categories. I'm looking under "BALLADS" and remembering the warm vibrato he had on "I'll Be Seeing You" and "Polka Dots and Moonbeams."

One Monday when I was in seventh grade, Pop was driving me home from dance class at nearby Glen Echo Park. (Yes, my Korean War vet father drove me to dance class: ballet, jazz, and modern.) Monday was also the night of his jam session. After dropping me off, he had to drive about forty-five minutes over to College Park to play with four or five other guys (George on trombone and Ray on the banjo are the ones I remember). But as he pulled in to the driveway to let me out of the car, my mother walked out on the front stoop. My father got out of the car, too, to see why.

"Dick Durfee died," she said. Dick was my father's best friend from the army. We'd seen him and his family only a few years earlier in Quincy, Illinois, when we were driving back home to Maryland from our summer vacation in New Orleans—where we went so that my father could hear live Dixieland. I'm not sure that Dick had even really been sick. He certainly wasn't old.

My father bowed his head. "I have to go to my jam session" was all I remember him saying. And with a very heavy heart—my father was very sensitive; a dead bird at the side of the road filled him with sorrow—he got back in the car and drove off to do the thing he loved. You didn't miss the jam session. You didn't let the guys down.

Just a couple of years ago I was guest-hosting a live variety show in New York backed by Jay Leonhart and his orchestra. Jay's son Michael Leonhart is a terrific trumpet player. Because I was thinking about writing about trumpet players for this book, I asked Michael if there was a certain personality trait that trumpeters shared.

"The thing about the trumpet," he said, "is that if you make a mistake, if you bust a note, everyone knows it. You can't cover it up like you can if you play the saxophone. To come back after embarrassing yourself like that, the very next night, you gotta be a certain kind of person."

It was such a keen observation. And it wasn't inconsistent with the stereotypes around trumpet players: volatile personalities like the great Lee Morgan, who was shot dead onstage at Slugs' Saloon in New York's East Village by the common-law wife he'd betrayed. There's a good reason why so many great trumpet players die before they hit thirty. They are bold.

My father was many things. He felt things very deeply. (When I was thirteen he took me and my best friend, Mario, to see the movie *Frances*, the tragic story of the actress Frances Farmer, starring Jessica Lange. During the scene when she's lobotomized he got up and waited in the lobby for the rest of the movie. He found her story just too sad to bear.) He was indulgent. (All those quarters he gave me to play *Ms. Pac-Man* at the drugstore.) My friends still talk about how warm and friendly he was. (I can still hear the hearty way he would say hello every single time to the Somali immigrants who worked at the 7-Eleven near our house. Sometimes I think they were startled!) He had a great laugh, especially for corny jokes. (*Never* dirty jokes.) But I hadn't thought of him also as the type of person willing, as Michael said, to bust a big note in public and get right back onstage, as someone so *bold*.

But of course he was bold. *He took up the trumpet at age fifty.* He and his buddies from the jam session formed a band called the Metrotones. They had vests made. They played at restaurants sometimes but mostly at retirement homes. But as far as my father was concerned, every gig might as well have been the Blue Note. He took it that seriously, was that nervous ahead of time and that happy while it was happening.

So often in writing this book my father sprang to mind. Partly because my love of obituaries comes from him. Partly because so many of the things he liked—old movies, the music of Jerome Kern, long car rides—are the things I like. When my boyfriend and I missed our flight to Buffalo—a very underrated summer vacation destination—I was not-so-secretly excited that we'd have to rent a car and drive eight hours from New York City.

But there's a larger sense in which he's been my guide through this endeavor. The greatest compliment I've received on the *Mobituaries* podcast has been that the subjects were treated with compassion—the "Siamese Twins" Chang and Eng, who were brought to America for exhibition; JFK impersonator Vaughn Meader, whose life fell apart at age twenty-seven; even the Auburn University tree killer. That's a compliment I most certainly share with the small group of talented producers who collaborated with me and worked their hearts out on it.

So much of my own capacity for compassion comes from my father. And my stick-to-itiveness (a word I love and wish autocorrect recognized). And my appreciation for talent. (You may have noticed a preponderance of artists profiled in this book.)

Writing a book is an optimistic act. My father was the most optimistic person I've ever known.

Did I mention he took up the trumpet at age fifty?

MO ROCCA
Sunday, June 16, 2019
Father's Day

ACKNOWLEDGMENTS

MO ROCCA

The ever-wise Jon Karp and I had talked for years about my doing a book, but only if the topic genuinely excited me. Book ideas are like organ transplants, he likes to say. They'll be rejected by the host body unless they're truly a match. So far, *Mobituaries* has taken. I am grateful to him and Rand Morrison for making both the book and the podcast possible.

Rand Morrison is more than the executive producer of *CBS Sunday Morning*; he is its heart and soul. Anyone who works on the show can attest to the profound joy he takes week in and week out in creating a ninety-minute broadcast. I have turned to him for guidance on every aspect of both the *Mobituaries* podcast and book. He is a model and mentor, and he is my friend.

I am so glad I ran into my old friend Jonathan Greenberg on the street two years ago in the West Village. He has been the perfect partner on this book. The afternoons we spent together on this were, more than anything else, fun. And both our heads are now stuffed with facts to the point of bursting.

From the start, my editor, Emily Graff, helped bring order to the whole. Seriously, at the beginning, I had no idea how the hell these pieces would fit together. I am grateful to her for her deep intelligence, her thoughtfulness, and her sense of humor. She never once lost confidence in me. (And if she did, she's a great actress.) Her recurring note to be direct with the reader is good life advice.

If you're looking for a great producer, you'd be lucky to find one half as good as Megan Marcus. Her work on the *Mobituaries* podcast and on the research side of the *Mobituaries* book have proved invaluable. Gideon Evans, Kate McAuliffe, Alison Byrne, David Fuchs, and Genia Stanescki—all of them outstanding—share credit in bringing the *Mobits* podcast to #1 during its first season. Thanks also to Mark Hudspeth, Lucie Kirk, Mike Levine, Kay Lim, and Harry Wood for joining the fun for season two.

I'm grateful for the cartooning genius of Mitch Butler, the razor-sharp wit of my friend Adam Felber, the imagination of Hank Greenberg, and the seriously deep well of old movie knowledge of Francisco Robaina and Steven Spanbauer. Thank you, Matthew Brown, for diagramming the first line of Bill Cosby's obit. And thank you, Kitty Burns Florey, for vetting said diagram.

My thanks to everyone at Simon & Schuster, including Carolyn Reidy, Lashanda Anakwah, Stephen Bedford, Jonathan Evans, Alison Forner, Cary Goldstein, Kimberly Goldstein, Larry Hughes, Ruth Lee-Mui, Beth Maglione, and Richard Rhorer.

acknowledgments

The *Mobituaries* podcast would not exist without the support of Susan Zirinsky and Charlie Pavlounis. I thank them and everyone at CBS News, including Dustin Gervais, Richard Huff, Dr. Jon LaPook, Emily Lazar, Allen Peng, and Craig Swagler.

Thank you to Jim Lichtenstein and my friends at Innovation Nation (that includes you, Erica!) for accommodating my trickier-than-usual schedule. Likewise, thank you to my friends at *Wait Wait . . . Don't Tell Me!*, including Doug Berman, Ian Chillag, Mike Danforth, Bill Kurtis, and the great Peter Sagal.

I could never have written a book without a corps of friends who were willing to listen to me complain. During the last year I have leaned in particular on Carol Bagnoli, Nell Benjamin, Ginna Carter, John Claflin, Catherine Collins, Mario Correa, Lisa Dallos, Tom de Kay, Julian Fleisher, Susan George, Mark Haug, Shannon Hill, Marilynn and John Hill, Bill Keith, Jim and Leslie Margolis, Madeline McIntosh, Erick Neher, Brian O'Brien, Larry O'Keefe, Faith Salie, Jennifer Simard, Jeanne Simpson, Stephanie Simpson, and Kelsey Wirth.

Samantha Lee was my dear friend and a brilliant editor. When she told me that the idea of *Mobituaries* was a good one, it mattered. I have thought of her often during the project and I will think of her long after.

Don Epstein is the agent you all wish you had for anything. He has taken such good care of me every step of the way for twenty years. We are common-law at this point. Thanks also to our partner-in-crime, my lawyer Peter Grant. (Wait, that didn't come out right.) And my gratitude to Kristen Sena, Jennifer Peykar, Juliet Gabriel, and Melissa Levitt for keeping my head from exploding over so many years.

My brother Lawrence did not hesitate to write a beautiful (and generous) remembrance of my short career in baseball. And he helped jog my memory on events from growing up. My brother Francis has encouraged me through the years and has been a great example. I'm grateful to them both.

One of the great pleasures of writing this book has been the extra time I was allowed to spend at home and with my wonderful mother. If I'd only listened more as a kid, I would have long ago realized how smart and funny she is. Having her so close by is a great gift. We're both very excited for the third season of *The Crown*.

Alberto Robaina is my more than other half. We laugh about how all-consuming this project has been for the both of us. (At least I hope he's still laughing.) If something in the podcast or the book made you laugh or moved you, there's a good chance he helped make it that way. Over the hours and hours (and hours) he's spent listening to cuts of the podcast and reading drafts of the book, I've learned just how smart, sensitive, and deeply intuitive he is—and how lucky I am. I'm saving all his notes.

JONATHAN GREENBERG

Working with Mo Rocca has been a delight, and has given me new respect for his generosity, work ethic, creativity, scrupulousness, and sense of humor. Kim Plaksin, a masters student at Montclair State University, provided critical research assistance for several essays. Hank Greenberg first suggested the comparison of Thomas Paine and T-Pain and a number of the deceased trees, and helped to compile

acknowledgments

the bibliography. Over coffee and trudging through the streets of Montclair, New Jersey, my running group—Andy Coccari, Andy Fried, Ed Gold, Pete Gutowski, Tony Ianuale, Harry Moskowitz, Terry Mullane, Tom Mullane, Patrick O'Neill, Jay Strong, John Thornton—kindly pretended to be interested in this project; it was Patrick who suggested that we do a Mobit for the fur coat. John Lasiter commented extensively and invaluably on the entirety of a long early draft. Conversations with many people enriched my thinking about this project: Bob Weisbuch, Dan Lawson, and Mike Gnojewski; Scott Stevenson and Suzanne Farkas; Adrienne Shulman and John Lasiter. Art Simon, Jeff Miller, David Greenberg, and Susan Wolfson lent scholarly expertise. Andrew Stuart of the Stuart Agency managed the business side of things with ease and grace.

And of course, where would I be without the love and support of my parents, Bob and Maida, and my siblings and my in-laws and their families—Judith, Ira, Claire, Sasha, David, Susanne, Leo, Liza, Gene, Peggy, Kate, Ken, Ellie, Nina, Stephen, Hillary, Spencer, Griffin, Carter. My own children, Hank and Maggie, served as cheerful sounding boards and even laughed when I read them favorite lines. Finally, my wife, Megan Blumenreich, read many different pieces at different stages of completion and ably addressed all kinds of questions, many of them inane, that I put to her during the writing of this book.

WORKS CONSULTED

DEATH OF THE FANTASTIC: DRAGONS

Consulted:

Borges, Jorge Luis, et al. *The Book of Imaginary Beings*. Dutton, 1969.

Broberg, Gunnar. "The Dragonslayer." *TijdSchrift voor Skandinavistiek* 29, no. 1 (2008). https://rjh.ub.rug.nl/tvs/article/view/10739/8310.

Brown, B. Ricardo. "The Paradoxa from the *Systema Natura* by Linnaeus." *Until Darwin Blog.* Nov. 24, 2012. https://until-darwin.blogspot.com/2012/11/the-paradoxa-from-systema-natura-by.html.

Cramer, Marc. "Fabulous Animal Frauds: An Exercise in Human Ingenuity and Fraudulence." *The Connoisseur: An Illustrated Magazine for Collectors* 203 (1980).

Dobbs, Betty Jo Teeter. "Newton's Alchemy and His Theory of Matter." *Isis* 73, no. 4 (1982): 511–28.

Hinge, George. "Dionysus and Hercules in Scythia." *HeroDot.Glossa.dk.* 2003. http://www.glossa.dk/herodot/orph.html.

McNeil, Donald G. "From Many Imaginations, One Fearsome Creature." *New York Times.* April 29, 2003.

"Natural History of Dragons." American Museum of Natural History. https://www.amnh.org/exhibitions/mythic-creatures/dragons/natural-history-of-dragons.

Senter, Phil, Uta Maddox, and Eid E. Haddad. "Snake to Monster: Conrad Gessner's Schlangenbuch and the Evolution of the Dragon in the Literature of Natural History." *Journal of Folklore Research* 53, no. 1 (2016): 67–124.

Silver, Carly. "A Match Made in Greek Legend: What Happened When Heracles Met the Snake Woman?" *Ancient Origins.* Stella Novus, Ltd. March 24, 2017. https://www.ancient-origins.net/myths-legends/match-made-greek-legend-what-happened-when-heracles-met-snake-woman-007771.

Waters, Hannah. "The Enchanting Sea Monsters on Medieval Maps." *Smithsonian Magazine.* Oct. 15, 2013. https://www.smithsonianmag.com/science-nature/the-enchanting-sea-monsters-on-medieval-maps-1805646/.

Quoted:

American Museum of Natural History. "Natural History of Dragons."

Borges, Jorge Luis. *The Book of Imaginary Beings.*

Brown. "The Paradoxa from the *Systema Natura* by Linnaeus."

Cramer. "Fabulous Animal Frauds."

works consulted

. . . and Other Mythological Creatures We Used to Think Were Real

Consulted:

Bane, Theresa. "Kishi." *Encyclopedia of Beasts and Monsters in Myth, Legend and Folklore.* McFarland Publishing, 2016, 192.

Browne, Sir Thomas. "Of Mermaids, Unicorns, Long-Tailed Bears, Flying Horses, and Other Pictures." *Pseudodoxia Epidemica, Book V.* Rpt. at University of Chicago. http://penelope .uchicago.edu/pseudodoxia/pseudo519.html.

Glinski, Mikolaj. "Was Van Helsing Originally from Poland?" *Culture.PL.* April 2, 2015. https:// culture.pl/en/article/was-van-helsing-originally-from-poland.

Lee, Henry. "Sea Fables Explained." 1883. Rpt. at AlternateWars.com. https://www.alternatewars .com/Mythology/Sea_Fables_Expl/Sea_Fables_Expl_II.htm.

Lewalski, Barbara, and Philip Schwyzer, eds. "The Unicorn: End of a Legend." A Web Companion to the *Norton Anthology of English Literature: The Early 17th Century.* https:// www.wwnorton.com/college/english/nael/noa/pdf/27636_17th_U46_Unicorn-1-5.pdf.

NOAA. "Are Mermaids Real?" National Ocean Service. June 25, 2018. https://oceanservice.noaa .gov/facts/mermaids.html.

Payne, John V. "Benign Red Pigmentation of Stool Resulting from Food Coloring in a New Breakfast Cereal (the Franken Berry Stool)." *Pediatrics* 49, no. 2 (February 1972). https:// pediatrics.aappublications.org/content/49/2/293.

Pliny the Elder. *Natural History*, Book 8, Ch. 31. Trans. John Bostock. Rpt. at Perseus Digital Library. Edited by Gregory Crane. Tufts University. http://www.perseus.tufts.edu/hopper /text?doc=Perseus%3Atext%3A1999.02.0137%3Abook%3D8%3Achapter%3D31.

Simon, Matt. "Fantastically Wrong: The Murderous, Sometimes Sexy History of the Mermaid." *Wired.* Oct. 15, 2014. https://www.wired.com/2014/10/fantastically-wrong-strange -murderous-sometimes-sexy-history-mermaid/.

Smith, K. Annabelle. "Franken Berry, the Beloved Halloween Cereal, Was Once Medically Found to Cause Pink Poop." *Smithsonian Magazine.* Oct. 30, 2013. https://www .smithsonianmag.com/arts-culture/franken-berry-the-beloved-halloween-cereal-was-once -medically-found-to-cause-pink-poop-7114570.

Sprat, Thomas. "Excerpt from *The History of the Royal Society*." In "The Unicorn: End of a Legend."

Stieber, Zachary. "Mermaids Are Real: Columbus, Shakespeare, and Pliny the Elder." *The Epoch Times.* Aug. 15, 2013. https://www.theepochtimes.com/mermaid-hoax-columbus -shakespeare-and-pliny-the-elder-say-mermaids-are-real_82540.html.

Quoted:

Lee, Henry. "Sea Fables Explained."

Payne, John V. "Benign Red Pigmentation."

Pliny the Elder. *Natural History.*

Sprat, Thomas. "Excerpt from *The History of the Royal Society*."

DEATH OF A FOUNDING FATHER: THOMAS PAINE

Consulted:

"Abolition of the Slave Trade." *BBC Norfolk*. Sept. 24, 2014. http://www.bbc.co.uk/norfolk /content/articles/2007/03/27/abolition_thomas_paine_20070327_feature.shtml.

Bragg, Melvyn, et al. "Thomas Paine's Common Sense." *In Our Time Podcast: BBC Radio 4*. Jan. 21, 2016. https://www.bbc.co.uk/programmes/b06wg9dw.

Cools, Amy. "Paine on Basic Income and Human Rights." Thomas Paine National Historical Association. http://thomaspaine.org/paine-on-basic-income-and-human-rights.html.

Davis, Burke. *George Washington and the American Revolution*. Random House, 1975.

Feron, James. "Paine Tombstone Uncovered Upstate Revives Mystery about Pamphleteer." *New York Times*. July 19, 1976.

Franklin, Benjamin. "From Benjamin Franklin to—, [13 Dec. 1757]." Founders Online. National Archives. https://founders.archives.gov/documents/Franklin/01-07-02-0130.

Getlen, Larry. "Wanna Piece of Me?" *New York Post*. March 10, 2013. https://nypost .com/2013/03/10/wanna-piece-of-me/.

Grimm, Kevin. "Thomas Paine." *George Washington's Mount Vernon*. https://www.mountvernon .org/library/digitalhistory/digital-encyclopedia/article/thomas-paine/.

Hitchens, Christopher. "Bones of Contention." *Guardian*. July 15, 2006. https://www .theguardian.com/books/2006/jul/15/featuresreviews.guardianreview28.

Lepore, Jill. "The Sharpened Quill." *New Yorker*. Oct. 16, 2006. https://www.newyorker.com /magazine/2006/10/16/the-sharpened-quill.

Lovejoy, Bess. *Rest in Pieces: The Curious Fates of Famous Corpses*. Simon & Shuster, 2013.

"The Macabre Legacy of the Heroes of the American Revolution." StrangeRemains.com. July 4, 2014. https://strangeremains.com/2014/07/04/the-macabre-legacy-of-the-heroes-of-the -american-revolution/.

Napolitano, Ann. "2. Thomas Paine (1737–1809)." AnnNapolitano.com. http://annnapolitano .com/2011/07/12/2-thomas-paine-1737-1809/.

Nelson, Craig. *Thomas Paine: Enlightenment, Revolution, and the Birth of Modern Nations*. Penguin, 2006.

Paine, Thomas. "African Slavery in America." *Pennsylvania Journal and the Weekly Advertiser*. March 8, 1775. Rpt. at Constitution Society. https://www.constitution.org/tp/afri.htm.

———. "Age of Reason Letters." *Writings*.

———. "Letter to George Washington, Jul. 30, 1796." *Writings*.

———. "Letter to George Washington, Sept 20, 1795." *Writings*.

———. "Rights of Man Part the First." *Writings*.

———. "Age of Reason: Part I." *Writings*.

———. "Letter to Thomas Jefferson, Dec 25, 1802." *Writings*.

———. *Writings*. Edited by Philip Foner. Rpt at. Thomas Paine National Historical Association. http://thomaspaine.org/pages/writings.html#.

Riggenbach, Jeff. "Thomas Paine: From Pirate to Revolutionary." Foundation for Economic Education. Sept. 28, 2016. https://fee.org/articles/thomas-paine-from-pirate-to-revolutionary/.

"This Day in History: December 28: An American Hero Is Arrested in France." History.com. Dec. 13, 2018. https://www.history.com/this-day-in-history/an-american-hero-is-arrested-in-france.

"Thomas Paine Honored After 100 Years." *New York Times.* May 8, 1910.

"Thomas Paine's Remains Are Still a Bone of Contention." *Los Angeles Times.* April 1, 2001.

"Twenty Celebrities You Didn't Know Were Muslim." Beliefnet.com. https://www.beliefnet.com/entertainment/celebrities/galleries/20-celebrities-you-didnt-know-were-muslim.aspx?p=17.

Untitled Obituary. *The New-York Evening Post.* Jun. 10, 1809. Rpt. at "Paine Relief." *Classic Works of Apologetics.* https://classicapologetics.com/special/painerelief.html.

Walsh, Kevin. "A Paine in the Village." *Forgotten New York.* May 1, 1999. http://forgotten-ny.com/1999/05/a-paine-in-the-village/.

Quoted:

Lepore, Jill. "The Sharpened Quill."

Nelson, Craig. *Thomas Paine.*

Paine, Thomas. "African Slavery in America."

———. *Writings.*

"Thomas Paine Honored After 100 Years." *New York Times.*

"Twenty Celebrities You Didn't Know Were Muslim." Beliefnet.com.

Untitled Obituary. *New-York Evening Post.*

In Memoriam: The Long s

"Lesson Materials: How to Speak and Write Eighteenth-Century Style." Colonial Williamsburg Foundation. 2011. https://www.history.org/history/teaching/enewsletter/volume10/sept11/images/letterslessonmaterials.pdf.

Lynch, Jack. "A Guide to Eighteenth-Century English Vocabulary." Jack Lynch. Rutgers University–Newark. April 14, 2006. https://andromeda.rutgers.edu/~jlynch/C18Guide.pdf.

West, Andrew. "The Rules for Long S." *Babelstone Blog.* June 12, 2006. http://babelstone.blogspot.com/2006/06/rules-for-long-s.html.

FORGOTTEN FORERUNNER: The Rosa Parks of New York: Elizabeth Jennings

Consulted:

"Aged Colored Teacher Dead." *New York Times.* June 8, 1901.

Alexander, Leslie M. *African or American? Black Identity and Political Activism in New York City, 1784–1861.* University of Illinois Press, 2008.

"City Items." *New-York Daily Tribune,* Feb. 23, 1855.

Hearth, Amy Hill. *Streetcar to Justice: How Elizabeth Jennings Won the Right to Ride in New York.* Greenwillow Books, 2018.

"Outrage upon Colored Persons." *New-York Daily Tribune.* July 19, 1854.

Weigley, Russell Frank, ed. *Philadelphia: A 300-Year History.* Norton, 1982.

"A Wholesome Verdict." *New York Tribune.* Feb. 23, 1855.

Quoted:

"Aged Colored Teacher Dead." *New York Times.*

Alexander, Leslie M. *African or American?*

"A Wholesome Verdict." *New York Tribune.*

Interviewed:

Alexander, Leslie.

Hearth, Amy Hill.

DEATH OF AN INFLUENCER: BEAU BRUMMELL

Consulted:

Baudelaire, Charles. "The Painter of Modern Life." *Selected Writings on Art and Literature.* Translated by P. E. Charvet. Penguin, 1993, 390–436.

"Beau Brummell." *Blackwood's Edinburgh Magazine.* 1844. Rpt. at Dandyism.net. Nov. 7, 2006. http://www.dandyism.net/beau-brummell/.

Bloy, Marjorie. "George Bryan ('Beau') Brummell." A Web of English History. Jan. 12, 2016. http://www.historyhome.co.uk/people/beaubrum.htm.

Dillon, Brian. "Inventory: A Poet of Cloth." *Cabinet*, Issue 21 (Spring 2006). http://www.cabinetmagazine.org/issues/21/dillon.php.

Fitzerman-Blue, Micah. "Beau Knows: Beau Brummell and the Birth of Fit." GQ.com. Oct. 31, 2012. https://www.gq.com/story/beau-knows-beau-brummel-and-the-birth-of-fit.

Kelly, Ian. *Beau Brummell: The Ultimate Dandy.* Hodder, 2006.

Knowles, Rachel. "The Rise and Fall of Beau Brummell." RegencyHistory.net. Nov. 14, 2012. https://www.regencyhistory.net/2012/11/the-rise-and-fall-of-beau-brummell-1778.html.

Lee, Christopher. "Beau Brummell: The Original Gentleman of Style." *Gentleman's Gazette*, Aug. 15, 2018. https://www.gentlemansgazette.com/beau-brummell-the-original/.

Lynch, Tony. "The Heretical Romantic Heroism of Beau Brummell." *European Romantic Review* 27, no. 5 (2016): 679–95.

Moers, Ellen. *The Dandy: Brummell to Beerbohm.* Viking, 1960.

Nigro, Jeffrey A., and William A. Phillips. "A Revolution in Masculine Style: How Beau Brummell Changed Jane Austen's World." *Persuasions* 36, no. 1 (2015). JASNA.org.

Quoted:

Baudelaire, Charles. "The Painter of Modern Life."

"Beau Brummell." *Blackwood's Edinburgh Magazine.*

Fitzerman-Blue, Micah. "Beau Knows."

Kelly, Ian. *Beau Brummell: The Ultimate Dandy.*

Knowles, Rachel. "The Rise and Fall of Beau Brummell."

DEATH OF AN AMERICAN STORY: CHANG AND ENG BUNKER

Consulted:

"Eng and Chang Bunker: The Original Siamese Twins." Surry Arts Council. http://www.surryarts.org/siamesetwins/index.html

Huang, Yunte. *Inseparable: The Original Siamese Twins and Their Rendezvous with American History.* Liveright, 2018.

Melville, Herman. *Moby-Dick.* Penguin Classics, 349.

Orser, Joseph Andrew. *The Lives of Chang and Eng: Siam's Twins in Nineteenth-Century America.* University of North Carolina Press, 2014.

Twain, Mark. "Personal Habits of the Siamese Twins." *Packard's Monthly.* August 1869. Rpt. at *Mark Twain in His Times.* Edited by Stephen Railton. University of Virginia Library Electronic Text Center. http://twain.lib.virginia.edu/wilson/siamese.html.

Quoted:

Melville, Herman. *Moby-Dick.*

Orser, Joseph Andrew. *The Lives of Chang and Eng.*

Twain, Mark. "Personal Habits of the Siamese Twins."

Interviewed:

Huang, Yunte.

LaPook, Joseph.

Orser, Joseph.

Sink, Alex.

. . . and Other "Sideshow" Sensations

Consulted:

Bates, Martin Van Buren. "Boy, Soldier, and Man." Rpt. in "A Brief History of Kona, Letcher County, Ky." Edited by William Thayer. 2009. University of Chicago: Bill Thayer's website. http://penelope.uchicago.edu/Thayer/E/Gazetteer/Places/America/United_States/Kentucky/Letcher/Kona/_Texts/Brief_History.html#Martin_VanBuren_Bates.

Gould, Stephen Jay. "The Hottentot Venus." *The Flamingo's Smile.* Norton, 1985, 291–305.

Parkinson, Justin. "The Significance of Sarah Baartman." *BBC News Magazine.* Jan. 7, 2016. https://www.bbc.com/news/magazine-35240987.

Plucker, Jonathan. "Jean-Marc Gaspard Itard." *Human Intelligence.* 2016. https://www.intelltheory.com/itard.shtml.

Wadsworth, Kimberly. "Lavinia Warren: Half of the 19th Century's Tiniest, Richest Power Couple." *Atlas Obscura.* June 30, 2015. https://www.atlasobscura.com/articles/lavinia-warren-half-of-the-19th-century-s-tiniest-richest-power-couple.

Quoted:

Bates, Martin Van Buren. "Boy, Soldier, and Man."

DEATH OF REPRESENTATION: THE BLACK CONGRESSMEN OF RECONSTRUCTION

Consulted:

Butler, Nic. "The South Carolina Constitutional Convention of 1868." Charleston County Public Library. March 2, 2018. https://www.ccpl.org/charleston-time-machine/south-carolina-constitutional-convention-1868.

Dray, Philp. *Capitol Men: The Epic Story of Reconstruction through the Lives of the First Black Congressmen.* Houghton Mifflin, 2010.

Foner, Eric. "South Carolina's Forgotten Black Political Revolution." *Slate.* Jan. 31, 2018. https://slate.com/human-interest/2018/01/the-many-black-americans-who-held-public-office-during-reconstruction-in-southern-states-like-south-carolina.html.

Gordon-Reed, Annette. "What If Reconstruction Hadn't Failed?" *The Atlantic*. Oct. 26, 2015. https://www.theatlantic.com/politics/archive/2015/10/what-if-reconstruction-hadnt -failed/412219/.

Griffith, D. W., dir. *The Birth of a Nation*. Epoch Producing Co., 1915.

Lineberry, Cate. *Be Free or Die: The Amazing Story of Robert Smalls' Escape from Slavery to Union Hero*. St. Martin's, 2017.

———. "The Thrilling Tale of How Robert Smalls Seized a Confederate Ship and Sailed it to Freedom." *Smithsonian Magazine*. June 13, 2017. https://www.smithsonianmag.com /history/thrilling-tale-how-robert-smalls-heroically-sailed-stolen-confederate-ship -freedom-180963689/.

Middleton, Stephen, ed. *Black Congressmen During Reconstruction: A Documentary Sourcebook*. Praeger, 2002.

"Revels, Hiram Rhodes." History, Art and Archives: United States House of Representatives. http://history.house.gov/People/Listing/R/REVELS,-Hiram-Rhodes-(R000166)/.

Quoted:

Butler, Nic. "The South Carolina Constitutional Convention of 1868."

Dray, Philp. *Capitol Men*.

. . . and Other Political Firsts Who Didn't Make Your High School History Book

Consulted:

Barron, James. "Shirley Chisholm, 'Unbossed' Pioneer in Congress, Is Dead at 80." *New York Times*. Jan. 3, 2005. https://www.nytimes.com/2005/01/03/obituaries/shirley-chisholm-unbossedpioneer-in-congress-is-dead-at-80.html.

Billington, Monroe. "Susanna Madora Salter: First Woman Mayor." *Kansas History: A Journal of the Central Plains* 21, no. 3 (Autumn 1954): 173–83. Rpt. Kansas Historical Society. www.kshs .org. https://www.kshs.org/p/kansas-historical-quarterly-susanna-madora-salter/13106.

Genini, Ronald, and Richard Hitchman. *Romualdo Pacheco: A Californio in Two Eras*. The Book Club of California, 1985.

Giteck, Lenny. "Harvey Milk's Original *Advocate* Obituary from 1979." *Advocate*, Nov. 27, 2018. https://www.advocate.com/politics/2018/11/27/harvey-milks-original-advocate -obituary-1979.

Hatfield, Mark O., with the Senate Historical Office. "Vice Presidents of the United States: Charles Curtis (1929–1933)." *Vice Presidents of the United States, 1789–1993*. U.S. Government Printing Office. 1997, 373–81. https://www.senate.gov/artandhistory/history/common /generic/VP_Charles_Curtis.htm.

Kansas Historical Society. "Prohibition." Nov. 2001, rev. Mar. 2014. https://www.kshs.org /kansapedia/prohibition/14523.

Michals, Debra. "Shirley Chisholm." National Women's History Museum. 2015. www .womenshistory.org/education-resources/biographies/shirley-chisholm.

Nichols, John. "Shirley Chisholm Deserves a Great Big Statue Honoring Her in the Capitol. *The Nation*. March 9, 2018. https://www.thenation.com/article/shirley-chisholm-deserves-a -great-big-statue-honoring-her-in-the-capitol/.

"Romualdo Pacheco." History, Art & Archives, United States House of Representatives. https://
www.govinfo.gov/content/pkg/GPO-CDOC-108hdoc225/pdf/GPO-CDOC-108hdoc225
-2-2-6.pdf, rpt. at https://history.house.gov/People/Listing/P/PACHECO,-Romualdo
-(P000003)/.

Roy, Anthony. "Ebenezer D. Bassett." Central Connecticut State University. https://www.ccsu
.edu/bassett/biography.html.

Teal, Christopher, "Ebenezer Bassett: The Legacy of America's First African-American
Diplomat." *Foreign Service Journal*. June 2018. Afsa.org. https://www.afsa.org/ebenezer
-bassett-legacy-americas-first-african-american-diplomat.

FORGOTTEN FORERUNNER: When a Woman Ruled Hollywood: Lois Weber

Consulted:

Brody, Richard. "Lois Weber's Vital Films of the Early Silent Era." *New Yorker*. July 19, 2018. https://
www.newyorker.com/culture/the-front-row/lois-webers-vital-films-of-the-early-silent-era.

Fuster, Jeremy. "Hollywood Studios Are Releasing Five Times More Films with Female Directors
This Year." *The Wrap*. Feb. 28, 2019. https://www.thewrap.com/female-director-woman
-hollywood-studio-progress-five-times-more-history/.

Hopper, Hedda. "Death Takes Lois Weber." *Los Angeles Times*. Nov. 14, 1939.

"Lois Weber (1879–1939)." Internet Movie Database. https://www.imdb.com/name/nm0916665/.

Planned Parenthood of New York City. "Our History: Planned Parenthood of New York City: A
Series of Firsts." 2019. https://www.plannedparenthood.org/planned-parenthood-new-york
-city/who-we-are/our-history.

Roosevelt, Theodore. "Speech before the Mothers' Congress, Washington, D.C., March 13, 1905."
A Compilation of the Messages and Speeches of Theodore Roosevelt, 1901–1905. Vol. 1. Edited
by Alfred Henry Lewis. Bureau of National Literature and Art, 1906.

Stamp, Shelley. "Profile: Lois Weber." *Women Film Pioneers Project*. Edited by Jane Gaines, Radha
Vatsal, and Monica Dall'Asta. Center for Digital Research and Scholarship. Columbia University
Libraries. Sep. 27, 2013. https://wfpp.cdrs.columbia.edu/pioneer/ccp-lois-weber/%20.

Weber, Lois, dir. *Hypocrites*. Bosworth Inc./Paramount Pictures. 1915.

Quoted:

Brody, Richard. "Lois Weber's Vital Films of the Early Silent Era."

Hopper, Hedda. "Death Takes Lois Weber."

Roosevelt, Theodore. "Speech before the Mothers' Congress."

Interviewed:

Stamp, Shelley.

DEATH OF MEDIEVAL SCIENCE

Consulted:

"Albertus Magnus and Astrology." *Daily Medieval*. Nov. 15, 2012. http://dailymedieval.blogspot
.com/2012/11/albertus-magnus-astrology.html.

"The Alchemy of Color in Medieval Manuscripts." The J. Paul Getty Museum. Oct. 11, 2016.
www.getty.edu/art/exhibitions/alchemy_of_color/index.html.

Bell, Timothy M. "A Brief History of Bloodletting." *Journal of Lancaster General Hospital* 11, no. 4 (Winter 2016): 119–23. http://www.jlgh.org/JLGH/media/Journal-LGH-Media-Library /Past%20Issues/Volume%2011%20-%20Issue%204/Bloodletting.pdf.

Bilyeau, Nancy. "Frankenstein and the Earl of Surrey." *English Historical Fiction Authors*. April 8, 2016. https://englishhistoryauthors.blogspot.com/2016/04/when-earl-of-surrey-met -frankenstein.html.

"Bloodletting." The Science Museum, London. http://broughttolife.sciencemuseum.org.uk /broughttolife/techniques/bloodletting.

Bond, Sarah. "Creating the Philosopher's Stone: The Medieval Science of Color and Alchemy." *Forbes*. Nov. 16, 2016. https://www.forbes.com/sites/drsarahbond/2016/11/16/creating-the -philosophers-stone-the-medieval-science-of-color-and-alchemy/#2249cb6c1501.

Cohen, Jennie. "A Brief History of Bloodletting." History.com. Aug. 29, 2018. https://www .history.com/news/a-brief-history-of-bloodletting.

Curran, Stuart. "Contexts—Science—Alchemy." University of Pennsylvania English. http://knarf .english.upenn.edu/Contexts/alchemy.html.

Dow, Travis J. "Paracelsus." *History of Alchemy*. Dec. 4, 2013. http://historyofalchemy.com/list -of-alchemists/paracelsus/.

Ferrario, Gabriele. "Al-Kimiya: Notes on Arabic Alchemy." *Science History Institute*. Oct. 15, 2007. https://www.sciencehistory.org/distillations/al-kimiya-notes-on-arabic-alchemy.

Gallegos, Fernando. "The Forgotten Art of Scrying." *Exploring Traditions*. Nov. 21, 2015. https:// www.exploringtraditions.com/the-art-of-scrying/.

Godwin, William. *Lives of the Necromancers: Or, an Account of the Most Eminent Persons in Successive Ages*. Chatto & Windus, 1876.

Greenstone, Gerry. "The History of Bloodletting." *British Columbia Medical Journal* 52, no. 1 (Jan.–Feb. 2010): 12–14. https://www.bcmj.org/premise/history-bloodletting.

Kerridge, Ian H., and Michael Lowe. "Bloodletting: The Story of a Therapeutic Technique." *Medical Journal of Australia* 163 (Dec. 1995): 631–33.

Krans, Brian, and Kathryn Wilson. "What Is Leech Therapy?" *HealthLine*. April 21, 2017. https:// www.healthline.com/health/what-is-leech-therapy.

"Medical Use of Medicinal Leeches." University of Connecticut, Department of Molecular and Cell Biology. http://web.uconn.edu/mcbstaff/graf/Medical.html.

"Medieval Astrology." British Library. https://www.bl.uk/learning/cult/bodies/astrology /astrologyhome.html.

O'Donoghue, Michael, et al. "Theodoric of York, Medieval Barber." *Saturday Night Live*. NBC. April 22, 1978. https://www.nbc.com/saturday-night-live/video/theodoric-of-york/n8661.

Pendergrast, Mark. *Mirror Mirror: A History of the Human Love Affair with Reflection*. Basic Books, 2004.

Pruitt, Sarah, "What Was the Philosopher's Stone?" History.com. Sept. 1, 2018. https://www .history.com/news/what-was-the-philosophers-stone.

"The Real Nicolas Flamel and the Philosopher's Stone." Pottermore.com. https://www .pottermore.com/features/the-real-nicolas-flamel-and-the-philosophers-stone.

Shelley, Mary. *Frankenstein*. Penguin, 2002.

Thomas, D. P. "The Demise of Bloodletting." *Journal of the Royal College of Physicians of Edinburgh* 44 (2014): 72–77. https://pdfs.semanticscholar.org/1e9e/1c396d21 18c4b0c196fbbac159c7cde72646.pdf.

Wheeler, L. Kip. "Medieval Numerology: A Brief Guide." *Dr. Wheeler's Website*. Carson-Newman University. https://web.cn.edu/kwheeler/documents/Numerology.pdf.

Quoted:

Ferrario, Gabriele. "Al-Kimiya: Notes on Arabic Alchemy."

Gallegos, Fernando. "The Forgotten Art of Scrying."

Godwin, William. *Lives of the Necromancers*.

O'Donoghue, Michael, et al. "Theodoric of York, Medieval Barber."

Shelley, Mary. *Frankenstein*.

DEATH OF A SPORTS TEAM: LOS DRAGONES DE CIUDAD TRUJILLO

Consulted:

Borges, Ron. "Baseball's Dirty Secret." *The National*. April 11, 2009. https://www.thenational.ae /sport/baseball-s-dirty-secret-1.495096.

Gilmore, Richard L., Jr. "A Historical Look at the Pittsburgh Crawfords and the Impact of Black Baseball on American Society." *Sloping Halls Review* 3 (1996): 63–71. Rpt. at *KiltHub*, Carnegie Mellon University. June 30, 2018. https://kilthub.cmu.edu/articles/A_Historical_Look_at_the _Pittsburgh_Crawfords_and_the_Impact_of_Black_Baseball_on_American_Society/6712472.

Hill, Justice B. "Traveling Show: Barnstorming Was Common Place [*sic*] in the Negro Leagues." *Negro Leagues Legacy*. MLB.com. http://mlb.mlb.com/mlb/history/mlb_negro_leagues_story .jsp?story=barnstorming.

"Martin Dihigo." National Baseball Hall of Fame. BaseballHall.org. https://baseballhall.org/hof /dihigo-mart%C3%ADn.

McKenna, Brian. "Gus Greenlee." *Society for American Baseball Research*. Sabr.org. https://sabr .org/bioproj/person/fabd8400.

"Negro League Baseball." Western Pennsylvania Sports Museum at the History Center. Heinz History Center. https://www.heinzhistorycenter.org/exhibits/negro-league-baseball.

Paige, Satchel. *Maybe I'll Pitch Forever*. University of Nebraska Press, 1993.

Pearson, Richard. "James 'Cool Papa' Bell, Baseball Legend, Dies." *Washington Post*. March 9, 1991.

"A Series under Siege." *The Washington Times*. Aug. 7, 2002. https://www.washingtontimes.com /news/2002/aug/7/20020807-035749-7581r/.

Smith, Averell "Ace." *The Pitcher and the Dictator: Satchel Paige's Unlikely Season in the Dominican Republic*. University of Nebraska Press, 2018.

Vago, Mike, "In 1937, a Dictator Assembled a Baseball Team for the Ages." *AV Club*. March 25, 2018. https://www.avclub.com/in-1937-a-dictator-assembled-a-baseball-team-for-the -a-1823978045.

Quoted:

"Martin Dihigo." National Baseball Hall of Fame.

Paige, Satchel. *Maybe I'll Pitch Forever.*

"A Series under Siege." *The Washington Times.*

. . . and Other Teams You Can't Root for Anymore

Consulted:

Berkow, Ira. "Hebrew Hoop Dreams." Review of *When Basketball Was Jewish: Voices of Those Who Played the Game* by Douglas Stark. *Moment.* Dec. 6, 2017. https://www.momentmag .com/book-review-basketball-jewish-voices-played-game/.

———. "Trump Building the Generals in His Own Style." *New York Times.* Jan. 1, 1984.

Cohen, Steve. "Once Upon a Time in the East." *Broad Street Review.* Jan. 14, 2012. http://www .broadstreetreview.com/dance/when_the_jews_ruled_basketball#.

Coll, Steve. "The Nationals Election." *The New Yorker.* Apr. 25, 2012. https://www.newyorker .com/news/daily-comment/the-nationals-election.

Gaines, Cork. "Inside Trump's 35-Year War with the NFL." *Business Insider.* June 10, 2018. https://www.businessinsider.com/trump-winning-pigskin-war-with-the-nfl-2018-6.

Goldstein, Gary. "Honoring Hebrew Hoopsters." *Los Angeles Times.* Nov. 9, 2008. http://articles .latimes.com/2008/nov/09/entertainment/ca-firstbasket9.

Guenther, Karen. "SPHAS." *Encyclopedia of Greater Philadelphia.* http:// philadelphiaencyclopedia.org/archive/sphas/.

Holmes, Linda. "Football and Donald Trump: It's a Long Story." NPR. Sept. 30, 2017. https:// www.npr.org/2017/09/30/554257688/football-and-donald-trump-its-a-long-story.

Jason. "Baseball Leaves the District (Again)." *Ghosts of DC.* May 3, 2012. https://ghostsofdc .org/2012/05/03/washington-senators-leave-dc-1971/.

Kelly, John. "Senators? Nationals? What's in a Name?" *Washington Post.* Oct. 6, 2012. https:// www.washingtonpost.com/local/senators-nationals-nats-whats-in-a-name/2012/10/05 /75e95352-0ef9-11e2-bd1a-b868e65d57eb_story.html.

Povich, Shirley. "1924: When Senators Were Kings." *Washington Post.* Oct. 22, 1994. http://www .washingtonpost.com/wp-srv/sports/longterm/general/povich/launch/senators1.htm.

Stark, Douglas. *The SPHAS: The Life and Times of Basketball's Greatest Jewish Team.* Temple University Press, 2011.

Vyorst, David, dir. *The First Basket: Jews and Basketball.* Film Trailer. Laemle/Zeller Films. JTN: Jewish Television Network. https://www.youtube.com/watch?v=Cd_6N_K4oeg.

Quoted:

Berkow, Ira. "Hebrew Hoop Dreams."

———. "Trump Building the Generals in His Own Style."

Coll, Steve. "The Nationals Election."

FORGOTTEN FORERUNNER: The Byronic Woman: Ada Lovelace

Consulted:

Campbell-Kelly, Martin. "The Origins of Computing." *Scientific American.* Sept. 2009, 62–69.

"Charles Babbage's Influence." *The Computer's Impact on Society.* http://thecomputersimpact .weebly.com/charles-babbages-influence.html.

Essinger, James. *Ada's Algorithm: How Lord Byron's Daughter Ada Lovelace Launched the Digital Age.* Melville House, 2014.

Harris, William. "Who Invented the Computer?" *How Stuff Works.* Jan. 12, 2011. https://science .howstuffworks.com/innovation/inventions/who-invented-the-computer.htm.

Kramer, Kyra C. "Ada Lovelace." KyraCKramer.com. Dec. 10, 2017. http://www.kyrackramer .com/2017/12/10/ada-lovelace/.

Rocca, Mo. "Horse Play." *Henry Ford's Innovation Nation*, Episode 28. Oct. 10, 2015. https:// www.thehenryford.org/explore/innovation-nation/episodes/horse-play/.

Swade, Doron. "Ada Lovelace." *Computer History Museum.* https://www.computerhistory.org /babbage/adalovelace/.

———. "The Babbage Engine." *Computer History Museum.* https://www.computerhistory.org /babbage/.

———. "Charles Babbage." *Computer History Museum.* https://www.computerhistory.org /babbage/charlesbabbage/.

Woolley, Benjamin. "Child of Poetry, Bride of Science." *The Guardian.* Aug. 13, 1999. https:// www.theguardian.com/books/1999/aug/14/books.guardianreview.

Quoted:

Essinger, James. *Ada's Algorithm.*

Swade, Doron. "Ada Lovelace."

Interviewed:

Gallerneaux, Kristen.

DEATH OF A COUNTRY: PRUSSIA

Consulted:

Amudsen, Michael. "The Forgotten Russian Enclave of Kaliningrad." Vice.com. May 8, 2013. https://www.vice.com/en_us/article/gqwayy/the-forgotten-russian-enclave-of-kaliningrad.

Bennetts, Marc. "Kaliningrad: The Russian Enclave with a Taste for Europe." *The Guardian.* May 31, 2018. https://www.theguardian.com/cities/2018/may/31/kaliningrad-the-russian-enclave -with-a-taste-for-europe.

Clark, Christopher. *Iron Kingdom: The Rise and Downfall of Prussia, 1600–1947.* Belknap Press of Harvard University Press, 2008.

Elon, Amos. "The Nowhere City." *New York Review of Books.* May 13, 1993.

Hadley, Kathryn. "Frederick the Great's Erotic Poem." HistoryToday.com. Sept. 21, 2011. https:// www.historytoday.com/frederick-greats-erotic-poem.

Mansel, Philip. "Atheist and Gay, Frederick the Great Was More Radical Than Most Leaders

Today." *Spectator*. Oct. 3, 2015. www.spectator.co.uk/2015/10/frederick-the-great-king-of-prussia
-is-a-great-read/.

Roy, James Charles. *The Vanished Kingdom: Travels through the History of Prussia*. Westview,
Connecticut, 2000.

Quoted:

Amudsen, Michael. "The Forgotten Russian Enclave of Kaliningrad."

Clark, Christopher. *Iron Kingdom*.

Elon, Amos. "The Nowhere City."

Mansel, Philip. "Atheist and Gay."

Roy, James Charles. *The Vanished Kingdom*.

. . . and Other Places You Won't Find on a Map

Consulted:

Davis, William C. "The History of the Short-Lived Independent Republic of Florida."
Smithsonian Magazine. May 2013. https://www.smithsonianmag.com/history/the-history
-of-the-short-lived-independent-republic-of-florida-28056078/.

Frye, Richard Nelson. "Assyria and Syria: Synonyms." *Journal of Near Eastern Studies* 51, no. 4
(October 1992): 281–85.

Josephs, John. "Assyria and Syria: Synonyms?" *Journal of Assyrian Academic Studies* 11, no. 2
(1997): 37–43. http://www.jaas.org/edocs/v11n2/JohnJoseph.pdf, http://www.fotuva.org
/newsletters/higgins_2.html.

Noble, Mariana. "Tuva: Explore Siberia's Remote and Undiscovered Treasure." Mir Corporation.
https://www.mircorp.com/reasons-to-travel-tuva-siberias-remote-and-undiscovered-treasure/.

Quoted:

Davis, William C. "The History of the Short-Lived Independent Republic of Florida."

Heroes of the New Jersey Turnpike

Consulted:

Berghaus, Bob. "Forty-five Years Ago, Lombardi Accepted a Gay Player." *Citizen Times*. Citizen
-times.com. Feb. 10, 2014. https://www.citizen-times.com/story/sports/2014/02/10/45-years
-ago-lombardi-accepted-a-gay-player/5381673/.

Fiedler, Leslie. *Love and Death in the American Novel*. Penguin, 1984.

Lachman, Charles. *A Secret Life: The Lies and Scandals of President Grover Cleveland*. Skyhorse
Publishing, 2013.

Maraniss, David. *When Pride Still Mattered: A Life of Vince Lombardi*. Simon & Schuster, 1999.

Nix, Elizabeth. "Who Was Molly Pitcher?" History.com. March 17, 2016. https://www.history
.com/news/who-was-molly-pitcher.

Schiff, Judith Ann. "Leatherstocking at Yale." *Yale Alumni Magazine*. Nov–Dec 2006. http://
archives.yalealumnimagazine.com/issues/2006_11/old_yale.html.

Teipe, Emily J. "Will the Real Molly Pitcher Please Stand Up?" *Prologue* 31, no. 2 (Summer 1999).
National Archives. https://www.archives.gov/publications/prologue/1999/summer/pitcher.html.

Quoted:

Maraniss, David. *When Pride Still Mattered.*

DEATH OF A FUNNY GIRL: FANNY BRICE

Consulted:

Bentley, Toni. *Sisters of Salome.* University of Nebraska Press, 2005.

"Fanny Brice." Jewish Virtual Library: A Project of AICE. www.jewishvirtuallibrary.org.

"Fanny Brice Under Knife: Jokes as Surgeons 'Trim' Her Nose 'Down to Normalcy.'" *New York Times.* Aug. 16, 1923, 2.

Frere-Jones, Sasha. "Stars." *New Yorker.* Dec. 2, 2009. https://www.newyorker.com/culture/sasha-frere-jones/stars.

Gabler, Neal. *Barbra Streisand: Redefining Beauty, Femininity, and Power.* Yale University Press, 2016.

———. "A Jew Becomes a Star." *Tablet.* May 18, 2016. https://www.tabletmag.com/jewish-arts-and-culture/books/202488/a-jew-becomes-a-star.

Goldman, Herbert G. *Fanny Brice: The Original Funny Girl.* Oxford University Press, 1993.

Grossman, Barbara. *Funny Woman: The Life and Times of Fanny Brice.* Indiana University Press, 1991.

Kenrick, John. "Funny Girl Debunked: The Truth about Fanny Brice." Barbra Streisand Archives Library. Barbra-Archives.com. Edited by Matt Howe. 2017. http://barbra-archives.com/bjs_library/60s/funny_girl_debunked.html.

Nachman, Gerald. *Showstoppers! The Surprising Backstage Stories of Broadway's Most Remarkable Songs.* Chicago Review Press, 2016.

Passafiume, Andrea. "Behind the Camera on Funny Girl." TCM.com. April 22, 1994. http://www.tcm.com/this-month/article/220494%7C0/Behind-the-Camera-Funny-Girl.html.

Popkin, Henry. "The Vanishing Jew of Our Popular Culture: The Little Man Who Is No Longer There." *Commentary.* July 1952, 46–55.

"Report: Surgeon's Art Gives Bard a New Nose: Fanny Brice Reported to Be Anxious to Get New Lineaments for Coming Play." *New York Times.* Aug. 2, 1923, 10.

Rocca, Mo. "Arthur Laurents: Musical Theater Master." *CBS Sunday Morning.* March 23, 2009. https://www.youtube.com/watch?v=z43jBcjfbQs.

Wagner, Kristen Anderson. "Fanny Brice's New Nose: Beauty, Ethnicity, and Liminality." *Hysterical! Women in American Comedy.* Edited by Linda Mizejewski and Victoria Sturtevant. University of Texas Press, 2017, 109–36.

Quoted:

Bentley, Toni. *Sisters of Salome.*

Frere-Jones, Sasha. "Stars."

Gabler, Neal. *Barbra Streisand.*

Goldman, Herbert G. *Fanny Brice.*

Grossman, Barbara. *Funny Woman.*

Nachman, Gerald. *Showstoppers!*

Popkin, Henry. "The Vanishing Jew of Our Popular Culture."

works consulted

Rocca, Mo. "Arthur Laurents: Musical Theater Master."

Wagner, Kristen Anderson. "Fanny Brice's New Nose."

. . . and Other Historical Figures Eclipsed by the Actors Who Played Them

Consulted:

Corliss, Richard. "That Old Feeling: Marlene's Siren Songs." Time.com. Jan. 27, 2002. http://content.time.com/time/arts/article/0,8599,197674-2,00.html.

Elliott, Felicia. "In Context: Cagney and Cohan." TheCinessential.com. May 31, 2017. http://www.thecinessential.com/yankee-doodle-dandy/in-context.

Eschner, Kat. "The Real-Life Story of Maria von Trapp." *Smithsonian Magazine.* Nov. 16, 2017. https://www.smithsonianmag.com/smart-news/real-life-story-maria-von-trapp-180967182/.

ESPN News Services. "Former Middleweight Champion Jake LaMotta Dies at 95." ABC News. Sept. 20, 2017. https://abcnews.go.com/Sports/middleweight-champion-jake-lamotta-dies-95/story?id=49978611.

Gearin, Joan. "Movie vs. Reality: The Real Story of the Von Trapp Family." *Prologue Magazine* 37, no. 4. July 19, 2017. https://www.archives.gov/publications/prologue/2005/winter/von-trapps.html.

Goldstein, Richard. "Jake LaMotta, 'Raging Bull' in and out of the Ring, Dies at 95." *New York Times.* Sept. 20, 2017.

Grant, Lee, dir. "Madeline Kahn: Part 3." *Lifetime Intimate Portrait.* Lifetime Network. 2001. YouTube. https://www.youtube.com/watch?v=V72ZbbDTNWM.

Gross, Terry, and Peter O'Toole. "The Camels Were 'Impossible': Peter O'Toole Remembers 'Arabia.'" *Fresh Air.* NPR. 1993. https://www.npr.org/templates/transcript/transcript.php?storyId=251610110.

Harvey, Ian. "Argentina's Juan Peron: His Harboring of Nazi War Criminals Did Not Bring about the Benefits He Expected for His Country." *Vintage News.* Feb. 21, 2017. https://www.thevintagenews.com/2017/02/21/argentinas-juan-peron-his-harboring-of-nazi-war-criminals-did-not-bring-about-the-benefits-he-expected-for-his-country/.

James, Bryan. "Calamity Jane." *The Films of Doris Day.* https://www.dorisday.net/calamity-jane/.

Kantor, Michael, dir. "PBS Broadway: George M. Cohan: All the Gang at 42nd Street." 2004. YouTube. https://www.youtube.com/watch?v=CeDDqYrfvt8.

Kent, Kathleen. "Calamity Jane: Explorer, Teamster, Prostitute." KathleenKent.com. Aug. 26, 2013. http://www.kathleenkent.com/2013/08/26/calamity-jane-explorer-teamster-prostitute/.

Kerr, Peter. "Maria von Trapp, Whose Life Was 'Sound of Music,' Is Dead." *New York Times.* March 29, 1987.

Kinetic Koncepts, LLC. "Black Twitter Erupts After Grammys Confuse the Hell Outta Them Over Patti Labelle." ILoveOldSchoolMusic.com. Jan. 29, 2018. https://www.iloveoldschoolmusic.com/black-twitter-erupts-after-grammys-confuse-the-hell-outta-them-over-patti-labelle/.

Larsen, Andrew. "Evita: Whose Narrative Is It Anyway?" AELarsen.wordpress.com. March 21, 2014. https://aelarsen.wordpress.com/2014/03/21/evita-whose-narrative-is-it-anyway/.

Madison, William V. *Madeline Kahn: Being the Music, a Life*. University Press of Mississippi, 2015.

Murray, Steve. "Former Argentines Issue Warning on 'Evita': Don't Believe It." *Chicago Tribune*, Jan. 24, 1997.

Pendergast, Tom, and Sara Pendergast. "George M. Cohan." *St. James Encyclopedia of Popular Culture*. St. James Press, 2000. Rpt. at *Broadway: The American Musical*. PBS.org. https://www.pbs.org/wnet/broadway/stars/george-m-cohan/.

Reed, Rex. "George Is on His Best Behavior Now." *New York Times*. March 29, 1970.

Review of "Spartacus." *BBC Home*. Aug. 25, 2000. http://www.bbc.co.uk/films/2000/08/25/spartacus_review.shtml.

Rotella, Carlo. "Jake LaMotta Was More than Just a 'Raging Bull.'" *New York Times*. Sept. 21, 2017.

Sandvick, Clinton, Edward Whalen, and Eric Lambrecht. "How Accurate Is Stanley Kubrick's 'Spartacus'?" DailyHistory.org. Jan. 6, 2019. https://dailyhistory.org/How_accurate_is_Stanley_Kubrick%27s_%27Spartacus%27%3F.

Sheward, David. *Rage and Glory: The Volatile Life and Career of George C. Scott*. Applause Theatre and Cinema Books, 2008.

Siskel, Gene. "Movie Legend James Cagney Dies." *Chicago Tribune*. March 31, 1986.

Snider, Eric D. "Fifteen Punchy Facts about Raging Bull." *Mental Floss*. Aug. 3, 2015. http://mentalfloss.com/article/66911/15-punchy-facts-about-raging-bull.

Woolf, Christopher. "Is Peter O'Toole's 'Lawrence of Arabia' Fact or Fiction?" *PRI's The World*. PRI.org. Dec. 16, 2013. https://www.pri.org/stories/2013-12-16/peter-otooles-lawrence-arabia-fact-or-fiction.

Quoted:

Corliss, Richard. "That Old Feeling."

Eschner, Kat. "The Real-Life Story of Maria von Trapp."

ESPN News Services. "Former Middleweight Champion Jake LaMotta Dies at 95."

Grant, Lee. "Madeline Kahn: Part 3."

James, Bryan. "Calamity Jane."

Kantor, Michael. *PBS Broadway: George M. Cohan*.

Reed, Rex. "George Is on His Best Behavior Now."

Rotella, Carlo. "Jake LaMotta Was More than Just a 'Raging Bull.'"

Sheward, David. *Rage and Glory*.

Siskel, Gene. "Movie Legend James Cagney Dies."

BEFORE AND AFTER: THE PRE-PRESIDENCY: HERBERT HOOVER AND THE POST-PRESIDENCY: JOHN QUINCY ADAMS

Consulted:

Adams, John. "Letter to John Quincy Adams, 18 February 1825." *Founders Online*, National Archives. https://founders.archives.gov/documents/Adams/99-03-02-4497.

Amistad Captives, Letter to John Quincy Adams. Tulane University Digital Library. https://digitallibrary.tulane.edu/islandora/object/tulane%3A53601.

Haltiwanger, John. "Trump Worries He'll Become a 'Hoover,' the President at the Beginning of the Great Depression." *Business Insider*. Dec. 24, 2018. https://www.businessinsider.com /trump-worries-about-being-compared-to-herbert-hoover-president-at-the-start-of-great -depression-2018-12.

"John Adams Was a Tiger Dad. So Was John Quincy." New England Historical Society. http:// www.newenglandhistoricalsociety.com/john-adams-tiger-dad-john-quincy/.

Myers, Walter Dean. *Amistad: A Long Road to Freedom*. Dutton Juvenile, 1998.

Nagel, Paul C. "Father Knew Best." *New York Times*. Dec. 3, 2005. https://www.nytimes .com/2005/12/03/opinion/father-knew-best.html.

Olson, Casey. "John Quincy Adams' Congressional Career." U.S. Capitol Historical Society, 2000. https://uschs.org/explore/historical-articles/john-quincy-adams-congressional-career/.

Remini, Robert. *John Quincy Adams: The American Presidents Series: The 6th President, 1825–1829*. Henry Holt, 2002.

Sam, Jim. "Herbert Hoover and the Great Mississippi Flood." May 19, 2011. https://www.hoover .org/research/herbert-hoover-and-great-mississippi-flood.

"Supreme Court Rules in Amistad Slave Ship Case." *VOA Learning English*. Voice of America. April 17, 2014. https://learningenglish.voanews.com/a/amistad-supreme-court -abolitionists/1894249.html.

Traub, James. *John Quincy Adams: Militant Spirit*. Basic Books, 2016.

Quoted:

Adams, John. "Letter to John Quincy Adams."

Haltiwanger, John. "Trump Worries He'll Become a 'Hoover.'"

"John Adams Was a Tiger Dad." New England Historical Society.

Remini, Robert. *John Quincy Adams*.

Sam, Jim. "Herbert Hoover and the Great Mississippi Flood."

Traub, James. *John Quincy Adams*.

Interviewed:

Hoover, Margaret.

Schwartz, Tom.

Whyte, Ken.

The Graveyard of Failed Presidential Candidates

Ansley, Laura. "When Politics Becomes Show Business: Gracie Allen Runs for President." Nursing Clio. Oct. 11, 2016. https://nursingclio.org/2016/10/11/when-politics-becomes -show-business-gracie-allen-runs-for-president/.

"Chicago Cops Squelch Piggy Nominations." *Montreal Gazette*. Aug. 23, 1968. https://news.google .com/newspapers?id=1IY1AAAAIBAJ&sjid=1Z8FAAAAIBAJ&pg=4960,4621941&dq= pigasus+yippies&hl=en.

Clymer, Adam. "John Anderson, Who Ran Against Reagan and Carter in 1980, Is Dead at 95." *New York Times*. Dec. 4, 2017.

Collins, Bob, dir. *Pat Paulsen for President*. 1968. https://vimeo.com/46296105.

"A Declaration of Conscience." *Senate Stories: 1941–1963.* United States Senate. https://www
.senate.gov/artandhistory/history/minute/A_Declaration_of_Conscience.htm.

"Pigasus the Immortal." *Porkopolis: Considering the Pig, a Single-Minded Bestiary.* http://www
.porkopolis.org/2008/pigasus/.

Widmer, Ted. "The Fringe Campaign of Dr. Spock." *The Boston Globe.* June 3, 2016. https://
www.bostonglobe.com/ideas/2016/06/03/widmer/DFtUEAHUdgMOubi4xuGtbM/story
.html.

Quoted:

Ansley, Laura. "When Politics Becomes Show Business."

Collins, Bob. *Pat Paulsen for President.*

FORGOTTEN FORERUNNER: Before Jackie: Moses Fleetwood Walker

Consulted:

"Fleet Walker." *Baseball Reference: Players.* Sports Reference, LLC. https://www.baseball
-reference.com/players/w/walkefl01.shtml.

Husman, John R. "Fleet Walker." *Society for American Baseball Research.* https://sabr.org/bioproj
/person/9fc5f867.

Lester, Larry. "The First Jackie: Moses Fleetwood Walker." Unpublished Essay, 2018.

Toledo City Council. "Moses Fleetwood Walker." City of Toledo/Ohio Historical
Society marker, 2003. Historical Marker Database. https://www.hmdb.org/marker
.asp?marker=94868.

Walker, M. F. *Our Home Colony: A Treatise on the Past, Present and Future of the Negro Race in
America.* Herald Printing Company, 1908.

Wilson, Brian. "Unfortunate Situation: Color Line Takes Stovey out of Big Leagues."
MLB.com. 2019. http://mlb.mlb.com/mlb/history/mlb_negro_leagues_profile
.jsp?player=stovey_george.

Zang, David. *Fleet Walker's Divided Heart: The Life of Baseball's First Black Major Leaguer.* Bison
Books, 1998.

Quoted:

Lester, Larry. "The First Jackie: Moses Fleetwood Walker."

Toledo City Council. "Moses Fleetwood Walker."

Walker, M. F. *Our Home Colony.*

Interviewed:

Lester, Larry.

Wiercinski, Rob.

DEATH OF A DIAGNOSIS: HOMOSEXUALITY AS A MENTAL ILLNESS

Consulted:

"Barbara Gittings (1932–)." *Out of the Past: 400 Years of Lesbian and Gay History in America.*
PBS. 1997. https://www.pbs.org/outofthepast/past/p5/gittings.html.

"Barbara Gittings: Gay Pioneer." *LGBT Civil Rights Movement: 50th Anniversary.* 2017. https://
lgbt50.org/barbara-gittings.

works consulted

Bayer, Ronald. *Homosexuality and American Psychiatry: The Politics of Diagnosis.* Princeton University Press, 1981.

Burton, Neel. "When Homosexuality Stopped Being a Mental Disorder." *Psychology Today.* Sept. 18, 2015. https://www.psychologytoday.com/us/blog/hide-and-seek/201509/when-homosexuality-stopped-being-mental-disorder.

Clendinen, Dudley. "Dr. John Fryer, 65, Psychiatrist Who Said in 1972 He Was Gay." *New York Times.* March 5, 2003.

Colville, Robert. "The Man Who Fried Gay People's Brains." *Independent.* July 6, 2016. https://www.independent.co.uk/life-style/health-and-families/health-news/the-man-who-fried-gay-people-s-brains-a7119181.html.

Drescher, Jack. "Out of DSM: Depathologizing Homosexuality." *Behavioral Science* 5, no. 4 (2015): 565–75. https://www.ncbi.nlm.nih.gov/pmc/articles/PMC4695779/#B48-behavsci-05-00565.

Dunlap, David W. "Franklin Kameny, Gay Rights Leader, Dies at 86." *New York Times.* Oct. 13, 2011.

"Frank Kameny: Gay Pioneer." *LGBT Civil Rights Movement: 50th Anniversary.* 2017. https://lgbt50.org/frank-kameny.

Freud, Sigmund. "Sigmund Freud Writes to Concerned Mother: 'Homosexuality Is Nothing to Be Ashamed Of.'" *Open Culture.* Sept. 26, 2014. http://www.openculture.com/2014/09/freud-letter-on-homosexuality.html.

Herek, Gregory. "Facts About Homosexuality and Mental Health." University of California at Davis. 2012. http://psychology.ucdavis.edu/rainbow/html/facts_mental_health.html.

Illustrated Films. "About Krafft-Ebing." *Psychopathia Sexualis: A Film by Bret Wood.* https://www.kinolorber.com/sites/psychopathia/history.html.

Krafft-Ebing, Richard. *Psychopathia Sexualis.* F.A. Davis Company, 1892. Archive.org. https://archive.org/details/PsychopathiaSexualis1000006945.

Scasta, David L. "John E. Fryer, MD, and the Dr. H. Anonymous Episode." *Journal of Gay and Lesbian Psychotherapy* 6, no. 4 (2003): 73–84.

Scot, Jamie. "Shock the Gay Away: Secrets of Early Gay Aversion Therapy Revealed." *Huffington Post.* June 28, 2013. https://www.huffingtonpost.com/jamie-scot/shock-the-gay-away-secrets-of-early-gay-aversion-therapy-revealed_b_3497435.html.

Singer, Bennett, and Patrick Sammon, dir. *Cured.* [Trailer.] Story Center Films. 2018. https://www.curedfilm.com/.

Susskind, David. *The David Susskind Show.* 1971.

Quoted:

Bayer, Ronald. *Homosexuality and American Psychiatry.*

Clendinen, Dudley. "Dr. John Fryer, 65, Psychiatrist Who Said in 1972 He Was Gay."

Drescher, Jack. "Out of DSM: Depathologizing Homosexuality."

"Frank Kameny: Gay Pioneer." *LGBT Civil Rights Movement: 50th Anniversary.*

Freud, Sigmund. "Sigmund Freud Writes to Concerned Mother."

Scasta, David L. "John E. Fryer, MD, and the Dr. H. Anonymous Episode."

Susskind, David. *The David Susskind Show.* 1971.

. . . and Other Defunct Diagnoses

Consulted:

Chase, Loretta, and Susan Holloway Scott. "A Cure for the Vapours. 1736." *Two Nerdy Girls*. June 16, 2013. http://twonerdyhistorygirls.blogspot.com/2013/06/a-cure-for-vapours-1736.html.

Cox, Savannah. "How Left-Handedness Came to Be Seen as Evil." *All That's Interesting*. Jan. 17, 2018. https://allthatsinteresting.com/left-handedness-evil.

Cruz, Gilbert. "Top Ten Redheads: Judas." *Time*. Nov. 7, 2010. http://content.time.com/time/specials/packages/article/0,28804,2029961_2029964_2029966,00.html.

Drescher, Jack. "Out of DSM: Depathologizing Homosexuality." *Behavioral Science* 5, no. 4 (2015): 565–75.

Eakin, Emily. "Bigotry as Mental Illness, or Just Another Norm." *New York Times*. Jan. 15, 2000.

Garcia, Michelle. "What Six Ridiculous Old-Timey Diseases All Have in Common." Mic.com. March 31, 2015. https://www.mic.com/articles/114114/what-6-ridiculous-old-timey-diseases-all-have-in-common#.BYruc05ig.

Kumar, Sanjaya, and David B. Nash. "Health Care Myth Busters: Is There a High Degree of Scientific Certainty in Modern Medicine?" *Scientific American*. March 25, 2011. https://www.scientificamerican.com/article/demand-better-health-care-book/.

Lombroso, Cesare, and Guglielmo Ferraro. *Criminal Woman, the Prostitute, and the Normal Woman*. Edited by Nicole Hahn Rafter. Duke University Press, 2004, 123–24.

McVean, Ada. "The History of Hysteria." McGill University Office for Science and Society. July 31, 2017. https://www.mcgill.ca/oss/article/history-quackery/history-hysteria.

Peart, Karen N. "Left-handed People More Likely to Have Mental Disorders like Schizophrenia." *Yale News*. Oct. 31, 2013. https://news.yale.edu/2013/10/31/left-handed-people-more-likely-have-mental-disorders-schizophrenia.

Ptak, John. "On Curing the Disability and Disease of Left-Handedness." *JF Ptak Science Books*. https://longstreet.typepad.com/thesciencebookstore/2014/06/on-curing-the-disability-of-left-handedness.html.

Shiel, William C. "Medical Definition of Consumption." *MedicineNet*. https://www.medicinenet.com/script/main/art.asp?articlekey=19050.

Summers, Montague. *The Vampire: His Kith and Kin*. Mockingbird Press, 2017.

Torrey, Tricia. "Historical Names of Diseases and Conditions." *Very Well Health*. May 21, 2019. https://www.verywellhealth.com/outdated-disease-names-2615295.

"When Did 'Consumption' Become 'Tuberculosis'?" *Stack Exchange*. Jan. 18, 2014. https://english.stackexchange.com/questions/146782/when-did-consumption-become-tuberculosis.

"A Word for What Ails You." *Merriam Webster: Words at Play*. Merriam-Webster.com. https://www.merriam-webster.com/words-at-play/illnesses-ailments-diseases-history-names.

Wypijewski, JoAnn. "Playing Doctor." *The Nation*. May 30, 2012. https://www.thenation.com/article/playing-doctor/.

Quoted:

> Summers, Montague. *The Vampire: His Kith and Kin.*
> Wypijewski, JoAnn. "Playing Doctor."

REPUTATION ASSASSINATION: GIACOMO MEYERBEER, ARNOLD BENNETT, AND DISCO

Consulted:

Ahmed, Samira. "Arnold Bennett: The Edwardian David Bowie?" *BBC Radio 4*. June 23, 2014. https://www.bbc.com/news/entertainment-arts-27920331.

Beale, Nigel. "Wyndham Lewis: Overlooked Scourge of Mediocrity." *The Guardian*. April 17, 2008. https://www.theguardian.com/books/booksblog/2008/apr/17/wyndham lewisoverlookedscour.

Boone, Brian. *I Love Rock 'n' Roll (Except When I Hate It): Extremely Important Stuff about the Songs and Bands You Love, Hate, Love to Hate, and Hate to Love.* Perigee, 2011.

Davis, Peter G. "Wagner's Anxiety of Influence." *New York Times*. July 22, 2009.

Easlea, Daryl. "Disco Inferno." *Independent*. Dec. 11, 2004. https://www.independent.co.uk/news/world/americas/disco-inferno-680390.html.

Echols, Alice. *Hot Stuff: Disco and the Remaking of American Culture*. Norton, 2011.

Flinn, Caryl. *Brass Diva: The Life and Legends of Ethel Merman*. University of California Press, 2009.

Harris, Garrett. "What Happened to Meyerbeer?" *San Diego Reader*. Sept. 26, 2011. https://www.sandiegoreader.com/news/2016/sep/29/blurt-what-happened-meyerbeer/.

Hynes, Samuel. "The Whole Contention between Mr. Bennett and Mrs. Woolf." *Novel: A Forum on Fiction* 1, no. 1 (Autumn 1967): 34–44.

Kenney, Edwin J. "The Moment, 1910: Virginia Woolf, Arnold Bennett, and Turn of the Century Consciousness." *Colby Quarterly* 13, no. 1 (March 1977).

Kennicott, Philip. "Barred Genius." *Opera News* 82, no. 8 (February 2018). https://www.operanews.com/Opera_News_Magazine/2018/2/Features/Barred_Genius.html.

Kot, Greg, and Jim DeRogatis. "Episode 668: Disco and Seymour Stein." *Sound Opinions* podcast. Sept. 14, 2018. https://www.soundopinions.org/show/668/.

Lehmann-Haupt, Christopher. Review of *Arnold Bennett*, by Margaret Drabble. *Books of the Times. New York Times*. Sept. 17, 1974.

Mattera, Adam. "How Disco Changed Music Forever." *The Guardian*. Feb. 25, 2012. https://www.theguardian.com/music/2012/feb/26/disco-changed-world-for-ever.

"Meyerbeer: Robert Le Diable." OperaToday.com. Nov. 28, 2006. http://www.operatoday.com/content/2006/11/meyerbeer_rober.php.

Mordden, Ethan. *Opera Anecdotes*. Oxford University Press, 1985.

Pound, Ezra. "Hugh Selwyn Mauberly." *Poetry Foundation*. https://www.poetryfoundation.org/poems/44915/hugh-selwyn-mauberley-part-i.

Powers, Richard, "The Disco Lifestyle." Stanford University. http://socialdance.stanford.edu/syllabi/disco_lifestyle.htm.

Ricks, Christopher. "To Bennett's Rescue." *New York Review of Books*. Nov. 3, 1966.

Ross, Alex. "The Dark Prophetic Vision of Giacomo Meyerbeer." *New Yorker*. Oct. 15, 2018.

Wagner, Richard. "Judaism in Music." Translated by William Ashton Ellis. From *The Theatre: Richard Wagner's Prose Works*, vol. 3, 79–100. Rpt. at https://archive.org/details /RichardWagner-JudaismInMusicdasJudenthumInDerMusik.

Wilson, Greg. "Life and Death on the New York City Dance Floor." *Greg Wilson: Being a DJ*. Aug. 30, 2016. https://blog.gregwilson.co.uk/2016/08/tim-lawrence-life-death-new-york -dance-floor/#more-10634.

Woolf, Virginia. "Modern Fiction." *Modernism and Literature: An Introduction and Reader*. Edited by Mia Carter and Warren Friedman. Routledge, 2013, 472–76.

———. "Mr. Bennett and Mrs. Brown." *Essentials of the Theory of Fiction*. Edited by Michael Hoffman and Patrick Murphy. Duke University Press, 1988, 24–39.

Woolfe, Zachary. "Heard of Giacomo Meyerbeer? He's on the Cusp of a Musical Renaissance." *New York Times*, Apr. 28, 2017.

Quoted:

Beale, Nigel. "Wyndham Lewis: Overlooked Scourge of Mediocrity."

Easlea, Daryl. "Disco Inferno."

Mattera, Adam. "How Disco Changed Music Forever."

Pound, Ezra. "Hugh Selwyn Mauberly."

Powers, Richard. "The Disco Lifestyle."

Ross, Alex. "The Dark Prophetic Vision of Giacomo Meyerbeer."

Wagner, Richard. "Judaism in Music."

Woolf, Virginia. "Modern Fiction."

———. "Mr. Bennett and Mrs. Brown."

Woolfe, Zachary. "Heard of Giacomo Meyerbeer?"

. . . and Other Ruined Reputations

Consulted:

Bloom, Harold. *The Western Canon: The Books and School of the Ages*. Harcourt, 1994.

Fischlin, Daniel. "Voltaire, Shakespeare, and Canada." *Canadian Adaptations of Shakespeare Project*. 2004. http://www.canadianshakespeares.ca/essays/voltaire.cfm.

Jones, Paul Anthony. "Five Writers Who Really Hated Shakespeare." *Mental Floss*. Nov. 5, 2015. http://mentalfloss.com/article/70783/5-writers-who-really-hated-shakespeare.

Kehr, Dave. "Restoring Fatty Arbuckle's Tarnished Reputation at MoMa." *New York Times*. April 16, 2006.

King, Gilbert. "The Skinny on the Fatty Arbuckle Trial." *Smithsonian Magazine*. Nov. 8, 2011. www.smithsonianmag.com/history/the-skinny-on-the-fatty-arbuckle-trial-131228859.

Milton, John. *Paradise Lost*. Edited by Thomas Luxon. 2018. https://www.dartmouth .edu/~milton/reading_room/pl/book_1/text.shtml.

Richard III Society. "Welcome." Richard III Society. www.RichardIII.net.

Shaw, George Bernard. "Letter from Mr. G. Bernard Shaw." *Tolstoy on Shakespeare*. Funk & Wagnalls, 1906. Rpt. at Project Gutenberg. Jan. 7, 2009. http://www.gutenberg.org /files/27726/27726-h/27726-h.htm#Page_166.

Sims, David. "The Internet Is Freaking out About Ira Glass Saying Shakespeare Sucks." *The Atlantic.* July 28, 2014. https://www.theatlantic.com/entertainment/archive/2014/07/the -internet-is-freaking-out-about-ira-glass-saying-shakespeare-sucks/375187/.

Stone, Phil. "Richard III: A Hero Maligned by Shakespeare." *Telegraph.* https://www.telegraph .co.uk/history/11484855/Richard-III-A-hero-maligned-by-Shakespeare.html.

Tertullian. "On the Apparel of Women: Book I." Edited by Roger Pearse. Feb. 3, 1998. http:// www.tertullian.org/anf/anf04/anf04-06.htm.

Quoted:

Bloom, Harold. *The Western Canon.*

Jones, Paul Anthony. "Five Writers Who Really Hated Shakespeare."

King, Gilbert. "The Skinny on the Fatty Arbuckle Trial."

Milton, John. *Paradise Lost.*

Richard III Society. "Welcome."

Shaw, George Bernard. "Letter from Mr. G. Bernard Shaw."

Sims, David. "The Internet Is Freaking out."

Stone, Phil. "Richard III: A Hero Maligned by Shakespeare."

Tertullian. "On the Apparel of Women."

FORGOTTEN FORERUNNER: Before AA: The Washingtonian Movement

Consulted:

Geiling, Natasha. "Long Before Jack Daniel's, George Washington Was a Whiskey Tycoon." *Smithsonian Magazine.* May 12, 2014. https://www.smithsonianmag.com/history/george -washington-whiskey-businessman-180951364/.

Grosh, A. B., editor. *Washingtonian Pocket Companion*, 2nd edition. B. S. Merrell, 1842.

L., John. "Washingtonian Forebears of Alcoholics Anonymous." AAagnostica.org. https:// aaagnostica.org/2012/07/15/washingtonian-forbears-of-alcoholics-anonymous/.

Lincoln, Abraham. "Temperance Address." Abraham Lincoln Online. Feb. 22, 1842. http://www .abrahamlincolnonline.org/lincoln/speeches/temperance.htm.

Maxwell, Milton A. "The Washingtonian Movement: The Baltimore Origins." *Quarterly Journal of Studies on Alcohol* 11 (1950): 410–52. Rpt. at SemanticScholar.org. https://pdfs .semanticscholar.org/d5f3/043f07c94c1bc34eb4f2cf6d8aee2c8f9aac.pdf.

O'Neill, Jenny. "The Washingtonians and the Nineteenth-Century Temperance Movement in Westport." Westport Historical Society. June 16, 2010. http://wpthistory.org/2010/06/ the_washingtoni/.

Quoted:

Grosh, A. B. *Washingtonian Pocket Companion.*

Lincoln, Abraham. "Temperance Address."

Maxwell, Milton A. "The Washingtonian Movement: The Baltimore Origins."

DEATH OF A BROTHER: BILLY CARTER

Consulted:

Carter, Billy, with Dan Rather. "Billy Carter Interview Transcript." *Dan Rather: American Journalist.* Dolph Briscoe Center for American History, University of Texas at Austin. Original air date Jan. 11, 1977. https://danratherjournalist.org/interviewer/whos-who /compilation-whos-who-interviews-transcripts/document-billy-carter-interview.

Carter, Billy, Sybil Carter, and Ken Estes. *Billy: Billy Carter's Reflections on His Struggle with Fame, Alcoholism and Cancer.* Edgehill, 1990.

Treadwell, David. "Billy Carter Is Dead of Cancer at 51: Ex-President's Brother Capitalized on Country Boy Image." *Los Angeles Times.* Sep. 26, 1988. https://www.latimes.com/archives /la-xpm-1988-09-26-mn-1791-story.html.

Quoted:

Carter, Billy, with Dan Rather. "Billy Carter Interview Transcript."

Carter, Billy, et al. *Billy.*

Treadwell, David. "Billy Carter Is Dead of Cancer at 51."

Interviewed:

Carter, Buddy.

Carter, Earl.

Carter, Mandy.

Carter, Sybil.

Rather, Dan.

. . . and Other Black Sheep Siblings

Handy, Bruce. "Glamour and Goulash." *Vanity Fair.* Oct. 4, 2010. https://www.vanityfair.com /news/2001/07/zsa-zsa-200107.

DEATH OF THE ENTERTAINER: SAMMY DAVIS JR.

Consulted:

Davis Jr., Sammy, as told to Trude B. Feldman. "Why I Became a Jew." *Ebony* (February 1960): 62–69.

Davis Jr., Sammy, Jane Boyar and Burt Boyar. *Yes I Can: The Story of Sammy Davis, Jr.* Farrar, Straus & Giroux, 2012.

Davis, Tracey, and Nina Bunche Pierce. *Sammy Davis Jr.: A Personal Journey with My Father.* Running Press, 2014.

DeCaprio, Al, and Robert Finkelstein, dir. *The Frank Sinatra Spectacular.* CBS Productions. 1965.

Pollard, Samuel D., dir. *Sammy Davis, Jr.: I've Gotta Be Me.* American Masters/Arte France. 2019.

"Sammy Davis, Jr." *CBS This Morning.* CBS. June 12, 1989.

Schlatter, George, prod. *Sammy Davis, Jr. 60th Anniversary Celebration.* ABC. Feb. 4, 1990.

Quoted:

Davis Jr., Sammy, and Jane Boyar and Burt Boyar. *Yes I Can.*

Davis, Tracey, and Nina Bunche Pierce. *Sammy Davis Jr.: A Personal Journey with My Father.*

DeCaprio, Al, and Robert Finkelstein. *The Frank Sinatra Spectacular.*

Pollard, Samuel D. *Sammy Davis, Jr.: I've Gotta Be Me.*

"Sammy Davis, Jr." *CBS This Morning.*

Schlatter, George. *Sammy Davis, Jr. 60th Anniversary Celebration.*

Interviewed:

Auerbach, Larry.

Brown, Willie.

Maslon, Laurence.

Rivera, Chita.

Vereen, Ben.

Warwick, Dionne.

. . . and Other One-Eyed Wonders

Quoted:

Nasr, Constantine, prod. *King Size Comedy: Tex Avery and the Looney Tunes Revolution.* Rivendell Films/Warner Home Video. 2012. YouTube. https://www.youtube.com /watch?v=uP9RMN0uSXg.

DEATH OF A SQUARE: LAWRENCE WELK

Consulted:

Destiny. "Lawrence Welk vs. the Hippies." 10zenmonkeys.com. March 13, 2008. http:// www.10zenmonkeys.com/2008/03/13/lawrence-welk-vs-the-hippies/.

Flint, Peter B. "Lawrence Welk, the TV Maestro of Champagne Music, Dies at 89." *New York Times.* May 19, 1992.

Gorman, Tom. "Lawrence Welk, Popular TV Bandleader, Dies at 89." *Los Angeles Times.* May 19, 1992.

Jacobson, Marion. *Squeeze This! A Cultural History of the Accordion in America.* University of Illinois Press, 2012.

Johnson, Victoria E. "Citizen Welk: Bubbles, Blue Hair, and Middle America." *The Revolution Wasn't Televised: Sixties Television and Social Conflict.* Edited by Lynn Spigel and Michael Curtin. Routledge, 2013.

———. *Heartland TV: Prime Time Television and the Struggle for U.S. Identity.* New York University Press, 2008.

Kirby, Doug, Ken Smith, and Mike Wilkins. "Lawrence Welk Museum." RoadsideAmerica.com. www.roadsideamerica.com/story/2035.

McManis, Sam. "Welk Resort a Legacy of the Champagne Music-Maker." *Sacramento Bee.* Jan. 3, 2015. https://www.sacbee.com/entertainment/living/travel/sam-mcmanis/article529 4391.html.

Welk, Lawrence. "Hippie Welk." *The Lawrence Welk Show.* YouTube. https://www.youtube.com /watch?v=oFmSv2WFDrs.

Quoted:

Johnson, Victoria E. *Heartland TV.*

Welk, Lawrence. "Hippie Welk."

. . . and Other Victims of the "Rural Purge"

Consulted:

Jay, Robert. "The Headmaster." TVObscurities.com. May 7, 2018. https://www.tvobscurities .com/articles/headmaster/.

MeTV Staff. "Nine Iconic Shows Canceled Due to the Rural Purge." MeTV.com. Oct. 12, 2016. https://www.metv.com/lists/9-iconic-shows-canceled-due-to-the-rural-purge.

Nowalk, Brandon. "A Beginner's Guide to Classic TV Westerns." *AV Club*. Jul. 10, 2014. https:// tv.avclub.com/a-beginner-s-guide-to-classic-tv-westerns-1798270445.

Quoted:

MeTV Staff. "Nine Iconic Shows."

DEATH OF AN ICON: AUDREY HEPBURN

Consulted:

"Audrey Hepburn." *CBS This Morning*. CBS. Nov. 29, 1989.

"Audrey Hepburn." *CBS This Morning*. CBS. June 3, 1991.

Hammond, Pete. "Oscars Q&A: Alan Arkin." *Deadline*. February 9, 2013. https://deadline .com/2013/02/oscars-qa-alan-arkin-on-argo-426062/.

James, Caryn. "Audrey Hepburn, Actress, Is Dead at 63." *New York Times*. Jan. 21, 1993.

Paris, Barry. *Audrey Hepburn*. Berkley Publishing Group, 1996.

The Tonight Show with Johnny Carson. NBC. March 30, 1976.

We the People. CBS. December 1951.

Quoted:

"Audrey Hepburn." *CBS This Morning*.

"Audrey Hepburn." *CBS This Morning*.

Hammond, Pete. "Oscars Q&A: Alan Arkin."

James, Caryn. "Audrey Hepburn, Actress, Is Dead at 63."

The Tonight Show with Johnny Carson.

We the People.

Interviewed:

Bogdanovich, Peter.

Clinton, William J.

Dotti, Luca.

Ephron, Nora.

Ferrer, Sean.

James, Caryn.

Katoh, Taki.

Schilling, Mark.

FORGOTTEN FORERUNNER: The Aviatrix: Bessie Coleman

Consulted:

Alexander, Kerri Lee. "Bessie Coleman." National Women's History Museum. 2018. https://www .womenshistory.org/education-resources/biographies/bessie-coleman.

Carriere, Dave. "Bessie Coleman: Remembering an Aviation Pioneer." FlyingMag.com. Jan. 26, 2017. https://www.flyingmag.com/remembering-aviation-pioneer-bessie-coleman/.

Cochrane, D., and P. Ramirez. "Women in Aviation and Space History: Bessie Coleman." Smithsonian Air and Space Museum. https://airandspace.si.edu/explore-and-learn/topics/women-in-aviation/coleman.cfm.

Hart, Philip S. *Flying Free: America's First Black Aviators*. Lerner Publishing, 1992.

"Negro Aviatrix Arrives: Bessie Coleman Flew Planes of Many Types in Europe." *New York Times*. Aug 14, 1922, 4.

Onkst, David H. "Air Shows: An International Phenomenon." *Centennial of Flight*. https://www.centennialofflight.net/essay/Social/airshows/SH20.htm.

———. "Barnstormers." *Centennial of Flight*. https://www.centennialofflight.net/essay/Explorers_Record_Setters_and_Daredevils/barnstormers/EX12.htm.

Rudd, Thelma. "Yesterday, Today and Tomorrow." BessieColeman.org. 2019. http://www.bessiecoleman.org/bio-bessie-coleman.php.

Rocca, Mo. "Floating Hammocks Featuring Female Aviators." *Henry Ford's Innovation Nation*, Episode 86. Nov. 11, 2017. https://www.thehenryford.org/explore/innovation-nation/episodes/.

Quoted:

Carriere, Dave. "Bessie Coleman: Remembering an Aviation Pioneer."

Rocca, Mo. "Floating Hammocks Featuring Female Aviators."

DEATH OF A CAREER: VAUGHN MEADER

Consulted:

Bunzel, Peter. "A Kennedy Spoof Full of 'Vigah.'" *Life*. Dec. 14, 1962, 83–86.

"Interview with Vaughn Meader." *P.S.* CBS Television. Aug. 17, 1998.

Kennedy, Jacqueline. *Jacqueline Kennedy: Historic Conversations on Life with John F. Kennedy*. Edited by Michael Beschloss. HarperCollins, 2011.

Maslon, Laurence, and Michael Kantor. "Comedy LPs." *Make 'Em Laugh: The Funny Business of America*. PBS. Dec. 1, 2008. https://www.pbs.org/wnet/makeemlaugh/comedys-evolution/history-comedy-lps/38/.

Meader, Vaughn. "Telegram to the President." June 26, 1962. John F. Kennedy Presidential Library and Museum Archives. https://www.jfklibrary.org/asset-viewer/archives/JFKWHCNF/1842/JFKWHCNF-1842-015.

Meader, Vaughn, et al. *Bob Booker & Earle Doud Present the First Family*. Cadence Records. Produced by Bob Booker, Earle Doud, and George Foster. November 1962.

Nabokov, Vladimir. *Strong Opinions*. McGraw-Hill, 1975.

"News Conference 46." December 12, 1962. John F. Kennedy Presidential Library and Museum Archives. https://www.jfklibrary.org/archives/other-resources/john-f-kennedy-press-conferences/news-conference-46.

Schlesinger Jr., Arthur. "Memorandum to the President." November 26, 1962. Arthur M. Schlesinger Personal Papers, John F. Kennedy Presidential Library and Museum Archives.

Talent Scouts. CBS. July 3, 1963.

Thomas, Bob. "Mimic of President Tries to Develop Other Shows." Associated Press. Nov. 22, 1963.

Quoted:

"Interview with Vaughn Meader." *P.S.*

Meader, Vaughn. "Telegram to the President."

Meader, Vaughn, et al. *Bob Booker & Earle Doud Present the First Family.*

Nabokov, Vladimir. *Strong Opinions.*

"News Conference 46."

Schlesinger Jr., Arthur. "Memorandum to the President."

Talent Scouts. CBS. July 3, 1963.

Thomas, Bob. "Mimic of President Tries to Develop Other Shows."

Interviewed:

Booker, Bob.

Meader, Sheila.

Where's Chuck?: The Graveyard of Disappeared and Dead Sitcom Characters

Consulted:

Dowd, A. A. "Read This: Behind 'the Single Coldest Moment in the History of Television.'" *AV Club.* July 13, 2016. https://news.avclub.com/read-this-behind-the-single-coldest-moment -in-the-his-1798249304.

Eichel, Molly. "'We All Feel Sad, Big Bird': When Sesame Street Confronted Death." AV Club. Nov. 10, 2014. https://tv.avclub.com/we-all-feel-sad-big-bird-when-sesame-street -confron-1798273912.

Gajewski, Ryan. "Jason Alexander: 'Seinfeld' Killed off Susan Because Actress Was 'F—ing Impossible' to Work with." HollwoodReporter.com. June 4, 2015. https://www .hollywoodreporter.com/live-feed/jason-alexander-seinfeld-killed-susan-800031.

Gross, Terry, and David Bianculli. "The Greatest Hits of 'The Platinum Age of Television.'" *Fresh Air.* NPR. Oct. 6, 2016. https://www.npr.org/2017/10/06/556103549/the-greatest-hits-of-the -platinum-age-of-television.

Jurgen, Lex. "The Death of Apu Nahasapeemapetilon and the End of Comedy." TerribleWords .com. Apr. 29, 2018. http://terriblewords.com/the-death-of-apu-nahasapeemapetilon-and-the -end-of-comedy/.

Lloyd, David. "Chuckles Bites the Dust." *Mary Tyler Moore Show.* Oct. 25, 1975. YouTube. https://www.youtube.com/watch?v=5ZrL4fuzz2w.

Markoutsas, Elaine. "NBC Faces Facts of Life: Chico and Freddie Are Gone." *Chicago Tribune,* Jan. 19, 1978.

Quoted:

Dowd, A. A. "Read This: Behind 'the Single Coldest Moment in the History of Television.'"

Gross, Terry, and David Bianculli. "The Greatest Hits of 'The Platinum Age of Television.'"

Lloyd, David. "Chuckles Bites the Dust."

Markoutsas, Elaine. "NBC Faces Facts of Life."

DIED THE SAME DAY: FARRAH FAWCETT AND MICHAEL JACKSON

Consulted:

Bennets, Leslie. "Beautiful People, Ugly Choices." *Vanity Fair.* Aug. 25, 2009. https://www
.vanityfair.com/culture/2009/09/farrah-fawcett200909.

Farber, Stephen. "A Change of Pace for Farrah Fawcett." *New York Times.* May 14, 1984.

Healy, Mark. "How a 1973 Shave Cream Ad Launched the $5 Million Super Bowl Commercial
Phenomenon." Ceros.com. Feb. 2, 2017. https://www.ceros.com/originals/super-bowl
-commercials/.

Nelson, Valerie J. "Farrah Fawcett Dies at 62: Actress Soared with, Then Went Beyond 'Charlie's
Angels.'" *Los Angeles Times.* June 26, 2009. https://www.latimes.com/local/obituaries/la-me
-farrah-fawcett26-2009jun26-story.html.

Ryan, Harriet, et al. "King of Pop Is Dead at 50." *Los Angeles Times.* June 26, 2009.

Stanley, Alessandra. "Farrah Fawcett, a Sex Symbol Who Aimed Higher." *New York Times.* June
25, 2009. https://www.nytimes.com/2009/06/26/arts/television/26appraisal.html.

Stewart, Susan. "Farrah Fawcett Dies of Cancer at 62." *New York Times.* June 26, 2009. https://
www.nytimes.com/2009/06/26/arts/television/26fawcett.html.

Vowell, Sarah. "Those Liberated Angels: How Farrah and Her Friends Made Me a Feminist." *Time.*
Nov. 6, 2000.

Wong, Wailin. "Michael Jackson: 1958–2009." *Chicago Tribune.* June 26, 2009.

Quoted:

Farber, Stephen. "A Change of Pace for Farrah Fawcett."

Interviewed:

Lansing, Sherry.

Reed, Rex.

. . . and Other Famous People Who Died the Same Day

Bergman, Ingmar. Interview with Jan Aghed. Quoted at "Bergman on Bergman and Others."
Tarkovsky Bergman. May 4, 2006. http://m.blog.sina.com.cn/s/blog_46c8225b0100031h
.html#page=2.

Wilkins, Frank. "The Death of Our Gang's Carl 'Alfalfa' Switzer." *Reel Reviews.* 2003. http://
reelreviews.com/shorttakes/alfalfa/alfalfa.htm.

DEATH OF A LEVIATHAN: THE STATION WAGON

Consulted:

Beato, Greg. "End of the Road: Some Thoughts on the Death of the Station Wagon." *Smart Set.*
March 9, 2011. https://thesmartset.com/article03091101/.

"Best Wagons." Edmunds.com. https://www.edmunds.com/wagon/.

DeLillo, Don. *White Noise.* Penguin, 1985.

Kwon, Amos. "The Demise of the Station Wagon." GearPatrol.com. July 29, 2013. https://
gearpatrol.com/2013/07/29/the-demise-of-the-station-wagon/.

Lewis, Sinclair. *Babbitt.* Oxford World's Classics, 2010.

Miller, Aaron. "The Ten Best Woody Wagons of All Time." ThrillList.com. May 16, 2014. https://www.thrillist.com/cars/the-10-best-woodies-of-all-time.

Motavalli, Jim. "R.I.P. to Station Wagons: The Death of a Noble Breed." CarTalk.com. March 18, 2011. https://www.cartalk.com/content/rip-station-wagons-death-noble-breed.

Ramis, Harold, dir. *National Lampoon's Vacation*. Warner Bros., 1983.

Taylor, Alex. "The Death of the Station Wagon." *Fortune*. Feb. 15, 2011. http://archive.fortune.com/2011/02/15/autos/death_station_wagon.fortune/index.htm.

Trotta, Mark. "Woodie Wagons." Classic-Car-History.com. 2019. http://www.classic-car-history.com/woodie-wagons.htm.

Quoted:

"Best Wagons." Edmunds.com.

DeLillo, Don. *White Noise*.

Kwon, Amos. "The Demise of the Station Wagon."

Lewis, Sinclair. *Babbitt*.

. . . and Other Things from the '70s That Could've Killed Us

Consulted:

Bellomo, Mark. "The Weird History of McDonaldland Toys." *Mental Floss*. Oct. 4, 2016. http://mentalfloss.com/article/69989/brief-history-mcdonaldland-and-toys-and-lawsuit-it-spawned.

"Carpet Dangers." Ecomall.com. https://www.ecomall.com/greenshopping/abscarpet.htm.

Carson, Alan, and John Caverly. "Urea Formaldehyde Foam Insulation." CarsonDunlop.com. Feb. 4, 2014. https://www.carsondunlop.com/inspection/blog/urea-formaldehyde-foam-insulation/.

"Dangerous Lead Content Reported in Paint on McDonald's Glasses." *New York Times*. July 9, 1977.

Denchak, Melissa. "All about Alar." NRDC.org. March 14, 2016. https://www.nrdc.org/stories/all-about-alar.

DePietro, MaryAnn. "Are Electric Blankets Safe?" SymptomFind.com. May 7, 2016. https://www.symptomfind.com/health/are-electric-blankets-safe/.

Griffith, Eric. "Nine Awesome but Super Dangerous Toys." PCmag.com. Sept. 15, 2015. https://www.pcmag.com/feature/337700/9-awesome-but-super-dangerous-toys.

"How They Lie, Part 4: The True Story of Alar, Part 2." *Rachel's Environment and Health News* #531. Jan. 29, 1997. http://www.rachel.org/files/rachel/Rachels_Environment_Health_News_592.pdf.

Schwartz, Sherwood. "The Honeymoon." *The Brady Bunch*. DailyMotion.com. https://www.dailymotion.com/video/x68vblv.

Uhlig, Robert. "Carpets Are Piled High with Toxic Pollutants." *The Telegraph*. May 3, 2001. https://www.telegraph.co.uk/news/science/science-news/4763062/Carpets-are-piled-high-with-toxic-pollutants.html.

Consulted:

"Dangerous Lead Content." *New York Times.*

Schwartz, Sherwood. "The Honeymoon."

Uhlig, Robert. "Carpets Are Piled High with Toxic Pollutants."

FORGOTTEN FORERUNNER: The First Great Wall: Hadrian's Wall
Consulted:

Achim, Mike. "Hadrian's Wall: Where Rome Meets Westeros." FeveredMutterings.com. Dec. 22, 2011. https://feveredmutterings.com/hadrians-wall-where-rome-meets-westeros.

Bragg, Melvyn, et al. "Hadrian's Wall." *In Our Time* podcast. BBC 4. July 12, 2012. https://www.bbc.co.uk/programmes/b01kkr42.

"Hadrian and Antinous: An Ancient Love Story." Planet Romeo. https://www.planetromeo.com/en/blog/gay-history-hadrian-antinous/.

Henderson, Tony. "How North England Became Cosmopolitan During Roman Times." *Chronicle Live.* Feb. 21, 2017. https://www.chroniclelive.co.uk/news/north-east-news/how-north-england-became-cosmopolitan-12634587.

Historia Augusta. "Life of Hadrian." Loeb Classical Library, 1921. Rpt. at University of Chicago: Bill Thayer's website. http://penelope.uchicago.edu/Thayer/E/Roman/Texts/Historia_Augusta/Hadrian/1*.html#note:other_translations.

"John Clayton (Town Clerk)." *Wikipedia.* May 12, 2019.

Mark, Joshua J. "Hadrian." *Ancient History Encyclopedia.* Sept. 2, 2009. https://www.ancient.eu/hadrian/.

McLaurin, Wayne. "A Conversation with George R. R. Martin." SF Site. Nov. 2000. https://www.sfsite.com/01a/gm95.htm.

"Places to Visit: Hadrian's Wall." English Heritage Press Office. https://www.english-heritage.org.uk/visit/places/hadrians-wall/.

Quoted:

Achim, Mike. "Hadrian's Wall: Where Rome Meets Westeros."

Bragg, Melvyn, et al. "Hadrian's Wall."

Historia Augusta. "Life of Hadrian."

McLaurin, Wayne. "A Conversation with George R. R. Martin."

CELEBRITIES WHO PUT THEIR BUTTS ON THE LINE
Elizabeth Taylor:
Consulted:

Altman, Lawrence K. "New Homosexual Disorder Worries Health Officials." *New York Times.* May 11, 1982.

———. "Rare Cancer Seen in 41 Homosexuals." *New York Times.* July 3, 1981.

Baker, Paige, ed. "A Timeline of HIV and AIDS." HIV.gov. https://www.hiv.gov/hiv-basics/overview/history/hiv-and-aids-timeline.

Chang, Alisa, and Urvashi Vaid. "Critics of President George H.W. Bush Reflect on His Handling of the AIDS Crisis." *All Things Considered.* National Public Radio. Dec. 4, 2018.

https://www.npr.org/2018/12/04/673398013/critics-of-president-george-h-w-bush
-reflect-on-his-handling-of-the-aids-crisis.

"Clinton Administration Record on HIV/AIDS." National Institutes of Health. NIH.gov. Dec. 1,
2000. https://aidsinfo.nih.gov/news/564/clinton-administration-record-on-hiv-aids.

Collins, Nancy. "Liz's AIDS Odyssey." *Vanity Fair*. Nov. 1, 1992. https://www.vanityfair.com
/news/1992/11/elizabeth-taylor-199211.

"Elizabeth Taylor Discusses Her Life and Career." *Larry King Live*. CNN. Jan. 15, 2001.

"History of HIV and AIDS Overview." *Avert: Global Information and Education on HIV and
AIDS*. Avert.org. Nov. 26, 2018.

"A Look Inside the Elizabeth Taylor AIDS Foundation." *UNAIDS*. Jan. 26, 2015. https://www
.unaids.org/en/resources/presscentre/featurestories/2015/january/20150126_ETAF.

Nelson, Harry. "Epidemic Affecting Gays Now Found in Heterosexuals." *Los Angeles Times*.
March 18, 1982.

O'Brien, Toby. "Celebrity Corner with Elizabeth Taylor." *Inner Toob*. April 5, 2011. http://
toobworld.blogspot.com/2011/04/celebrity-corner-with-elizabeth-taylor.html.

Padamsee, Tasleem J. "Fighting an Epidemic in Political Context: Thirty-Five Years of HIV/
AIDS Policy Making in the United States." *Social History of Medicine*. Dec. 28, 2018, 1–28.

Panem, Sandra. *The AIDS Bureaucracy: Why Society Failed to Meet the AIDS Crisis and How We
Might Improve Our Response*. Harvard University Press, 1988.

Shilts, Randy. *And the Band Played On: Politics, People, and the AIDS Epidemic*. Macmillan,
2000.

Taraborrelli, J. Randy. *Elizabeth*. Warner Books, 2007.

Taylor, Elizabeth. "Acceptance Speech: Jean Hersholt Humanitarian Award." Mar. 29, 1992.
Academy of Motion Pictures Arts and Sciences: Academy Award Acceptance Speech
Database. http://aaspeechesdb.oscars.org/link/065-25/.

Quoted:

Altman, Lawrence K. "New Homosexual Disorder."

Collins, Nancy. "Liz's AIDS Odyssey."

"Elizabeth Taylor Discusses Her Life and Career." *Larry King Live*.

"A Look Inside the Elizabeth Taylor AIDS Foundation." *UNAIDS*.

Nelson, Harry. "Epidemic Affecting Gays Now Found in Heterosexuals."

O'Brien, Toby. "Celebrity Corner with Elizabeth Taylor."

Shilts, Randy. *And the Band Played On*.

Taylor, Elizabeth. "Acceptance Speech: Jean Hersholt Humanitarian Award."

Interviewed:

Sager, Carole Bayer.

Marlene Dietrich:

Bernard, Marie Lyn. "Top 10 Sexually Prolific Lesbians and Bisexuals of Old Hollywood."
AutoStraddle.com. July 7, 2016. https://www.autostraddle.com/10-old-hollywood-stars-who
-enjoyed-scissoring-343227.

works consulted

Dalke, Anne, and Laura Blankenship. "Marlene Dietrich and Technology: Did She Shape Herself, or Did It Shape Her?" *Gender and Technology*. Bryn Mawr College. Spring 2009. http://gandt.blogs.brynmawr.edu/web-papers/final-papersprojects/marlene-dietrich-and -technology-did-she-shape-herself-or-did-it-shape-her/.

Foldessy, Gabor. "A Foreign 'Affair' on the Domestic Scene: Marlene Dietrich's Contributions to U.S. Cinema, Society, and Culture." *Americana: E-Journal of American Studies in Hungary* 13, no. 1 (Spring 2017). http://americanaejournal.hu/vol13no1/foldessy.

Goran, David. "Thirteen Famous People Who Were Actually Spies and They Were Good at It." *Vintage News*. Dec. 21, 2015. https://www.thevintagenews.com/2015/12/21/41772/.

Heing, Bridey. "Marlene Dietrich: The Femme Fatale Who Fought Social and Sexual Oppression." CNN. June 19, 2017. https://www.cnn.com/style/article/marlene-dietrich -dressed-for-the-image/index.html.

Helm, Toby. "Film Star Felt Ashamed of Belsen Link." *Telegraph*. June 24, 2000. https://www .telegraph.co.uk/news/worldnews/europe/1344765/Film-star-felt-ashamed-of-Belsen-link .html.

Hunt, Chris, dir. *No Angel: The Life of Marlene Dietrich*. Iambic Productions, 1996.

Leafe, David. "Did Marlene Dietrich Plot to Murder Hitler? She Seduced John Wayne, James Stewart, and JFK, but the German Siren had Grander Designs on History." *Daily Mail*. April 15, 2011. https://www.dailymail.co.uk/femail/article-1377378/Marlene-Dietrichs-plot -murder-Hitler.html.

"Marlene Dietrich: The Bisexual Goddess." *Lesbian News*. Oct. 16, 2015. https://www .lesbiannews.com/marlene-dietrich-the-bisexual-goddess/.

McKee, Abaigh. "Marlene Dietrich." *Music and the Holocaust*. http://holocaustmusic.ort.org /politics-and-propaganda/dietrich-marlene-1901-1992/.

Roth Pierpont, Claudia. "Bombshells." *New Yorker*. Oct. 12, 2015.

Spring, Kelly A. "Marlene Dietrich." National Women's History Museum. 2017. https://www .womenshistory.org/education-resources/biographies/marlene-dietrich.

Thomson, David. "I Have Been Photographed to Death." *The Guardian*. Dec. 27, 2001. https:// www.theguardian.com/film/2001/dec/28/artsfeatures.dvdreviews.

Tindle, Hannah. "Ten Things You Might Not Know about Femme Fatale Marlene Dietrich." AnotherMag.com. April 10, 2018. https://www.anothermag.com/fashion-beauty/10744/ten -things-you-might-not-know-about-femme-fatale-marlene-dietrich.

Quoted:

Dalke, Anne, and Laura Blankenship. "Marlene Dietrich and Technology."

Hunt, Chris. *No Angel: The Life of Marlene Dietrich*.

Interviewed:

Riva, Peter.

Lord Byron:

Consulted:

Barton, Anne. "Byron." *The Cambridge Companion to English Poets*. Edited by Claude Rawson. Cambridge University Press, 2011.

Beaton, Roderick. "In Greece, and for Greece." *History Today* 63, no. 6 (June 6, 2013). https://www.historytoday.com/archive/%E2%80%98-greece-and-greece%E2%80%99.

Chrysopoulos, Phillip. "Lord Byron: The Romantic Poet Who Died for Greece." *Greek Reporter.* April 19, 2018. https://greece.greekreporter.com/2018/04/19/lord-byron-the-romantic-poet-who-died-for-greece/.

Douglass, Paul. "Byron's Life and His Biographers." *Cambridge Companion to Byron.* Edited by Drummond Bone. Cambridge University Press, 2004.

Drummond, Clara. "Lord Byron, 19th-Century Bad Boy." British Library. May 15, 2014. https://www.bl.uk/romantics-and-victorians/articles/lord-byron-19thcentury-bad-boy.

Hanson, Marilee. "Lord Byron; The Life of George Noel Gordon: Facts and Information." EnglishHistory.net. Feb. 1, 2015. https://englishhistory.net/byron/life-of-lord-byron/.

"Lord Byron (George Gordon)." *Poetry Foundation.* https://www.poetryfoundation.org/poets/lord-byron.

MacCarthy, Fiona. "Poet of All the Passions." *The Guardian.* Nov. 8, 2002. https://www.theguardian.com/books/2002/nov/09/classics.poetry.

O'Brien, Edna. "'Mad, Bad' Byron." *On Point.* WBUR.org. Jul. 22, 2009. https://www.wbur.org/onpoint/2009/07/22/the-loves-of-lord-byron.

Pallardy, Richard. "War of Greek Independence." *Encyclopedia Britannica.* https://www.britannica.com/event/War-of-Greek-Independence.

St. Clair, William. *Lord Elgin and the Marbles.* Oxford University Press, 1983, 261.

Weiss, Michael. "Poet and Rake Lord Byron Was Also an Interventionist with Brains and Savvy." *Daily Beast.* Feb. 16, 2014. https://www.thedailybeast.com/poet-and-rake-lord-byron-was-also-an-interventionist-with-brains-and-savvy.

Wolfson, Susan J. *Romantic Interactions: Social Being and the Turns of Literary Action.* Johns Hopkins University Press, 2010.

Quoted:

Drummond, Clara. "Lord Byron, 19th-Century Bad Boy."

Weiss, Michael. "Poet and Rake Lord Byron Was Also an Interventionist."

Wolfson, Susan J. *Romantic Interactions.*

DEATH OF A TREE: THE LIVE OAKS OF TOOMER'S CORNER

Consulted:

Auburn University Athletics. "Rolling Toomer's Oaks." AuburnTigers.com. https://auburntigers.com/sports/2019/3/28/rolling-toomers.aspx.

Barra, Alan. "The Integration of College Football Didn't Happen in One Game." *The Atlantic.* Nov. 15, 2013. https://www.theatlantic.com/entertainment/archive/2013/11/the-integration-of-college-football-didnt-happen-in-one-game/281557/.

Crepea, James. "Auburn Fans Roll Toomer's Corner Oaks One Last Time." *USA Today.* June 10, 2013. https://www.usatoday.com/story/sports/ncaaf/sec/2013/04/21/auburn-tigers-a-game-toomers-corner-oaks-rolls-toilet-paper-spring-game/2100365/.

Keever, Gary. "The Poisoning of the Toomer's Oaks: A Rivalry Gone Awry." Auburn University

Agriculture: Horticulture. 2019. https://hort.auburn.edu/news-and-events/a-rivalry-gone
-awry/.

Kemper, Kurt Edward. *College Football and American Culture in the Cold War Era*. University of
Illinois Press, 2009, 126.

National Archives and Records Administration et al. "Transcript of Morrill Act (1862)."
OurDocuments.gov. https://www.ourdocuments.gov/print_friendly.php?flash
=true&page=transcript&doc=33&title=Transcript+of+Morrill+Act+%281862%29.

Seinfeld, Jerry, and David Letterman. "Rooting for Laundry." *The David Letterman Show*. 1994.
Vimeo. https://vimeo.com/47283296.

Stone, Larry. "The Psychology of Being a Sports Fan." *Seattle Times*. Feb. 16, 2014. https://www
.seattletimes.com/sports/the-psychology-of-being-a-sports-fan/.

Tarver, Erin C. *The I in Team: Sports Fandom and the Reproduction of Identity*. University of
Chicago Press, 2017, 2.

Thamel, Pete. "Newton Leads Auburn to Comeback Win." *New York Times*. Nov. 26, 2010.
https://www.nytimes.com/2010/11/27/sports/ncaafootball/27alabama.html.

Tomlinson, Tommy. "Lasting Memories at Toomer's Corner." *Sports on Earth*. April 22, 2013.
http://www.sportsonearth.com/article/45458306/.

———. "Something Went Very Wrong at Toomer's Corner." *Sports Illustrated: The Vault*. Aug.
15, 2011. https://www.si.com/vault/2011/08/15/106097882/something-went-very-wrong-at
-toomers-corner.

Tracy, Marc. "Alabama Win in 1926 Rose Bowl Put Southern Stamp on College Football." *New
York Times*. Dec. 27, 2016. https://www.nytimes.com/2016/12/27/sports/ncaafootball
/alabama-crimson-tide-washington-huskies.html.

Quoted:

Kemper, Kurt Edward. *College Football and American Culture*.

National Archives and Records Administration et al. "Transcript of Morrill Act (1862)."

Seinfeld, Jerry, and David Letterman. "Rooting for Laundry."

Tarver, Erin C. *The I in Team*.

Tomlinson, Tommy. "Lasting Memories at Toomer's Corner."

Interviewed:

Finebaum, Paul.

Keever, Gary.

Updyke Jr., Harvey.

. . . and Other Trees Felled Too Soon

Abumrad, Jad, et al. "Be Careful What You Plan For." *RadioLab* podcast. June 28, 2010. https://
www.wnycstudios.org/story/91722-be-careful-what-you-plan-for.

"Anne Frank Tree Falls in Heavy Winds Despite 'Rescue' Battle." *Telegraph*. Aug. 23, 2010.
https://www.telegraph.co.uk/history/world-war-two/7960315/Anne-Frank-tree-falls-in
-heavy-winds-despite-rescue-battle.html.

works consulted

"April 1: 1957: BBC Fools the Nation." *On This Day: 1950–2005*. BBC.com. http://news.bbc.co
.uk/onthisday/hi/dates/stories/april/1/newsid_2819000/2819261.stm.

Ball, Lauren. "The Woman Who Burned Down the 'Senator' Finally Sentenced." *Orlando Weekly*.
June 5, 2014. https://www.orlandoweekly.com/Blogs/archives/2014/06/05/the-woman-who
-burned-down-the-senator-finally-sentenced.

Barnes, Alison. "The First Christmas Tree." *History Today* 56, no. 12 (December 2006). https://
www.historytoday.com/archive/first-christmas-tree.

Dimbleby, Richard. "The Great Spaghetti Harvest Hoax of 1957." *Public Access America* podcast.
June 2, 2016. YouTube. https://www.youtube.com/watch?v=ZXvou6RcWzM.

Dononoske, Camila. "Iconic Sequoia 'Tunnel Tree' Brought Down by California Storm." NPR.
Jan. 9, 2017. https://www.npr.org/sections/thetwo-way/2017/01/09/508919216/iconic
-sequoia-tunnel-tree-brought-down-by-california-storm.

"L'Arbre du Ténéré (2)." *Internet Archive Wayback Machine*. https://web.archive.org/web/2009
0302080214/http://www.the153club.org/tenere2.html.

Martyn-Hemphill, Richard, and Joanna Berendt. "Who Tossed on the First Tinsel? Two Baltic
Capitals Disagree." *New York Times*. Dec. 22, 2016.

Ravitz, Jessica. "Anne Frank's Tree, Now Dying, Still Inspires Hope and New Life." CNN.
April 30, 2010. http://www.cnn.com/2010/US/04/30/anne.frank.tree/index.html.

Richardson, Jay. "The Cherry Tree Myth." Washington Library Center for History. Mount
Vernon.org. https://www.mountvernon.org/library/digitalhistory/digital-encyclopedia
/article/cherry-tree-myth/.

"The Sapling Project." Anne Frank Center for Mutual Respect. AnneFrank.com. 2018. https://
www.annefrank.com/sapling-project.

Stutzman, Rene. "Woman Who Burned Down Giant Tree Going to Prison." *Orlando Sentinel*.
March 31, 2016. https://www.orlandosentinel.com/news/breaking-news/os-tree-burner-sara
-barnes-pleads-guilty-20160331-story.html.

Wilde, Oscar. "The Decay of Lying." *The Decay of Lying and Other Essays*. Penguin, 2010.

Quoted:

Ball, Lauren. "The Woman Who Burned Down the 'Senator' Finally Sentenced."

Dimbleby, Richard. "The Great Spaghetti Harvest Hoax of 1957."

"L'Arbre du Ténéré (2)." *Internet Archive Wayback Machine*.

Ravitz, Jessica. "Anne Frank's Tree, Now Dying, Still Inspires Hope and New Life."

Wilde, Oscar. "The Decay of Lying."